The
Classic 1000
Microwave
Recipes

The Classic 1000 Microwave Recipes

Sonia Allison

foulsham
LONDON • NEW YORK • TORONTO • SYDNEY

foulsham

The Publishing House, Bennetts Close,
Cippenham, Slough, Berkshire, SL1 5AP, England

With grateful thanks to Magimix and Schwartz
herbs and spices for their help and
co-operation over the years.

ISBN 0-572-01945-9

Copyright © 1998 Strathearn Publishing Ltd in
association with Sonia Allison

Cover photographs © Food Features

Printed in Great Britain by St Edmundsbury Press, Bury St Edmunds, Suffolk

Contents

Introduction

Since the mid-seventies, microwave cooking has become part and parcel of my busy everyday life and given me more flexibility and freedom in and out of the kitchen than I ever imagined possible. Speedy, cool, hygienic, reliable and undemanding, the microwave works like a charm, cooks like a dream and uses only minimal electricity, a major consideration in times of rising energy costs and the need to make savings where we can.

It is an accepted fact that microwave ovens cannot completely replace conventional ovens and hobs but they do go a long way towards it. Used to full capacity, a microwave can become the most efficient, valued and respected piece of equipment in your kitchen, and my intention in writing this book is to put together a package of innovative recipes in addition to old favourites, proving that a wide range of dishes can be microwaved successfully. I have sometimes given an alternative method of cooking some of the ingredients used in a specific recipe to save time, or suggested finishing off a dish under the grill (broiler) to crisp skin or brown a topping. In these instances, your microwave will work in perfect harmony with your conventional oven.

I have to admit that some dishes are not at their best if given the microwave treatment. Yorkshire pudding collapses. Pancakes fare no better, though they reheat to perfection. Soufflés and éclairs fail with irritating predictability. Meringues just about work but take so long you might just as well bake them conventionally and have done with it. And deep-frying is taboo because it is impossible to control the temperature of the fat or oil.

Some people still regard the microwave as something to use only for defrosting and reheating. A pity, because they're missing out. Many grow to love microwave cookery and soon come to understand and appreciate its seemingly magical properties ... Over to you.

Guide to Microwave Cooking

What are Microwaves?

Based on the principle of radar, microwaves are a form of energy that comprises electro-magnetic, short-length, non-ionising, high-frequency radio waves at the top end of the radio band. They arc close to infra-red rays but not as powerful and the frequency is 2450 megahertz (MHz), which translates into literally millions of cycles or vibrations per second. The word 'hertz' comes from Heinrich Hertz, the scientist who first discovered the nature of the waves.

Inside the cavity of a microwave oven, with its extraordinary number of compulsory cut-outs and safety devices, the microwaves are completely confined and are unable to leak out and attack you. In any event, microwaves are an altogether different kettle of fish from X-rays, gamma-rays and ultra-violet rays, which are ionising and known to cause dangerous cellular alterations to the body with minimal or no temperature change. Microwaves have none of these effects and, more importantly, are non-cumulative. Leaks can occur only if the oven is worn, damaged or mishandled, and for safety reasons it should be checked from time to time by a qualified engineer to make sure the door fits snugly, the seal around the door is secure, and the hinges are not rusty. If the door front fractures, stop using the oven at once and request a service call as soon as possible. So what would happen if one were, briefly, exposed to microwaves? The answer is a burn, which is never pleasant. Therefore look after your oven, keep it serviced and clean it regularly.

7

How Microwaves Cook Food

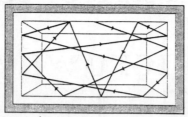

Microwaves deflecting in an oven

When the microwave is plugged into a socket, the door closed and oven switched on, microwaves are emitted from a magnetron (or microwave energy generator) usually on one side at the top, protected by a cover, generally plastic. The microwaves are transmitted into the inside of the oven cavity down a channel called a waveguide, bounce off the sides and 'beam' on to the food from all directions. Instantaneously, the food absorbs the microwaves, which cause the water molecules within the food to vibrate. The result is excessively rapid friction that creates enough heat to cook food. For a simple demonstration of how friction makes heat, rub your hands together vigorously and feel how warm they become. Now imagine this multiplied umpteen times and you will understand how the microwaves work.

For even cooking, most models are fitted with a wave stirrer, stirrer blade or paddle (concealed at the top) which helps to distribute the waves. Most also have a rotating turntable so dishes do not need turning during cooking. However, turntables do restrict the shape and size of dishes, so consider buying a model where the turntable can be switched off or removed if necessary.

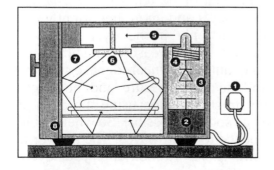

1. Flexible cord;
2. Power transformer;
3. High voltage rectifier and capacitor;
4. Magnetron;
5. Waveguide;
6. Wave stirrer (paddle);
7. Oven cavity;
8. Oven door and frame with special seals.

Successful Cooking

Because microwaves are short-length, high-frequency radio waves, they are able to penetrate only 2.5 cm/1 in of the food in all directions. Thus shallow containers are better than deep ones except those used for some cakes and puddings that need headroom for satisfactory rising. Round dishes give the best results, followed by oval. Sometimes food in rectangular or square dishes cooks unevenly, especially at the corners. The food will also cook more effectively if thick pieces are arranged towards the outside edge of the dish and not piled up. Stirring during the cooking cycle helps to distribute heat and, where practical, this has been recommended in the recipes. If possible, whole potatoes and other similar-sized foods (apples for example) should be arranged, on a plate or in a dish, in a hollow triangle, square or circle. If your microwave is an older model without a turntable, make sure you turn the dishes several times during cooking.

Resting and Standing Times

For heat to penetrate the food and work its way gently from the outside to the centre, it is recommended that the food be allowed to rest and stand after or during cooking. Some dishes, especially large quantities, turkeys, etc., if cooked without a rest, would become overcooked on the outside but remain undercooked in the middle. Depending on what is more convenient, food may be left to rest or stand inside or outside the microwave. Individual recipes give guidance on resting and standing. As a further precaution, it is preferable to return an undercooked dish briefly to the oven rather than add extra time initially. The microwaves act so swiftly that even a few too many seconds could spoil the food.

Seasonings

As salt toughens microwaved meat, poultry and vegetables, it should be added half-way through or at the end of cooking. Other seasonings, such as herbs and spices, may be added at the beginning.

Caution

Never operate the oven while empty because without food or liquid to absorb the microwaves they will bounce straight back to the magnetron and shorten its life span. Similarly, melting 5–10 ml/ 1–2 tsp of fat, or heating just a tiny amount of liquid, will have the same effect, so it is best to place a cup or tumbler of water in the oven at the same time. Just in case it gets switched on by accident, it is a wise safety measure always to keep a container of water inside an empty oven until it is needed for cooking.

Cleaning

Suggestions for cleaning have been given in Hints and Tips (page 392). As fresh food spills are so easy to remove from the cool interior of a microwave (nothing burns on in the conventional sense), a wipe over with a damp cloth immediately after use will ensure that it stays spotless and fresh.

Cookware

Metal containers reflect microwaves away from the food and prevent it cooking so metal containers or tins (pans) of any sort should *never* be used in the microwave. It is also important to note that crockery with metal trims or with the manufacturers' name or pattern design printed in gold or silver underneath could cause arcing – an effect like tiny flashes of lightning. This arcing not only damages the magnetron but also ruins the metallic decorations. The exceptions here are small amounts of foil used to cover poultry wing tips and ends of legs to prevent scorching, and metal kebab skewers that are well covered by the surrounding food. However, you must ensure that the skewers do not come into direct contact with any part of the oven interior.

In order for the microwaves to reach the food and subsequently cook it, the dishes chosen should be made of materials through which the microwaves can pass most readily – like rays of sun through a window pane. These are listed below and, although most stay cool or even cold, some kinds absorb heat from the cooked

*A selection of
microwave containers*

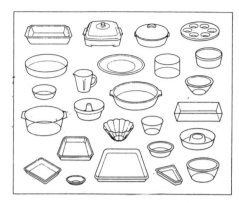

food and feel hot to the touch. For comfort, the cookware should be removed from the oven using oven gloves.

Baskets
These may be used for brief reheating of rolls, etc. Prolonged spells in the microwave cause dryness and cracking.

Clingfilm
Clingfilm (plastic wrap) is excellent for covering and lining dishes. To prevent the film from ballooning up in the oven and bursting, or being sucked back on to the food (the latter is a disaster if it happens to a pudding that is supposed to rise), I have recommended puncturing the film twice with the tip of a knife to allow steam to escape. By puncturing, I mean making a small slit and not a tiny pin-prick.

Glass
Not your best crystal but Pyrex-type glassware is ideal. Corning ware, which is ceramic glass, is also excellent. Other, sturdy, glass may also be used.

Paper
Kitchen towel or paper napkins may be used to line the oven base if food is to be cooked directly on it (paper is a great absorber), and also to cover food to prevent spluttering.

Plastic

Use only rigid plastic; yoghurt or cottage cheese containers or thin plastic may collapse. Look for special microwave utensils made by firms like Lakeland or other reliable makes stocked by specialist kitchen shops, supermarkets and department stores. Note that plastic spatulas are useful as they can be left in, say, a sauce during cooking to use for stirring when required.

Pottery and Porcelain

Both may be used – but not your best china. Avoid dark utensils and ironstone as they absorb heat and take it away from the food.

Roasting Bags

Roasting bags, also called boiling bags, have a hundred and one uses; see-through plastic roasting bags are convenient to use and also clean. They are ideal for cooking joints of meat or poultry. Close the tops with elastic bands or string, not metal ties.

Waxed Paper Products

Like basketware, these dry out in the microwave and should be used only for brief reheating.

Wood

Like basketware, wood dries out in the microwave and should be used only for brief reheating.

Extras

Browning dish: this is a white ceramic dish, the base of which is coated with a special tin oxide material. It becomes very hot indeed when preheated, making it possible to sear food prior to microwave cooking. This gives the food the browned finish associated with conventional grilling (broiling) or frying (sautéing). As the dish needs to be preheated, empty, for varying lengths of time depending on the food being cooked, be guided by your own microwave oven instruction book. As a general rule, the preheating time should be around 6 minutes for steaks and chops and 2–3 minutes for eggs. It should never be preheated for longer than 8 minutes, nor used in a conventional oven. If you are cooking in batches, the browning dish will need cleaning and preheating for half the initial length of time between batches. Although it will take on a yellowy tinge when hot, the dish will return to its original colour when cool. Preheating this type of dish does not harm the oven.

Temperature probe: this looks like a thick knitting needle attached to a plastic-coated lead and is generally available with the more sophisticated models of microwave ovens to register the internal temperature of food. One end slots into the side of the oven while the sharp end is inserted into the food to be cooked. The cooking cycle is therefore geared to temperature and not time and when, for example, a joint of well-done beef registers 160°C, the oven will switch off automatically. As every model varies, please refer to your own microwave book before using the probe and setting the temperature.

Thermometer: thermometers for use in microwave ovens are now obtainable and, like temperature probes, they must be used according to the manufacturers' instructions. Never use a conventional meat thermometer in a microwave, although it can be used to test the meat for doneness when the joint is resting after cooking.

Choice of Microwave Ovens

People often ask me which model I would recommend and I always find this a difficult question to answer. Those who are not technically minded will do best with a fairly basic model that is straightforward to operate and does its job efficiently. Others might find the new models a joy in that they bear some relation to computers and can be easily programmed and manipulated to suit all purposes. The only advice I can give on the selection front is to suggest a visit to your electricity supply retail store or a department store to have a thorough look at as many ovens as you can and ask for a demonstration. You will then be in a good position to buy what suits you, not what looks fabulous, is very expensive and turns out to be more to cope with than you bargained for.

Power Controls

Most domestic microwave ovens vary between 500 and 850 watt output.

All recipes in this book have been prepared in a 650 watt output oven, and usually use only two power settings: Full, which is 100 per cent power (650 watts), and Defrost, which is 50 per cent (325 watts). If your oven has a different output, the guide below may prove useful. Be warned: if you have a higher wattage output oven, make sure you do reduce cooking times and check a little before the end of your calculated cooking time. You can always cook for a few seconds more.

● For a 500/550 watt output oven, increase the cooking time by about 20 per cent, e.g. 10 minutes becomes 12 minutes.

● A 600 watt output oven will be much the same as a 650 watt one.

● For a 700 watt output oven, decrease the cooking time by about 20 per cent, e.g. 10 minutes becomes 8 minutes.

● For a 850 watt output oven, decrease the cooking time by about 30 per cent, e.g. 10 minutes becomes 7 minutes.

Using these figures will give a fairly accurate conversion time but for greater accuracy refer to your own microwave oven recipe book. Note that some manufacturers call Defrost 30 per cent power. Check your manual if yours does and you have a 650 watt or less output microwave, in which case use Medium (50 per cent) power where a recipe calls for Defrost. If you have a higher output (650–850 watts), use 30 per cent power instead of Defrost.

There are now technically advanced microwave ovens with variable power settings ranging from 1–10 or from 1–5 (see figures in brackets in the Summary of Settings on pages 15–16). The variable settings enable some dishes to be cooked more slowly than others and some users find this advantageous, especially when making stews and casseroles. Some models have a system whereby the power comes on and off automatically; listen and you can hear it happening. Other models have an automatic reduction in output at the lower settings but this is silent.

Colour

Foods cooked in the microwave can look pale and insipid. Hence my inclusion of bastes (pages 332–3) for roast meat and poultry, a few shakes of soy sauce or a dusting of paprika, beef stock cubes for stews and casseroles, and icings (frostings) for cakes. I have also incorporated a number of other tricks – like using Red Leicester cheese for toppings instead of Cheddar. As you will find out when you make up the recipes in the book, none lacks colour.

Summary of Settings

Setting 1 (1) equates to 10 per cent of power output and is used to keep cooked dishes warm or to take the chill off cold ones. It is called either warm or low.

Setting 2 equates to 20 per cent of power output and is recommended for warming or very gentle simmering. It is called either warm or low.

Setting 3 (2) equates to 30 per cent of power output and is used for defrosting and simmering. It is called either defrost, medium-low, simmer or soften.

Setting 4 equates to 40 per cent of power output and is often chosen for defrosting, braising and stewing. It is called either slow cook, medium, low defrost, stew, simmer or braise.

Setting 5 (3) equates to 50 per cent of power output and is used for defrosting and also for simmering and stewing. It is called either medium, defrost, simmer or stew.

Setting 6 equates to 60 per cent of power output and is used chiefly for reheating cooked dishes, baking or simmering. This setting is called either reheat, bake or simmer.

Setting 7 (4) equates to 70 per cent of power output and is used primarily for roasting. It is called either medium-high, bake or roast.

Setting 8 equates to 80 per cent of power output and is also used for reheating and baking. It is called either reheat or bake.

Setting 9 equates to 90 per cent of power output and is used for fast cooking of vegetables in fat (i.e. when making a stew). It is called either medium-high, roast or fast reheat, or sometimes sauté.

Setting 10 (5) equates to 100 per cent of power output and is used for the majority of recipes in this book. It is called either full, high maximum or fast cook.

Even if you have a microwave with variable power settings such as listed above, do not try to convert my recipes, which were all cooked at Full or 50 per cent power.

Reheating
Conventional reheating of meat and poultry, or keeping plates of food warm in a cool oven, can sometimes cause a build-up of bacteria, resulting in mild food poisoning. With a microwave oven, the action is so fast that germs have no time to breed, and the food stays fresh and moist without looking frayed round the edges.

Bonuses
Freshness of flavour and colour, plus retention of nutrients, characterise most foods cooked in a microwave oven. The foods also tend to shrink less, and cooking smells are reduced.

It is encouraging to know that when cooking in the microwave the electricity saved is between 50 and 70 per cent. Also no preheating is necessary and there is minimal residual heat in the oven cavity. It has been estimated that using a microwave is four times as efficient as conventional cooking because all the energy is directed to the food, with no 'overspill'.

Notes on the Recipes

- Always check food is piping hot all the way through before serving.

- When following a recipe, use either metric, imperial or American measures, never a combination.

- All spoon measures are level: 1 tsp = 5 ml; 1 tbsp = 15 ml.

- Always wash and peel, if necessary, fresh produce before preparation.

- Adjust strong-flavoured ingredients and seasonings to taste.

- Herbs are fresh unless otherwise stated. You can substitute dried for fresh, as long as the herb is not for garnishing, but halve the quantity stated in the recipe as they are more pungent.

- Eggs are medium unless otherwise stated.

- Never preheat a microwave.

- Dishes used for cooking sandwich-type cakes, deep cakes, flans, quiches and tarts should be the same depth as traditional baking tins (pans).

Convenience Food Labels

Microwave Oven Labels

More recent microwave ovens have a symbol on the front that ties in with the heating instructions on some small food packs like ready-made meals. Matching the information on the pack with that on the oven will enable you to calculate the heating time required.

the microwave symbol

the power output (watts)

the heating category for small packs

Heating categories range from A to E: A is for the lowest wattage ovens (500w), E for the highest (850w). If your oven displays a C, for example, on the label it will heat more quickly than an A or B category oven, but not as fast as a D or E.

Food Pack Labels

Most packaged foods suitable for microwaving have a label similar to the one below:

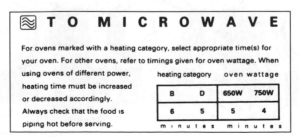

☒ **T O   M I C R O W A V E**

For ovens marked with a heating category, select appropriate time(s) for your oven. For other ovens, refer to timings given for oven wattage. When using ovens of different power, heating time must be increased or decreased accordingly. Always check that the food is piping hot before serving.

heating category		oven wattage	
B	D	650W	750W
6	5	5	4
m i n u t e s		m i n u t e s	

In the illustration, information is given for B and D category ovens only.

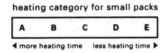

heating category for small packs

A	B	C	D	E

◄ more heating time   less heating time ►

- For C category ovens, you would need to choose a time midway between B and D – in this case 5½ minutes.
- For A category ovens, you would need to heat the food for a little longer than B – in this case 6½ minutes.
- For E category ovens, you would need to heat the food for slightly less than D – in this case 4½ minutes.*

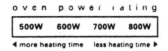

oven power rating

500W	600W	700W	800W

◄ more heating time   less heating time ►

It also shows only 650w and 750w output. The same applies as above: you will need to add on a proportionate amount of time for lower wattage ovens and decrease the time proportionally for higher wattage ovens.

Helpline

If you're at all confused or would like more information, phone the freephone foodline at the Food Safety Advisory Centre.

0800 282407

* Reproduced by permission of MAFF, based on A *Guide to the New Microwave Labels*.

Meat and Poultry

Most meat and poultry responds well to microwave cooking but, where possible, prime cuts should be chosen as they tenderise more readily than the less expensive and muscular parts of the animal traditionally recommended for braises, stews and hot-pots. This may sound extravagant but 450g/1 lb of rump steak, with additions, will make a generous and richly flavoured meal for 4–6 people, lengthy cooking time is not needed and the saving in fuel is substantial.

Many microwave cookery writers don't recommend cooking large joints in the microwave – I disagree. The meat remains moist, succulent and often more tender than a joint cooked conventionally. It isn't easy to achieve but for skilled microwave users it's worth persevering. Other, more cautious, converts may prefer to part-cook the joint in the microwave, then finish off conventionally in a hot oven to give the crisp, browned appearance we associate with a roast. Obviously, as with all meat, it must be completely defrosted before cooking (see the defrosting table on pages 24–26).

Meat stewed or braised in the microwave can be cooked in its own serving dish which saves on washing up, and the whole process is clean and fast, no sticking or burning occurs, and strong smells rarely filter through the house. But I have to stress that there are still a few provisos: meat should be cut into 1 cm/½ in cubes, smaller than is usually suggested for braising or stewing; it is advisable to 'dry' cook meat or poultry for a given length of time before liquid is added as this technique helps to soften the meat; seasonings, and salt in particular, have a toughening effect and are therefore best added half-way through or at the very end of cooking. Minced (ground) meat behaves perfectly in the microwave because its tiny pieces tenderise easily.

Another tip to note is that kosher meat, eaten by the Orthodox Jewish community, is salted by the butcher and reacts unfavourably to microwave cooking, the only exceptions being mince, poultry and offal such as liver.

Standing time is necessary to allow heat from the outside to transfer through to the centre, particularly when dealing with large joints. If standing times were not allowed or were carried out only at the end, the outside of the meat would become dry and hard, leaving the centre area raw, cold or both.

Understanding the Tables

If you are at all uncertain about the cooking and standing times given in the cooking tables on pages 27-29, let me explain in more detail. Large joints, as the table shows, require 7 minutes' cooking time on Full and 5 minutes' standing time for every 450 g/1 lb. Thus you should cook a 3 kg/7 lb joint for an initial 21 minutes, leave it to stand for 15 minutes (inside or outside the microwave, whichever is more convenient), cook it for a further 21 minutes, then leave it to stand for another 15 minutes, completing the cooking and standing cycle as given in the tables. To hold in heat and moisture, the joint should be drained and then wrapped in foil or left in its roasting bag for the last part of the standing time.

Joints of up to 1 kg/2 lb can be cooked for 14 minutes, with no standing time between, and then left to stand as above for 10 minutes at the end.

Times

The times given in the tables for cooking and standing are fairly general. Pork and veal should have 2 minutes per 450 g/1 lb added to the cooking time given, as should meat taken straight from the refrigerator. Medium–rare beef may be cooked for 1–1½ minutes less per 450 g/1 lb, but the standing time remains the same. If your microwave oven has a temperature probe to denote the degree of doneness of the joint, use it according to the instructions given in your own microwave oven guide book. Alternatively, buy a microwave meat thermometer.

Roasting Tips

- The more regular the shape of the joint the better and more evenly it will cook. As this is not always a viable proposition, wrap the narrow end of a joint (the bony part of a leg of lamb for example) with foil during the first half of the cooking time to prevent frizzle and overcooking. The foil will have no detrimental effect on the workings of the oven, because there is so much more meat in relation to the foil. If choice is possible, settle for the fillet end of pork or lamb, and a boned and rolled piece of beef or veal.
- Roasting bags are perfect for microwaved lamb, beef and veal and seem to encourage browning. Simply season and/or baste the joint, slide it into a roasting bag and close the top with an elastic band, a piece of string or any other non-metallic tie. Cook and stand as directed in the table on pages 27–29.
- If not using a roasting bag, stand the joint in a dish, cover it with clingfilm (plastic wrap) and puncture it twice with the tip of a knife. If the cooking time recommended is 15 minutes or over at full power, the joint will brown slightly of its own accord so, if you prefer, you need not baste it prior to cooking.
- For very fat joints, stand a plastic trivet or two inverted saucers in a dish and place the meat on top. Cover with clingfilm as above.
- If the joint has fat on one side only, place it in a bag or dish with the fat side down. Turn over half-way through cooking.
- For crisp crackling on pork, rub sunflower or corn oil and salt well into the scored rind. 'Open' roast by standing in a dish and covering closely with paper to prevent spluttering and soiling the oven interior with grease splashes. Do not turn the joint at half time but keep it crackling-side uppermost all the time. Be warned, the crackling can become very hard and crisp – so watch your teeth!

Poultry Tips

- The same defrosting and cooking rules apply to poultry as to meat but for a golden-brown effect, a chicken or turkey should be brushed with a baste (pages 332–3) prior to cooking. If the bird is of the self-basting variety, a light brushing of soy sauce or a sprinkling of paprika is all that is necessary.
- Wing tips and the ends of legs should be foil-wrapped to prevent overcooking.
- Stuff the crop end only and leave the body cavity empty. Prepared stuffings may be heated up separately in a greased dish. Times will vary from 3 to 6 minutes at Full, depending on the quantity and on whether the mixture is hot, warm, cold or chilled.
- Most microwaves can accommodate a bird of up to only 4.5 kg/ 10 lb.

Defrosting Hints

- To prevent slight cooking of the outside, large joints or birds are best left to defrost naturally, either overnight in a refrigerator or for several hours in the kitchen. Alternatively, partially defrost in the microwave, then finish off at room temperature.
- When defrosting fairly large joints and birds, refer to the defrosting table on pages 24–26 and add up the number of minutes' standing time required. If it works out at about 40 minutes, rest for 20 minutes at half time, then rest for a further 20 minutes at the end of the defrosting period. If the joint or bird is still partially frozen, leave it to thaw at room temperature or in a sink of cold water.
- As soon as chops, steaks and poultry joints have defrosted enough to be separated, arrange them in a single layer in a ring round the edge of plate or in a dish. Never heap them up.
- Cover meat or poultry with clingfilm (plastic wrap) or kitchen paper or put into a roasting bag as these speed up defrosting and help keep in the moisture.

Browning Dish

For a grilled (broiled) or fried (sautéed) effect, use a browning dish for steaks, chops, etc., following the directions in your own microwave oven guide book or any that came with the dish itself.

- In general the dish should be heated for 5–6 minutes at Full if small and 7–8 minutes if large. It should then be brushed with melted fat or oil (unless it's non-stick), then the food added.
- For steaks weighing up to 225 g/8 oz, allow 3–5 minutes at Full, according to doneness preferred, turning them over once.
- For two pork chops, each weighing 200–225 g/7–8 oz, allow a total of 15 minutes' cooking time at Full, turning them over after 5 minutes, then again after a further 5 minutes.
- For 450 g/1 lb of chicken joints, allow a total of 9–10 minutes, placing them skin side down initially, turning them over after 3 minutes, then again after 7 minutes.
- Clean the dish thoroughly after every batch of cooking. It should then be regreased and reheated for half the original time.

Defrosting Meat and Poultry

	Defrost Setting	Comments
Joints for Roasting on the bone	9 minutes per 450 g/ 1 lb, allowing the same standing time at the end. (Thus a 450 g/1 lb joint should stand for 9 minutes after defrosting, a 900 g/ 2 lb joint 18 minutes, and so on.)	Stand the joint on an upturned plate or trivet in a shallow dish. Turn it over half-way through defrosting. Wrap in foil before standing.
off the bone	10 minutes per 450 g/ 1 lb, allowing the same standing time at the end as above.	As above.

	Defrost Setting	Comments
Chops **125 g/4 oz**	3 minutes; stand for 3 minutes	Place on a plate and cover loosely with kitchen paper.
175 g/6 oz	4 minutes; stand for 4 minutes	As above.
225 g/8 oz	5 minutes; stand for 5 minutes	As above.
Minced (Ground) Meats	10 minutes per 450 g/ 1 lb; stand for 10 minutes	Remove the mince from the wrapper and stand on a plate. Cover with a second inverted plate or a pudding basin. As the outside edges thaw, scrape away the soft mince and transfer it to another plate. This prevents the outside meat from starting to cook before the inside has thawed. Free-flow mince can be cooked from frozen.
Stewing Cubes	8 minutes per 450 g/ 1 lb; stand for 8 minutes	Stand in a shallow dish and cover with a plate. Turn the cubes over half-way through.
Steaks **225 g/8 oz**	6 minutes; stand for 6 minutes. Reduce the time for smaller steaks.	Place on a plate and cover loosely with kitchen paper.
Liver **225 g/8 oz**	2½ minutes; stand for 8 minutes	Place in a covered dish. Separate the slices before standing.
450 g/1 lb	4 minutes; stand for 12 minutes	As above.
Chicken, whole	8 minutes per 450 g/ 1 lb, allowing the same standing time at the end	Stand in a shallow dish or leave in its bag, metal tie removed and the end of the bag snipped off. Remove the giblets. Turn over half-way through.

	Defrost Setting	Comments
Chicken Portions **225 g/8 oz**	6 minutes; stand for 6 minutes	Stand in a shallow dish and cover loosely with kitchen paper. Turn over half-way through defrosting.
350 g/12 oz	8 minutes; stand for 8 minutes	As above.
Duck, whole	7 minutes per 450 g/ 1 lb, allowing the same standing time at the end	Stand in a shallow dish or defrost in its bag as for chicken. Turn over half-way through defrosting.
Duck Portions **225 g/8 oz**	5 minutes; stand for 5 minutes	Stand in a shallow dish and cover loosely with kitchen paper. Turn over half-way through defrosting.
350 g/12 oz	7 minutes; stand for 7 minutes	As above.
Goose **(about 4.5 kg/** **10 lb max)**	4 minutes per 450 g/ 1 lb	Stand in a large shallow dish and cover loosely with kitchen paper. Turn over once during defrosting. Remove any giblets as soon as possible. Wrap the goose in aluminium foil and stand overnight at room temperature until completely defrosted.
Turkey **(about 4.5 kg/** **10 lb max)**	45 minutes initially; stand for 45 minutes, then defrost for a further 60 minutes	Leave in its bag, metal tie removed. Remove the giblet bag after the initial defrosting and standing, if possible. If not, turn the bird over half way through the second defrosting and remove the giblet bag. Make sure the body cavity is entirely free of ice crystals after the second defrosting. Rinse thoroughly and dry on kitchen paper.

Cooking Meat and Poultry

	Cook/Heat/Full Power	Comments
Joints for Roasting on the bone	7 minutes per 450 g/ 1 lb, allowing 5 minutes per 450 g/1 lb standing time. This should take place half-way through the cooking time for large joints with further standing time at the end. Small joints may be left to stand just at the end.	Place in a shallow dish, cover with clingfilm (plastic wrap) and slit it twice. Turn the dish several times during cooking. When standing at the end, wrap the joint in foil. Alternatively, cook and leave to stand in a roasting bag.
off the bone	8 minutes per 450 g/ 1 lb, allowing 5 minutes per 450 g/1 lb standing time as above. For pork or veal, allow an extra 2 minutes per 450 g/ 1 lb. For pink lamb or beef, reduce the cooking time by 1–1½ minutes per 450 g/1 lb.	As above.
Chops 125 g/4 oz	3 minutes; stand for 3 minutes	Wash and dry the chops and trim off surplus fat. Place on a plate or in a shallow dish. Cover with clingfilm (plastic wrap) and slit it twice. Turn the plate or dish half-way through cooking. Drain off the melted fat before serving. Alternatively, cook in a browning dish, following the instructions given with the dish or those in your own microwave oven guide book.
175 g/6 oz	4 minutes; stand for 4 minutes	As above.
225 g/8 oz	5 minutes; stand for 5 minutes	As above.

	Cook/Heat/Full Power	Comments
Steaks **200 g/8 oz**	3–5 minutes; stand for 5 minutes. For smaller steaks, cook as chops.	Wash and dry the steaks. Place on a plate and cover with kitchen paper. Turn over half-way through cooking. Alternatively, cook in a browning dish, following the instructions given with the dish or those in your own microwave oven guide book.
Liver **225 g/8 oz**	3 minutes	Wash and dry the liver. Place in a greased shallow dish and cover with a plate or matching lid. Stir and turn the liver over half-way through cooking. Season at the end.
450 g/1 lb	6 minutes	As above.
Chicken, whole	8 minutes per 450 g/ 1 lb, allowing 5 minutes per 450 g/1 lb standing time. This should take place half-way through the cooking time for large chickens with further standing time at the end. Small chickens may be left to stand just at the end.	Wash and drain the chicken. Remove giblets. Stand the chicken in shallow dish and brush with a baste. Cover with clingfilm (plastic wrap) and slit it twice. After the standing time, remove the film and lift the chicken out of the dish, retaining the hot juices for gravy, soup, etc. Skim off the fat before use. If preferred, cook in a roasting bag, starting breast-side down for larger birds and then turning over half-way through.
Chicken Portions **225 g/8 oz**	4 minutes; stand for 5 minutes	Wash and dry the portions. Stand on a plate, cover with clingfilm (plastic wrap) and slit it twice. If several portions, place thin parts towards the centre of the plate.
350 g/12 oz	6 minutes; stand for 5 minutes	As above.

	Cook/Heat/Full Power	Comments
Duck, whole	8 minutes per 450 g/ 1 lb, allowing 5 minutes per 450 g/1 lb standing time. For detailed technique, see chicken above.	Wash and drain the duck. Stand on a rack in a shallow dish, breast-side down. Cover with clingfilm (plastic wrap) and slit it twice. Half-way through cooking, remove the clingfilm and carefully turn the duck over. Re-cover with clingfilm and slit it twice. After cooking, remove the film. Wrap the duck in foil for the duration of the standing time. Do not use a roasting bag or the duck will be greasy. Crisp the skin by placing the bird under a hot grill (broiler) for a few minutes, if liked.
Duck Portions	As for chicken portions.	As for chicken portions. Drain after standing.
Goose (about 4.5 kg/ 10 lb max)	7 minutes per 450 g/ 1 lb, allowing 5 minutes per 450 g/1 lb standing time. For detailed technique, see chicken above.	Wash and drain the goose. Remove giblets. Place in a large roasting bag and close the end with an elastic band or a non-metallic tie. Stand the bag on a large plate, shallow dish or on the turntable. Turn over once during cooking, taking care that no juices run out of the bag. Carefully lift out the goose, still on its plate, dish or turntable and stand it on a draining board. Open up the bag and allow the juices to trickle out into a bowl placed in the sink. Transfer the goose to a carving board and wrap in foil. Leave to rest for the remaining standing time. Crisp the skin as for duck, if liked.
Turkey	See full instructions on page 26.	

Vegetables

If you refer to the tables, you will see how easy it is to cook a wide selection of both fresh and frozen vegetables in the microwave with no loss of colour, flavour or texture. And because the amount of cooking water is minimal in most instances, valuable nutrients are retained instead of being drained away at the end.

Use of flavourings and additions has been left to your imagination, but cooked vegetables can be served with sauces from pages 316–330, tossed or coated with melted butter or margarine, flavoured to taste and garnished with a shower of chopped parsley, chives or other fresh herbs or spices, or even sprinkled with chopped nuts or grated lemon rind. Always season vegetables after cooking as salt tends to toughen them during cooking.

For simplicity, when cooking smallish packs of frozen vegetables leave them in their original bags. Puncture each bag with a knife two or three times and stand in a dish. Cook for the length of time given in the tables or on the bag itself, then drain and serve. If cooking a block of frozen vegetables, open out, place in a a dish and cook as directed.

A small selection of vegetable dishes is included in the recipes, from Dauphine Potatoes (page 221) and Red Cabbage with Apple (page 218) to Fennel in Sherry (page 232) and Ratatouille (page 221). Even Creamed Potatoes (page 225), with its hundred and one uses, has been included.

Cooking Vegetables from Frozen

	Cook/Heat/Full Power	Comments
Asparagus Spears 225 g/8 oz	6 minutes	Place in a rectangular dish. Add 15 ml/1 tbsp boiling water. Cover with a plate or lid. Half-way through cooking, separate the spears. Season after cooking and remove from the dish with a fish slice to prevent the spears breaking.
450 g/1 lb	10 minutes	As above, adding 45 ml/3 tbsp boiling water.
Beans, Broad (Lima) 225 g/8 oz	5 minutes	Place in a bowl or dish. Add 15 ml/1 tbsp boiling water. Cover with a plate or lid. Stir half-way through cooking. Season after cooking and drain before serving.
450 g/1 lb	9 minutes	As above, adding 45 ml/3 tbsp boiling water.
Beans, Green, Cut or Whole 225 g/8 oz	6 minutes	Place in a bowl or dish. Add 15 ml/1 tbsp boiling water. Cover with a plate or lid. Stir half-way through cooking. Season after cooking and drain before serving.
450 g/1 lb	10 minutes	As above, adding 45 ml/3 tbsp boiling water.

	Cook/Heat/Full Power	Comments
Beans, Green, Sliced **225 g/8 oz**	5 minutes	Place in a bowl or dish. Add 15 ml/1 tbsp) boiling water. Cover with a plate or lid. Stir half-way through cooking. Season after cooking and drain before serving.
450 g/1 lb	9 minutes	As above, adding 45 ml/3 tbsp boiling water.
Broccoli Spears **400 g/14 oz pack**	8 minutes	Place in a rectangular dish. Add 30 ml/2 tbsp boiling water. Cover with a plate or lid. Separate half-way through cooking. Season after cooking and drain before serving.
2 × 400 g/14 oz packs	14 minutes	As above, adding 60 ml/4 tbsp boiling water.
Brussels Sprouts **225 g/8 oz**	5 minutes	Place in a bowl or dish. Add 15 ml/1 tbsp boiling water. Cover with a plate or lid. Stir half-way through cooking. Season after cooking and drain before serving.
450 g/1 lb	9 minutes	As above, adding 45 ml/3 tbsp boiling water.
Carrots, Baby **225 g/8 oz**	8 minutes	Place in a bowl or dish. Add 15 ml/1 tbsp boiling water. Cover with a plate or lid. Stir half-way through cooking. Season after cooking and drain before serving.
450 g/1 lb	15 minutes	As above, adding 45 ml/3 tbsp boiling water.

	Cook/Heat/Full Power	Comments
Carrots, Sliced **225 g/8 oz**	5 minutes	Place in a bowl or dish. Add 15 ml/1 tbsp boiling water. Cover with a plate or lid. Stir half-way through cooking. Season after cooking and drain before serving.
450 g/1 lb	9 minutes	As above, adding 45 ml/3 tbsp boiling water.
Cauliflower **Florets** **225 g/8 oz**	6 minutes	Place in a bowl or dish. Add 15 ml/1 tbsp boiling water. Cover with a plate or lid. Stir half-way through cooking. Season after cooking and drain before serving.
450 g/1 lb	10 minutes	As above, adding 45 ml/3 tbsp boiling water.
Corn on the Cob **1 head**	6 minutes	Place on a plate. Cover with kitchen paper. Turn over twice during cooking.
2 heads	8–9 minutes	As above, turning over three times during cooking.
Courgettes **(Zucchini), sliced** **225 g/8 oz**	5 minutes	Place in a bowl or dish. Add 15 ml/1 tbsp boiling water. Cover with a plate or lid. Stir half-way through cooking. Season after cooking and drain before serving.
450 g/1 lb	9 minutes	As above, adding 45 ml/3 tbsp boiling water

	Cook/Heat/Full Power	Comments
Macedoine (Diced Mixed Vegetables with Peas) **225 g/8 oz**	5 minutes	Place in a bowl or dish. Add 15 ml/1 tbsp boiling water. Cover with a plate or lid. Stir half-way through cooking. Season after cooking and drain before serving.
450 g/1 lb	9 minutes	As above, adding 45 ml/3 tbsp boiling water.
Mangetout (Snow Peas) **225 g/8 oz**	5 minutes	Place in a bowl or dish. Add 15 ml/1 tbsp boiling water. Cover with a lid or plate. Stir half-way through cooking. Season after cooking and drain before serving.
450 g/1 lb	9 minutes	As above, adding 45 ml/3 tbsp boiling water.
Mexican Mix **225 g/8 oz**	5 minutes	Place in a bowl or dish. Add 15 ml/1 tbsp boiling water. Cover with a plate or lid. Stir half-way through cooking. Season after cooking and drain before serving.
450 g/1 lb	9 minutes	As above, adding 45 ml/3 tbsp boiling water.
Mixed Vegetables, Farmhouse-style **225 g/8 oz**	5 minutes	Place in a bowl or dish. Add 15 ml/1 tbsp boiling water. Cover with a plate or lid. Stir half-way through cooking. Season, drain and serve.
450 g/1 lb	9 minutes	As above, adding 45 ml/3 tbsp boiling water.

	Cook/Heat/Full Power	Comments
Onions, Sliced **225 g/8 oz**	3–4 minutes	Place in a bowl or dish with no added liquid. Cover with a plate or lid. Stir half-way through cooking. Season after cooking and drain before serving.
Peas, Garden **225 g/8 oz**	5 minutes	Place in a a bowl or dish. Add 15 ml/1 tbsp boiling water. Cover with a plate or lid. Stir half-way through cooking. Season after cooking and drain before serving.
450 g/1 lb	9 minutes	As above, adding 45 ml/3 tbsp boiling water.
Peppers (Bell **Peppers), Mixed** **Sliced** **225 g/8 oz**	2–3 minutes	Place in a bowl or dish. Add 15 g /½ oz/1 tbsp butter or margarine but no liquid. Cover with a plate or lid. Stir half-way through cooking. Season after cooking. Do not drain.
Spinach, Chopped **225 g/8 oz**	5 minutes	Place in a a bowl or dish. Add 15 ml/1 tbsp boiling water. Cover with a plate or lid. Stir half-way through cooking. Season after cooking and drain well before serving.
450 g/1 lb	9 minutes	As above, adding 45 ml/3 tbsp boiling water.
Sweetcorn (Corn) **225 g/8 oz**	5 minutes	Place in a bowl or dish. Add 30 ml/2 tbsp boiling water. Stir half-way through cooking. Season after cooking and drain well before serving.
450 g/1 lb	9 minutes	As above, adding 45 ml/3 tbsp boiling water.

Tips on Cooking Fresh Vegetables

Microwaved vegetables should be cooked in either a mixing bowl or, for convenience, a dish suitable for serving. The bowl or dish should be covered with clingfilm (plastic wrap), punctured twice, or with a matching lid or a plate if stirring or rearranging is required during cooking.

Weights given are for vegetables *before* trimming, peeling, etc. It is advisable to leave firm vegetables to stand for 2–3 minutes after cooking but soft vegetables, such as sliced cabbage, tomato halves or mushrooms, may be served straight away. Always season after cooking, but before standing, to avoid toughening.

Some vegetables take longer in the microwave than on the hob, but you will avoid a steamy kitchen and save on washing up.

Blanching in the Microwave

This operation is carried out prior to freezing fresh vegetables. Allow 150 ml/¼ pt/⅔ cup of water to every 450 g/1 lb of prepared vegetables. Place both in a dish, cover with clingfilm (plastic wrap), punctured twice, and cook for only half the time given in the tables. Then drain the vegetables and rinse under cold water. Pack as directed in your freezer instruction book or manual.

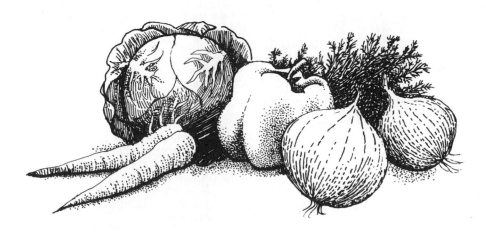

Cooking Fresh Vegetables

	Cook/Heat/Full Power	Comments
Artichokes, Globe 4	20–30 minutes, depending on size	Cut off and discard the stems and leaf tips. Soak in cold water for 1 hour with the leaves pointing downwards. Drain. Stand upright in a large glass or pottery dish. Add 2.5 cm/1 in boiling water. Cover with clingfilm (plastic wrap) and slit it twice. Drain before serving.
Artichokes, Jerusalem 450 g/1 lb	12–14 minutes	Peel and wash the artichokes. Place in a dish or bowl with 15 ml/1 tbsp lemon juice (to prevent browning) and 90 ml/6 tbsp boiling water. Cover with clingfilm (plastic wrap) and slit it twice. Season after cooking and drain before serving.
Asparagus Spears medium–thin 225 g/8 oz	10 minutes	Wash, leave whole and place in a dish. Add 30 ml/2 tbsp water. Cover with clingfilm (plastic wrap) and slit it twice. Season after cooking and drain before serving. Tip: Cut a thin sliver off the root end of each asparagus spear before washing and cooking. If the spears are thick, scrape downwards from the tips to remove a thin layer from the outside of each.
thick 225 g/8 oz	12 minutes	As above.

	Cook/Heat/Full Power	Comments
Aubergines (Eggplants) 450 g/1 lb	6 minutes	Leave unpeeled. Cut off and discard the tops (stem ends) and slice. Place in a dish or bowl with 60 ml/4 tbsp water and 10 ml/2 tsp lemon juice (to retain the flavour). Cover with a plate or matching lid. Stir half-way through cooking. Season after cooking and drain before serving.
Beans, Broad (Lima), French (Green) or Runner 450 g/1 lb	8–10 minutes	Prepare according to the type of bean. Place in a shallow dish with 30 ml/2 tbsp water (60 ml/4 tbsp for broad beans). Cover with a plate or matching lid. Stir half-way through cooking. Season after cooking and drain before serving.
Broccoli Spears 3–4	11 minutes	Wash and shake dry. Split the spears lengthways. Place in a shallow dish with 60 ml/4 tbsp water. Cover with clingfilm (plastic wrap) and slit it twice. Season after cooking and drain before serving.
Brussels Sprouts 225 g/8 oz	10 minutes	Wash the sprouts and remove any bruised outer leaves. Cut a cross in the stem end of each. Place in a shallow dish with 30 ml/2 tbsp water. Cover with a plate or matching lid. Stir half-way through cooking. Season after cooking and drain before serving.

	Cook/Heat/Full Power	Comments
Cabbage **450 g/1 lb**	10 minutes	Remove any damaged or bruised outer leaves. Wash and shred the cabbage. Place in a dish or bowl with 30 ml/2 tbsp water. Cover with a plate or matching lid. Stir half-way through cooking. Season after cooking and drain before serving.
Carrots, **New** **225 g/8 oz**	12–14 minutes	Scrape the carrots and leave whole. Place in a shallow dish with 60 ml/4 tbsp boiling water. Cover with clingfilm (plastic wrap) and slit it twice. Season after cooking and drain before serving.
Old **225 g/8 oz**	8½ –10 minutes	Peel and slice the carrots. Place in a shallow dish with 60 ml/4 tbsp boiling water. Cover with a plate or matching lid. Stir half-way through cooking. Season after cooking and drain before serving.
Cauliflower **675 g/1½ lb**	10–12 minutes	Wash the cauliflower and cut the head into small florets. Place in a dish or bowl with 60 ml/4 tbsp water. Cover with a plate or matching lid. Stir half-way through cooking. Season after cooking and drain before serving.
Celery **350 g/12 oz**	10 minutes	Wash and scrub the celery, then slice. Place in a shallow dish with 30 ml/2 tbsp water. Cover with clingfilm (plastic wrap) and slit it twice. Season after cooking and drain before serving.

	Cook/Heat/Full Power	Comments
Chicory (Belgian Endive) **225 g/8 oz**	8 minutes	Remove a cone-shaped core from the base of each chicory head. Wash the heads gently, removing any damaged outer leaves. Place in a dish with 15 ml/1 tbsp lemon juice (for a pale colour) and 45 ml/3 tbsp water. Cover with clingfilm (plastic wrap) and slit it twice. Season after cooking and drain before serving.
Corn on the Cob **1** **2** **3**	2 minutes 4–4 minutes 6–7 minutes	Cook in the cob's own husk and silk for maximum flavour and moistness. Alteratively, wrap each in clingfilm (plastic wrap), slitting in two or three places. Allow to stand for 5 minutes after cooking, then unwrap and serve.
Courgettes (Zucchini) **450 g/1 lb**	7–8 minutes	Leave unpeeled. Top and tail, then wash and slice. Place in a shallow dish with no added liquid. Cover with a plate or matching lid. Stir half-way through cooking. Season before serving, if liked.
Cucumber **225 g/8 oz**	4 minutes	Peel and dice the cucumber. Place in a shallow dish with 15 ml/1 tbsp water. Cover with a plate or matching lid. Stir half-way through cooking. Season after cooking and drain before serving.

	Cook/Heat/Full Power	Comments
Leeks **450 g/1 lb**	10 minutes	Slit the leeks and wash thoroughly. Trim and slice. Place in a dish or bowl with 30 ml/2 tbsp water. Cover with a plate or matching lid. Stir half-way through cooking. Season lightly after cooking. Drain thoroughly before serving.
Marrow (Squash) **450 g/1 lb**	8–9 minutes	Peel. Slice into rings and remove the centre cores of seeds and fibres. Cut each empty ring into small cubes. Place in a shallow dish with no added liquid. Cover with a plate or matching lid. Stir half-way through cooking. Season after cooking. If necessary, drain before serving.
Mushrooms **225 g/8 oz**	6 minutes	Wash the mushrooms and peel if necessary. Place in a shallow dish with 15 ml/1 tbsp water. Cover with a plate or matching lid. Stir half-way through cooking. Season after cooking and drain before serving. If preferred, omit the water and cook in 15 ml/1 tbsp melted butter or margarine; do not drain after cooking but serve with the juices.
Okra (Ladies' **Fingers)** **450 g/1 lb**	7–8 minutes	Wash the okra and top and tail. Place in a shallow dish with 30 ml/2 tbsp melted butter or margarine. Cover with a plate or matching lid. Stir gently half-way through cooking. Do not drain before serving.

	Cook/Heat/Full Power	Comments
Onions **450 g/1 lb**	8–10 minutes	Peel the onions and halve or quarter if large. Place in a dish or bowl. Add 30 ml/2 tbsp water and a knob of butter or margarine. Cover with clingfilm (plastic wrap) and slit it twice. Season after cooking and drain if necessary before serving.
Parsnips **450 g/1 lb**	8–10 minutes	Peel and dice the parsnips. Place in a shallow dish with 45 ml/3 tbsp water. Cover with a plate or matching lid. Stir half-way through cooking. Season after cooking and drain before serving.
Peas **450 g/1 lb**	9 minutes	Shell the peas. Place in a shallow dish with 30 ml/2 tbsp water. Add a pinch of sugar and a mint sprig, if liked. Cover with a plate or matching lid. Stir half-way through cooking. Season after cooking and drain before serving.
Potatoes, New **small, in their** **skins** **450 g/1 lb**	11 minutes	Thoroughly wash and scrub the potatoes. Place in a shallow dish with 30 ml/2 tbsp water and a mint sprig, if liked. Cover with a plate or matching lid. Stir half-way through cooking. Season after cooking and drain before serving.

	Cook/Heat/Full Power	Comments
Potatoes, Old in their jackets 1 (about 125 g/4 oz)	5–6 minutes; stand for 5 minutes wrapped in foil or a tea towel (dish cloth)	Thoroughly wash and dry the potatoes. Slit or prick the skins in several places. Stand on a plate or kitchen paper and cover with more kitchen paper. Turn over two or three times during cooking. When cooking more than one potato, leave 25 cm/1 in between each. Arrange 3 potatoes in triangle; 4 in a square; 5–8 round the edge of a plate or piece of kitchen paper. After cooking, the potatoes should feel soft when squeezed gently. Note: the cooking times can vary enormously, depending on variety and size; these are the minimum you can expect. For 5–8 potatoes, increase the cooking times accordingly (approx. 3 minutes for each extra potato).
2	6½ –8 minutes; stand for 5 minutes as above.	
3	9–11 minutes; stand for 5 minutes as above.	
4	12–14 minutes; stand for 5 minutes as above.	
Spinach 450 g/1 lb	7–8 minutes	Wash very thoroughly to remove grit. Tear the leaves into small pieces. Place in a dish with no added liquid. Cover with a plate or matching lid. Stir half-way through cooking. Season after cooking and drain if necessary.
Spring Greens (Collard Greens) 450 g/1 lb	7–9 minutes	Tear the leaves off the stalks, wash and shake until almost dry. Shred coarsely and place in a shallow dish. Cover with a plate or matching lid. Stir half-way through cooking. Season after cooking and drain before serving.

	Cook/Heat/Full Power	Comments
Swede (Rutabaga) 450 g/1 lb	10 minutes	Peel the swede and dice. Place in a shallow dish with 60 ml/ 4 tbsp water. Cover with a plate or matching lid. Stir half-way through cooking. Season after cooking and drain before serving.
Peppers (Bell Peppers) 450 g/1 lb	8 minutes	Halve the peppers and remove the cores and seeds. Slice or coarsely chop. Place in a bowl with 30 ml/2 tbsp water. Cover with clingfilm (plastic wrap) and slit it twice. Season after cooking and drain before serving.
Tomatoes 450 g/1 lb	6–7 minutes	Wash and halve the tomatoes. Place in a shallow dish, cut sides uppermost, with no added liquid. Cover with clingfilm (plastic wrap) and slit it twice. If liked, brush the cut sides with melted butter or margarine and sprinkle with sugar. Season before serving.
Turnips 450 g/1 lb	10–12 minutes	Peel the turnips and dice. Place in a shallow dish with 60 ml/4 tbsp water. Cover with a plate or matching lid. Stir half-way through cooking. Season after cooking and drain before serving.

Fruit

Fruit, like vegetables, behaves extremely well in the microwave. Defrosting from frozen is quick and efficient and cooking fresh fruit couldn't be simpler. You used to have to stew fruit in quite heavy syrup to preserve its colour and texture, but in the microwave you need only sweeten to taste as the fruit will keep its shape and colour.

Defrosting Frozen Fruit

	Defrost Setting	Comments
Apples 450 g/1 lb	7 minutes; stand for 8 minutes	Place in a dish or bowl. Cover with a plate or matching lid. Stir gently when partially thawed, bringing the softer fruit from the edge to the centre of the dish.
Blackberries 450 g/1 lb	8 minutes; stand for 7 minutes	As above.
Blackcurrants 450 g/1 lb	5 minutes; stand for 6 minutes	As above.
Cherries 450 g/1 lb	4 minutes; stand for 5 minutes	As above.
Gooseberries 450 g/1 lb	7–8 minutes; stand for 7 minute	As above.
Rhubarb 450 g/1 lb	8 minutes; stand for 8 minutes	As above.
Strawberries 450 g/1 lb	6 minutes; stand for 6 minutes	As above.

Cooking Fresh Fruit

	Cook/Heat/Full Power	Comments
Apples **450 g/1 lb**	7–8 minutes	Peel, core and slice the apples. Place in a dish or bowl with 30 ml/2 tbsp boiling water. Sprinkle to taste with caster (superfine) sugar. Cover with a plate or matching lid. Stir during cooking. For pulpy fruit allow 1 minute less cooking time than suggested, beat the fruit to a purée, then stir in sugar to taste. Cover and reheat for 1½ minutes until the sugar has dissolved completely. Remove from the oven and stir round.
Apricots **450 g/1 lb**	8–9 minutes	Halve, stone (pit) and wash the apricots. Place in a dish or bowl with 60 ml/4 tbsp boiling water. Sprinkle to taste with caster (superfine) sugar. Cover with a plate or matching lid. Stir during cooking. For pulpy fruit, see apples.
Blackberries **450 g/1 lb**	5–7 minutes	Hull the berries and wash well. Place in a dish or bowl with 30 ml/2 tbsp boiling water. Sprinkle to taste with caster (superfine) sugar. Cover with a plate or matching lid. Stir during cooking. For pulpy fruit, see apples.

	Cook/Heat/Full Power	Comments
Blackcurrants **450 g/1 lb**	8–10 minutes	Remove the currants from the stalks and wash well. Place in a dish or bowl with 60 ml/ 4 tbsp boiling water. Sprinkle to taste with caster (superfine) sugar. Cover with a plate or matching lid. Stir during cooking. If the skins remain tough, cook for a further 30 seconds. For pulpy fruit, see apples, then blend in a food processor or blender to a smooth purée.
Damsons **450 g/1 lb**	8–10 minutes	Wash the damsons and slit each with a sharp knife. Place in a dish or bowl with 60 ml/ 4 tbsp boiling water. Sprinkle liberally to taste with caster (superfine) sugar. Cover with a plate or matching lid. Stir during cooking. Do not pulp because of the stones (pits).
Gooseberries **450 g/1 lb**	6–7 minutes	Top and tail the gooseberries and wash. Place in a dish or bowl with 60 ml/4 tbsp boiling water. Sprinkle liberally to taste with caster (superfine) sugar. Cover with a plate or matching lid. Stir during cooking. For pulpy fruit, see apples.

	Cook/Heat/Full Power	Comments
Peaches **450 g/1 lb**	5–7 minutes	Halve, stone (pit) and wash the peaches. Place in a dish or bowl with 30 ml/2 tbsp boiling water and 15 ml/1 tbsp lemon juice. Sprinkle to taste with caster (superfine) sugar. Cover with a plate or matching lid. Stir during cooking. For pulpy fruit, see apples.
Pears **450 g/1 lb**	8–10 minutes	Peel, halve and core the pears. Arrange in a dish or bowl. Put 45 ml/3 tbsp boiling water into a jug. Partially dissolve 50 g/2 oz sugar in the water and add 3 or 4 cloves. Pour over the fruit and cover the bowl with a plate or matching lid. Stir during cooking but take care not to break up the pear halves. Do not pulp.
Plums and **Greengages** **450 g/1 lb**	5–7 minutes	Stone (pit) and wash the fruit. Place in a dish or bowl with 60 ml/4 tbsp boiling water. Sprinkle to taste with caster (superfine) sugar and the grated peel of ½ lemon. Cover with a plate or matching lid. Stir during cooking. For pulpy fruit, see apples.
Rhubarb **450 g/1 lb**	7–9 minutes	Trim and wash the rhubarb and cut into small pieces. Place in a dish or bowl with 30 ml/2 tbsp boiling water. Sprinkle liberally with caster (superfine) sugar and the grated peel of 1 lemon or small orange. Cover with a plate or matching lid. Stir during cooking. For pulpy fruit, see apples.

Convenience Foods

Cooking Convenience Foods from Frozen

	Defrost Setting	Cook/Heat/ Full Power	Comments
Bacon Rashers (Slices) 225 g/8 oz	3 minutes; stand for 6 minutes	5 minutes, turning over after 3 minutes	Separate the rashers after defrosting. Transfer to a microwave rack over a large plate, arranging the rashers in a single layer. Cover with kitchen or greaseproof (waxed) paper.
Beefburgers 2 × 50 g/2 oz	2 minutes; stand for 30 seconds	1½ minutes	Put on a microwave rack over a plate to defrost and cook. Cover with kitchen or greaseproof (waxed) paper. Turn over once during cooking.
4 × 50 g/2 oz	3 minutes; stand for 1 minute	2½ –3 minutes	As above.
2 × 100 g/ 3½ oz	3 minutes; stand for 2 minutes	3 minutes	As above.
4 × 100 g/ 3½ oz	6 minutes; stand for 3 minutes	5½ –6 minutes	As above.

	Defrost Setting	Cook/Heat/ Full Power	Comments
Beef, Roast in Gravy **225 g/8 oz**	6 minutes; stand for 4 minutes	4 minutes	Remove from foil container. Place in a glass or pottery dish. Cover with clingfilm (plastic wrap), slit twice, or with a matching lid.
350 g/12 oz	8 minutes; stand for 4 minutes	6 minutes	As above.
Bread **1 slice**	20–30 seconds; stand for 1 minute		Stand on kitchen paper or a plate. Time depends on thickness of slice.
2 slices	30–40 seconds; stand for 1 minute		As above.
4 slices	1–1½ minutes; stand for 1½ –2 minutes		As above.
6 slices	2 minutes; stand for 2 minutes		As above.
Small loaf	4 minutes; stand for 5–6 minutes		Wrap loaf in kitchen paper.
Large loaf	6–8 minutes; stand for 8–10 minutes		As above.
Bread Rolls **2**	30–60 seconds		Place on a plate and cover with kitchen paper.

	Defrost Setting	Cook/Heat/ Full Power	Comments
Burger Buns **2**	30–60 seconds		Place on a plate and cover with kitchen paper.
4	1½–2 minutes		As above.
Croissants **2**	30–60 seconds	30 seconds	Place on a plate and cover with kitchen paper.
4	1½–2 minutes	45–60 seconds	As above.
Cakes and Puddings **Cake 1 slice**	45 seconds–1¼ minutes		Place on kitchen paper or a plate. Defrosting time will depend on the size of the slice.
Individual Cream Cake/ Pastry	45 seconds; stand for 3 minutes		Place on kitchen paper or a plate.
Cream Sponge **275 g/10 oz**	1–1½ minutes; stand for 20–25 minutes		Place on kitchen paper or a plate. Allow to stand until the cream has thawed through.
Three-layer Cake **475 g/17 oz**	1–1½ minutes; stand for 2–3 minutes		Place on a plate.
Cheesecake **275 g/10 oz**	1½–2½ minutes; stand for 10 minutes		Remove from foil container. Place on kitchen paper or a plate.
475–525 g/ 17–19 oz	2–4 minutes; stand for 10–15 minutes		As above.

	Defrost Setting	Cook/Heat/ Full Power	Comments
Doughnut, Cream			
1	30 seconds; stand for 4 minutes		Place on kitchen paper or a plate. Check that the cream is not thawing too fast.
2	45 seconds; stand for 5 minutes		As above.
4	45–60 seconds; stand for 8 minutes		As above.
Doughnut, Jam			
1	30–60 seconds; stand for 3 minutes		Place on kitchen paper or a plate.
2	1 minute; stand for 5 minutes		As above.
4	1–1½ minutes; stand for 8 minutes		As above.
Cannelloni 400 g/14 oz	7 minutes; stand for 4 minutes	5–6 minutes	Remove from foil container and place in a similar-sized dish. Cover with clingfilm (plastic wrap) and slit it twice.
Chicken, Coated and Fried (Sautéed) 2 or 3 pieces (200–250 g/ 7–9 oz)	4 minutes; stand for 4 minutes	2–3 minutes; stand for 2–3 minutes	Separate the pieces and arrange on a plate or dish with the thickest pieces round the edge. Cover with kitchen paper. Rearrange the pieces half-way through the cooking time and re-cover.

	Defrost Setting	Cook/Heat/ Full Power	Comments
Chicken Cordon Bleu 350 g/12 oz	4 minutes; stand for 4 minutes	6 minutes	Remove the wrapping and place on a plate. Cover with kitchen paper. Note: all crumb-coated portions can be crisped under a hot grill (broiler) after cooking.
Chicken Kiev 350 g/12 oz	As above.	As above.	As above.
Chipolatas 225 g/8 oz	3 minutes; stand for 2 minutes	3 minutes	Stand on kitchen paper or a microwave rack on a plate. Cover with greaseproof (waxed) or kitchen paper.
450 g/1 lb	5 minutes; stand for 3 minutes	4½ minutes	As above.
Chocolate Eclairs 4	1–1½ minutes; stand for 15–20 minutes		Stand on kitchen paper on a plate. Check to ensure the cream does not thaw too quickly or it will run.
Cottage/ Shepherd's Pie individual	3 minutes; stand for 2 minutes	3 minutes	Transfer from foil to a plate or dish and cover with a lid or kitchen paper.
450 g/1 lb	8 minutes; stand for 4 minutes	7 minutes	Transfer from foil to a similar-sized dish. Cover with clingfilm (plastic wrap), slit twice, or a matching lid.

	Defrost Setting	Cook/Heat/ Full Power	Comments
Cream **300 ml/½ pt/** **1¼ cups**	1½ minutes and stand for 5 minutes, then a further 30 seconds and stand for 2 minutes. Repeat until almost thawed.		Remove lid if in a carton. Transfer to a bowl as soon as the cream can be removed and break up with a fork while thawing. Don't overheat but allow the last few ice crystals to melt naturally.
Faggots in Sauce **4** **(375 g/13 oz)**	3 minutes; stand for 3 minutes	4½–5 minutes	Remove from foil container and place in a dish. Cover with clingfilm (plastic wrap), slit twice, or a matching lid. When defrosted, uncover and arrange the faggots round the edge of the dish. Re-cover and cook.
6 **(500 g/18 oz)**	5 minutes; stand for 5 minutes	7–9 minutes	As above.
Fish Cakes **4**	3 minutes; stand for 2 minutes	1½–2 minutes	Place on a plate and cover with kitchen paper. Turn over half-way through defrosting time.
Fish Fingers **4**	2 minutes; stand for 1 minute	2 minutes	Place on a plate and cover with kitchen paper. Turn over half-way through cooking time.
8	4 minutes; stand for 2 minutes	2 minutes	As above.

	Defrost Setting	Cook/Heat/ Full Power	Comments
Fish in Sauce (Boil-in-Bag Cod, Plaice, etc.) **1 × 175 g/ 6 oz** **2 × 175 g/ 12 oz**	4–4½ minutes; stand for 2 minutes 6–6½ minutes; stand for 2 minutes	2½–3 minutes 4½–5 minutes	Place on a plate. Slit the corner of each bag with scissors to prevent the bag ballooning up and bursting. Cook one bag at a time because the sauce heats up faster than the fish and may seep out if cooked for longer. After cooking, the sauce will be hot, so cut the bag open carefully along the slit end and slide the contents out on to the same plate.
Fruit Juice, to soften 175 ml/6 fl oz/ ¾ cup	3 minutes		If the container has a metal top or bottom or a metallic lining, soften the block by running under warm water, then transfer to a jug or bowl to defrost. Otherwise, remove the lid of the container and stand upright on kitchen paper. Break up as soon as possible and stir frequently to thaw fast.
Haddock, Buttered, Smoked 200 g/7 oz	4 minutes; stand for 4 minutes	4 minutes	Place on a plate. Slit the corner of the bag with scissors to prevent the bag ballooning up and bursting. After cooking the butter will be hot, so cut the bag open carefully along the slit end and slide the contents out on to the same plate.

	Defrost Setting	Cook/Heat/ Full Power	Comments
Ice Cream, to soften 1 litre/1¾ pt/ 4¼ cups)	30–45 seconds		Leave, covered, in original container. Check every 10 seconds to ensure that it is not melting too rapidly.
Kipper Fillets, in Bag with Butter 175–225 g/ 6–8 oz	4 minutes; stand for 2 minutes	2–3 minutes	Place on a plate. Slit the corner of each bag with scissors to prevent the bag ballooning up and bursting. Cook one bag at a time because the sauce heats up faster than the fish and may seep out if cooked for longer. After cooking, the sauce will be hot, so cut the bag open carefully along the slit end and slide the contents out on to the same plate.
275 g/10 oz	6 minutes; stand for 2 minutes	5 minutes	
Lasagne 450 g/1 lb	8 minutes; stand for 4 minutes	6 minutes	Remove from foil container and place in a similar-sized dish. Cover with clingfilm (plastic wrap), slit twice, or a matching lid.

	Defrost Setting	Cook/Heat/ Full Power	Comments
Mackerel Fillets, smoked 2 × 225 g/8 oz to serve cold	2–2½ minutes; stand for 2–3 minutes		Place on a plate and cover with kitchen paper.
to serve hot	2–2½ minutes; stand for 2–3 minutes	2–3 minutes	As above.
Mackerel Fillets, Buttered and Smoked (Boil-in-Bag) 175 g/6 oz	4 minutes; stand for 2 minutes	3 minutes	Cook one bag at a time because the sauce heats up faster than the fish and may seep out if cooked for longer. After cooking, the sauce will be hot, so cut the bag open carefully along the slit end and slide the contents out on to the same plate.
Moussaka 400 g/14 oz	7 minutes; stand for 4 minutes	5–6 minutes	Remove from foil container and place in a similar-sized dish. Cover with clingfilm (plastic wrap), slit twice, or cover with a matching lid.
Mousse, individual	30 seconds; stand for 15 minutes		Remove lid.

	Defrost Setting	Cook/Heat/ Full Power	Comments
Oven Chips 225 g/8 oz		Cook from frozen for 6–7 minutes, rearrange after 2½ minutes; stand for 3 minutes	Arrange in a single layer on a 25 cm/10 in plate. Cover with kitchen paper. If liked flash briefly under a hot grill (broiler), turning once, to crisp.
Pancakes, Filled 4	5 minutes	1½–2 minutes	Place on a plate and cover with kitchen paper.
Pastry (Pie Crust) 397 g/14 oz	2 minutes; stand for 5–10 minutes		Stand until soft enough to roll out.
Pâté 1 portion	2–2½ minutes; stand for 5–10 minutes		Transfer to a plate and cover with kitchen paper. Take care not to heat.
Pizza 12.5 cm/5 in (200 g/7 oz)	2 minutes; stand for 2 minutes	2 minutes	Snip the wrapping after defrosting and before cooking/heating or remove completely, according to the packet instructions.
18 cm/7 in (250–275 g/ 9–10 oz)	3 minutes; stand for 2 minutes	2½ minutes	As above.

	Defrost Setting	Cook/Heat/ Full Power	Comments
Pizza, French Bread 2 pieces	2 minutes; stand for 2 minutes	2 minutes	Snip the wrapping after defrosting and before cooking/heating or remove completely according to the packet instructions. Note: if any of the above are not wrapped top and bottom, stand on a plate and cover with kitchen paper while defrosting and cooking/heating.
Pizza Buns 2	1 minute; stand for 1½ minutes	2 minutes	As above.
Plate Meal, home-prepared and frozen	1 minute; stand for 5 minutes	4½–5 minutes	If covered with clingfilm (plastic wrap), slit it twice before defrosting and cooking. If not, cover with kitchen paper.
Pork Pies individual	1 minute; stand for 15 minutes		Place on kitchen paper on a plate. Do not overheat or the jelly will melt.
Prepared Meals, shop-bought e.g. Sweet and Sour Chicken 175–225 g/ 6–8 oz	3–4 minutes; stand for 3 minutes	3–4 minutes	Remove from container and place in a suitable dish. Cover with clingfilm (plastic wrap), slit twice, or a matching lid. Stir before serving.

	Defrost Setting	Cook/Heat/ Full Power	Comments
Salmon, Smoked Slices, 200 g/ 7 oz pack	45 seconds; stand for 25–30 minutes		Turn over after 20 seconds, defrosting. Take care not to heat.
Sausage Rolls, Cooked 1	45 seconds; stand for 2 minutes	15 seconds	Stand on kitchen paper on a plate. Cover with more paper.
4	1½–2 minutes; stand for 3 minutes	45 seconds	As above.
Sausages, large (6 per 450 g/1 lb) 2	2 minutes; stand for 2 minutes	3½ minutes	Stand on kitchen paper on a microwave rack or plate. Brush with a baste (pages 332–3). Cover with greaseproof (waxed) paper or an inverted bowl or use a browning dish for the best results.
4	2 minutes; stand for 2 minutes	5 minutes	As above.
medium (8 per 450 g/ 1 lb) 2	1½ minutes; stand for 1 minute	2½ minutes	As above.
4	2 minutes; stand for 2 minutes	3½ minutes	As above.

	Defrost Setting	Cook/Heat/ Full Power	Comments
Sausages, Cocktail or Chipolata **225 g/8 oz**	3 minutes; stand for 2 minutes	3 minutes	As for large sausages above.
450 g/1 lb	5 minutes; stand for 3 minutes	4½ minutes	As above.
Trifles, Individual Shop-bought	1–2 minutes; stand for 5 minutes		Remove lid.
Waffles **2**		1–2 minutes; stand for 2 minutes	Place on kitchen paper, cover with more paper. Flash under a hot grill (broiler) to crisp, if liked.
Yoghurt Individual	2–3 minutes; stand for 5 minutes		Remove lid. Stir before serving

Cooking Canned Convenience Foods

	Cook/Heat/Full Power	Comments
Casserole, Soya-type Chunks or Meat **439 g/15½ oz**	4 minutes; stand for 2 minutes	Place in a bowl and cover with a plate. Stir after 2 minutes' cooking.
Sweetcorn (Corn) **350 g/12 oz**	4–4½ minutes	Place in a bowl. Cover with clingfilm (plastic wrap), slit twice, or a plate or lid.

	Cook/Heat/Full Power	Comments
Custard **to warm** **425 g/15 oz**	1½–2 minutes	Pour the custard into jug or bowl and cover with a plate. Stir once or twice. Do not allow to boil.
to heat until hot **425 g/15 oz**	3½ minutes	As above.
500 ml/17 fl oz/ **2¼ cups**	4–4½ minutes	As above.
Pasta, Spaghetti Hoops, etc. **439 g/15½ oz**	3 minutes; stand for 2 minutes	Place in a bowl and cover with a plate. Stir once or twice.
Rice Pudding **439 g/15½ oz**	3 minutes	Place in a bowl and cover with a plate. Stir once or twice.
Soup **condensed** **about 295 g/10 oz**	6–6½ minutes	Empty the soup into bowl. Add 1 can of cold water and mix well. Cover with a plate. Stir every minute while cooking. Do not allow to boil. The cooking time will vary depending on the consistency of the soup.
ready-to-serve **425 g/15 oz**	4–5 minutes	Place in mugs or bowls. Cover with plates. Stir every minute while cooking. The cooking time will depend on personal taste in hot soup, but do not allow to boil vigorously.
Sponge Pudding **225–275 g/8–10 oz**	1½–2 minutes	Remove from the can and place in a bowl. Cover with clingfilm (plastic wrap), slit twice, or a plate.

	Cook/Heat/Full Power	Comments
Steak and Kidney Pudding **439 g/15½ oz**	4–5 minutes; stand for 5 minutes	Remove from the can and place in a bowl. Cover with clingfilm (plastic wrap), slit twice, or a plate.
Vegetables **Small (peas, beans, etc.)** **225–275 g/8–10 oz**	2–3½ minutes; stand for 2 minutes	Pour 30 ml/2 tbsp of liquid from the can into a serving dish or bowl and drain off and discard the rest of the liquid, but do not drain if the vegetable is in sauce, e.g. baked beans. Put the vegetables into the dish and cover with clingfilm (plastic wrap), slit twice, or with a plate. Stir the vegetables at least once during cooking/heating. Drain before serving.
400–439 g/ **14–15½ oz**	3–4 minutes; stand for 3 minutes	As above.
Large (artichoke, asparagus, etc.) **425–439 g/** **15–15½ oz**	4–5 minutes; stand for 3 minutes	As above but do not stir.

Miscellaneous Convenience Foods

	Defrost Setting	Cook/Heat/ Full Power	Comments
Butter **125 g/4 oz**	15 seconds and stand for 15 seconds, then a further 10 seconds and stand for 15 seconds		Remove from any foil. Place on a plate. Repeat the 10 seconds defrosting and 15 seconds standing until thawed. Check often to ensure the butter does not become too soft.
225 g/8 oz	30 seconds and stand for 30 seconds, then a further 15 seconds and stand for 30 seconds		As above.
to melt from room temp **15 g/½ oz/** **1 tbsp**	40–50 seconds		Put into a cup or jug. Cover with a plate. Allow extra time if chilled.
25 g/1 oz/ **2 tbsp**	1–1½ minutes		As above.
50 g/2 oz/ **¼ cup**	1½–2 minutes		As above.
75 g/3 oz/ **⅓ cup**	2–2½ minutes		As above.
125 g/4 oz/ **½ cup**	2½–3 minutes		As above.
225 g/8 oz/ **1 cup**	3–3½ minutes		As above.
to soften from chilled **225 g/8 oz**	40–50 seconds		Remove from foil wrapping. Stand on a plate.

	Defrost Setting	Cook/Heat/ Full Power	Comments
Christmas Pudding, to heat from room temp **1 portion**		45 seconds; stand for 1 minute	Stand on a plate and cover with kitchen paper.
450 g/1 lb		3–4 minutes; stand for 2 minutes	Cook in bowl, covered with kitchen paper or a plate.
900 g/2 lb		5 minutes; stand for 5 minutes	Cook in bowl, covered with kitchen paper or a plate.
Cheese, to bring to serving temp from chilled **Firm Cheese** **225 g/8 oz**	30–45 seconds		Put uncovered on a plate.
Soft Cheese **225 g/8 oz**	15–45 seconds		As above.
Chocolate, to melt from room temp **100 g/3½ oz bar**	3–3½ minutes		Break into pieces and place in a bowl. Stir once during cooking and watch carefully to stop as soon as it starts to melt. Overheated chocolate may become granular or burn (allow a further 30–60 seconds if chilled).
200 g/7 oz bar	4–5 minutes		As above.

	Defrost Setting	Cook/Heat/ Full Power	Comments
Gelatine, to dissolve 1 × 15 ml/ 1 tbsp sachet	1½–1¾ minutes		Add 30 ml/2 tbsp cold liquid to the granules in a jug or bowl. Cover with a plate. Swirl round after 1 minute. Stir thoroughly after cooking to ensure the gelatine has dissolved. Do not allow to boil.
Jelly, to melt 1 × 135 g/ 4¾ oz packet	2–2½ minutes		Break into cubes and place in a jug. Cover with a plate.
Meat Pie individual		45 seconds– 1¼ minutes	Remove from foil tray. Stand on kitchen paper and cover with more paper.
family size (450 g/1 lb)		3 minutes; stand for 4 minutes	As above.
Mince Pies, cooked 1		15 seconds; stand for 1–2 minutes	Stand on paper. Leave uncovered.
4		1 minute; stand for 2–3 minutes	As above.
Plate Meal, from chilled 1 serving		4–4½ minutes; stand for 30–40 seconds	Cover with clingfilm (plastic wrap) if not already done. Slit it twice. Alternatively, cover with an inverted plate.

Starters

This world-wide selection of easy-to-prepare starters and nibbles covers old favourites like quiches, pâtés, Egg Mayonnaise, Potted Shrimps and the typically English Scotch Woodcock, still served in City of London gentlemen's clubs. All of them make the most of the microwave. For anyone into more exotic taste sensations, the microwave makes light work of bean salads, aubergine (egg plant) and avocado combinations, Pickled Mushrooms and hearty and substantial snacks from Germany and Holland. The warm and trendy Leafy Salad with Goat's Cheese and Warm Dressing also takes a bow, as do Stuffed Tomatoes, a buttery Rich Liver Pâté and Devilled Nuts to munch with drinks.

Minted Aubergine Dip

SERVES 6–8

750 g/1½ lb aubergines
(eggplants)
Juice of 1 lemon
20 ml/4 tsp olive oil
1–2 garlic cloves, crushed
250 ml/8 fl oz/1 cup fromage frais
or quark
15 ml/1 tbsp chopped mint leaves
1.5 ml/¼ tsp caster (superfine)
sugar
7.5–10 ml/1½–2 tsp salt

Top and tail the aubergines and halve them lengthways. Arrange them on a large plate, cut sides down, and cover with kitchen paper. Cook on Full for 8–9 minutes or until soft. Scoop the flesh out of the skins directly into a food processor and add the remaining ingredients. Process to a smooth and creamy purée. Spoon into a serving bowl, cover and chill lightly before serving.

Aubergine Dip with Tomatoes and Mixed Herbs

SERVES 6–8

750 g/1½ lb aubergines
(eggplants)
5 ml/1 tsp chopped mint leaves
75 ml/3 tsp chopped coriander
(cilantro) leaves
5 ml/1 tsp chopped parsley
3 tomatoes, blanched, skinned,
seeded and finely chopped

Top and tail the aubergines and halve them lengthways. Arrange them on a large plate, cut sides down, and cover with kitchen paper. Cook on Full for 8–9 minutes or until soft. Scoop the flesh out of the skins directly into a food processor and add the remaining ingredients except the tomatoes. Process to a smooth and creamy purée. Stir in the tomatoes, then spoon into a serving bowl, cover and chill lightly before serving.

Middle Eastern Aubergine and Tahini Dip

SERVES 6–8

750 g/1½ lb aubergines (eggplants)
45 ml/3 tbsp tahini (sesame seed paste)
Juice of 1 small lemon
1 garlic clove, thinly sliced
25 ml/1½ tbsp olive oil
1 small onion, sliced
60 ml/4 tbsp coarsely chopped coriander (cilantro) leaves
5 ml/1 tsp caster (superfine) sugar
5–10 ml/1–2 tsp salt

Top and tail the aubergines and halve them lengthways. Arrange them on a large plate, cut sides down, and cover with kitchen paper. Cook on Full for 8–9 minutes or until soft. Scoop the flesh out of the skins directly into a food processor. Add the remaining ingredients and salt to taste. Process to a smooth and creamy purée. Spoon into a serving bowl and serve at room temperature.

Turkish Aubergine Dip

SERVES 6–8

750 g/1½ lb aubergines (eggplants)
30 ml/2 tbsp olive oil
Juice of 1 large lemon
2.5–5 ml/½–1 tsp salt
2.5 ml/½ tsp caster (superfine) sugar
Black olives, red (bell) pepper strips and tomato wedges, to garnish

Top and tail the aubergines and halve them lengthways. Arrange them on a large plate, cut sides down, and cover with kitchen paper. Cook on Full for 8–9 minutes or until soft. Scoop the flesh out of the skins directly into a food processor and add the remaining ingredients. Process to a semi-smooth purée. Pile into a serving dish and garnish with olives, red pepper and tomato wedges.

Greek Aubergine Dip

SERVES 6–8

750 g/1½ lb aubergines (eggplants)
1 small onion, coarsely grated
2 garlic cloves, thinly sliced
5 ml/1 tsp malt vinegar
5 ml/1 tsp lemon juice
150 ml/¼ pt/⅔ cup mild olive oil
2 large tomatoes, blanched, seeded and coarsely chopped
Parsley, green or red (bell) pepper rings and small black olives, to garnish

Top and tail the aubergines and halve them lengthways. Arrange them on a large plate, cut sides down, and cover with kitchen paper. Cook on Full for 8–9 minutes or until soft. Scoop the flesh out of the skins directly into a food processor and add the onion, garlic, vinegar, lemon juice and oil. Process to a smooth purée. Spoon into a large bowl and mix in the tomatoes. Pile into a serving dish and garnish with parsley, pepper rings and olives.

Bagna Cauda

SERVES 4–6

An immensely rich and unique anchovy dip from Italy which, once made, should be kept warm over a spirit stove on the dining table. The dunks are generally raw or cooked vegetables. Use only mild and delicate pale gold extra virgin olive oil, otherwise the flavour may be too strong.

30 ml/2 tbsp olive oil
25 g/1 oz/2 tbsp unsalted (sweet)
  butter
1 garlic clove, crushed
50 g/2 oz/1 small can anchovy
  fillets in oil
60 ml/4 tbsp finely chopped
  parsley
15 ml/1 tbsp finely chopped basil
  leaves

Put the oil, butter and garlic into a non-metallic flameproof bowl. Add the oil from the can of anchovies, the parsley and basil. Finely chop the anchovies and add to the bowl. Part-cover the bowl with a plate and cook on Defrost for 3–4 minutes until the dip is just warmed. Transfer to a lit spirit stove and keep warm while eating.

Bagna Cauda with Cream

SERVES 6

Prepare as for Bagna Cauda, but add 150 ml/¼ pt/⅔ cup crème fraîche to the butter mixture with the anchovies. Cook for an extra 1½ minutes.

Aubergine Casserole

SERVES 4

A Louisiana recipe, which returned with me from this steamy part of North America.

2 aubergines (eggplants), about
  550 g/1¼ lb in all
1 celery stalk, finely chopped
1 large onion, finely chopped
½ green (bell) pepper, seeded and
  finely chopped
30 ml/2 tbsp sunflower or corn oil
3 tomatoes, skinned and chopped
75 g/3 oz/1½ cups fresh white
  breadcrumbs
Salt and freshly ground black
  pepper
50 g/2 oz/½ cup Cheddar cheese,
  grated

Using a sharp knife, score the skin of each aubergine lengthways all the way round. Place on a plate, cover with kitchen paper and cook on Full for 6 minutes, turning once. They should feel tender but, if not, cook for a further 1–2 minutes. Halve each along the scoring, then scoop the pulp into blender or food processor and discard the skins. Process to a purée. Put the celery, onion, green pepper and oil into a 2 litre/3½ pt/8½ cup casserole dish (Dutch oven), cover with a plate and cook on Full for 3 minutes. Mix in the aubergine purée, tomatoes, breadcrumbs and salt and pepper to taste and cook on Full for a further 3 minutes. Uncover, sprinkle with the cheese and reheat, uncovered, on Full for 2 minutes. Allow to stand for 2 minutes before serving.

Pickled Cocktail Mushrooms

••••••••••••••••••••••••••••••
SERVES 8

60 ml/4 tbsp red wine vinegar
60 ml/4 tbsp sunflower or corn oil
1 onion, very thinly sliced
5 ml/1 tsp salt
15 ml/1 tbsp chopped coriander
    (cilantro) leaves
5 ml/1 tsp mild made mustard
15 ml/1 tbsp light soft brown
    sugar
5 ml/1 tsp Worcestershire sauce
Cayenne pepper
350 g/12 oz button mushrooms

Put the vinegar, oil, onion, salt, coriander, mustard, sugar and Worcestershire sauce into a 2 litre/ 3½ pt/8½ cup casserole dish (Dutch oven) with a sprinkling of cayenne pepper. Cover with a plate and heat on Full for 6 minutes. Stir in the mushrooms. When cold, cover and chill for about 12 hours. Drain and serve with a creamy dip.

Stuffed Baked Aubergines with Eggs and Pine Nuts

••••••••••••••••••••••••••••••
SERVES 2

2 aubergines (eggplants), about
    550 g/1¼ lb in all
10 ml/2 tsp lemon juice
75 g/3 oz/1½ cups fresh white or
    brown breadcrumbs
45 ml/3 tbsp toasted pine nuts
    (page 205)
7.5 ml/1½ tsp salt
1 garlic clove, crushed
3 hard-boiled (hard-cooked) eggs,
    chopped
60 ml/4 tbsp milk
5 ml/1 tsp dried mixed herbs
20 ml/4 tsp olive oil

Using a sharp knife, score the skin of each aubergine lengthways all the way round. Place on a plate, cover with kitchen paper and cook on Full for 6 minutes, turning once. They should feel tender but, if not, cook for a further 1–2 minutes. Halve each along the scoring, then scoop the pulp into a blender or food processor, leaving the skins intact. Add the lemon juice and process to a smooth purée. Scrape into a bowl and mix in all the remaining ingredients except the oil. Spoon into the aubergine skins, then arrange on a plate with the narrow ends towards the centre. Trickle the oil over the top, cover with kitchen paper and reheat on Full for 4 minutes. Eat hot or cold.

Greek Mushrooms

••••••••••••••••••••••••••••••
SERVES 4

1 bouquet garni sachet
1 garlic clove, crushed
2 bay leaves
60 ml/4 tbsp water
30 ml/2 tbsp lemon juice
15 ml/1 tbsp wine vinegar
15 ml/1 tbsp olive oil
5 ml/1 tsp salt
450 g/1 lb button mushrooms
30 ml/2 tbsp chopped parsley

Put all the ingredients except the mushrooms and parsley into a large bowl. Cover with a plate and heat on Full for 4 minutes. Stir in the mushrooms, cover as before and cook on Full for a further 3½ minutes. Cool, cover, then chill for several hours. Remove the bouquet garni then, using a draining spoon, lift the mushrooms on to four plates, sprinkle each with the parsley and serve.

Artichokes Vinaigrette
•••••••••••••••••••••••••••••
SERVES 4

450g/1lb Jerusalem artichokes
Vinaigrette dressing, home-made
  or bought
10 ml/2 tsp chopped parsley
5 ml/1 tsp chopped tarragon

Put the artichokes and a little water into a dish and cover with a plate. Cook on Full for 10 minutes, turning the dish twice. Drain thoroughly and slice thickly. Coat with the vinaigrette dressing while still warm. Divide between four plates and sprinkle with the parsley and tarragon.

Caesar Salad
•••••••••••••••••••••••••••••
SERVES 4

A unique salad, created in the twenties by Caesar Cardini, which unusually features coddled eggs. It's a superbly simple starter yet has classic chic.

1 cos (romaine) lettuce, chilled
1 garlic clove, crushed
60 ml/4 tbsp extra virgin olive oil
Salt and freshly ground black
  pepper
2 large eggs
5 ml/1 tsp Worcestershire sauce
Juice of 2 lemons, strained
90 ml/6 tbsp freshly grated
  Parmesan cheese
50 g/2 oz/1 cup garlic croûtons

Cut the lettuce across into 5 cm/2 in pieces and place in a salad bowl with the garlic, oil and seasoning to taste. Toss gently. To coddle the eggs, line a cereal bowl with clingfilm (plastic wrap) and break in the eggs. Cook, uncovered, on Defrost for 1½ minutes. Add to the salad bowl with all the remaining ingredients and toss again until thoroughly mixed. Arrange on dinner plates and serve straight away.

Dutch Chicory with Egg and Butter
•••••••••••••••••••••••••••••
SERVES 4

8 heads chicory (Belgian endive)
30 ml/2 tbsp lemon juice
75 ml/5 tbsp boiling water
5 ml/1 tsp salt
75 g/3 oz/⅓ cup butter, at kitchen
  temperature and quite soft
4 hard-boiled (hard-cooked) eggs
  (pages 98–9) , chopped

Trim the chicory and cut out a cone-shaped piece from the base of each to prevent a bitter taste. Arrange the chicory in a single layer in a 20 cm/8 in diameter dish and add the lemon juice and water. Sprinkle with the salt. Cover with clingfilm (plastic wrap) and slit it twice to allow the steam to escape. Cook on Full for 15 minutes. Allow to stand 3 minutes, then drain. While the chicory is cooking, beat the butter until light and creamy. Mix in the eggs. Arrange the chicory on four warmed plates and top with the egg mixture. Eat straight away.

Egg Mayonnaise
•••••••••••••••••••••••••••••
SERVES 1

One of France's standard starters, Egg Mayonnaise is reliably appetising and can be varied according to taste.

Shredded lettuce leaves
1–2 hard-boiled (hard-cooked)
  eggs (pages 98–9), halved
Mayonnaise Sauce (page 319), or
  use bought mayonnaise
4 canned anchovy fillets in oil
1 tomato, cut into wedges

Arrange the lettuce on a plate. Top with the eggs, cut sides down. Coat fairly thickly with the mayonnaise, then garnish to taste with the anchovies and tomato wedges.

Eggs with Skordalia Mayonnaise

SERVES 4

A simplified version of a complex garlic and breadcrumb mayonnaise sauce that complements the full flavour and texture of the eggs.

150 ml/¼ pt/⅔ cup Mayonnaise
*   Sauce (page 319)*
1 garlic clove, crushed
10 ml/2 tsp fresh white
*   breadcrumbs*
15 ml/1 tbsp ground almonds
10 ml/2 tsp lemon juice
10 ml/2 tsp chopped parsley
Shredded lettuce leaves
2 or 4 hard-boiled (hard-cooked)
*   eggs (pages 98–9), halved*
1 red onion, very thinly sliced
Small Greek black olives, to
*   garnish*

Mix together the mayonnaise, garlic, breadcrumbs, almonds, lemon juice and parsley. Arrange the lettuce on a plate, then top with the egg halves. Coat with the mayonnaise mixture, then garnish with the onion slices and olives.

Scotch Woodcock

SERVES 4

This belongs to the old league of City gentlemen's clubs and, served hot, remains one of the most up-market of canapés.

4 slices bread
Butter
Gentleman's Relish or anchovy
*   paste*
2 quantities Extra Creamy
*   Scrambled Eggs (pages 99–100)*
A few canned anchovy fillets in oil,
*   to garnish*

Toast the bread, then spread with butter. Spread thinly with Gentleman's Relish or anchovy paste, cut each slice into quarters and keep warm. Make the Extra Creamy Scrambled Eggs and spoon on to the toast quarters. Garnish with anchovy fillets.

Eggs with Swedish Mayonnaise

SERVES 4

Shredded lettuce leaves
1–2 hard-boiled (hard-cooked)
*   eggs (pages 98–9), halved*
25 ml/1½ tbsp apple purée (apple
*   sauce)*
Caster (superfine) sugar
150 ml/¼ pt/⅔ cup Mayonnaise
*   Sauce (page 319), or use*
*   bought mayonnaise*
5 ml/1 tsp horseradish sauce
5–10 ml/1–2 tsp black or orange
*   mock caviare*
1 red-skinned eating (dessert)
*   apple, thinly sliced*

Arrange the lettuce on a plate. Top with the eggs, cut sides down. Sweeten the apple purée lightly with caster sugar, then mix into the mayonnaise with the horseradish sauce. Coat the eggs with this mixture, then garnish with the mock caviare and a band of apple slices.

Turkish Bean Salad

SERVES 6

This is called *fesulya plaki* in Turkey, and is essentially a mix of canned haricot (navy) beans and a helping of Mediterranean vegetables. It's an economical starter and begs for crusty bread on the side.

75 ml/5 tbsp olive oil
2 onions, finely grated
2 garlic cloves, crushed
1 large ripe tomato, blanched, skinned, seeded and chopped
1 green (bell) pepper, seeded and very finely chopped
10 ml/2 tsp caster (superfine) sugar
75 ml/5 tbsp water
2.5–5 ml/½–1 tsp salt
30 ml/2 tbsp chopped dill (dill weed)
400 g/14 oz/1 large can haricot beans, drained

Put the oil, onions and garlic into a 1.75 litre/3 pt/7½ cup dish and cook, uncovered, on Full for 5 minutes, stirring twice. Mix in the tomato, green pepper, sugar, water and salt. Two-thirds cover with a plate and cook on Full for 7 minutes, stirring twice. Allow to cool completely, then cover and chill for several hours. Stir in the dill and beans. Cover again and chill for a further hour.

Bean Salad with Egg

SERVES 6

Prepare as for Turkish Bean Salad but garnish each portion with wedges of hard-boiled (hard-cooked) egg (pages 98–9).

Potted Kipper

SERVES 6

275 g/10 oz kipper fillets
75 g/3 oz/⅓ cup cream cheese
Juice of ½ lemon
2.5 ml/½ tsp English or continental made mustard
1 garlic clove, thinly sliced (optional)
Hot toast or savoury biscuits (crackers), to serve

Microwave the kippers as directed on page 56. Remove the skin and bones and flake up the flesh. Transfer to a food processor with the remaining ingredients and process until the mixture forms a paste. Spoon into a small dish and level the top. Cover and chill until firm. Serve spread on to hot toast or savoury biscuits.

Slimmers' Potted Kipper

SERVES 6

Prepare as for Potted Kipper, but substitute fromage frais for the cream cheese.

Buttery Potted Kipper

SERVES 6

Prepare as for Potted Kipper, but substitute unsalted (sweet) butter for the cream cheese.

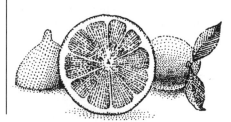

Potted Shrimp

SERVES 4

Another typically British revivalist recipe. Serve with freshly made thin white toast.

175 g/6 oz/¾ cup unsalted (sweet)
  butter
225 g/8 oz/2 cups tiny shrimps
A pinch of allspice
White pepper
Toast, to serve

Put the butter into bowl and cover with a plate. Microwave on Full for about 2–3 minutes until melted. Combine two-thirds of the butter with the shrimps, then season with the allspice and pepper to taste. Spoon into four individual pots or ramekin dishes (custard cups). Coat evenly with the rest of the butter. Chill until the butter is set. Turn out on to plates and eat with toast.

Potted Smoked Salmon

SERVES 4

Prepare as for Potted Shrimp, but substitute coarsely chopped smoked salmon for the shrimps.

Potted Smoked Mackerel

SERVES 4

Prepare as for Potted Shrimp, but substitute flaked smoked mackerel for the shrimps.

Baked Stuffed Egg Avocados

SERVES 4

A neglected recipe from the seventies, often chosen then for a light meal or substantial starter.

2 celery stalks, finely chopped
60 ml/4 tbsp fresh white
  breadcrumbs
2.5 ml/½ tsp finely grated lemon
  peel
5 ml/1 tsp onion salt
2.5 ml/½ tsp paprika
45 ml/3 tbsp single (light) cream
Freshly ground black pepper
2 medium–large just-ripe avocados
2 large hard-boiled (hard-cooked)
  eggs (pages 98–9), chopped
20 ml/4 tsp toasted breadcrumbs
20 ml/4 tsp melted butter

Combine the celery, white breadcrumbs, lemon peel, onion salt, paprika and cream and add pepper to taste. Halve the avocados and remove the stones (pits). Scoop out some of the flesh to make room for the filling and mash coarsely. Add the flesh to the crumb mixture with the eggs. Mix well and pile into the avocado shells. Arrange on a plate with the pointed ends towards the centre. Sprinkle with the toasted breadcrumbs, then trickle the butter over the top. Cover with kitchen paper and warm on Full for 4–5 minutes. Eat straight away.

Baked Stuffed Avocados with Prawns

SERVES 4

Prepare as for Baked Stuffed Egg Avocados, but substitute 175 g/6 oz/ 1½ cups peeled prawns (shrimp), coarsely chopped, for the eggs.

Baked Stuffed Avocados with Parma Ham and Walnuts

SERVES 4

Prepare as for Baked Stuffed Egg Avocados, but substitute 100 g/ 3½ oz/1 cup coarsely chopped Parma ham and 30 ml/2 tbsp finely chopped walnuts for the eggs.

Tomato and Cheese-stuffed Avocados

SERVES 2 AS A MAIN MEAL,
4 AS A STARTER

A glorious mix, perfect for vegetarians and anyone else thinking along those lines.

2 large ripe avocados
Juice of ½ lime
50 g/2 oz/1 cup soft brown breadcrumbs
1 small onion, finely grated
2 tomatoes, blanched, skinned and chopped
Salt and freshly ground black pepper
50 g/2 oz/½ cup hard cheese, grated
Paprika
8 toasted hazelnuts (page 205)

Halve the avocados and carefully scoop out the flesh directly into a bowl. Add the lime juice and mash finely with a fork. Stir in the breadcrumbs, onion and tomatoes with salt and pepper to taste. Place in the avocado shells and sprinkle with the cheese and paprika. Top each half with two hazelnuts. Arrange on a large plate with the pointed ends towards the centre. Cover loosely with kitchen paper and cook on Full for 5–5½ minutes. Serve straight away.

Sturdy Max

SERVES 1

A recipe from old Berlin

Butter a large slice of German rye bread and top with a slice of German air-dried ham (*schinken*). Top with two fried eggs (page 99), sprinkle with chopped parsley or chives and serve straight away.

Scandinavian Rollmop and Apple Salad

SERVES 4

75 g/3 oz dried apple rings
150 ml/¼ pt/⅔ cup water
3 rollmops with onions
150 ml/¼ pt/⅔ cup whipping or double (heavy) cream
Crispbread, to serve

Wash the apple rings, snap into chunks, put into a medium-sized bowl and add the water. Cover with a plate and heat on Full for 5 minutes. Allow to stand for 5 minutes, then drain thoroughly. Undo the rollmops and cut them into diagonal strips. Add to the apple with the onions and mix in the cream. Cover and marinate overnight in the refrigerator. Stir before serving, then arrange on individual plates and serve with crispbread.

Rollmop and Apple Salad with Curry Sauce

SERVES 4

Prepare as for Scandinavian Rollmop and Apple Salad, but substitute half mayonnaise and half crème fraîche for the cream. Flavour with curry paste to taste.

Leafy Salad with Goat's Cheese and Warm Dressing

SERVES 4

12 small round lettuce leaves
1 box cress
20 rocket leaves
4 individual goat's cheeses
90 ml/6 tbsp grapeseed oil
30 ml/2 tbsp hazelnut oil
10 ml/2 tsp orange flower water
10 ml/2 tsp Dijon mustard
45 ml/3 tbsp rice or cider vinegar
10 ml/2 tsp caster (superfine) sugar
5 ml/1 tsp salt

Wash and dry the lettuce leaves. Trim, wash and dry the cress. Wash and drain the rocket. Arrange these three attractively on four individual plates and place a cheese in the centre of each. Place all the remaining ingredients in a bowl and heat, uncovered, on Defrost for 3 minutes. Stir to mix, then spoon over each salad.

Dutch Egg Snack

SERVES 1

A filling starter, unpronounceable by its Dutch name – uitsmijter.

Butter a large slice of white or brown bread and top with a thick slice of ham or thinly sliced rare roast beef. Top with two freshly fried eggs (page 99) and garnish with tomato wedges, baby gherkins (cornichons) and any salad leaves.

Jellied Tomato Sundaes

SERVES 4

4 tomatoes, blanched, skinned and chopped
5 ml/1 tsp finely chopped fresh root ginger
5 ml/1 tsp finely grated lime peel
20 ml/4 tsp powdered gelatine
750 ml/1¼ pt/3 cups chicken stock
30 ml/2 tbsp tomato purée (paste)
5 ml/1 tsp Worcestershire sauce
5 ml/1 tsp caster (superfine) sugar
5 ml/1 tsp celery salt
20 ml/4 tsp crème fraîche
Toasted sesame seeds (page 206), for sprinkling
Cheese biscuits (crackers), to serve

Divide the tomatoes equally between four large wine glasses, then sprinkle with the ginger and lime peel. Put the gelatine into a 1.5 litre/2½ pt/6 cup bowl with 75 ml/5 tbsp stock and leave to soften for 5 minutes. Melt, uncovered, on Defrost for about 2 minutes. Stir in the remaining stock with the tomato purée, Worcestershire sauce, sugar and celery salt. Whisk gently until evenly combined, then chill only until just beginning to thicken slightly. Spoon over the tomatoes, then chill to set. Top each with 5 ml/1 tsp crème fraîche and a sprinkling of sesame seeds before serving with cheese biscuits.

Stuffed Tomatoes

SERVES 4

A sound but uncomplicated starter, delicious served on rounds of buttered toast or rounds of bread fried (sautéed) in garlic butter.

6 tomatoes
1 onion, grated
50 g/2 oz/1 cup fresh white breadcrumbs
5 ml/1 tsp made mustard
5 ml/1 tsp salt
15 ml/1 tbsp chopped chives or parsley
50 g/2 oz/½ cup chopped cold cooked meat or poultry, chopped prawns (shrimp) or grated cheese
1 small egg, beaten

Halve the tomatoes and scoop the centres into a bowl, discarding the hard cores. Stand the shells upside-down on kitchen paper to drain. Put all the remaining ingredients into a bowl and add the tomato pulp. Stir well with a fork to mix, then spoon back into the tomato halves. Arrange in two rings, one inside the other, round the edge of a dinner plate. Cover with kitchen paper and cook on Full for 7 minutes, turning the plate three times. Serve hot, allowing three halves per portion.

Italian Stuffed Tomatoes

SERVES 4

6 tomatoes
75 g/3 oz/1½ cups fresh brown breadcrumbs
175 g/6 oz/1½ cups Mozzarella cheese, grated
2.5 ml/½ tsp dried oregano
2.5 ml/½ tsp salt
10 ml/2 tsp chopped basil leaves
1 garlic clove, crushed
1 small egg, beaten

Halve the tomatoes and scoop the centres into a bowl, discarding the hard cores. Stand the shells upside-down on kitchen paper to drain. Put all the remaining ingredients into a bowl and add the tomato pulp. Stir well with a fork to mix, then spoon back into the tomato halves. Arrange in two rings, one inside the other, round the edge of a dinner plate. Cover with kitchen paper and cook on Full for 7–8 minutes, turning the plate three times. Serve hot or cold, allowing three halves per portion.

French Stuffed Tomatoes

SERVES 4

Prepare as for Italian Stuffed Tomatoes, but substitute blue Roquefort cheese for the Mozzarella and 5 ml/1 tsp dried herbes de Provence for the oregano and basil.

Quiche Lorraine

SERVES 4–6

The original French quiche or savoury flan, with a 'family' of variations.

For the pastry (paste):
175 g/6 oz/1½ cups plain (all-purpose) flour
1.5 ml/¼ tsp salt
100 g/3½ oz/scant ½ cup butter mixed with margarine, white cooking fat or lard, or use all margarine
1 small egg yolk
For the filling:
6 rashers (slices) streaky bacon
3 eggs
300 ml/½ pt/1¼ cups full-cream milk or single (light) cream
2.5 ml/½ level tsp salt
Freshly ground black pepper
Grated nutmeg

To make the pastry, sift the flour and salt into a bowl. Rub in the fat until the mixture resembles fine breadcrumbs, then mix to a firm dough with cold water. Wrap in foil and chill for ½–¾ hour. Turn out on to a floured surface and knead quickly and lightly until smooth. Roll out into a thin circle and use to line a 20 cm/8 in diameter glass, china or pottery flan dish. Pinch the top edge into tiny flutes, then prick all over with fork. Cook uncovered on Full for 6 minutes, turning the dish twice. If the pastry has bulged in places, press down gently with a hand protected by an oven glove. Brush all over with the egg yolk and cook on Full for 1 minute to seal any holes. Leave to stand while preparing the filling.

Arrange the bacon rashers on a plate lined with kitchen paper, cover with another sheet of kitchen paper and cook on Full for 5 minutes, turning once. Drain and allow to cool slightly. Cut each rasher into three pieces and place over the base of the pastry case. Beat the eggs with the milk or cream and season with the salt and pepper to taste. Strain carefully into the flan over the bacon and sprinkle with nutmeg. Cook uncovered on Full, turning the dish four times, for 10–12 minutes or until bubbles just begin to break across the centre. Allow to stand for 10 minutes before cutting. Eat warm or cold.

Cheese and Bacon Quiche

SERVES 4–6

Prepare as for Quiche Lorraine, but use four bacon rashers (slices) instead of six to cover the base of the flan. After straining in the egg and milk mixture, sprinkle the top with 50 g/2 oz/½ cup grated hard cheese in addition to the nutmeg.

Cheese and Mushroom Quiche

SERVES 4–6

Prepare as for Quiche Lorraine, but substitute 50 g/2 oz sliced mushrooms for the bacon. Season the egg and milk mixture with 5 ml/1 tsp made mustard before straining it into the flan. Sprinkle the top with 50 g/2 oz/½ cup grated hard cheese in addition to the nutmeg.

Cheese and Tomato Quiche

SERVES 4–6

Prepare as for Quiche Lorraine, but substitute three skinned and sliced tomatoes for the bacon.

Smoked Salmon Quiche

SERVES 4–6

Prepare as for Quiche Lorraine, but substitute 175 g/6 oz smoked salmon, cut into strips, for the bacon.

Prawn Quiche

SERVES 4–6

Prepare as for Quiche Lorraine, but substitute 175 g/6 oz/1½ cups chopped prawns (shrimp) for the bacon.

Spinach Quiche

SERVES 4–6

Prepare as for Quiche Lorraine, but cover the base of the flan with 175 g/6 oz cooked spinach, from which all the water has been wrung out, instead of the bacon. (The spinach must be as dry as possible or the pastry (paste) will become soggy.)

Mediterranean Quiche

SERVES 4–6

Prepare as for Quiche Lorraine, but cover the base of the flan with 185 g/6½ oz/1 small can flaked tuna and its oil, 12 stoned (pitted) black olives and 20 ml/4 tsp tomato purée (paste) instead of the bacon.

Asparagus Quiche

SERVES 4–6

Prepare as for Quiche Lorraine, but substitute 350 g/12 oz/1 large can asparagus spears for the bacon. Drain thoroughly, reserve six spears and chop the remainder. Use to cover the base of the flan. Garnish with the reserved spears.

Devilled Walnuts

SERVES 4–6

225 g/8 oz/2 cups walnut halves
50 g/2 oz/¼ cup butter
10 ml/2 tsp corn oil
5 ml/1 tsp mustard powder
5 ml/1 tsp paprika
5 ml/1 tsp celery salt
5 ml/1 tsp onion salt
2.5 ml/½ tsp chilli powder
Salt

Toast the walnut halves as described on page 205. Heat the butter and oil in a shallow dish, uncovered, on Full for 1½ minutes. Add the nuts and toss gently with the butter and oil until well mixed. Leave uncovered and cook on Full for 3–4 minutes, turning often and watching carefully in case they start to over-brown. Drain on kitchen paper. Toss in a plastic bag with the mustard powder, paprika, celery salt, onion salt, chilli powder and salt to taste. Store in an airtight container.

Curried Brazil Nuts

SERVES 4–6

225 g/8 oz/2 cups brazil nuts,
*   thickly sliced*
50 g/2 oz/¼ cup butter
10 ml/2 tsp corn oil
20 ml/4 tsp mild, medium or hot
*   curry powder*
Salt

Toast the brazil nuts as described on page 205. Heat the butter and oil in a shallow dish, uncovered, on Full for 1½ minutes. Add the nuts and toss gently with the butter and oil until well mixed. Leave uncovered and cook on Full for 3–4 minutes, turning often and watching carefully in case they start to over-brown. Drain on kitchen paper. Toss in a plastic bag with the curry powder and salt to taste. Store in an airtight container.

Tomato and Chicken Salad Cups

SERVES 4

450 ml/¾ pt/2 cups chicken stock
15 ml/1 tbsp powdered gelatine
30 ml/2 tbsp tomato purée (paste)
1 small onion, finely grated
5 ml/1 tsp caster (superfine) sugar
1 small green (bell) pepper, cut into tiny cubes
175 g/6 oz/1½ cups cold cooked meat, finely chopped
1 carrot, grated
2 canned pineapple rings (not fresh or the jelly won't set)
2 hard-boiled (hard-cooked) eggs (pages 98–9), grated

Pour half the stock into a 1.5 litre/ 2½ pt/6 cup bowl. Stir in the gelatine and leave to soften for 5 minutes. Melt, uncovered, on Defrost for 2–2½ minutes. Add the remaining stock, stirring well to mix. Cover and chill until cold and just beginning to thicken, then fold in all the remaining ingredients except the eggs. Divide between four glass bowls and chill until set. Before serving, sprinkle with the egg.

Vegetarian Tomato Salad Cups

SERVES 4

Prepare as for Tomato and Chicken Salad Cups, but substitute 175 g/ 6 oz/¾ cup cottage cheese for the chicken and use vegetable stock.

Chopped Egg and Onion

SERVES 4 AS A STARTER,
6 AS AN APPETISER

A spectacular all-year-round Jewish classic, best eaten with crisp biscuits such as traditional matzos. The big advantage is microwaving the eggs – no steamed-up kitchen and no saucepan to wash up. Butter or any margarine is suggested here, but the orthodox community would use only vegetable margarine.

5 hard-boiled (hard-cooked) eggs (pages 98–9), shelled and finely chopped
40 g/1½ oz/3 tbsp butter or margarine, softened
1 onion, finely grated
Salt and freshly ground black pepper
Salad leaves or parsley, to garnish

Combine the chopped eggs with the butter or margarine. Stir in the onion and season to taste. Pile on to four plates and garnish each with salad leaves or parsley.

Chopped Egg with Parsley

SERVES 4 AS A STARTER,
6 AS AN APPETISER

Prepare as for Chopped Egg and Onion, but add 60 ml/4 tbsp chopped parsley to the egg mixture.

Blue Cheese and Pecan Flan

SERVES 4–6

A sophisticated addition to the quiche family.

For the pastry (paste):
175 g/6 oz/1½ cups plain (all-purpose) flour
1.5 ml/¼ tsp salt
100 g/3½ oz/scant ½ cup butter mixed with margarine, white cooking fat or lard, or use all margarine
45 ml/3 tbsp finely chopped pecan nuts
1 small egg yolk
For the filling:
200 g/7 oz/scant 1 cup full-fat cream cheese
30–45 ml/2–3 tbsp snipped chives or spring onions (scallions)
125 g/4 oz/generous 1 cup blue cheese, crumbled
5 ml/1 tsp paprika
3 eggs
60 ml/4 tbsp full-cream milk or single (light) cream
Salt and freshly ground black pepper

To make the pastry, sift the flour and salt into a bowl. Rub in the fat until the mixture resembles fine breadcrumbs, then add the chopped nuts. Mix to a firm dough with cold water. Wrap in foil and chill for ½–¾ hour. Turn out on to a floured surface and knead quickly and lightly until smooth. Roll out into a thin circle and use to line a 20 cm/8 in diameter glass, china or pottery flan dish. Pinch the top edge into tiny flutes, then prick all over with a fork. Cook uncovered on Full for 6 minutes, turning the dish twice. If the pastry has bulged in places, press down gently with a hand protected by an oven glove. Brush all over with the egg yolk and cook on Full for 1 minute to seal any holes. Leave to stand while preparing the filling.

Put the filling ingredients into a food processor, seasoning to taste with salt and pepper, and process until the mixture is smooth. Spread smoothly into the flan case (pie shell). Cook on Defrost for 14 minutes, turning the dish three times. Allow to stand for 5 minutes. Eat warm or cold.

Rich Liver Pâté

SERVES 8–10

Excellent served with hot toast at parties or special dinners.

250 g/9 oz/generous 1 cup butter
1 garlic clove, crushed
450 g/1 lb chicken livers
1.5 ml/¼ tsp grated nutmeg
Salt and freshly ground black pepper

Put 175 g/6 oz/¾ cup of the butter into a 1.75 litre/3 pt/7½ cup dish and melt, uncovered, on Full for 2 minutes. Stir in the garlic. Pierce each piece of chicken liver with the tip of a knife and add to the dish. Mix well with the butter. Cover with a plate and cook on Full for 8 minutes, stirring twice. Mix in the nutmeg, then season well to taste. In two batches, work to a smooth paste in a blender or food processor. Spread smoothly into a soufflé-type dish. Melt the remaining butter, uncovered, on Full for 2 minutes. Pour over the liver to make an airtight seal, then allow to stand until the butter has set. Cover and store in the refrigerator for up to five days.

Cottage Cheese and Onion Tart
SERVES 4–6

For the pastry (paste):
175 g/6 oz/1½ cups plain (all-purpose) flour
1.5 ml/¼ tsp salt
100 g/3½ oz/scant ½ cup butter mixed with margarine, white cooking fat or lard, or use all margarine
1 small egg yolk
For the filling:
25 g/1 oz/2 tbsp butter or margarine
1 onion, grated
350 g/12 oz/1½ cups cottage cheese
3 eggs
60 ml/4 tbsp full-cream milk or single (light) cream
Salt and freshly ground black pepper

To make the pastry, sift the flour and salt into a bowl. Rub in the fat until the mixture resembles fine bread-crumbs, then mix to a firm dough with cold water. Wrap in foil and chill for ½–¾ hour. Turn out on to a floured surface and knead quickly and lightly until smooth. Roll out into a thin circle and use to line a 20 cm/8 in diameter glass, china or pottery flan dish. Pinch the top edge into tiny flutes, then prick all over with fork. Cook uncovered on Full for 6 minutes, turning the dish twice. If the pastry has bulged in places, press down gently with a hand protected by an oven glove. Brush all over with the egg yolk and cook on Full for 1 minute to seal any holes. Leave to stand while preparing the filling.

Melt the butter or margarine, uncovered, on Full for 1 minute. Add the onion and cook, uncovered, on Full for 3 minutes, stirring once. Transfer to a food processor with the remaining ingredients, seasoning to taste with salt and pepper, and process until the mixture is smooth. Spread smoothly into the flan case (pie shell). Cook on Defrost for 14 minutes, turning the dish three times. Allow to stand for 5 minutes. Eat warm or cold.

Popadoms

Place one 18 cm/7 in diameter popadom on a dinner plate. Cook on Full for 55–60 seconds, turning over once. Transfer to a clean tea towel (dish cloth) and leave to cool. Eat when cold and crisp with dips and Indian dishes, allowing one or two per person.

Winter Fruit Cocktail
SERVES 4–6

Just before a heavy meal around Christmas time and the New Year, there is no better starter than this seasonal and unusual fruit cocktail.

300 ml/½ pt/1¼ cups cranberry juice
75 g/3 oz/⅓ cup caster (superfine) sugar
350 g/12 oz melon, cut into 1.5 cm/½ in cubes
350 g/12 oz peeled pineapple, cut into 1.5 cm/½ in cubes
2 sharon fruit, finely diced
2 kiwi fruit, peeled and thinly sliced
2 star anise

Put the cranberry juice and sugar in a 2.5 litre/4½ pt/11 cup bowl. Heat, uncovered, on Defrost for 4–5 minutes, stirring two or three times, until the sugar dissolves. Mix in all the fruit and the star anise. Cover when cold and chill until ready to serve.

Soups

Summer and winter, come rain or shine, soups never fail to please and there are some beauties that can be turned round in the microwave in minutes without mess and steam everywhere. Try French and Belgian-style purée soups, mostly vegetable-based, with croûtons and a swirl of cream. There's also a range of other international favourites: Chinese Hot and Sour Soup, a memorable Minestrone and many more.

Hot and Sour Crab Soup

SERVES 6

An opulent contribution from China, an easily made pleasure.

1 litre/1¾ pts/4¼ cups poultry
   stock
225 g/7 oz/1 small can water
   chestnuts, coarsely chopped
225 g/7 oz/1 small can sliced
   bamboo shoots in water
75 g/3 oz mushrooms, thinly sliced
150 g/5 oz tofu, cut into small
   cubes
175 g/6 oz/1 small can crabmeat
   in brine, undrained and meat
   flaked
15 ml/1 tbsp cornflour
15 ml/1 tbsp water
30 ml/2 tbsp malt vinegar
15 ml/1 tbsp soy sauce
5 ml/1 tsp sesame oil
2.5 ml/½ tsp salt
1 large egg, beaten

Pour the stock into a 2 litre/3½ pt/ 8½ cup bowl. Add the contents of the cans of water chestnuts and bamboo shoots. Add the mushrooms and tofu and the contents of the can of crabmeat. Stir. Cover the bowl with clingfilm (plastic wrap) and slit it twice to allow steam to escape. Cook on Full for 15 minutes. Uncover carefully to prevent steam burns and stir well to mix. Blend the cornflour smoothly with the water and vinegar, then stir in the remaining ingredients. Gently whisk into the soup. Cover as before and cook on Full for 4 minutes. Stir round and cover with large plate or saucepan lid. Allow to stand for 2 minutes. Serve hot in china bowls.

Easy Oriental Soup

SERVES 3–4

400 ml/16 fl oz/1 large can
   mulligatawny soup
400 ml/16 fl oz/1 large can
   coconut milk
Salt
Chilli powder
Chopped coriander (cilantro)
Popadoms, to serve

Pour the soup and coconut milk into a 1.75 litre/3 pt/7½ cup bowl. Add salt to taste. Heat, uncovered, on Full for 7–8 minutes, stirring twice. Pour into warm bowls, sprinkle with chilli powder and coriander and serve with popadoms.

Liver Dumpling Soup

SERVES 4

**50 g/2 oz/1 cup fresh white
breadcrumbs
50 g/2 oz/½ cup chicken livers,
minced (ground)
15 ml/1 tbsp very finely chopped
parsley, plus extra to garnish
5 ml/1 tsp grated onion
1.5 ml/¼ tsp marjoram
1.5 ml/¼ tsp salt
Freshly ground black pepper
½ egg, beaten
750 ml/1¼ pts/3 cups clear beef or
chicken stock or diluted canned
concentrated consommé**

Place all the ingredients, except the stock or consommé, into a mixing bowl. Mix thoroughly and shape into 12 small dumplings. Pour the stock or consommé into a deep 1.5 litre/2½ pt/ 6 cup bowl and cover with a plate. Heat on Full to boiling, allowing about 8–10 minutes. Add the dumplings. Cook, uncovered, for 3–4 minutes until the dumplings have risen and float to the top of the soup. Ladle into warm bowls, sprinkle with the extra parsley and serve straight away.

Cream of Carrot Soup

SERVES 6

**30 ml/2 tbsp cornflour
(cornstarch)
550 g/1¼ lb/1 large can carrots
450 ml/¾ pt/2 cups cold milk
7.5–10 ml/1½–2 tsp salt
300 ml/½ pt/1¼ cups hot water
60 ml/4 tbsp single (light) cream**

Place the cornflour in a 3 litre/5¼ pt/ 12 cup bowl. Mix smoothly with the liquid from the can of carrots. Blend the carrots to a purée in a blender or food processor. Add to the bowl with the milk and salt. Cook, uncovered, on Full for 12 minutes until thickened, whisking gently four or five times to ensure smoothness. Thin down with the hot water. Spoon into warmed bowls and swirl 10 ml/2 tsp cream into each portion.

Chilled Carrot and Leek Soup

SERVES 6

**1 large leek, slit and thoroughly
washed
4 large carrots, thinly sliced
3 small–medium potatoes, cut into
small cubes
150 ml/¼ pt/⅔ cup hot water
600 ml/1 pt/2½ cups vegetable
stock
300 ml/½ pt/1¼ cups single (light)
cream
Salt and freshly ground black
pepper
Chopped watercress**

Coarsely chop the leek. Put all the vegetables in a 2 litre/3½ pt/8½ cup dish with the hot water. Cover with clingfilm (plastic wrap) and slit it twice to allow steam to escape. Cook on Full for 15 minutes until the vegetables are tender. Transfer to a blender or food processor with the liquid from the dish and work to a smooth purée, adding a little of the stock if necessary. Scrape into a large bowl and stir in the remaining stock. Cover and chill. Before serving, gently whisk in the cream and season to taste. Ladle into soup cups and sprinkle each with cress.

Carrot and Coriander Soup

SERVES 6

Prepare as for Cream of Carrot Soup, but add a handful of fresh coriander (cilantro) leaves to the blender or food processor with the carrots. The cream can be added as an optional extra.

Carrot with Orange Soup

SERVES 6

Prepare as for Cream of Carrot Soup, but add 10 ml/2 tsp grated orange peel to the soup half-way through cooking. Top each portion with whipped cream to which a little Grand Marnier has been added.

Lettuce Cream Soup

SERVES 6

75 g/3 oz/⅓ cup butter or
  margarine
2 onions, grated
225 g/8 oz round soft lettuce, cut
  into strips
600 ml/1 pt/2½ cups full-cream
  milk
30 ml/2 tbsp cornflour
  (cornstarch)
300 ml/½ pt/1¼ cups hot water or
  vegetable stock
2.5 ml/½ tsp salt

Melt 50 g/2 oz/¼ cup of the butter or margarine in a 1.75 litre/ 3 pt/7½ cup bowl on Defrost for 2 minutes. Mix in the onions and lettuce. Cover with a plate and cook on Full for 3½ minutes. Transfer to a blender with one-third of the milk. Work to a smooth purée. Return to the bowl. Mix the cornflour smoothly with 60 ml/ 4 tbsp of the remaining milk. Add to the soup with all the remaining milk, the hot water or stock and the salt. Cook, uncovered, on Full for 15 minutes, whisking frequently to ensure smoothness. Serve in warmed bowls with 5 ml/1 tsp butter added to each.

Green Purée Soup

SERVES 4–6

1 large round lettuce
125 g/4 oz watercress or young
  spinach
1 leek, white part only, sliced
300 ml/½ pt/1¼ cups hot water
60 ml/4 tbsp cornflour
  (cornstarch)
300 ml/½ pt/1¼ cups cold milk
25 g/1 oz/2 tbsp butter or
  margarine
Salt
Croûtons, to serve

Thoroughly wash the lettuce and watercress or spinach and shred. Place in a 1.5 litre/2½ pt/6 cup bowl with the leek and water. Cover with clingfilm (plastic wrap) and slit it twice to allow steam to escape. Cook on Full for 10 minutes, turning the bowl twice. Allow to cool for 10 minutes. Transfer to a blender and work to a smooth purée. Return to the bowl. Blend the cornflour smoothly with the milk. Add to the bowl with the butter or margarine and salt to taste. Cook, uncovered, on Full, stirring three times for 8–10 minutes or until piping hot and slightly thickened. Ladle into warmed soup bowls and add croûtons to each.

Parsnip and Parsley Soup with Wasabi

SERVES 6

With a subtle kick of horseradish from the wasabi, this is an intriguingly flavoured, highly original soup with just a hint of sweetness from the parsnips.

30 ml/2 tbsp corn or sunflower oil
450 g/1 lb parsnips, peeled and
*   sliced*
900 ml/1½ pts/3¾ cups well-
*   flavoured hot vegetable or*
*   chicken stock*
10 ml/2 tsp Japanese wasabi
*   powder*
30 ml/2 tbsp chopped parsley
150 ml/¼ pt/⅔ cup single (light)
*   cream*

Pour the oil into a 2 litre/3½ pt/ 8½ cup dish. Add the parsnips. Cover with clingfilm (plastic wrap) and slit it twice to allow steam to escape. Cook on Full for 7 minutes, turning the dish twice. Add the stock and wasabi powder. Cover with a plate and cook on Full for 6 minutes. Allow to cool slightly, then purée until smooth in a blender. Return to the bowl. Stir in the parsley. Cover as before and cook on Full for 5 minutes. Stir in the cream and serve.

Sweet Potato Soup

SERVES 6

Prepare as for Parsnip and Parsley Soup with Wasabi, but substitute chopped, orange-fleshed sweet potatoes for the parsnips.

Cream of Vegetable Soup

SERVES 4–6

A very useful soup – use any combination of vegetables you fancy or have available.

450 g/1 lb mixed fresh vegetables
1 onion, chopped
25 g/1 oz/2 tbsp butter or
*   margarine or 30 ml/2 tbsp*
*   sunflower oil*
175 ml/6 fl oz/¾ cup water
450 ml/¾ pt/2 cups milk or milk
*   and water mixed*
15 ml/1 tbsp cornflour
*   (cornstarch)*
2.5 ml/½ tsp salt
Chopped parsley

Prepare the vegetables according to type and cut into small pieces. Put into 2 litre/3½ pt/8½ cup bowl with the onion, butter, margarine or oil and 30 ml/2 tbsp of the water. Cover with a plate and cook on Full for 12–14 minutes until tender, stirring four times. Purée until smooth in a blender. Return to the bowl with three-quarters of the milk or milk and water. Mix the cornflour smoothly with the remaining liquid and add to the bowl with the salt. Cook, uncovered, on Full for 6 minutes, stirring four times. Ladle into soup bowls and sprinkle each with parsley.

Green Pea Soup

SERVES 4–6

Prepare as for Cream of Vegetable Soup, but substitute 450 g/1 lb frozen garden peas for the mixed vegetables and onion. Garnish lightly with chopped mint instead of parsley.

Squash Soup

SERVES 4–6

Prepare as for Cream of Vegetable Soup, but substitute 450 g/1 lb peeled and diced courgettes (zucchini), marrow, pumpkin, butternut or turban squash for the mixed vegetables and onion. Sprinkle each serving with grated nutmeg instead of parsley.

Cream of Mushroom Soup

SERVES 4–6

Prepare as for Cream of Vegetable Soup, but substitute mushrooms for the mixed vegetables and onion.

Cream of Pumpkin Soup

SERVES 6–8

For Hallowe'en mostly, but the soup is glorious chilled so freeze any leftovers, or make an extra batch while pumpkins are in season, and keep for the beginning of summer.

1.75 kg/4 lb fresh pumpkin, either in the piece or a whole one
2 onions, coarsely chopped
15–20 ml/3–4 tsp salt
600 ml/1 pt/2½ cups full-cream milk
15 ml/1 tbsp cornflour (cornstarch)
30 ml/2 tbsp cold water
2.5 ml/½ tsp grated nutmeg
Croûtons, to serve (optional)

Cut the pumpkin into wedges like melon. Remove the seeds and wash and dry them. Arrange on a plate in a single layer. Toast lightly, uncovered, on Full for 4 minutes. Allow to cool, then crack open the husks and remove the inside seeds. Reserve. Peel the pumpkin and cut the flesh into fairly large cubes. Put into a large bowl with the onions and toss well to mix. Cover closely with clingfilm (plastic wrap) but do not slit. Cook on Full for 30 minutes, turning the bowl four times. Remove from the oven and allow to stand for 10 minutes. Work the pumpkin, onions and cooking liquid to a purée, in several batches, in a blender or food processor. Return to the bowl. Stir in the salt and milk. Mix the cornflour smoothly with the water and add to the purée with the nutmeg. Reheat, uncovered, on Full for 7 minutes, whisking every minute. Ladle the soup into bowls or cups and sprinkle with the toasted pumpkin seeds and/or croûtons.

Cock-a-leekie Soup

SERVES 6–8

4 chicken portions
4 leeks, coarsely shredded
1.25 litre/2¼ pts/5½ cups hot water
10 ml/2 tsp salt
1 bouquet garni sachet
50 g/2 oz/¼ cup easy-cook long-grain rice
12 stoned (pitted) prunes

Wash the chicken and place in a 20 cm/8 in diameter deep casserole dish (Dutch oven). Add the leeks. Cover with clingfilm (plastic wrap) and slit it twice to allow steam to escape. Cook on Full for 12 minutes. Lift the chicken out of the dish, remove the meat from the bones and cut into bite-sized pieces. Reserve. Pour the water into a second, large dish. Add the salt and bouquet garni with the rice, leeks and the liquid from the casserole dish. Cover with a plate and cook on Full for 18 minutes. Stir in the chicken and prunes. Cover as before and cook for a further 3 minutes. Eat while very hot.

Scotch Broth

SERVES 6

30 ml/2 tbsp pearl barley
225 g/8 oz neck of lamb fillet, cut
    into bite-sized cubes
1.2 litres/2 pts/5 cups hot water
1 large onion, chopped
1 carrot, cut into small cubes
1 small turnip, cut into small
    cubes
1 small leek, shredded
Salt and freshly ground black
    pepper
Chopped parsley

Soak the barley for 4 hours in 75 ml/
5 tbsp cold water. Drain. Place the
lamb in a 2.25 litre/4 pt/10 cup bowl.
Add the hot water and barley. Cover
with a plate and cook on Full for 4
minutes. Skim. Add the prepared vegetables and salt and pepper to taste.
Cover as before and cook on Full for
25–30 minutes until the barley is soft.
Allow to stand for 5 minutes. Ladle
into warmed soup bowls and sprinkle
each thickly with parsley.

Israeli Chicken and Avocado Soup

SERVES 4–5

900 ml/1½ pts/3¾ cups well-
    flavoured chicken stock
1 large ripe avocado, peeled and
    stoned
30 ml/2 tbsp fresh lemon juice

Pour the chicken stock into a
1.5 litre/2½ pt/6 cup bowl. Cover
with a plate and heat on Full for 9 minutes. Mash the avocado flesh with the
lemon juice to a coarse purée. Stir into
the hot stock. Cover as before and
reheat on Full for 1 minute. Serve hot.

Avocado Soup with Beetroot

SERVES 4–5

Prepare as for Israeli Chicken and
Avocado Soup and garnish each
portion with 7.5 ml/1½ tsp grated
cooked beetroot (red beets).

Bortsch

SERVES 6

450 g/1 lb raw beetroot (red beets)
75 ml/5 tbsp water
1 large carrot, peeled and grated
1 small turnip, peeled and grated
1 onion, peeled and grated
750 ml/1¼ pts/3 cups hot beef or
    vegetable stock
125 g/4 oz white cabbage,
    shredded
15 ml/1 tbsp lemon juice
5 ml/1 tsp salt
Freshly ground black pepper
90 ml/6 tbsp soured (dairy sour)
    cream

Wash the beetroot thoroughly but
leave unpeeled. Place in a
shallow 20 cm/ 8 in diameter dish, in a
single layer, with the water. Cover with
clingfilm (plastic wrap) and slit it twice
to allow steam to escape. Cook on Full
for 15 minutes. Place the carrot, turnip and onion in a 2 litre/3½ pt/
8½ cup bowl. Drain and peel the beetroot and slice. Add to the bowl of vegetables with 150 ml/¼ pt/⅔ cup stock.
Cover as before and cook on Full for
10 minutes. Mix in the remaining
stock and all the remaining ingredients except the soured cream, seasoning to taste. Cover with a plate and
cook on Full for 10 minutes, stirring
four times. Ladle into warmed soup
bowls and top each with 15 ml/1 tbsp
soured cream.

Cold Bortsch

SERVES 6

Prepare as for Bortsch and allow to cool. Strain when cold. Add 150 ml/ ¼ pt/⅔ cup cold water and 1 large cooked beetroot, coarsely shredded. Allow to stand for 15 minutes. Strain again. Sharpen with extra lemon juice to taste. Chill for several hours before serving.

Creamy Cold Bortsch

SERVES 6

Prepare as for Cold Bortsch. After the second straining, blend in a blender or food processor with 250 ml/ 8 fl oz/1 cup half-fat crème fraîche. Chill.

Orange Lentil Soup

SERVES 4–5

125 g/4 oz/½ cup orange lentils
1 large onion, grated
1 large carrot, grated
½ small turnip, grated
1 potato, grated
20 ml/4 tsp butter or margarine
5 ml/1 tsp corn or sunflower oil
30 ml/2 tbsp chopped parsley, plus
*   extra for garnishing*
900 ml/1½ pts/3¾ cups hot
*   chicken or vegetable stock*
Salt and freshly ground black
*   pepper*

Wash and drain the lentils. Place the vegetables, butter or margarine and oil in a 2 litre/3½ pt/8½ cup bowl. Add the parsley. Cook, uncovered, on Full for 5 minutes, stirring three times. Stir in the lentils and one-third of the hot stock. Season to taste. Cover with clingfilm (plastic wrap) and slit it twice to allow steam to escape. Cook on Full for 10 minutes until the lentils are tender. (If not, cook for a further 5–6 minutes.) Transfer to a blender or food processor and work to a coarse purée. Return to the bowl with the remaining stock. Cover with a plate and reheat on Full for 6 minutes, stirring three times. Serve straight away, sprinkling each portion with extra parsley.

Orange Lentil Soup with Cheese and Toasted Cashews

SERVES 4–5

Prepare as for Orange Lentil Soup, but stir in 60 ml/4 tbsp grated Edam cheese and 60 ml/4 tbsp coarsely chopped toasted cashew nuts (page 205) after the final reheating.

Lentil Soup with Tomato Garnish

SERVES 4–5

Prepare as for Orange Lentil Soup, but instead of sprinkling with parsley, top each portion with 5 ml/1 tsp sun-dried tomato paste, then float in a slice of fresh tomato.

Yellow Pea Soup

SERVES 6–8

A Swedish version of pea soup, eaten every Thursday in Sweden. It is customarily followed by pancakes and jam.

350 g/12 oz/1½ cups yellow split peas, washed
900 ml/1½ pts/3¾ cups cold water
5 ml/1 tsp marjoram
1 ham bone, about 450–500 g/1 lb
750 ml/1¼ pts/3 cups hot water
5–10 ml/1–2 tsp salt

Place the split peas in a mixing bowl. Add the cold water. Cover with a plate and cook on Full for 6 minutes. Allow to stand for 3 hours. Transfer the peas and soaking water to a 2.5 litre/ 4½ pt/11 cup bowl. Stir in the marjoram and add the ham bone. Cover with clingfilm (plastic wrap) and slit it twice to allow steam to escape. Cook on Full for 30 minutes. Mix in half the hot water. Cover as before and cook on Full for a further 15 minutes. Remove the bone. Take the meat off the bone and cut it into small pieces. Return to the soup with the remaining hot water. Season to taste with the salt. Stir well. Cover with a plate and reheat on Full for 3 minutes. The soup can be thinned, if preferred, with extra boiling water.

French Onion Soup

SERVES 6

30 ml/2 tbsp butter, margarine or sunflower oil
4 onions, thinly sliced and separated into rings
20 ml/4 tsp cornflour (cornstarch)
900 ml/1½ pts/3¾ cups hot beef stock or consommé
Salt and freshly ground black pepper
6 slices French bread, diagonally sliced
90 ml/6 tbsp grated Gruyère (Swiss) or Jarlsberg cheese
Paprika

Place the butter, margarine or oil in a 2 litre/3½ pt/8½ cup dish. Heat, uncovered, on Full for 2 minutes. Stir the onion rings into the dish. Cook, uncovered, on Full for 5 minutes. Stir in the cornflour. Gradually blend in half the hot stock. Cover the dish with clingfilm (plastic wrap) and slit it twice to allow steam to escape. Cook on Full for 30 minutes, turning the dish four times. Mix in the remaining stock and season to taste. Stir well. Ladle the soup into six bowls and add a slice of bread to each. Sprinkle with the cheese and paprika. Return each bowl individually to the microwave and heat on Full for 1½ minutes until the cheese is melted and bubbling. Eat straight away.

Minestrone

••••••••••••••••••••••••••••••••
SERVES 8–10

350 g/12 oz courgettes (zucchini),
thinly sliced
225 g/8 oz carrots, thinly sliced
225 g/8 oz onions, coarsely
chopped
125 g/4 oz white cabbage,
shredded
125 g/4 oz green cabbage,
shredded
3 celery stalks, thinly sliced
3 potatoes, cubed
125 g/4 oz/1 cup fresh or frozen
peas
125 g/4 oz fresh or frozen sliced
green beans
400 g/14 oz/1 large can tomatoes
30 ml/2 tbsp tomato purée (paste)
50 g/2 oz macaroni, broken into
short lengths
1 litre/1¾ pts/4¼ cup hot water
15–20 ml/3–4 tsp salt
100 g/3½ oz/1 cup grated
Parmesan cheese

Place all the prepared vegetables in a 3.5 litre/6 pt/15 cup bowl. Stir in the remaining ingredients except the water and salt, breaking up the tomatoes against the side of the bowl with the back of a wooden spoon. Cover with a large plate and cook on Full for 15 minutes, stirring three times. Mix in about three-quarters of the hot water. Cover as before and cook on Full for 25 minutes, stirring four or five times. Remove from the microwave. Stir in the remaining water and the salt to taste. If the soup seems too thick, dilute with extra boiling water. Ladle into deep bowls and serve with the Parmesan cheese handed separately.

Minestrone Milanese

••••••••••••••••••••••••••••••••
SERVES 8–10

Prepare as for Minestrone, but substitute risotto rice for the macaroni.

Minestrone Genovese

••••••••••••••••••••••••••••••••
SERVES 8–10

Prepare as for Minestrone, but stir in 30 ml/2 tbsp ready-prepared green pesto before serving.

Italian Potato Soup

••••••••••••••••••••••••••••••••
SERVES 4–5

1 large onion, chopped
30 ml/2 tbsp olive or sunflower oil
4 large potatoes
1 small cooked ham bone
1.25 litres/2¼ pts/5½ cups hot
chicken stock
Salt and freshly ground black
pepper
60 ml/4 tbsp single (light) cream
Grated nutmeg
30 ml/2 tbsp chopped parsley

Place the onion and oil in a 2.25 litre/4 pt/10 cup bowl. Cook, uncovered, on Defrost for 5 minutes, stirring twice. Meanwhile, peel and grate the potatoes. Stir into the onions and add the ham bone, hot stock and salt and pepper to taste. Cover with a plate and cook on Full for 15–20 minutes, stirring twice, until the potatoes are soft. Mix in the cream, ladle into soup bowls and sprinkle with nutmeg and the parsley.

Fresh Tomato and Celery Soup

SERVES 6–8

900 g/2 lb ripe tomatoes,
blanched, skinned and
quartered
50 g/2 oz/¼ cup butter or
margarine or 30 ml/2 tbsp olive
oil
2 celery stalks, finely chopped
1 large onion, finely chopped
30 ml/2 tbsp dark soft brown
sugar
5 ml/1 tsp soy sauce
2.5 ml/½ tsp salt
300 ml/½ pt/1¼ cups hot water
30 ml/2 tbsp cornflour
(cornstarch)
150 ml/¼ pt/⅔ cup cold water
Medium sherry

Purée the tomatoes in a blender or food processor. Place the butter, margarine or oil in a 1.75 litre/3 pt/ 7½ cup dish. Heat on Full for 1 minute. Mix in the celery and onion. Cover with a plate and cook on Full for 3 minutes. Add the puréed tomatoes, sugar, soy sauce, salt and hot water. Cover as before and cook on Full for 8 minutes, stirring four times. Meanwhile, mix the cornflour smoothly with the cold water. Stir into the soup. Cook, uncovered, on Full for 8 minutes, stirring four times. Ladle into soup bowls and add a dash of sherry to each.

Gingered Tomato Soup

SERVES 6–8

Prepare as for Fresh Tomato and Celery Soup, but add 5 cm/2 in root ginger, finely chopped, and 1 garlic clove, crushed, with the celery and onion. Garnish each portion with chopped spring onions (scallions).

Tomato Soup with Avocado Dressing

SERVES 8

2 ripe avocados
Juice of 1 small lime
1 garlic clove, crushed
30 ml/2 tbsp mustard mayonnaise
45 ml/3 tbsp crème fraîche
5 ml/1 tsp salt
A pinch of turmeric
600 ml/20 fl oz/2 cans condensed
tomato soup
600 ml/1 pt/2½ cups warm water
2 tomatoes, blanched, skinned,
seeded and quartered

Peel and halve the avocados, removing the stones (pits). Finely mash the flesh, then combine with the lime juice, garlic, mayonnaise, crème fraîche, salt and turmeric. Cover and chill until needed. Pour both cans of soup into a 1.75 litre/3 pt/7½ cup dish. Gently whisk in the water. Cut the tomato flesh into strips and add two-thirds to the soup. Cover the dish with a plate and cook on Full for 9 minutes until very hot, stirring four or five times. Ladle into soup bowls and add a scoop of avocado dressing to each. Garnish with the remaining tomato strips.

Chilled Cheese and Onion Soup

SERVES 6–8

25 g/1 oz/2 tbsp butter or
  margarine
2 onions, chopped
2 celery stalks, finely chopped
30 ml/2 tbsp plain (all-purpose)
  flour
900 ml/1½ pts/3¾ cups warm
  chicken or vegetable stock
45 ml/3 tbsp dry white wine or
  white port
Salt and freshly ground black
  pepper
125 g/4 oz/1 cup blue cheese,
  crumbled
125 g/4 oz/1 cup Cheddar cheese,
  grated
150 ml/¼ pt/⅔ cup whipping cream
Finely chopped sage, to garnish

Place the butter or margarine in a 2.25 litre/4 pt/10 cup dish. Melt, uncovered, on Defrost for 1½ minutes. Mix in the onions and celery. Cover with a plate and cook on Full for 8 minutes. Remove from the microwave. Stir in the flour, then gradually blend in the stock and wine or port. Cover as before and cook on Full for 10–12 minutes, whisking every 2–3 minutes, until the soup is smooth, thickened and hot. Season to taste. Add the cheeses and stir until melted. Cover and allow to cool, then chill for several hours or overnight. Before serving, stir round and gently whisk in the cream. Ladle into cups or bowls and sprinkle each lightly with sage.

Swiss-style Cheese Soup

SERVES 6–8

25 g/1 oz/2 tbsp butter or
  margarine
2 onions, chopped
2 celery stalks, finely chopped
30 ml/2 tbsp plain (all-purpose)
  flour
900 ml/1½ pts/3¾ cups warm
  chicken or vegetable stock
45 ml/3 tbsp dry white wine or
  white port
5 ml/1 tsp caraway seeds
1 garlic clove, crushed
Salt and freshly ground black
  pepper
225 g/8 oz/2 cups Emmental or
  Gruyère (Swiss) cheese, grated
150 ml/¼ pt/⅔ cup whipping cream
Croûtons

Place the butter or margarine in a 2.25 litre/4 pt/10 cup dish. Melt, uncovered, on Defrost for 1½ minutes. Mix in the onions and celery. Cover with a plate and cook on Full for 8 minutes. Remove from the microwave. Stir in the flour, then gradually blend in the stock and wine or port. Stir in the caraway seeds and garlic. Cover as before and cook on Full for 10–12 minutes, whisking every 2–3 minutes, until the soup is hot, smooth and thickened. Season to taste. Add the cheese and stir until melted. Mix in the cream. Ladle into cups or bowls and serve hot, garnished with croûtons.

Avgolemono Soup
•••••••••••••••••••••••••••••••••
SERVES 6
___

1.25 litres/2¼ pts/5½ cups hot
  chicken stock
60 ml/4 tbsp risotto rice
Juice of 2 lemons
2 large eggs
Salt and freshly ground black
  pepper

Pour the stock into a deep 1.75 litre/
3 pt/7½ cup dish. Stir in the rice.
Cover with a plate and cook on Full for
20–25 minutes until the rice is tender.
Thoroughly beat together the lemon
juice and eggs in a soup tureen or
other large serving dish. Gently whisk
in the stock and rice. Season to taste
before serving.

Cream of Cucumber Soup with Pastis
•••••••••••••••••••••••••••••••••
SERVES 6–8
___

900 g/2 lb cucumber, peeled
45 ml/3 tbsp butter or margarine
30 ml/2 tbsp cornflour (cornstarch)
600 ml/1 pt/2½ cups chicken or
  vegetable stock
300 ml/½ pt/1¼ cups whipping
  cream
7.5–10 ml/1½–2 tsp salt
10 ml/2 tsp Pernod or Ricard
  (pastis)
Freshly ground black pepper
Chopped dill (dill weed)

Slice the cucumber very thinly using
a grater or the slicing disc of a food
processor. Place in a bowl, cover and
leave to stand for 30 minutes to allow
some of the moisture to seep out.
Wring as dry as possible in a clean tea
towel (dish cloth). Place the butter or
margarine in a 2.25 litre/4 pt/10 cup
dish. Melt, uncovered, on Defrost for
1½ minutes. Mix in the cucumber.
Cover with a plate and cook on Full for
5 minutes, stirring three times. Mix the
cornflour smoothly with some of the
stock, then add the remaining stock.
Gradually stir into the cucumber.
Cook, uncovered, on Full for about 8
minutes, stirring three or four times,
until the soup is hot, smooth and
thickened. Add the cream, salt and
pastis and mix thoroughly. Reheat,
uncovered, on Full for 1–1½ minutes.
Season to taste with pepper. Ladle into
soup bowls and sprinkle each portion
with dill.

Curry Soup with Rice
•••••••••••••••••••••••••••••••••
SERVES 6
___

A pleasantly mild Anglo-Indian
chicken soup.

30 ml/2 tbsp groundnut or
  sunflower oil
1 large onion, chopped
3 celery stalks, finely chopped
15 ml/1 tbsp mild curry powder
30 ml/2 tbsp medium-dry sherry
1 litre/1¾ pts/4¼ cups chicken or
  vegetable stock
125 g/4 oz/½ cup long-grain rice
5 ml/1 tsp salt
15 ml/1 tbsp soy sauce
175 g/6 oz/1½ cups cooked
  chicken, cut into strips
Thick plain yoghurt or crème
  fraîche, to serve

Pour the oil into a 2.25 litre/4 pt/
10 cup dish. Heat, uncovered, on
Full for 1 minute. Add the onions and
celery. Cook, uncovered, on Full for 5
minutes, stirring once. Mix in the curry
powder, sherry, stock, rice, salt and
soy sauce. Cover with a plate and cook
on Full for 10 minutes, stirring twice.
Add the chicken. Cover as before and
cook on Full for 6 minutes. Ladle into
bowls and top each with a swirl of
yoghurt or crème fraîche.

Vichyssoise

•••••••••••••••••••••••••••••••••••••
SERVES 6

An up-market and chilled version of leek and potato soup, invented by the American chef Louis Diat early in the twentieth century.

2 leeks
350 g/12 oz potatoes, peeled and sliced
25 g/1 oz/2 tbsp butter or margarine
30 ml/2 tbsp water
450 ml/³⁄₄ pt/2 cups milk
15 ml/1 tbsp cornflour (cornstarch)
150 ml/¼ pt/⅔ cup cold water
2.5 ml/½ tsp salt
150 ml/¼ pt/⅔ cup single (light) cream
Snipped chives, to garnish

Trim the leeks, cutting away most of the green. Slit the remainder and wash thoroughly. Slice thickly. Place in a 2 litre/3½ pt/8½ cup dish with the potatoes, butter or margarine and water. Cover with a plate and cook on Full for 12 minutes, stirring four times. Transfer to a blender, add the milk and work to a purée. Return to the dish. Mix the cornflour smoothly with the water and add to the dish. Season to taste with the salt. Cook, uncovered, on Full for 6 minutes, beating every minute. Allow to cool. Stir in the cream. Cover and chill thoroughly. Ladle into bowls and sprinkle each serving with chives.

Chilled Cucumber Soup with Yoghurt

•••••••••••••••••••••••••••••••••••••
SERVES 6–8

25 g/1 oz/2 tbsp butter or margarine
1 large garlic clove
1 cucumber, peeled and coarsely grated
600 ml/1 pt/2½ cups plain yoghurt
300 ml/½ pt/1¼ cups milk
150 ml/¼ pt/⅔ cup cold water
2.5–10 ml/½–2 tsp salt
Chopped mint, to garnish

Place the butter or margarine in a 1.75 litre/3 pt/7½ cup dish. Heat, uncovered, on Full for 1 minute. Crush in the garlic and add the cucumber. Cook, uncovered, on Full for 4 minutes, stirring twice. Remove from the microwave. Whisk in all the remaining ingredients. Cover and chill for several hours. Ladle into bowls and sprinkle each serving with mint.

Chilled Spinach Soup with Yoghurt

SERVES 6–8

25 g/1 oz/2 tbsp butter or
margarine
1 large garlic clove
450 g/1 lb young spinach leaves,
shredded
600 ml/1 pt/2½ cups plain yoghurt
300 ml/½ pt/1¼ cups milk
150 ml/¼ pt/⅔ cup cold water
2.5–10 ml/½–2 tsp salt
Juice of 1 lemon
Grated nutmeg or ground walnuts,
to garnish

Place the butter or margarine in a 1.75 litre/3 pt/7½ cup dish. Heat, uncovered, on Full for 1 minute. Crush in the garlic and add the spinach. Cook, uncovered, on Full for 4 minutes, stirring twice. Remove from the microwave. Blend to a coarse purée in a blender or food processor. Whisk in all the remaining ingredients. Cover and chill for several hours. Ladle into bowls and dust each serving with nutmeg or ground walnuts.

Sherried Chilled Tomato Soup

SERVES 4–5

300 ml/½ pt/1¼ cups water
300 ml/10 fl oz/1 can condensed
tomato soup
30 ml/2 tbsp dry sherry
150 ml/¼ pt/⅔ cup double (heavy)
cream
5 ml/1 tsp Worcestershire sauce
Snipped chives, to garnish

Pour the water into a 1.25 litre/2¼ pt/5½ cup bowl and heat, uncovered, on Full for 4–5 minutes until it just begins to bubble. Whisk in the tomato soup. When completely smooth, thoroughly stir in the remaining ingredients. Cover and chill for 4–5 hours. Stir round, ladle into glass dishes and sprinkle each with chives.

New England Fish Chowder

SERVES 6–8

Always served in North America for Sunday brunch, Clam Chowder is the ultimate classic but, as clams are not that easy to come by, white fish has been substituted.

5 streaky bacon rashers (slices),
coarsely chopped
1 large onion, peeled and grated
15 ml/1 tbsp cornflour
(cornstarch)
30 ml/2 tbsp cold water
450 g/1 lb potatoes, cut into
1 cm/½ in cubes
900 ml/1½ pts/3¾ cups hot full-
cream milk
450 g/1lb firm white fish fillets,
skinned and cut into bite-sized
pieces
2.5 ml/½ tsp ground nutmeg
Salt and freshly ground black
pepper

Place the bacon in a 2.5 litre/4½ pt/11 cup bowl. Add the onion and cook, uncovered, on Full for 5 minutes. Mix the cornflour smoothly with the water and stir into the bowl. Mix in the potatoes and half the hot milk. Cook, uncovered, on Full for 6 minutes, stirring three times. Mix in the remaining milk and cook, uncovered, on Full for 2 minutes. Add the fish with the nutmeg and season to taste. Cover with a plate and cook on Full for 2 minutes until the fish is tender. (Do not worry if the fish has begun to flake.) Ladle into deep bowls and eat straight away.

Crab Soup

SERVES 4

**25 g/1 oz/2 tbsp unsalted (sweet)
butter**
**20 ml/4 tsp plain (all-purpose)
flour**
**300 ml/½ pt/1¼ cups warmed full-
cream milk**
300 ml/½ pt/1¼ cups water
**2.5 ml/½ tsp English made
mustard**
A dash of hot pepper sauce
**25 g/1 oz/¼ cup Cheddar cheese,
grated**
**175 g/6 oz light and dark
crabmeat**
**Salt and freshly ground black
pepper**
45 ml/3 tbsp dry sherry

Place the butter in a 1.75 litre/
3 pt/7½ cup dish. Melt on Defrost
for 1–1½ minutes. Stir in the flour.
Cook, uncovered, on Full for 30 seconds. Gradually mix in the milk and
water. Cook, uncovered, on Full for
5–6 minutes until smooth and thickened, beating every minute. Stir in all
the remaining ingredients. Cook,
uncovered, on Full for 1½–2 minutes,
stirring twice, until hot.

Crab and Lemon Soup

SERVES 4

Prepare as for Crab Soup, but add
5 ml/1 tsp finely grated lemon peel
with the remaining ingredients. Dust
each serving with a little grated
nutmeg.

Lobster Bisque

SERVES 4

Prepare as for Crab Soup, but substitute single (light) cream for the
milk and chopped lobster meat for the
crabmeat.

Dried Packet Soup

Tip the packet contents into a
1.25 litre/2¼ pt/5½ cup dish.
Gradually stir in the recommended
amount of cold water. Cover and allow
to stand for 20 minutes to soften the
vegetables. Stir. Cover with a plate and
cook on Full for 6–8 minutes, stirring
twice, until the soup comes to the boil
and thickens. Allow to stand for 3 minutes. Stir round and serve.

Canned Condensed Soup

Tip the soup into a 1.25 litre/2¼ pt/
5½ cup measuring jug. Add 1 can of
boiling water and whisk thoroughly.
Cover with a plate or saucer and heat
on Full for 6–7 minutes, whisking
twice, until the soup just comes to the
boil. Pour into bowls and serve.

Reheating Soups

For successful results, reheat clear
or thin soups on Full and creamy
soups and broths on Defrost.

Dairy Specialities

Dairy treats galore can be made in a fraction of the time it took before microwaves. Remember rubbery, overcooked scrambled eggs that leaked, and those horrible, burnt fried (sautéed) ones? Omelettes that misbehaved and broke apart, poached eggs that sprawled all over the place and cold eggs that did their best to curdle creamed cake mixtures? No more. From boiling to warming, eggs behave beautifully.

Warming Eggs for Cooking

Invaluable if you decide at the last minute to do some baking and need eggs at room temperature.

For 1 egg: break the egg into a small dish or cup. Puncture the yolk twice with a skewer or the tip of a knife to prevent the skin bursting and yolk exploding. Cover the dish or cup with a saucer. Warm on Defrost for 30 seconds.
For 2 eggs: as for 1 egg but warm for 30–45 seconds.
For 3 eggs: as for 1 egg but warm for 1–1¼ minutes.

Boiled Eggs

Although special egg boilers for use in microwave ovens are available the following method, which I have been using for years, works well and requires only minimal washing up. Wash the cup or basin immediately after use as egg white congeals quickly.

Soft-boiled (Soft-cooked) Egg

For 1 egg: butter a cup or, if the egg is to be turned, you can line the cup itself closely with clingfilm (plastic wrap) instead. Carefully break the egg into the cup and puncture the yolk twice with a skewer or the tip of a knife to prevent the skin bursting and yolk exploding. Cover with a saucer and cook on Defrost for 1 minute. Swirl round gently. Re-cover and cook for a further 30 seconds. Allow to stand for 30 seconds. Eat from the cup as though it were an egg cup or invert on to toast or a plate.

Medium-boiled (Soft-cooked) Egg

For 1 egg: as for soft-boiled but cook for 2 minutes initially.

Hard-boiled (Hard-cooked) Egg

For 1 egg: as for soft-boiled but cook for about 2½ minutes initially, depending on the size of the egg. Allow to stand for 45 seconds. Eat hot or cold.

For 2 eggs: tip the eggs into a small buttered pudding basin. Cover with a saucer and cook on Defrost for 4 minutes. Swirl round gently. Re-cover and cook for a further 30 seconds. Allow to stand for 1 minute.

For 3 eggs: as for 2 eggs but cook for 5½ minutes.

Poached Eggs

These are best cooked individually in their own dishes.

For 1 egg: pour 90 ml/6 tbsp hot water into a shallow dish. Add 2.5 ml/ ½ tsp mild vinegar to prevent the white spreading. Carefully slide in 1 egg, first broken into a cup. Puncture the yolk twice with a skewer or the tip of a knife. Cover with a plate and cook on Full for 45 seconds–1¼ minutes, depending on how firm you like the whites. Allow to stand for 1 minute. Lift out of the dish with a perforated fish slice.

For 2 eggs cooked in 2 dishes simultaneously: cook on Full for 1½ minutes. Allow to stand for 1¼ minutes. If the whites are too runny, cook for a further 15–20 seconds.

For 3 eggs cooked in 3 dishes simultaneously: cook on Full for 2–2½ minutes. Allow to stand for 2 minutes. If the whites are too runny, cook for a further 20–30 seconds.

Fried (Sautéed) Eggs

The microwave does a superb job here and the eggs turn out soft and tender, always sunny-side up and with a fringe of white that never frizzles. Frying more than 2 eggs at a time is not recommended as the yolks would cook more quickly than the whites and become hard. This is due to the longer cooking time needed to set the whites.

Use china or pottery without any hint of decoration, as they do in France.

For 1 egg: brush a small china or pottery dish lightly with melted butter, margarine or a trace of delicate olive oil. Break the egg into a cup, then slide it into the prepared dish. Puncture the yolk twice with a skewer or the tip of a knife. Sprinkle lightly with salt and freshly ground black pepper. Cover with a plate and cook on Full for 30 seconds. Allow to stand for 1 minute. Continue to cook for a further 15–20 seconds. If the white is not sufficiently set cook for a further 5–10 seconds.

For 2 eggs: as for 1 egg, but cook on Full for 1 minute initially, then stand for 1 minute. Cook for a further 20–40 seconds. If the whites are not sufficiently set, allow a further 6–8 seconds.

Scrambled Eggs

These work to perfection in the microwave and become thick and creamy yet light and soft in texture with the minimum of effort and no messy saucepans to clean. If the eggs have been taken straight from the refrigerator, allow a few seconds more cooking time.

For 2 eggs: break 2 eggs into a glass dish. Beat in 20 ml/4 tsp milk or cream. Season with salt and freshly ground black pepper and add a knob of butter or margarine. Cook, uncovered, on Full for 45 seconds. Stir briskly. Cook for a further 20–30 seconds until almost set. Stir briskly, then cover and allow to stand for 2 minutes before serving.

For 3 eggs: break 3 eggs into a glass dish. Beat in 30 ml/2 tbsp milk or cream. Season with salt and freshly ground black pepper and add a knob of butter or margarine. Cook, uncovered, on Full for 1 minute. Stir briskly. Cook for a further 35–50 seconds until almost set. Stir briskly, then cover and allow to stand for 2 minutes before serving.

For 4 eggs: break 4 eggs into a glass dish. Beat in 45 ml/3 tbsp milk or cream. Season with salt and freshly ground black pepper and add a knob of butter or margarine. Cook, uncovered, on Full for 1½ minutes. Stir briskly. Cook for a further 1–1½ minutes until almost set. Stir briskly, then cover and allow to stand for 2 minutes before serving.

Extra-creamy Scrambled Eggs

Prepare as for Scrambled Eggs but double the amount of milk or cream.

Flavoured Scrambled Eggs

Add any of the following to the beaten eggs before scrambling: curry powder; paprika; a little tomato purée (paste) or sun-dried tomato paste; a little pesto sauce; snipped chives; chopped parsley; grated cheese; sliced mushrooms, lightly cooked in butter.

Piperade

SERVES 4

30 ml/2 tbsp olive oil
3 onions, very thinly sliced
2 green (bell) peppers, seeded and finely chopped
6 tomatoes, blanched, skinned, seeded, and chopped
15 ml/1 tbsp chopped basil leaves
Salt and freshly ground black pepper
6 large eggs
60 ml/4 tbsp double (heavy) cream
Toast, to serve

Pour the oil into a deep 25 cm/10 in diameter dish and heat, uncovered, on Full for 1 minute. Stir in the onions and peppers. Cover with a plate and cook on Defrost for 12–14 minutes until the vegetables are tender. Stir in the tomatoes and basil and season to taste. Cover as before and cook on Full for 3 minutes. Thoroughly beat together the eggs and cream and season to taste. Pour into the dish and combine with the vegetables. Cook, uncovered, on Full for 4–5 minutes until lightly scrambled, stirring every minute. Cover and allow to stand for 3 minutes before serving with crisp toast.

Piperade with Gammon

SERVES 4

Prepare as for Piperade but serve spooned on portions of fried (sautéed) bread and top each with a grilled (broiled) or microwaved gammon rasher (slice).

Piperada

SERVES 4

Spain's version of Piperade.

Prepare as for Piperade, but add 2 garlic cloves, crushed, with the onions and green (bell) peppers and add 125 g/4 oz/1 cup coarsely chopped ham to the cooked vegetables. Garnish each portion with sliced stuffed olives.

Eggs Florentine

SERVES 4

450 g/1lb freshly cooked spinach
60 ml/4 tbsp whipping cream
4 poached eggs, cooked 2 at a
time (page 99)
300 ml/½ pt/1¼ cups hot Cheese
Sauce or Mornay Sauce (page
317)
50 g/2 oz/½ cup grated cheese

Work together the spinach and cream in a food processor or blender. Arrange in a buttered shallow heatproof 18 cm/7 in diameter dish. Cover with a plate and heat on Full for 1½ minutes. Arrange the eggs on top and coat with the hot sauce. Sprinkle with the cheese and brown under a hot grill (broiler).

Poached Egg Rossini

SERVES 1

This makes for an elegant light lunch with a leafy side salad.

Fry (sauté) or toast de-crusted slices of wheatmeal bread. Spread with a smooth liver pâté containing, if cost permits, some truffle. Top with a freshly cooked poached egg (page 99) and serve immediately.

Aubergine Egg Scramble

SERVES 4

An Israeli idea that converts well to the microwave. The flavour is curiously powerful.

750 g/1½ lb aubergines
(eggplants)
15 ml/1 tbsp lemon juice
15 ml/1 tbsp corn or sunflower oil
2 onions, finely chopped
2 garlic cloves, crushed
4 large eggs
60 ml/4 tbsp milk
Salt and freshly ground black
pepper
Hot buttered toast, to serve

Top and tail the aubergines and halve them lengthways. Arrange on a large plate, cut sides down, and cover with kitchen paper. Cook on Full for 8–9 minutes or until soft. Scoop the flesh out of the skins directly into a food processor with the lemon juice and work to a coarse purée. Place the oil in a 1.5 litre/2½ pt/6 cup dish. Heat, uncovered, on Full for 30 seconds. Stir in the onions and garlic. Cook, uncovered, on Full for 5 minutes. Beat the eggs with the milk and season thoroughly to taste. Pour into the dish and scramble with the onions and garlic on Full for 2 minutes, stirring every 30 seconds. Mix in the onions and garlic and add the aubergine purée. Continue to cook, uncovered, on Full for 3–4 minutes, stirring every 30 seconds, until the mixture thickens and the eggs are scrambled. Serve on hot buttered toast.

Classic Omelette

••••••••••••••••••••••••••••••
SERVES 1

A light-textured omelette that can be served plain or filled (pages 102–3).

Melted butter or margarine
3 eggs
20 ml/4 tsp salt
Freshly ground black pepper
30 ml/2 tbsp cold water
Parsley or watercress, to garnish

Brush a shallow 20 cm/8 in diameter dish with melted butter or margarine. Beat the eggs very thoroughly with all the remaining ingredients except the garnish. (Lightly breaking up the eggs, as for traditional omelettes, is not enough.) Pour into the dish, cover with a plate and transfer to the microwave. Cook on Full for 1½ minutes. Uncover and stir the egg mixture gently with a wooden spoon or fork, bringing the partially set edges to the centre. Cover as before and return to the microwave. Cook on Full for 1½ minutes. Uncover and continue to cook for 30–60 seconds or until the top is just set. Fold into three and slide out on to a warmed plate. Garnish and serve immediately.

Flavoured Omelettes

••••••••••••••••••••••••••••••
SERVES 1

Parsley Omelette: prepare as for Classic Omelette, but sprinkle the eggs with 30 ml/2 tbsp chopped parsley after the omelette has cooked for the initial 1½ minutes.

Chive Omelette: prepare as for Classic Omelette, but sprinkle the eggs with 30 ml/2 tbsp snipped chives after the omelette has cooked for the initial 1½ minutes.

Watercress Omelette: prepare as for Classic Omelette, but sprinkle the eggs with 30 ml/2 tbsp chopped watercress after the omelette has cooked for the initial 1½ minutes.

Omelette aux Fines Herbes: prepare as for Classic Omelette, but sprinkle the eggs with 45 ml/3 tbsp mixed chopped parsley, chervil and basil after the omelette has cooked for the initial 1½ minutes. A little fresh tarragon may also be added.

Curried Omelette with Coriander: prepare as for Classic Omelette, but beat the eggs and water with 5–10 ml/1–2 tsp curry powder in addition to the salt and pepper. Sprinkle the eggs with 30 ml/2 tbsp chopped coriander (cilantro) after the omelette has cooked for the initial 1½ minutes.

Cheese and Mustard Omelette: prepare as for Classic Omelette, but beat the eggs and water with 5 ml/1 tsp made mustard and 30 ml/2 tbsp very finely grated and well-flavoured hard cheese in addition to the salt and pepper.

Filled Omelettes

••••••••••••••••••••••••••••••
SERVES 1

Filled Omelettes should be folded in half, not into three.

Asparagus Omelette: warm 30–45 ml/2–3 tbsp asparagus tips in 10 ml/2 tsp butter on Defrost for 1½–2 minutes. Use to cover half a Classic Omelette, fold over and slide on to a plate.

Avocado Omelette: cut ½ a small ripe avocado into small cubes and toss with 5 ml/1 tsp each lemon juice and Worcestershire sauce. Season with salt and a dash of hot pepper sauce (optional). Use to cover half a Classic Omelette, fold over and slide on to a plate.

Bacon Omelette: chop 2 rashers (slices) lean bacon and heat with 5 ml/1 tsp butter or margarine on Full for 1½–2 minutes. Use to cover half a Classic Omelette, fold over and slide on to a plate.

Cheese Omelette: cover half a Classic Omelette with 60 ml/4 tbsp grated cheese, fold over and slide on to a plate.

Crab Omelette: cover half a Classic Omelette with 30–45 ml/2–3 tbsp dressed crab and a squeeze of lime juice. Fold over and slide on to a plate.

Croûton Omelette: cover half a Classic Omelette with 30 ml/2 tbsp small garlic or herb-flavoured croûtons, fold over and slide on to a plate.

Ham Omelette: cover half a Classic Omelette with 30–45 ml/2–3 tbsp coarsely chopped ham, fold over and slide on to a plate.

Italian Omelette: prepare a Classic Omelette, but beat the eggs and water with 15 ml/1 tbsp finely grated Parmesan cheese in addition to the seasoning. Cover half the omelette with 30 ml/2 tbsp chopped Parma ham, fold over and slide on to a plate.

Mushroom Omelette: melt 10 ml/2 tsp butter or margarine in a 750 ml/1¼ pt/3 cup dish on Full for 20 seconds. Add 75 g/3 oz sliced mushrooms. Cover loosely with kitchen paper and cook on Full for 2½ minutes. Use to cover half a Classic Omelette, fold over and slide on to a plate.

Tomato Omelette: slice two blanched and skinned tomatoes. Put on to a plate and top with a few flakes of butter or margarine. Cover loosely with kitchen paper and heat through on Full for 1½ minutes. Sprinkle with salt, freshly ground black pepper and a trace of caster (superfine) sugar. Use to cover half a Classic Omelette, fold over and slide on to a plate.

Cheese and Tomato Omelette: prepare as for Tomato Omelette but top the tomatoes with 30–45 ml/2–3 tbsp grated or crumbled cheese before folding over.

Blue Cheese Omelette: use 30–45 ml/2–3 tbsp crumbled Stilton or other blue cheese to cover half a Classic Omelette. Fold over and slide on to a plate.

Brunch Omelette
SERVES 1–2

A North American-style omelette, traditionally served at Sunday brunches. The Brunch Omelette may be flavoured and filled as for the Classic Omelette.

Prepare as for Classic Omelette (page 102), but substitute 45 ml/3 tbsp cold milk for the 30 ml/2 tbsp water. After uncovering, cook on Full for 1–1½ minutes. Fold into three and carefully slide on to a plate.

Poached Egg with Melted Cheese

SERVES 1

1 slice hot buttered toast
45 ml/3 tbsp cream cheese
Tomato ketchup (catsup)
1 poached egg (page 99)
60–75 ml/4–5 tbsp grated cheese
Paprika

Spread the toast with the cream cheese, then with tomato ketchup. Place on a plate. Top with the poached egg, then shower with the grated cheese and dust with paprika. Heat, uncovered, on Defrost for 1–1½ minutes until the cheese is just beginning to melt. Eat straight away.

Eggs Benedict

SERVES 1–2

No North American Sunday brunch would be complete without Eggs Benedict, a wickedly rich egg concoction that defies all calorie and cholesterol restrictions.

Split and toast a muffin or bap. Top with a rasher (slice) of conventionally grilled (broiled) mild bacon, then top both halves with a freshly poached egg. Coat with Hollandaise Sauce (page 318), then dust lightly with paprika. Eat straight away.

Omelette Arnold Bennett

SERVES 2

Said to have been created by a chef at London's Savoy Hotel in honour of the famous writer, this is a monumental and memorable omelette for every high day and feast day.

175 g/6 oz smoked haddock or cod
fillet
45 ml/3 tbsp boiling water
120 ml/4 fl oz/½ cup crème fraîche
Freshly ground black pepper
Melted butter or margarine, for
brushing
3 eggs
45 ml/3 tbsp cold milk
A pinch of salt
50 g/2 oz/½ cup coloured Cheddar
or Red Leicester cheese, grated

Place the fish in a shallow dish with the water. Cover with a plate and cook on Full for 5 minutes. Allow to stand for 2 minutes. Drain and flake up the flesh with a fork. Work in the crème fraîche and season to taste with pepper. Brush a 20 cm/8 in diameter shallow dish with melted butter or margarine. Beat the eggs thoroughly with the milk and salt. Pour into the dish. Cover with a plate and cook on Full for 3 minutes, moving the setting edges into the centre half-way through cooking. Uncover and cook on Full for a further 30 seconds. Spread with the fish and cream mixture and sprinkle with the cheese. Cook, uncovered, on Full for 1–1½ minutes until the omelette is hot and the cheese has melted. Divide into two servings and serve straight away.

Tortilla

SERVES 2

The renowned Spanish Omelette is round and flat as a pancake. It teams comfortably with chunks of bread or rolls and a crisp green salad.

15 ml/1 tbsp butter, margarine or olive oil
1 onion, finely chopped
175 g/6 oz cooked potatoes, diced
3 eggs
5 ml/1 tsp salt
30 ml/2 tbsp cold water

Put the butter, margarine or oil in a deep 20 cm/8 in diameter dish. Heat on Defrost for 30–45 seconds. Mix in the onion. Cover with a plate and cook on Defrost for 2 minutes. Stir in the potatoes. Cover as before and cook on Full for 1 minute. Remove from the microwave. Beat the eggs thoroughly with the salt and water. Pour evenly over the onions and potatoes. Cook, uncovered, on Full for 4½ minutes, turning the dish once. Allow to stand for 1 minute, then divide into two and transfer each portion to a plate. Eat straight away.

Spanish Omelette with Mixed Vegetables

SERVES 2

30 ml/2 tbsp butter, margarine or olive oil
1 onion, finely chopped
2 tomatoes, skinned and chopped
½ small green or red (bell) pepper, finely chopped
3 eggs
5–7.5 ml/1–1½ tsp salt
30 ml/2 tbsp cold water

Put the butter, margarine or oil in a deep 20 cm/8 in diameter dish. Heat on Defrost for 1½ minutes. Mix in the onion, tomatoes and chopped pepper. Cover with a plate and cook on Defrost for 6–7 minutes until tender. Beat the eggs thoroughly with the salt and water. Pour evenly over the vegetables. Cover with a plate and cook on Full for 5–6 minutes until the eggs are set, turning the dish once. Divide into two and transfer each portion to a plate. Eat straight away.

Spanish Omelette with Ham

SERVES 2

Prepare as for Spanish Omelette with Mixed Vegetables, but add 60 ml/4 tbsp coarsely chopped air-dried Spanish ham and 1–2 garlic cloves, crushed, to the vegetables and cook for 30 seconds longer.

Cheesy Eggs in Celery Sauce

SERVES 4

A short-cut lunch or supper dish, providing an ample meal for vegetarians.

6 large hard-boiled (hard-cooked) eggs (pages 98–9), shelled and halved
300 ml/10 fl oz/1 can condensed celery soup
45 ml/3 tbsp full-cream milk
175 g/6 oz/1½ cups Cheddar cheese, grated
30 ml/2 tbsp finely chopped parsley
Salt and freshly ground black pepper
15 ml/1 tbsp toasted breadcrumbs
2.5 ml/½ tsp paprika

Arrange the egg halves in a deep 20 cm/8 in diameter dish. In a separate bowl or dish, gently mix together the soup and milk. Heat, uncovered, on Full for 4 minutes, whisking every minute. Mix in half the cheese and heat, uncovered, on Full for 1–1½ minutes until melted. Stir in the parsley, season to taste, then spoon over the eggs. Sprinkle with the remaining cheese, the breadcrumbs and paprika. Brown under a hot grill (broiler) before serving.

Eggs Fu Yung

SERVES 2

5 ml/1 tbsp butter, margarine or corn oil
1 onion, finely chopped
30 ml/2 tbsp cooked peas
30 ml/2 tbsp cooked or canned bean sprouts
125 g/4 oz mushrooms, sliced
3 large eggs
2.5 ml/½ tsp salt
30 ml/2 tbsp cold water
5 ml/1 tsp soy sauce
4 spring onions (scallions), finely sliced

Put the butter, margarine or oil in a deep 20 cm/8 in diameter dish and heat, uncovered, on Defrost for 1 minute. Mix in the chopped onion, cover with a plate and cook on Full for 2 minutes. Stir in the peas, bean sprouts and mushrooms. Cover as before and cook on Full for 1½ minutes. Remove from the microwave and stir. Beat the eggs thoroughly with the salt, water and soy sauce. Pour evenly over the vegetables. Cook, uncovered, on Full for 5 minutes, turning twice. Allow to stand for 1 minute. Divide into two and transfer each to a warmed plate. Garnish with the spring onions and serve straight away.

Pizza Omelette

SERVES 2

A novelty pizza, the base made from a flat omelette instead of yeast dough.

15 ml/1 tbsp olive oil
3 large eggs
45 ml/3 tbsp milk
2.5 ml/½ tsp salt
4 tomatoes, blanched, skinned and sliced
125 g/4 oz/1 cup Mozzarella cheese, grated
8 canned anchovies in oil
8–12 stoned (pitted) black olives

Put the oil in a deep 20 cm/8 in diameter dish and heat, uncovered, on Defrost for 1 minutes. Beat the eggs very thoroughly with the milk and salt. Pour into the dish and cover with a plate. Cook on Full for 3 minutes, moving the setting edges to the centre of the dish half-way through cooking. Uncover and cook on Full for a further 30 seconds. Spread with the tomatoes and cheese, then garnish with the anchovies and olives. Cook, un-covered, on Full for 4 minutes, turning twice. Divide into two and serve straight away.

Soufflé Omelette

SERVES 2

45 ml/3 tbsp jam (conserve)
Icing (confectioners') sugar
Melted butter
3 drops lemon juice
3 large eggs, separated
15 ml/1 tbsp caster (superfine) sugar

Spoon the jam into a small dish or cup. Cover with a saucer and heat on Defrost for 1½ minutes. Carefully remove from the microwave, leave covered and set aside. Cover a large sheet of greaseproof (waxed) paper with sifted icing sugar. Brush a deep 25 cm/10 in diameter dish with melted butter. Add the lemon juice to the egg whites and beat until stiffly peaking. Add the caster sugar to the egg yolks and beat until thick, pale and creamy. Gently whisk the beaten whites into the yolks until smooth and evenly combined. Spoon into the prepared dish. Cook, uncovered, on Full for 3½ minutes. Invert on to the sugared paper, score a line down the centre with a knife and spread the warm jam over half the omelette. Gently fold in half, cut into two portions and eat straight away.

Lemon Soufflé Omelette

SERVES 2

Prepare as for Soufflé Omelette, but add 5 ml/1 tsp finely grated lemon rind to the beaten egg yolks and sugar.

Orange Soufflé Omelette

SERVES 2

Prepare as for Soufflé Omelette, but add 5 ml/1 tsp finely grated orange rind to the beaten egg yolks and sugar.

Almond and Apricot Soufflé Omelette

SERVES 2

Prepare as for Soufflé Omelette, but add 2.5 ml/½ tsp almond essence (extract) to the beaten egg yolks and sugar. Fill with warmed smooth apricot jam (conserve).

Raspberry Soufflé Omelette

SERVES 2

Prepare as for Soufflé Omelette (page 107), but add 2.5 ml/½ tsp vanilla essence (extract) to the beaten egg yolks and sugar. Fill with 45–60 ml/ 3–4 tbsp coarsely crushed raspberries mixed with icing (confectioners') sugar to taste and a dash of Kirsch or gin.

Strawberry Soufflé Omelette

SERVES 2

Prepare as for Soufflé Omelette (page 107), but add 2.5 ml/½ tsp vanilla essence (extract) to the beaten egg yolks and sugar. Fill with 45–60 ml/ 3–4 tbsp thinly sliced strawberries mixed with icing (confectioners') sugar to taste and 15 ml/1 tbsp chocolate or orange liqueur.

Soufflé Omelette with Toppings

SERVES 2

Prepare as for Soufflé Omelette (page 107), but instead of folding and cutting the omelette into halves, leave flat and cut into two portions. Transfer each to a plate and top with either warmed stewed fruit or a fruit coulis (pages 334–5). Serve straight away.

Baked Egg with Cream

SERVES 1

This way of preparing eggs is highly esteemed in France, where it is called *oeufs en cocotte*. It is certainly a top-drawer starter for dinner parties but it also makes a stylish lunch with toast or crackers and a green salad. To ensure success, it is advisable to cook one egg at a time in an individual dish.

1 egg
Salt and freshly ground black
*   pepper*
15 ml/1 tbsp double (heavy) cream
*   or crème fraîche*
5 ml/1 tsp very finely chopped
*   parsley, chives or coriander*
*   (cilantro)*

Brush a small ramekin dish (custard cup) or individual soufflé dish with melted butter or margarine. Gently break in the egg and puncture the yolk twice with a skewer or the tip of a knife. Season well to taste. Coat with the cream and sprinkle with the herbs. Cover with a saucer and cook on Defrost for 3 minutes. Allow to stand for 1 minute before eating.

Baked Egg Neapolitan

SERVES 1

Prepare as for Baked Egg with Cream, but coat the egg with 15 ml/ 1 tbsp passata (sieved tomatoes) and two finely chopped black olives or capers.

Cheese Fondue

•••••••••••••••••••••••••••••
SERVES 6

Born in Switzerland, Cheese Fondue is the *après-ski* darling of Alpine resorts or anywhere else with deep snow on high peaks. Dipping your bread into a communal pot of aromatic melted cheese is one of the most convivial, entertaining and relaxing ways of enjoying a meal with friends and there is no better kitchen helper for this than the microwave. Serve with small tots of Kirsch and cups of hot lemon tea for an authentic atmosphere.

1–2 garlic cloves, peeled and halved
175 g/6 oz/1½ cups Emmental cheese, grated
450 g/1 lb/4 cups Gruyère (Swiss) cheese, grated
15 ml/1 tbsp cornflour (cornstarch)
300 ml/½ pt/1¼ cups Mosel wine
5 ml/1 tsp lemon juice
30 ml/2 tbsp Kirsch
Salt and freshly ground black pepper
Cubed French bread, for dipping

Press the cut sides of the garlic halves against the sides of a deep 2.5 litre/4½ pt/11 cup glass or pottery dish. Alternatively, for a stronger taste, crush the garlic directly into the dish. Add both cheeses, the cornflour, wine and lemon juice. Cook, uncovered, on Full for 7–9 minutes, stirring four times, until the fondue begins to bubble gently. Remove from the microwave and mix in the Kirsch. Season well to taste. Bring the dish to the table and eat by spearing a cube of bread on to a long fondue fork, swirling it round in the cheese mixture, then lifting it out.

Fondue with Cider

•••••••••••••••••••••••••••••
SERVES 6

Prepare as for Cheese Fondue, but substitute dry cider for the wine and calvados for the Kirsch and serve cubes of red-skinned apple as well as the bread cubes for dipping.

Fondue with Apple Juice

•••••••••••••••••••••••••••••
SERVES 6

A non-alcoholic Fondue with a mellow taste and suitable for all ages.

Prepare as for Cheese Fondue, but substitute apple juice for the wine and omit the Kirsch. If necessary, thin down with a little hot water.

Pink Fondue

•••••••••••••••••••••••••••••
SERVES 6

Prepare as for Cheese Fondue, but substitute 200 g/7 oz/1¾ cups each white Cheshire cheese, Lancashire cheese and Caerphilly cheese for the Emmental and Gruyère (Swiss) cheeses and rosé wine for the white wine.

Smoky Fondue

•••••••••••••••••••••••••••••
SERVES 6

Prepare as for Cheese Fondue, but substitute 200 g/7 oz/1¾ cups smoked cheese for half the Gruyère (Swiss) cheese. The quantity of Emmental cheese is unchanged.

German Beer Fondue

•••••••••••••••••••••••••••••
SERVES 6

Prepare as for Cheese Fondue, but substitute beer for the wine and brandy for the Kirsch.

Fondue with Fire

SERVES 6

Prepare as for Cheese Fondue (page 109), but add 2–3 red chillies, seeded and very finely chopped, just after the cornflour (cornstarch).

Curried Fondue

SERVES 6

Prepare as for Cheese Fondue (page 109), but add 10–15 ml/2–3 tsp mild curry paste with the cheeses and substitute vodka for the Kirsch. Use pieces of warmed Indian bread for dipping.

Fonduta

SERVES 4–6

An Italian version of Cheese Fondue, inordinately luscious.

Prepare as for Cheese Fondue (page 109), but substitute Italian Fontina cheese for the Gruyère (Swiss) and Emmental cheeses, dry white Italian wine for the Mosel, and marsala for the Kirsch.

Mock Cheese and Tomato Fondue

SERVES 4–6

225 g/8 oz/2 cups mature Cheddar cheese, grated
125 g/4 oz/1 cup Lancashire or Wensleydale cheese, crumbled
300 ml/10 fl oz/1 can condensed tomato soup
10 ml/2 tsp Worcestershire sauce
A dash of hot pepper sauce
45 ml/3 tbsp dry sherry
Warmed ciabatta bread, to serve

Place all the ingredients except the sherry in a 1.25 litre/2¼ pt/5½ cup glass or pottery dish. Cook, uncovered, on Defrost for 7–9 minutes, stirring three or four times, until the fondue is smoothly thickened. Remove from the microwave and stir in the sherry. Eat with pieces of warm ciabatta bread.

Mock Cheese and Celery Fondue

SERVES 4–6

Prepare as for Mock Cheese and Tomato Fondue, but substitute condensed celery soup for the tomato soup and flavour with gin instead of sherry.

Italian Cheese, Cream and Egg Fondue

SERVES 4–6

1 garlic clove, crushed
50 g/2 oz/¼ cup unsalted (sweet) butter, at kitchen temperature
450 g/1 lb/4 cups Fontina cheese, grated
60 ml/4 tbsp cornflour (cornstarch)
300 ml/½ pt/1¼ cups milk
2.5 ml/½ tsp grated nutmeg
Salt and freshly ground black pepper
150 ml/¼ pt/⅔ cup whipping cream
2 eggs, beaten
Cubed Italian bread, to serve

Place the garlic, butter, cheese, cornflour, milk and nutmeg in a deep 2.5 litre/4½ pt/11 cup glass or pottery dish. Season to taste. Cook, uncovered, on Full for 7–9 minutes, stirring four times, until the fondue begins to bubble gently. Remove from the microwave and mix in the cream.

Cook, uncovered, on Full for 1 minute. Remove from the microwave and gradually beat in the eggs. Serve with Italian bread for dipping.

Dutch Farmhouse Fondue

SERVES 4–6

A soft and gentle fondue, mild enough for children.

1 garlic clove, crushed
15 ml/1 tbsp butter
450 g/1 lb/4 cups Gouda cheese, grated
15 ml/1 tbsp cornflour (cornstarch)
20 ml/4 tsp mustard powder
A pinch of grated nutmeg
300 ml/½ pt/1¼ cup full-cream milk
Salt and freshly ground black pepper
Cubed bread, to serve

Place all the ingredients in a deep 2.5 litre/4½ pt/11 cup glass or pottery dish, seasoning well to taste. Cook, uncovered, on Full for 7–9 minutes, stirring four times, until the fondue begins to bubble gently. Bring the dish to the table and eat by spearing a cube of bread on to a long fondue fork, swirling it round in the cheese mixture, then lifting it out.

Farmhouse Fondue with a Kick

SERVES 4–6

Prepare as for Dutch Farmhouse Fondue, but stir in 30–45 ml/2–3 tbsp Genever (Dutch gin) after cooking.

Baked Egg Flamenco Style

SERVES 1

Melted butter or margarine
1 small tomato, blanched, skinned and chopped
2 spring onions (scallions), chopped
1–2 stuffed olives, sliced
5 ml/1 tsp oil
15 ml/1 tbsp cooked ham, finely chopped
1 egg
Salt and freshly ground black pepper
15 ml/1 tbsp double (heavy) cream or crème fraîche
5 ml/1 tsp very finely chopped parsley, chives or coriander (cilantro)

Brush a small ramekin dish (custard cup) or individual soufflé dish with melted butter or margarine. Add the tomato, spring onions, olives, oil and ham. Cover with a saucer and heat through on Full for 1 minute. Gently break in the egg and puncture the yolk twice with a skewer or the tip of a knife. Season well to taste. Coat with the cream and sprinkle with the herbs. Cover as before and cook on Defrost for 3 minutes. Allow to stand for 1 minute before eating.

Bread and Butter Cheese and Parsley Pudding

SERVES 4–6

4 large slices white bread
50 g/2 oz/¼ cup butter, at kitchen
temperature
175 g/6 oz/1½ cups orange-
coloured Cheddar cheese
45 ml/3 tbsp chopped parsley
600 ml/1 pt/2½ cups cold milk
3 eggs
5 ml/1 tsp salt
Paprika

Spread the bread with the butter and cut each slice into four squares. Thoroughly butter a 1.75 litre/3 pt/7½ cup dish. Arrange half the bread squares, buttered sides up, over the base of the dish. Sprinkle with two-thirds of the cheese and all the parsley. Arrange the remaining bread on top, buttered sides up. Pour the milk into a jug and warm, uncovered, on Full for 3 minutes. Beat the eggs until foamy, then gradually whisk in the milk. Stir in the salt. Pour gently over the bread and butter. Sprinkle the remaining cheese on top and dust with paprika. Cover with kitchen paper and cook on Defrost for 30 minutes. Allow to stand for 5 minutes, then brown under a hot grill (broiler), if liked, before serving.

Bread and Butter Cheese and Parsley Pudding with Cashew Nuts

SERVES 4–6

Prepare as for Bread and Butter Cheese and Parsley Pudding, but add 45 ml/3 tbsp cashew nuts, toasted (page 205) and coarsely chopped, with the cheese and parsley.

Four-cheese Bread and Butter Pudding

SERVES 4–6

Prepare as for Bread and Butter Cheese and Parsley Pudding, but use a mixture of grated Cheddar, Edam, Red Leicester and crumbled Stilton cheeses. Substitute four chopped pickled onions for the parsley.

Cheese and Egg Crumpets

SERVES 4

300 ml/10 fl oz/1 can condensed
mushroom soup
45 ml/3 tbsp single (light) cream
125 g/4 oz/1 cup Red Leicester
cheese, grated
4 hot toasted crumpets
4 freshly poached eggs (page 99)

Put the soup, cream and half the cheese into a 900 ml/1½ pt/3¾ cup bowl. Heat, uncovered, on Full for 4–5 minutes until hot and smooth, beating every minute. Put each crumpet on a warmed plate and top with an egg. Coat with the mushroom mixture, sprinkle with the remaining cheese and heat one at a time on Full for about 1 minute until the cheese is melted and bubbling. Eat straight away.

Upside-down Cheese and Tomato Pudding
••••••••••••••••••••••••••••••••••
SERVES 4

225 g/8 oz/2 cups self-raising (self-rising) flour
5 ml/1 tsp mustard powder
5 ml/1 tsp salt
125 g/4 oz/½ cup butter or margarine
125 g/4 oz/1 cup Edam or Cheddar cheese, grated
2 eggs, beaten
150 ml/¼ pt/⅔ cup cold milk
4 large tomatoes, blanched and skinned and chopped
15 ml/1 tbsp chopped parsley or coriander (cilantro)

Grease a deep round 1.75 litre/3 pt/7½ cup pudding basin with butter. Sift the flour, mustard powder and 2.5 ml/½ tsp of the salt into a bowl. Rub in the butter or margarine finely, then toss in the cheese. Mix to a soft consistency with the eggs and milk. Spread smoothly into the prepared basin. Cook, uncovered, on Full for 6 minutes. Mix the tomatoes with the remaining salt. Place in a shallow bowl and cover with a plate. Remove the pudding from the oven and carefully invert into a shallow dish. Cover with kitchen paper and cook on Full for a further 2 minutes. Remove from the oven and cover with a piece of foil to retain the heat. Put the tomatoes in the microwave and heat on Full for 3 minutes. Spoon over the pudding, sprinkle with the herbs and serve hot.

Pizza Crumpets
••••••••••••••••••••••••••••••••••••••
SERVES 4

45 ml/3 tbsp tomato purée (paste)
30 ml/2 tbsp olive oil
1 garlic clove, crushed
4 hot toasted crumpets
2 tomatoes, thinly sliced
175 g/6 oz Mozzarella cheese, sliced
12 black olives

Mix together the tomato purée, olive oil and garlic and spread on to the crumpets. Arrange the tomato slices on top. Cover with the cheese and stud with the olives. Heat one at a time on Full for about 1–1½ minutes until the cheese is starting to melt. Eat straight away.

Fish and Seafood

All the great chefs are of one voice: fish needs gentle, tender treatment, and unless you're talking fried (sautéed) fish, steaming and poaching are among the best ways of cooking it. Because the microwave doubles as both a steamer and poacher nothing betters it for fish – as this handsome assortment of mixed dishes proves.

Gingered Sea Bass with Onions

SERVES 8

A Cantonese speciality and a typical Chinese buffet dish.

2 sea bass, 450 g/1 lb each, cleaned but heads left on
8 spring onions (scallions)
5 ml/1 tsp salt
2.5 ml/½ tsp sugar
2.5 cm/1 in piece fresh root ginger, peeled and finely chopped
45 ml/3 tbsp soy sauce

Wash the fish inside and out. Dry with kitchen paper. Make three diagonal slashes with a sharp knife, about 2.5 cm/1 in apart, on both sides of each fish. Place head-to-tail in a 30 × 20 cm/12 × 8 in dish. Top and tail the onions, cut each into threads along its length and sprinkle over the fish. Thoroughly mix together the remaining ingredients and use to coat the fish. Cover the dish with clingfilm (plastic wrap) and slit it twice to allow steam to escape. Cook on Full for 12 minutes, turning the dish once. Transfer the fish to a serving plate and coat with the onions and juices from dish.

Trout Packets

SERVES 2

Professional chefs call this *truites en papillote*. The parcels of simply prepared delicate trout make a smart fish course.

2 large cleaned trout, 450 g/1 lb each, washed but heads left on
1 onion, thickly sliced
1 small lemon or lime, thickly sliced
2 large dried bay leaves, coarsely crumbled
2.5 ml/½ tsp herbes de Provence
5 ml/1 tsp salt

Prepare two rectangles of baking parchment, 40 × 35 cm/16 × 14 in each. Place the onion and lemon or lime slices in the cavities of the fish with the bay leaves. Transfer to the parchment rectangles and sprinkle with the herbs and salt. Wrap each trout individually, then put both parcels together in a shallow dish. Cook on Full for 14 minutes, turning the dish once. Allow to stand for 2 minutes. Transfer each to a warmed plate and open out the parcels at the table.

Shining Monkfish with Slender Beans

SERVES 4

125 g/4 oz French (green) or
Kenya beans, topped and tailed
150 ml/¼ pt/⅔ cup boiling water
450 g/1 lb monkfish
15 ml/1 tbsp cornflour
(cornstarch)
1.5–2.5 ml/¼–½ tsp Chinese five
spice powder
45 ml/3 tbsp rice wine or medium
sherry
5 ml/1 tsp bottled oyster sauce
2.5 ml/½ tsp sesame oil
1 garlic clove, crushed
50 ml/2 fl oz/3½ tbsp hot water
15 ml/1 tbsp soy sauce
Egg noodles, to serve

Halve the beans. Place in a round 1.25 litre/2¼ pt/5½ cup dish. Add the boiling water. Cover with clingfilm (plastic wrap) and slit it twice to allow steam to escape. Cook on Full for 4 minutes. Drain and set aside. Wash the monkfish and cut it into narrow strips. Mix the cornflour and spice powder with the rice wine or sherry until smooth. Stir in the remaining ingredients. Transfer to the dish in which the beans were cooked. Cook, uncovered, on Full for 1½ minutes. Stir until smooth, then mix in the beans and monkfish. Cover as before and cook on Full for 4 minutes. Allow to stand for 2 minutes, then stir round and serve.

Shining Prawns with Mangetout

SERVES 4

Prepare as for Shining Monkfish with Slender Beans, but substitute mangetout (snow peas) for the beans

and cook them for only 2½–3 minutes as they should remain crisp. Substitute shelled prawns (shrimp) for the monkfish.

Normandy Cod with Cider and Calvados

SERVES 4

50 g/2 oz/¼ cup butter or
margarine
1 onion, very thinly sliced
3 carrots, very thinly sliced
50 g/2 oz mushrooms, trimmed
and thinly sliced
4 large cod steaks, about 225 g/
8 oz each
5 ml/1 tsp salt
150 ml/¼ pt/⅔ cup cider
15 ml/1 tbsp cornflour
(cornstarch)
25 ml/1½ tbsp cold water
15 ml/1 tbsp calvados
Parsley, to garnish

Place half the butter or margarine in a deep 20 cm/8 in diameter dish. Melt, uncovered, on Full for 45–60 seconds. Mix in the onion, carrots and mushrooms. Arrange the fish in a single layer on top. Dust with the salt. Pour the cider into the dish and dot the steaks with the remaining butter or margarine. Cover with clingfilm (plastic wrap) and slit it twice to allow steam to escape. Cook on Full for 8 minutes, turning the dish four times. Carefully pour off the cooking liquor and reserve. Mix the cornflour smoothly with the water and calvados. Add the fish juices. Cook, uncovered, on Full for 2–2½ minutes until the sauce thickens, whisking every 30 seconds. Arrange the fish on a warmed serving plate and top with the vegetables. Coat with the sauce and garnish with parsley.

Fish Paella

SERVES 6–8

Spain's foremost rice dish, known worldwide through international travel.

900 g/2 lb skinned salmon fillet, cubed
1 packet saffron powder
60 ml/4 tbsp hot water
30 ml/2 tbsp olive oil
2 onions, chopped
2 garlic cloves, crushed
1 green (bell) pepper, seeded and coarsely chopped
225 g/8 oz/1 cup Italian or Spanish risotto rice
175 g/6 oz/1½ cups frozen or fresh peas
600 ml/1 pt/2½ cups boiling water
7.5 ml/1½ tsp salt
3 tomatoes, blanched, peeled and quartered
75 g/3 oz/¾ cup cooked ham, diced
125 g/4 oz/1 cup peeled prawns (shrimp)
250 g/9 oz/1 large can mussels in brine
Lemon wedges or slices, to garnish

Arrange the salmon cubes round the edge of a 25 cm/10 in diameter casserole dish (Dutch oven), leaving a small hollow in the centre. Cover the dish with clingfilm (plastic wrap) and slit it twice to allow steam to escape. Cook on Defrost for 10–11 minutes, turning the dish twice, until the fish looks flaky and just cooked. Drain off and reserve the liquid and set aside the salmon. Wash and dry the dish. Empty the saffron into a small bowl, add the hot water and leave to soak for 10 minutes. Pour the oil into the cleaned dish and add the onions, garlic and green pepper. Cook, un-covered, on Full for 4 minutes. Add the rice, saffron and soaking water, peas, salmon cubes, reserved salmon liquid, boiling water and salt. Mix thoroughly but gently. Cover as before and cook on Full for 10 minutes. Allow to stand in the microwave for 10 minutes. Cook on Full for a further 5 minutes. Uncover and carefully mix in the tomatoes and ham. Garnish with the prawns, mussels and lemon and serve.

Soused Herrings

SERVES 4

4 herring, about 450 g/1 lb each, filleted
2 large bay leaves, coarsely crumbled
15 ml/1 tbsp mixed pickling spice
2 onions, sliced and separated into rings
150 ml/¼ pt/⅔ cup boiling water
20 ml/4 tsp granulated sugar
10 ml/2 tsp salt
90 ml/6 tbsp malt vinegar
Buttered bread, to serve

Roll up each herring fillet from the head to the tail end, skin sides inside. Arrange round the edge of a deep 25 cm/10 in diameter dish. Sprinkle with the bay leaves and spice. Arrange the onion rings between the herrings. Thoroughly mix together the remaining ingredients and spoon over the fish. Cover with clingfilm (plastic wrap) and slit it twice to allow steam to escape. Cook on Full for 18 minutes. Allow to cool, then chill. Eat cold with bread and butter.

Moules Marinières

•••••••••••••••••••••••••••••••
SERVES 4

Belgium's national dish, always served with a side dish of chips (fries).

**900 ml/2 pts/5 cups fresh mussels
15 g/½ oz/l tbsp butter or
  margarine
1 small onion, chopped
1 garlic clove, crushed
150 ml/¼ pt/⅔ cup dry white wine
1 bouquet garni sachet
1 dried bay leaf, crumbled
7.5 ml/1½ tsp salt
20 ml/4 tsp fresh white
  breadcrumbs
20 ml/4 tsp chopped parsley**

Wash the mussels under cold running water. Scrape away any barnacles, then cut off the beards. Discard any mussels with cracked shells or those that are open; they can cause food poisoning. Wash again. Put the butter or margarine in a deep bowl. Melt, uncovered, on Full for about 30 seconds. Mix in the onion and garlic. Cover with a plate and cook on Full for 6 minutes, stirring twice. Add the wine, bouquet garni, bay leaf, salt and mussels. Stir gently to mix. Cover as before and cook on Full for 5 minutes. Using a slotted spoon, transfer the mussels into four deep bowls or soup plates. Stir the breadcrumbs and half the parsley into the cooking liquid, then spoon over the mussels. Sprinkle with the remaining parsley and serve straight away.

Mackerel with Rhubarb and Raisin Sauce

•••••••••••••••••••••••••••••••
SERVES 4

The prettily coloured sweet-sour sauce balances the rich mackerel beautifully.

**350 g/12 oz young rhubarb,
  coarsely chopped
60 ml/4 tbsp boiling water
30 ml/2 tbsp raisins
30 ml/2 tbsp granulated sugar
2.5 ml/½ tsp vanilla essence
  (extract)
Finely grated zest and juice of
  ½ small lemon
4 mackerel, cleaned, boned and
  heads discarded
50 g/2 oz/¼ cup butter or
  margarine
Salt and freshly ground black
  pepper**

Place the rhubarb and water in a casserole dish (Dutch oven). Cover with clingfilm (plastic wrap) and slit it twice to allow steam to escape. Cook on Full for 6 minutes, turning the dish three times. Uncover and mash the rhubarb to a pulp. Stir in the raisins, sugar, vanilla essence and lemon zest, then set aside. With the skin sides facing you, fold each mackerel in half crossways from head to tail. Put the butter or margarine and lemon juice in a deep 20 cm/8 in diameter dish. Melt on Full for 2 minutes. Add the fish and coat with the melted ingredients. Sprinkle with salt and pepper. Cover with clingfilm (plastic wrap) and slit it twice to allow steam to escape. Cook on Medium for 14–16 minutes until the fish looks flaky. Allow to stand for 2 minutes. Heat through the rhubarb sauce on Full for 1 minute and serve with the mackerel.

Herring with Apple Cider Sauce

SERVES 4

Prepare as for Mackerel with Rhubarb and Raisin Sauce (page 117), but substitute peeled and cored cooking (tart) apples for the rhubarb and boiling cider in place of the water. Omit the raisins.

Carp in Jellied Sauce

SERVES 4

1 very fresh carp, cleaned and cut
into 8 thin slices
30 ml/2 tbsp malt vinegar
3 carrots, thinly sliced
3 onions, thinly sliced
600 ml/1 pt/2½ cups boiling water
10–15 ml/ 2–3 tsp salt

Wash the carp, then soak for 3 hours in enough cold water with the vinegar added to cover the fish. (This removes the muddy taste.) Place the carrots and onions in a deep 23 cm/9 in diameter dish with the boiling water and salt. Cover with clingfilm (plastic wrap) and slit it twice to allow steam to escape. Cook on Full for 20 minutes, turning the dish four times. Drain, reserving the liquid. (The vegetables can be used elsewhere in fish soup or stir-fries.) Pour the liquid back into the dish. Add the carp in a single layer. Cover as before and cook on Full for 8 minutes, turning the dish twice. Allow to stand for 3 minutes. Using a fish slice, transfer the carp to a shallow dish. Cover and chill. Transfer the liquid into a jug and chill until lightly jellied. Spoon the jelly over the fish and serve.

Rollmops with Apricots

SERVES 4

75 g/3 oz dried apricots
150 ml/¼ pt/⅔ cup cold water
3 bought rollmops with sliced
onions
150 g/5 oz/⅔ cup crème fraîche
Mixed salad leaves
Crispbread

Wash the apricots and cut into bite-sized pieces. Place in a bowl with the cold water. Cover with an inverted plate and heat on Full for 5 minutes. Allow to stand for 5 minutes. Drain. Cut the rollmops into strips. Add to the apricots with the onions and crème fraîche. Mix well. Cover and leave to marinate in the refrigerator for 4–5 hours. Serve on salad leaves with crispbread.

Poached Kipper

SERVES 1

Microwaving stops the smell permeating the house and leaves the kipper juicy and tender.

1 large undyed kipper, about
450 g/1 lb
120 ml/4 fl oz/½ cup cold water
Butter or margarine

Trim the kipper, discarding the tail. Soak for 3–4 hours in several changes of cold water to reduce saltiness, if wished, then drain. Place in a large, shallow dish with the water. Cover with clingfilm (plastic wrap) and slit it twice to allow steam to escape. Cook on Full for 4 minutes. Serve on a warmed plate with knob of butter or margarine.

Prawns Madras

SERVES 4

25 g/1 oz/2 tbsp ghee or 15 ml/
  1 tbsp groundnut (peanut) oil
2 onions, chopped
2 garlic cloves, crushed
15 ml/1 tbsp hot curry powder
5 ml/1 tsp ground cumin
5 ml/1 tsp garam masala
Juice of 1 small lime
150 ml/¼ pt/⅔ cup fish or
  vegetable stock
30 ml/2 tbsp tomato purée (paste)
60 ml/4 tbsp sultanas (golden
  raisins)
450 g/1 lb/4 cups peeled prawns
  (shrimp), thawed if frozen
175 g/6 oz/¾ cup long-grain rice,
  boiled
Popadoms (page 82)

Put the ghee or oil in a deep 20 cm/
8 in diameter dish. Heat, uncovered, on Full for 1 minute.
Thoroughly mix in the onions and garlic. Cook, uncovered, on Full for 3
minutes. Add the curry powder, cumin,
garam masala and lime juice. Cook,
uncovered, on Full for 3 minutes, stirring twice. Add the stock, tomato
purée and sultanas. Cover with an
inverted plate and cook on Full for 5
minutes. Drain the prawns if necessary, then add to the dish and stir
round to combine. Cook, uncovered,
on Full for 1½ minutes. Serve with the
rice and popadoms.

Martini Plaice Rolls with Sauce

SERVES 4

8 plaice fillets, 175 g/6 oz each,
  washed and dried
Salt and freshly ground black
  pepper
Juice of 1 lemon
2.5 ml/½ tsp Worcestershire sauce
25 g/1 oz/2 tbsp butter or
  margarine
4 shallots, peeled and chopped
100 g/3½ oz/1 cup cooked ham,
  cut into strips
400 g/14 oz mushrooms, thinly
  sliced
20 ml/4 tsp cornflour (cornstarch)
20 ml/4 tsp cold milk
250 ml/8 fl oz/1 cup chicken stock
150 g/¼ pt/⅔ cup single (light)
  cream
2.5 ml/½ tsp caster (superfine)
  sugar
1.5 ml/¼ tsp turmeric
10 ml/2 tsp martini bianco

Season the fish with salt and pepper.
Marinate in the lemon juice and
Worcestershire sauce for 15–20 minutes. Melt the butter or margarine in a
saucepan (skillet). Add the shallots
and fry (sauté) gently until soft and
semi-transparent. Add the ham and
mushrooms and stir-fry for 7 minutes.
Blend the cornflour with the cold milk
until smooth and add the remaining
ingredients. Roll up the plaice fillets
and spear with cocktail sticks (toothpicks). Arrange in a deep 20 cm/8 in
diameter dish. Coat with the mushroom mixture. Cover with clingfilm
(plastic wrap) and slit it twice to allow
steam to escape. Cook on Full for 10
minutes.

Shellfish Ragout with Walnuts

••••••••••••••••••••••••••••••••••
SERVES 4

30 ml/2 tbsp olive oil
1 onion, peeled and chopped
2 carrots, peeled and finely diced
3 celery stalks, cut into narrow strips
1 red (bell) pepper, seeded and cut into strips
1 green (bell) pepper, seeded and cut into strips
1 small courgette (zucchini), trimmed and thinly sliced
250 ml/8 fl oz/1 cup rosé wine
1 bouquet garni sachet
325 ml/11 fl oz/1⅓ cups vegetable or fish stock
400 g/14 oz/1 large can chopped tomatoes
125 g/4 oz squid rings
125 g/4 oz cooked shelled mussels
200 g/7 oz lemon sole or flounder fillet, cut into chunks
4 giant prawns (jumbo shrimp), cooked
50 g/2 oz/½ cup walnuts, coarsely chopped
30 ml/2 tbsp stoned (pitted) black olives
10 ml/2 tsp gin
Juice of ½ small lemon
2.5 ml/½ tsp granulated sugar
1 baguette
30 ml/2 tbsp coarsely chopped basil leaves

Pour the oil into a 2.5 litre/4½ pt/ 11 cup dish. Heat, uncovered, on Full for 2 minutes. Add the prepared vegetables and toss in the oil to coat. Cover with clingfilm (plastic wrap) and slit it twice to allow steam to escape. Cook on Full for 5 minutes. Add the wine and bouquet garni. Cover as before and cook on Full for 5 minutes. Add the stock, tomatoes and fish. Re-cover and cook on Full for 10 minutes. Mix in all the remaining ingredients except the basil. Re-cover and cook on full for 4 minutes. Scatter with the basil and serve hot.

Cod Hot-pot

••••••••••••••••••••••••••••••••••
SERVES 4

25 g/1 oz/2 tbsp butter or margarine
1 onion, peeled and chopped
2 carrots, peeled and finely diced
2 celery stalks, thinly sliced
150 ml/¼ pt/⅔ cup medium-dry white wine
400 g/14 oz skinned cod fillet, cut into large cubes
15 ml/1 tbsp cornflour (cornstarch)
75 ml/5 tbsp cold milk
350 ml/12 fl oz/1½ cups fish or vegetable stock
Salt and freshly ground black pepper
75 ml/5 tbsp chopped dill (dill weed)
300 ml/½ pt/1¼ cups double (heavy) cream, softly whipped
2 egg yolks

Place the butter or margarine in a 20 cm/8 in diameter casserole dish (Dutch oven). Heat, uncovered, on Full for 2 minutes. Mix in the vegetables and wine. Cover with clingfilm (plastic wrap) and slit it twice to allow steam to escape. Cook on Full for 5 minutes. Allow to stand for 3 minutes. Uncover. Add the fish to the vegetables. Mix the cornflour with the cold milk until smooth, then add to the casserole with the stock. Season. Cover as before and cook on Full for 8 minutes. Add the dill. Thoroughly mix the cream with the egg yolks and stir into the casserole. Cover and cook on Full for 1½ minutes.

Smoked Cod Hot-pot

SERVES 4

Prepare as for Cod Hot-pot but substitute smoked cod fillet for fresh.

Monkfish in Golden Lemon Cream Sauce

SERVES 6

300 ml/½ pt/1¼ cups full-cream
milk
25 g/1 oz/2 tbsp butter or
margarine, at kitchen
temperature
675 g/1½ lb monkfish fillets, cut
into bite-sized chunks
45 ml/3 tbsp plain (all-purpose)
flour
2 large egg yolks
Juice of 1 large lemon
2.5–5 ml/½ –1 tsp salt
2.5 ml/½ tsp finely chopped
tarragon
Cooked vol-au-vent cases (patty
shells) or toasted ciabatta bread
slices

Pour the milk into a jug and warm, uncovered, on Full for 2 minutes. Place the butter or margarine in a deep 20 cm/8 in diameter dish. Melt, uncovered, on Defrost for 1½ minutes. Coat the fish chunks in flour and add to the butter or margarine in the dish. Gently pour in the milk. Cover with clingfilm (plastic wrap) and slit it twice to allow steam to escape. Cook on Full for 7 minutes. Beat together the egg yolks, lemon juice and salt and stir into the fish. Cook, uncovered, on Full for 2 minutes. Allow to stand for 5 minutes. Stir round, sprinkle with the tarragon and serve in vol-au-vent cases or with slices of toasted ciabatta.

Sole in Golden Lemon Cream Sauce

SERVES 6

Prepare as for Monkfish in Golden Lemon Cream Sauce, but substitute sole, cut into strips, for the monkfish chunks.

Salmon Hollandaise

SERVES 4

4 salmon steaks, 175–200 g/
6–7 oz each
150 ml/¼ pt water/⅔ cup water or
dry white wine
2.5 ml/½ tsp salt
Hollandaise Sauce (page 318)

Arrange the steaks round the sides of a deep 20 cm/8 in diameter dish. Add the water or wine. Sprinkle the fish with the salt. Cover with clingfilm (plastic wrap) and slit it twice to allow steam to escape. Cook on Defrost (to prevent the salmon spitting) for 16–18 minutes. Allow to stand for 4 minutes. Lift out on to four warmed plates with a fish slice, draining off the liquid. Coat each with the Hollandaise Sauce.

Salmon Hollandaise with Coriander

SERVES 4

Prepare as for Salmon Hollandaise, but add 30 ml/2 tbsp chopped coriander (cilantro) to the sauce as soon as it has finished cooking. For additional flavour, mix in 10 ml/2 tsp chopped lemon balm.

Salmon Mayonnaise Flake

SERVES 6

*900 g/2 lb fresh salmon fillet,
  skinned*
*Salt and freshly ground black
  pepper*
*Melted butter or margarine
  (optional)*
*50 g/2 oz/½ cup flaked (slivered)
  almonds, toasted (page 205)*
1 small onion, finely chopped
*30 ml/2 tbsp finely chopped
  parsley*
5 ml/1 tsp chopped tarragon
*200 ml/7 fl oz/scant 1 cup French-
  style mayonnaise*
Lettuce leaves
Fennel sprays, to garnish

Divide the salmon into four portions. Arrange round the edge of a
deep 25 cm/10 in diameter dish.
Sprinkle with salt and pepper and
trickle a little melted butter or margarine over the top if wished. Cover
with clingfilm (plastic wrap) and slit it
twice to allow steam to escape. Cook
on Defrost for 20 minutes. Allow to
cool to lukewarm, then flake the fish
with two forks. Transfer to a bowl, add
half the almonds and the onion, parsley and tarragon. Gently stir in the
mayonnaise until well mixed and
moist. Line a long serving dish with
lettuce leaves. Arrange a line of
salmon mayonnaise on top. Sprinkle
with the remaining almonds and
garnish with fennel.

Mediterranean-style Salmon Roast

SERVES 6–8

*1.5 kg/3lb portion middle-cut
  salmon*
60 ml/4 tbsp olive oil
60 ml/4 tbsp lemon juice
60 ml/4 tbsp tomato purée (paste)
15 ml/1 tbsp chopped basil leaves
7.5 ml/1½ tsp salt
45 ml/3 tbsp small capers, drained
45 ml/3 tbsp chopped parsley

Wash the salmon, ensuring all
scales are scraped off. Place in a
deep 20 cm/8 in diameter dish. Whisk
together the remaining ingredients
and spoon over the fish. Cover with a
plate and leave to marinate in the
refrigerator for 3 hours. Cover with
clingfilm (plastic wrap) and slit it twice
to allow steam to escape. Cook on Full
for 20 minutes, turning the dish twice.
Divide into portions to serve.

Kedgeree with Curry

SERVES 4

Once a breakfast dish, particularly associated with colonial days in India around the turn of the century, kedgeree is now more often served for lunch.

350 g/12 oz smoked haddock or cod fillet
60 ml/4 tbsp cold water
50 g/2 oz/¼ cup butter or margarine
225 g/8 oz/1 cup basmati rice
15 ml/1 tbsp mild curry powder
600 ml/1 pt/2½ cups boiling water
3 hard-boiled (hard-cooked) eggs
150 ml/¼ pt/⅔ cup single (light) cream
15 ml/1 tbsp chopped parsley
Salt and freshly ground black pepper
Parsley sprigs, to garnish

Put the fish into a shallow dish with the cold water. Cover with clingfilm (plastic wrap) and slit it twice to allow steam to escape. Cook on Full for 5 minutes. Drain. Flake up the flesh with two forks, removing the skin and bones. Place the butter or margarine in a round 1.75 litre/3 pt/7½ cup heatproof serving dish and melt on Defrost for 1½–2 minutes. Stir in the rice, curry powder and boiling water. Cover as before and cook on Full for 15 minutes. Chop two of the eggs and stir into the dish with the fish, cream and parsley, seasoning to taste. Fork round, cover with an inverted plate and reheat on Full for 5 minutes. Slice the remaining egg. Remove the dish from the microwave and garnish with the sliced egg and parsley sprigs.

Kedgeree with Smoked Salmon

SERVES 4

Prepare as for Kedgeree with Curry, but substitute 225 g/8 oz smoked salmon (lox), cut into strips, for the smoked haddock or cod. Smoked salmon does not need precooking.

Smoked Fish Quiche

SERVES 6

175 g/6 oz shortcrust pastry (basic pie crust)
1 egg yolk, beaten
125 g/4 oz smoked fish such as mackerel, haddock, cod or trout, cooked and flaked
3 eggs
150 ml/¼ pt/⅔ cup soured (dairy sour) cream
30 ml/2 tbsp mayonnaise
Salt and freshly ground black pepper
75 g/3 oz/¾ cup Cheddar cheese, grated
Paprika
Mixed salad

Lightly butter a fluted 20 cm/8 in diameter glass or china flan dish. Roll out the pastry and use to line the greased dish. Prick well all over, especially where the side meets the base. Cook, uncovered, on Full for 6 minutes, turning the dish twice. If any bulges appear, press down with fingers protected by oven gloves. Brush the inside of the pastry case (pie shell) with the egg yolk. Cook on Full for 1 minute to seal any holes. Remove from the oven. Cover the base with the fish. Beat the eggs with the cream and mayonnaise, seasoning to taste. Pour into the quiche and sprinkle with the cheese and paprika. Cook, uncovered, on Full for 8 minutes. Serve warm with salad.

Louisiana Prawn Gumbo

SERVES 8

3 onions, chopped
2 garlic cloves
3 celery stalks, finely chopped
1 green (bell) pepper, seeded and
    finely chopped
50 g/2 oz/¼ cup butter
60 ml/4 tbsp plain (all-purpose)
    flour
900 ml/1½ pt/3¾ cups hot
    vegetable or chicken stock
350 g/12 oz okra (ladies' fingers),
    topped and tailed
15 ml/1 tbsp salt
10 ml/2 tsp ground coriander
    (cilantro)
5 ml/1 tsp turmeric
2.5 ml/½ tsp ground allspice
30 ml/2 tbsp lemon juice
2 bay leaves
5–10 ml/1–2 tsp Tabasco sauce
450 g/1 lb/4 cups cooked peeled
    prawns (shrimp), thawed if frozen
350 g/12 oz/1½ cups long-grain
    rice, boiled

Place the onions in a 2.5 litre/4½ pt/ 11 cup bowl. Crush the garlic over the top. Add the celery and green pepper. Melt the butter on Full for 2 minutes. Stir in the flour. Cook, uncovered, on Full for 5–7 minutes, stirring four times and watching carefully in case of burning, until the mixture is a light biscuit-coloured roux. Gradually blend in the stock. Set aside. Cut the okra into chunks and add to the vegetables with all the remaining ingredients except the Tabasco and prawns but including the roux mix. Cover with clingfilm (plastic wrap) and slit it twice to allow steam to escape. Cook on Full for 25 minutes. Allow to stand for 5 minutes. Stir in the Tabasco and prawns. Spoon into warmed deep bowls and add a mound of freshly cooked rice to each. Eat straight away.

Monkfish Gumbo

SERVES 8

Prepare as for Louisiana Prawn Gumbo, but substitute the same weight of boned monkfish, cut into strips, for the prawns (shrimp). Cover with clingfilm (plastic wrap) and cook on Full for 4 minutes before transferring to serving bowls.

Mixed Fish Gumbo

SERVES 8

Prepare as for Louisiana Prawn Gumbo, but substitute assorted cubed fish fillets for the prawns (shrimp).

Trout with Almonds

SERVES 4

50 g/2 oz/¼ cup butter
15 ml/1 tbsp lemon juice
4 medium trout
50 g/2 oz/½ cup flaked (slivered)
    almonds, toasted (page 205)
Salt and freshly ground black
    pepper
4 lemon wedges
Parsley sprigs

Melt the butter on Defrost for 1½ minutes. Stir in the lemon juice. Place the trout, head-to-tail, in a buttered 25 × 20 cm/10 × 8 in dish. Coat the fish with the butter mixture and sprinkle with the almonds and seasoning. Cover with clingfilm (plastic wrap) and slit it twice to allow steam to escape. Cook on Full for 9–12 minutes, turning the dish twice. Allow to stand for 5 minutes. Transfer to four warmed plates. Pour over the cooking liquid and garnish with the lemon wedges and parsley sprigs.

Prawns Provençale

SERVES 4

225 g/8 oz/1 cup easy-cook long-
  grain rice
600 ml/1 pt/2½ cups hot fish or
  chicken stock
5 ml/1 tsp salt
15 ml/1 tbsp olive oil
1 onion, grated
1–2 garlic cloves, crushed
6 large very ripe tomatoes,
  blanched, skinned and chopped
15 ml/1 tbsp chopped basil leaves
5 ml/1 tsp dark soft brown sugar
450 g/1 lb/4 cups frozen peeled
  prawns (shrimp), unthawed
Salt and freshly ground black
  pepper
Chopped parsley

Place the rice in a 2 litre/3½ pt/
8½ cup dish. Stir in the hot stock
and salt. Cover with clingfilm (plastic
wrap) and slit it twice to allow steam
to escape. Cook on Full for 16 minutes. Allow to stand for 8 minutes for
the rice to absorb all the moisture.
Pour the oil into a 1.75 litre/3 pt/
7½ cup serving dish. Heat, uncovered,
on Full for 1½ minutes. Stir in the
onion and garlic. Cook, uncovered, on
Full for 3 minutes, stirring twice. Add
the tomatoes with the basil and sugar.
Cover with a plate and cook on Full for
5 minutes, stirring twice. Mix in the
frozen prawns and seasoning to taste.
Cover as before and cook on Full for 4
minutes, then gently separate the
prawns. Re-cover and cook on Full for
a further 3 minutes. Allow to stand.
Cover the rice with a plate and reheat
on Defrost for 5–6 minutes. Spoon on
to four warmed plates and top with the
fish and tomato mixture. Sprinkle with
parsley and serve hot.

Plaice in Celery Sauce with Toasted Almonds

SERVES 4

8 plaice fillets, total weight about
  1 kg/2¼ lb
300 ml/10 fl oz/1 can condensed
  cream of celery soup
150 ml/¼ pt/⅔ cup boiling water
15 ml/1 tbsp finely chopped parsley
30 ml/2 tbsp flaked (slivered)
  almonds, toasted (page 205)

Roll up the fish fillets from head to
tail, skin sides inside. Arrange
round the edge of a deep 25 cm/10 in
diameter buttered dish. Gently whisk
together the soup and water and stir in
the parsley. Spoon over the fish. Cover
the dish with clingfilm (plastic wrap)
and slit it twice to allow steam to
escape. Cook on Full for 12 minutes,
turning the dish twice. Allow to stand
for 5 minutes. Cook on Full for a further 6 minutes. Spoon on to warmed
plates and serve, sprinkled with the
almonds.

Fillets in Tomato Sauce with Marjoram

SERVES 4

Prepare as for Plaice in Celery Sauce
with Toasted Almonds, but substitute condensed tomato soup for celery
and 2.5 ml/½ tsp dried marjoram for
the parsley.

Fillets in Mushroom Sauce with Watercress

SERVES 4

Prepare as for Plaice in Celery Sauce
with Toasted Almonds, but substitute condensed mushroom soup for
celery and 30 ml/2 tbsp chopped
watercress for the parsley.

Hashed Cod with Poached Eggs
••••••••••••••••••••••••••••••••••
SERVES 4

This was found in a handwritten nineteenth-century notebook, belonging to the grandmother of an old friend.

675 g/1½ lb skinned cod fillet
10 ml/2 tsp melted butter or
*   margarine or sunflower oil*
Paprika
Salt and freshly ground black
*   pepper*
50 g/2 oz/¼ cup butter or
*   margarine*
8 large spring onions (scallions),
*   trimmed and chopped*
350 g/12 oz cold cooked potatoes,
*   diced*
150 ml/¼ pt/⅔ cup single (light)
*   cream*
5 ml/1 tsp salt
4 eggs
175 ml/6 fl oz/¾ cup hot water
5 ml/1 tsp vinegar

Arrange the fish in a shallow dish. Brush with some of the melted butter or margarine or oil. Season with paprika, salt and pepper. Cover with clingfilm (plastic wrap) and slit it twice to allow steam to escape. Cook on Defrost for 14–16 minutes. Flake up the fish with two forks, removing the bones. Put the remaining butter, margarine or oil into a 20 cm/8 in diameter casserole dish (Dutch oven). Heat, uncovered, on Defrost for 1½ –2 minutes. Mix in the onions. Cover with a plate and cook on Full for 5 minutes. Stir in the fish with the potatoes, cream and salt. Cover as before and reheat on Full for 5–7 minutes until very hot, stirring once or twice. Keep hot. To poach the eggs, gently break two into a small dish and add half the water and half the vinegar. Puncture the yolks with the tip of a knife. Cover with a plate and cook on Full for 2 minutes. Allow to stand for 1 minute. Repeat with the remaining eggs, hot water and vinegar. Spoon helpings of the hash on to four warmed plates and top each with an egg.

Haddock and Vegetables in Cider Sauce
••••••••••••••••••••••••••••••••••
SERVES 4

50 g/2 oz/¼ cup butter or
*   margarine*
1 onion, thinly sliced and
*   separated into rings*
3 carrots, thinly sliced
50 g/2 oz button mushrooms,
*   sliced*
4 pieces filleted and skinned
*   haddock or other white fish*
5 ml/1 tsp salt
150 ml/¼ pt/⅔ cups medium-sweet
*   cider*
10 ml/2 tsp cornflour (cornstarch)
15 ml/1 tbsp cold water

Place half the butter or margarine in a deep 20 cm/8 in diameter dish. Melt, uncovered, on Defrost for about 1½ minutes. Add the onion, carrots and mushrooms. Arrange the fish on top. Sprinkle with the salt. Pour the cider gently over the fish. Dot with the remaining butter or margarine. Cover with clingfilm (plastic wrap) and slit it twice to allow steam to escape. Cook on Full for 8 minutes. In a glass jug, blend the cornflour smoothly with the cold water and gently strain in the fish liquor. Cook, uncovered, on Full for 2½ minutes until thickened, whisking every minute. Pour over the fish and vegetables. Spoon on to warmed plates and eat straight away.

Seaside Pie

•••••••••••••••••••••••••••••••
SERVES 4

For the topping:
**700 g/1½ lb floury potatoes,
    unpeeled weight**
75 ml/5 tbsp boiling water
15 ml/1 tbsp butter or margarine
**75 ml/5 tbsp milk or single (light)
    cream**
Salt and freshly ground pepper
Grated nutmeg
For the sauce:
300 ml/½ pt/1¼ cups cold milk
30 ml/2 tbsp butter or margarine
**20 ml/4 tsp plain (all-purpose)
    flour**
**75 ml/5 tbsp Red Leicester or
    coloured Cheddar cheese, grated**
5 ml/1 tsp wholegrain mustard
5 ml/1 tsp Worcestershire sauce
For the fish mixture:
**450 g/1 lb skinned white fish
    fillet, at kitchen temperature**
Melted butter or margarine
Paprika
**60 ml/4 tbsp Red Leicester or
    coloured Cheddar cheese, grated**

To make the topping, wash and peel the potatoes and cut into large cubes. Put in a 1.5 litre/2½ pt/6 cup dish with the boiling water. Cover with clingfilm (plastic wrap) and slit it twice to allow steam to escape. Cook on Full for 15 minutes, turning the dish twice. Allow to stand for 5 minutes. Drain and mash thoroughly with the butter or margarine and milk or cream, beating until fluffy. Season to taste with salt, pepper and nutmeg.

To make the sauce, heat the milk, uncovered, on Full for 1½ minutes. Set aside. Melt the butter or margarine, uncovered, on Defrost for 1–1½ minutes. Stir in the flour. Cook, uncovered, on Full for 30 seconds. Gradually blend in the milk. Cook on

Full for about 4 minutes, beating every minute to ensure smoothness, until the sauce is thickened. Stir in the cheese with the remaining sauce ingredients.

To make the fish mixture, arrange the fillets in a shallow dish and brush with melted butter or margarine. Season with paprika, salt and pepper. Cover with clingfilm (plastic wrap) and slit it twice to allow steam to escape. Cook on Full for 5–6 minutes. Flake up the fish with two forks, removing any bones. Transfer to a buttered 1.75 litre/ 3 pt/7½ cup dish. Mix in the sauce. Cover with the potatoes and sprinkle with the cheese and extra paprika. Reheat, uncovered, on Full for 6–7 minutes.

Smoky Fish Toppers

•••••••••••••••••••••••••••••••
SERVES 2

**2 frozen smoked haddock
    portions, 175 g/6 oz each**
Freshly ground black pepper
1 small courgette (zucchini), sliced
1 small onion, thinly sliced
**2 tomatoes, blanched, skinned and
    chopped**
**½ red (bell) pepper, seeded and cut
    into strips**
15 ml/1 tbsp snipped chives

Arrange the fish in a deep 18 cm/7 in diameter dish. Season with pepper. Cover with clingfilm (plastic wrap) and slit it twice to allow steam to escape. Cook on Full for 8 minutes. Spoon the juices over the fish, then allow to stand for 1 minute. Place the vegetables in another medium-sized casserole dish (Dutch oven). Cover with a plate and cook on Full for 5 minutes, stirring once. Spoon the vegetables over the fish. Cover as before and cook on Full for 2 minutes. Sprinkle with the chives and serve.

Coley Fillets with Leek and Lemon Marmalade

SERVES 2

An off-beat arrangement from Edinburgh's Sea Fish Authority, which also donated the next three recipes.

15 ml/1 tbsp butter
1 garlic clove, peeled and crushed
1 leek, slit and thinly sliced
2 coley fillets, 175 g/6 oz each,
  skinned
Juice of ½ lemon
10 ml/2 tsp lemon marmalade
Salt and freshly ground black pepper

Place the butter, garlic and leek in a deep 18 cm/7 in diameter dish. Cover with clingfilm (plastic wrap) and slit it twice to allow steam to escape. Cook on Full for 2½ minutes. Uncover. Arrange the fillets on top and sprinkle with half the lemon juice. Cover as before and cook on Full for 7 minutes. Transfer the fish to two warmed plates and keep hot. Mix the remaining lemon juice, the marmalade and seasoning into the fish juices and leek. Cover with a plate and cook on Full for 1½ minutes. Spoon over the fish and serve.

Seafish in a Jacket

SERVES 4

4 baking potatoes, unpeeled but
  well scrubbed
450 g/1 lb white fish fillet,
  skinned and cubed
45 ml/3 tbsp butter or margarine
3 spring onions (scallions),
  trimmed and chopped
30 ml/2 tbsp wholegrain mustard
1.5 ml/¼ tsp paprika, plus extra
  for dusting
30–45 ml/2–3 tbsp plain yoghurt
Salt

Stand the potatoes directly on the turntable, cover with kitchen paper and cook on Full for 16 minutes. Wrap in a clean tea towel (dish cloth) and set aside. Place the fish in an 18 cm/7 in diameter casserole dish (Dutch oven) with the butter or margarine, spring onions, mustard and paprika. Cover with a plate and cook on Full for 7 minutes, stirring twice. Allow to stand for 2 minutes. Mix in the yoghurt and salt to taste. Cut a cross on top of each potato and squeeze gently to open out. Fill with the fish mixture, dust with paprika and eat hot.

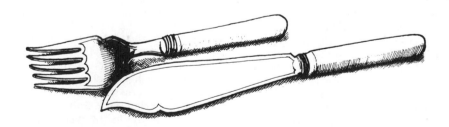

Swedish Cod with Melted Butter and Egg

SERVES 4

300 ml/½ pt/1¼ cups cold water
3 whole cloves
5 juniper berries
1 bay leaf, crumbled
2.5 ml/½ tsp mixed pickling spice
1 onion, quartered
10 ml/2 tsp salt
4 middle-cut fresh cod steaks,
    225 g/8 oz each
75 g/3 oz/⅓ cup butter
2 hard-boiled (hard-cooked) eggs
    (pages 98–9), shelled and
    chopped

Put the water, cloves, juniper berries, bay leaf, pickling spice, onion quarters and salt in a glass jug. Cover with clingfilm (plastic wrap) and slit it twice to allow steam to escape. Cook on Full for 15 minutes. Strain. Place the fish in a deep 25 cm/10 in diameter dish and pour in the strained liquid. Cover with clingfilm and slit it twice to allow steam to escape. Cook on Full for 10 minutes, turning the dish twice. Transfer the fish to a warmed dish, using a fish slice, and keep hot. Melt the butter, uncovered, on Defrost for 2 minutes. Pour over the fish. Sprinkle with the chopped eggs and serve.

Seafood Stroganoff

SERVES 4

30 ml/2 tbsp butter or margarine
1 garlic clove, crushed
1 onion, sliced
125 g/4 oz button mushrooms
700 g/1½ lb white fish fillet,
    skinned and cubed
150 ml/¼ pt/⅔ cup soured (dairy
    sour) cream or crème fraîche
Salt and freshly ground black
    pepper
30 ml/2 tbsp chopped parsley

Place the butter or margarine in a 20 cm/8 in diameter casserole dish (Dutch oven). Melt, uncovered, on Defrost for 2 minutes. Add the garlic, onion and mushrooms. Cover with clingfilm (plastic wrap) and slit it twice to allow steam to escape. Cook on Full for 3 minutes. Add the fish cubes. Cover as before and cook on Full for 8 minutes. Stir in the cream and season with salt and pepper. Cover again and cook on Full for 1½ minutes. Serve sprinkled with the parsley.

Fresh Tuna Stroganoff

SERVES 4

Prepare as for Seafood Stroganoff, but substitute very fresh tuna for the white fish.

White Fish Ragout Supreme

SERVES 4

30 ml/2 tbsp butter or margarine
1 onion, chopped
2 carrots, finely diced
6 celery stalks, thinly sliced
150 ml/¼ pt/⅔ cup white wine
400 g/14 oz skinned cod or
    haddock fillet, cubed
10 ml/2 tsp cornflour (cornstarch)
90 ml/6 tbsp single (light) cream
150 ml/¼ pt/⅔ cup vegetable stock
Salt and freshly ground black
    pepper
2.5 ml/½ tsp anchovy essence
    (extract) or Worcestershire
    sauce
30 ml/2 tbsp chopped dill (dill
    weed)
300 ml/½ pt/1¼ cups whipping
    cream
2 egg yolks

Place the butter or margarine in a 20 cm/8 in diameter casserole dish (Dutch oven). Heat, uncovered, on Full for 2 minutes. Add the vegetables and wine. Cover with clingfilm (plastic wrap) and slit it twice to allow steam to escape. Cook on Full for 5 minutes. Allow to stand for 3 minutes. Add the fish to the vegetables. Blend the cornflour smoothly with the cream, then mix in the stock. Season with salt, pepper and the anchovy essence or Worcestershire sauce. Pour over the fish. Cover as before and cook on Full for 8 minutes. Mix in the dill, then beat together the cream and egg yolks and stir into the fish mixture. Cover as before and cook on Defrost for 3 minutes.

Salmon Mousse

SERVES 8

30 ml/2 tbsp powdered gelatine
150 ml/¼ pt/⅔ cup cold water
418 g/15 oz/1 large can red salmon
150 ml/¼ pt/⅔ cup creamy
    mayonnaise
15 ml/1 tbsp mild made mustard
10 ml/2 tsp Worcestershire sauce
30 ml/2 tbsp fruit chutney,
    chopped if necessary
Juice of ½ large lemon
2 large egg whites
A pinch of salt
Cress, cucumber slices, salad
    greens and slices of fresh lime,
    to garnish

Stir the gelatine into 75 ml/5 tbsp of the cold water and allow to stand for 5 minutes to soften. Melt, uncovered, on Defrost for 2½–3 minutes. Stir again and mix in the remaining water. Tip the contents of the can of salmon into a fairly large bowl and flake with a fork, removing any skin and bones, then mash fairly finely. Mix in the melted gelatine, the mayonnaise, mustard, Worcestershire sauce, chutney and lemon juice. Cover and chill until just beginning to thicken and set round the edges. Beat the egg whites to stiff peaks. Beat one-third into the setting salmon mixture with the salt. Fold in the remaining egg whites and transfer the mixture to a 1.5 litre/2½ pt/6 cup ring mould, first rinsed with cold water. Cover with clingfilm (plastic wrap) and chill for 8 hours until firm. Before serving, quickly dip the mould up to its rim in and out of cold water to loosen. Run a wet knife gently round the sides, then invert on to a large wetted serving dish. (The wetting stops the jelly sticking.) Garnish attractively with plenty of cress, cucumber slices, salad greens and lime slices.

Dieters' Salmon Mousse

SERVES 8

Prepare as for Salmon Mousse, but substitute fromage frais or quark for the mayonnaise.

Crab Mornay

SERVES 4

300 ml/½ pt/1¼ cups full-cream
  milk
10 ml/2 tsp mixed pickling spice
1 small onion, cut into 8 wedges
2 parsley sprigs
A pinch of nutmeg
30 ml/2 tbsp butter
30 ml/2 tbsp plain (all-purpose)
  flour
Salt and freshly ground black pepper
75 g/3 oz/¾ cup Gruyère (Swiss)
  cheese, grated
5 ml/1 tsp continental mustard
350 g/12 oz prepared light and
  dark crabmeat
Toast slices

Pour the milk into a glass or plastic jug and stir in the pickling spice, onion wedges, parsley and nutmeg. Cover with a plate and heat on Full for 5–6 minutes until the milk just begins to shiver. Strain. Put the butter into a 1.5 litre/2½ pt/6 cup bowl and melt on Defrost for 1½ minutes. Mix in the flour. Cook on Full for 30 seconds. Gradually blend in the warm milk. Cook on Full for about 4 minutes, whisking every minute, until the sauce comes to the boil and thickens. Season with salt and pepper and stir in the cheese and mustard. Cook on Full for 30 seconds or until the cheese melts. Stir in the crabmeat. Cover with a plate and reheat on Full for 2–3 minutes. Serve on freshly made toast.

Tuna Mornay

SERVES 4

Prepare as for Crab Mornay, but substitute canned tuna in oil for the crabmeat. Flake up the flesh with two forks and add to the sauce with the oil from the can.

Red Salmon Mornay

SERVES 4

Prepare as for Crab Mornay, but substitute canned red salmon, drained and flaked, for the crabmeat.

Seafood and Walnut Combo

SERVES 4

45 ml/3 tbsp olive oil
1 onion, chopped
2 carrots, sliced
2 celery stalks, thinly sliced
1 red (bell) pepper, seeded and cut into strips
1 green (bell) pepper, seeded and cut into strips
1 small courgette (zucchini), thinly sliced
250 ml/8 fl oz/1 cup white wine
A pinch of mixed spice
300 ml/½ pt/1¼ cups fish or vegetable stock
450 g/1 lb ripe tomatoes, blanched, skinned and chopped
125 g/4 oz squid rings
400 g/14 oz plaice or lemon sole fillet, cut into squares
125 g/4 oz cooked mussels
4 large cooked prawns (shrimp)
50 g/2 oz/½ cup walnut halves or pieces
50 g/2 oz/⅓ cup sultanas (golden raisins)
A dash of sherry
Salt and freshly ground black pepper
Juice of 1 lemon
30 ml/2 tbsp chopped parsley

Heat the oil in a 2.5 litre/4½ pt/ 11 cup casserole dish (Dutch oven) on Full for 2 minutes. Add all the vegetables. Cook, uncovered, on Full for 5 minutes, stirring twice. Add the wine, spice, stock and tomatoes with all the fish and seafood. Cover with clingfilm (plastic wrap) and slit it twice to allow steam to escape. Cook on Full for 10 minutes. Stir in all the remaining ingredients except the parsley. Cover as before and cook on Full for 4 minutes. Uncover, sprinkle with the parsley and serve straight away.

Salmon Ring with Dill

SERVES 8–10

125 g/4 oz/3½ slices loose-textured white bread
900 g/2 lb skinned fresh salmon fillet, cubed
10 ml/2 tsp bottled anchovy sauce
5–7.5 ml/1–1½ tsp salt
1 garlic clove, crushed
4 large eggs, beaten
25 g/1 oz fresh dill (dill weed)
White pepper

Lightly butter a deep 23 cm/9 in diameter dish. Crumb the bread in a food processor. Add all remaining ingredients. Pulse the machine until the mixture is just combined and the fish coarsely minced. Avoid over-mixing or the mixture will be heavy and dense. Spread smoothly into the prepared dish and push a baby jam (conserve) jar or straight-sided egg cup into the centre so that the mixture forms a ring. Cover with clingfilm (plastic wrap) and slit it twice to allow steam to escape. Cook on Full for 15 minutes, turning the dish twice. (The ring will shrink away from the side of the dish.) Allow to stand until cool, then re-cover and chill. Cut into wedges and serve. Leftovers can be used in sandwiches.

Mixed Fish Ring with Parsley

SERVES 8–10

Prepare as for Salmon Ring with Dill, but substitute a mixture of skinned fresh salmon fillet, halibut and haddock for the salmon and 45 ml/3 tbsp chopped parsley for the dill.

Cod Casserole with Bacon and Tomatoes

SERVES 6

30 ml/2 tbsp butter or margarine
225 g/8 oz gammon, coarsely chopped
2 onions, sliced
1 large green (bell) pepper, seeded and cut into strips
2 × 400 g/2 × 14 oz/2 large cans tomatoes
15 ml/1 tbsp mild continental mustard
45 ml/3 tbsp Cointreau or Grand Marnier
Salt and freshly ground black pepper
700 g/1½ lb skinned cod fillet, cubed
2 garlic cloves, crushed
60 ml/4 tbsp toasted brown breadcrumbs
15 ml/1 tbsp groundnut (peanut) or sunflower oil

Put the butter or margarine in a 2 litre/3½ pt/8½ cup casserole dish (Dutch oven). Heat, uncovered, on Full for 1½ minutes. Mix in the gammon, onions and pepper. Cook, uncovered, on Defrost for 10 minutes, stirring twice. Remove from the microwave. Work in the tomatoes, breaking them down with a fork, and stir in the mustard, liqueur and seasoning. Cover with clingfilm (plastic wrap) and slit it twice to allow steam to escape. Cook on Full for 6 minutes. Add the fish and garlic. Cover as before and cook on Medium for 10 minutes. Sprinkle with the breadcrumbs and trickle the oil over the top. Heat, uncovered, on Full for 1 minute.

Slimmers' Fish Pot

SERVES 2

Tinged with a hottish jalapeno sauce and assertively spiced, enjoy this luxury fish feast with crusty French bread and rustic red wine.

2 onions, coarsely chopped
2 garlic cloves, crushed
15 ml/1 tbsp olive oil
400 g/14 oz/1 large can chopped tomatoes
200 ml/7 fl oz/scant 1 cup rosé wine
15 ml/1 tbsp Pernod or Ricard (pastis)
10 ml/2 tsp jalapeno sauce
2.5 ml/½ tsp hot pepper sauce
10 ml/2 tsp garam masala
1 bay leaf
2.5 ml/½ tsp dried oregano
2.5–5 ml/½–1 tsp salt
225 g/8 oz monkfish or skinned halibut, cut into strips
12 large cooked prawns (shrimp)
2 large scallops, cut into strips
30 ml/2 tbsp chopped coriander (cilantro), to garnish

Place the onions, garlic and oil in a 2 litre/3½ pt/8½ cup casserole dish (Dutch oven). Cover with a plate and cook on Full for 3 minutes. Mix in the remaining ingredients except the fish, shellfish and coriander. Cover as before and cook on Full for 6 minutes, stirring three times. Mix in the monkfish or halibut. Cover as before and cook on Defrost for 4 minutes until the fish whitens. Stir in the prawns and scallops. Cover as before and cook on Defrost for 1½ minutes. Stir round, ladle into deep plates and sprinkle each with coriander. Serve straight away.

Poultry and Game

Poultry has become our most favoured meat and this is the reason the section is so packed, taking in everything from a simple roast chicken to exotic curries and satays from the Far East and even South Africa's warm-hearted bredie. There's a generous selection of adapted Chinese classics, French Chicken Veronique and Danish roast chicken.

Roast Chicken

Microwaved chicken can be succulent and attractively flavoured if it's treated with a suitable baste and left unstuffed.

1 oven-ready chicken, size as required
For the baste:
25 g/1 oz/2 tbsp butter or margarine
5 ml/1 tsp paprika
5 ml/1 tsp Worcestershire sauce
5 ml/1 tsp soy sauce
2.5 ml/½ tsp garlic salt or 5 ml/1 tsp garlic paste
5 ml/1 tsp tomato purée (paste)

Stand the washed and dried chicken in a dish big enough to hold it comfortably and also to fit the microwave. (It needn't be deep.) To make the baste, melt the butter or margarine on Full for 30–60 seconds. Stir in the remaining ingredients and spoon over the chicken. Cover with clingfilm (plastic wrap) and slit it twice to allow steam to escape. Cook on Full for 8 minutes per 450 g/1 lb, turning the dish every 5 minutes. Half-way through cooking, switch off the microwave and allow the bird to stand inside for 10 minutes, then complete the cooking. Allow to stand for a further 5 minutes. Transfer to a carving board, cover with foil and allow to stand for 5 minutes before carving.

Glazed Roast Chicken

Prepare as for Roast Chicken, but add 5 ml/1 tsp black treacle (molasses), 10 ml/2 tsp brown sugar, 5 ml/1 tsp lemon juice and 5 ml/1 tsp brown sauce to the baste. Allow an extra 30 seconds' cooking time.

Tex-Mex Chicken

Prepare as for Roast Chicken. After cooking, divide the bird into portions and put in a clean dish. Coat with bought salsa, medium to hot according to taste. Sprinkle with 225 g/8 oz/ 2 cups grated Cheddar cheese. Reheat, uncovered, on Defrost for about 4 minutes until the cheese melts and bubbles. Serve with canned refried beans and slices of avocado sprinkled with lemon juice.

Coronation Chicken

1 Roast Chicken
45 ml/3 tbsp white wine
30 ml/2 tbsp tomato purée (paste)
30 ml/2 tbsp mango chutney
30 ml/2 tbsp sieved (strained)
  apricot jam (conserve)
30 ml/2 tbsp water
Juice of ½ lemon
10 ml/2 tsp mild curry paste
10 ml/2 tsp sherry
300 ml/½ pt/1¼ cups thick
  mayonnaise
60 ml/4 tbsp whipped cream
225 g/8 oz/1 cup long-grain rice,
  boiled
Watercress

Follow the recipe for Roast Chicken, including the baste. After cooking, remove the meat from the bones and cut into bite-sized pieces. Put into a mixing bowl. Pour the wine into a dish and add the tomato purée, chutney, jam, water and lemon juice. Heat, uncovered, on Full for 1 minute. Allow to cool. Work in the curry paste, sherry and mayonnaise and fold in the cream. Combine with the chicken. Arrange a bed of rice on a large serving dish and spoon the chicken mixture over. Garnish with watercress.

Chicken Veronique

1 Roast Chicken
1 onion, finely grated
25 g/1 oz/2 tbsp butter or
  margarine
150 ml/¼ pt/⅔ cup crème fraîche
30 ml/2 tbsp white port or
  medium-dry sherry
60 ml/4 tbsp thick mayonnaise
10 ml/2 tsp made mustard
5 ml/1 tsp tomato ketchup
  (catsup)
1 small celery stalk, chopped
75 g/3 oz seedless green grapes
Small bunches of green or red
  seedless grapes, to garnish

Follow the recipe for Roast Chicken, including the baste. After cooking, remove the meat from the bones and cut into bite-sized pieces. Put into a mixing bowl. Put the onion in a small bowl with the butter or margarine and cook, uncovered, on Full for 2 minutes. In a third bowl, beat together the crème fraîche, port or sherry, mayonnaise, mustard, tomato ketchup and celery. Fold into the chicken with the cooked onion and the grapes. Spoon neatly into a serving dish and garnish with the bunches of grapes.

Chicken in Vinegar Sauce with Tarragon

Adapted from a recipe discovered in a top restaurant in Lyons, France, in the early seventies.

1 Roast Chicken (page 134)
25 g/1 oz/2 tbsp butter or
 margarine
30 ml/2 tbsp cornflour
 (cornstarch)
15 ml/1 tbsp tomato purée (paste)
45 ml/3 tbsp double (heavy) cream
45 ml/3 tbsp malt vinegar
Salt and freshly ground black
 pepper

Follow the recipe for Roast Chicken, including the baste. Cut the cooked bird into six portions, cover with foil and keep hot on a plate. To make the sauce, pour the chicken cooking juices into a measuring jug and make up to 250 ml/8 fl oz/1 cup with hot water. Put the butter or margarine in a separate dish and heat, uncovered, on Full for 1 minute. Stir in the cornflour, tomato purée, cream and vinegar, and season to taste with salt and freshly ground black pepper. Gradually blend in the hot chicken juices. Cook, uncovered, on Full for 4–5 minutes until thickened and bubbly, whisking every minute. Pour over the chicken and serve straight away.

Danish Roast Chicken with Parsley Stuffing

Prepare as for Roast Chicken (page 134), but make several slits in the uncooked chicken skin and pack with small parsley sprigs. Put 25 g/1 oz/ 2 tbsp garlic butter in the body cavity. Then proceed as in the recipe.

Chicken Simla

An Anglo-Indian speciality belonging to the days of the Raj.

1 Roast Chicken (page 134)
15 ml/1 tbsp butter
5 ml/1 tsp finely chopped root
 ginger
5 ml/1 tsp garlic purée (paste)
2.5 ml/½ tsp turmeric
2.5 ml/½ tsp paprika
5 ml/1 tsp salt
300 ml/½ pt/1¼ cups whipping
 cream
Fried (sautéed) onion rings, home-
 made or bought, to garnish

Follow the recipe for Roast Chicken, including the baste. After cooking, divide the bird into six pieces and keep hot on a large plate or in a dish. Heat the butter in a 600 ml/1 pt/2½ cup dish on Full for 1 minute. Add the ginger and garlic purée. Cook, uncovered, on Full for 1½ minutes. Mix in the turmeric, paprika and salt, then the cream. Heat, uncovered, on Full for 4–5 minutes until the cream begins to bubble, whisking at least four times. Pour over the chicken and garnish with onion rings.

Spicy Chicken with Coconut and Coriander
SERVES 4

A delicately spiced curry dish from southern Africa.

8 chicken portions, 1.25 kg/2¾ lb
*   in all*
45 ml/3 tbsp desiccated (shredded)
*   coconut*
1 green chilli, about 8 cm/3 in
*   long, seeded and chopped*
1 garlic clove, crushed
2 onions, grated
5 ml/1 tsp turmeric
5 ml/1 tsp ground ginger
10 ml/2 tsp mild curry powder
90 ml/6 tbsp coarsely chopped
*   coriander (cilantro)*
150 ml/¼ pt/⅔ cup canned coconut
*   milk*
125 g/4 oz/½ cup cottage cheese
*   with chives*
Salt
175 g/6 oz/¾ cup long-grain rice,
*   boiled*
Chutney, to serve

Skin the chicken. Arrange round the edge of a deep 25 cm/10 in diameter dish, pushing the pieces closely together so they fit snugly. Cover with clingfilm (plastic wrap) and slit it twice to allow steam to escape. Cook on Full for 10 minutes, turning the dish twice. Place the coconut in a bowl with all the remaining ingredients except the rice. Stir well. Uncover the chicken and coat with the coconut mixture. Cover as before and cook on Full for 10 minutes, turning the dish four times. Serve in deep plates on a mound of rice with chutney handed separately.

Spicy Rabbit
SERVES 4

Prepare as for Spicy Chicken with Coconut and Coriander, but substitute eight rabbit portions for the chicken.

Spicy Turkey
SERVES 4

Prepare as for Spicy Chicken with Coconut and Coriander, but substitute eight 175 g/6 oz pieces of boned turkey breast fillet for the chicken.

Chicken Bredie with Tomatoes
SERVES 6

A South African stew, using the people's most popular combination of ingredients.

30 ml/2 tbsp sunflower or corn oil
3 onions, finely chopped
1 garlic clove, finely chopped
1 small green chilli, seeded and
*   chopped*
4 tomatoes, blanched, skinned and
*   sliced*
750 g/1¼ lb boned chicken
*   breasts, cut into small cubes*
5 ml/1 tsp dark soft brown sugar
10 ml/2 tsp tomato purée (paste)
7.5–10 ml/1½ –2 tsp salt

Pour the oil into a deep 25 cm/10 in diameter dish. Add the onions, garlic and chilli and mix in thoroughly. Cook, uncovered, for 5 minutes. Add the remaining ingredients to the dish and make a small hollow in the centre with an egg cup so the mixture forms a ring. Cover with clingfilm (plastic wrap) and slit it twice to allow steam to escape. Cook on Full for 14 minutes, turning the dish four times. Allow to stand for 5 minutes before serving.

137

Chinese Red Cooked Chicken

SERVES 4

A sophisticated Chinese stew, the chicken taking on a mahogany colour as it simmers in the sauce. Eat with plenty of boiled rice to absorb the salty juices.

6 Chinese dried mushrooms
8 large chicken drumsticks,
1 kg/2¼ lb in all
1 large onion, grated
60 ml/4 tbsp finely chopped
preserved ginger
75 ml/5 tbsp sweet sherry
15 ml/1 tbsp black treacle
(molasses)
Grated peel from 1 tangerine or
similar loose-skinned citrus
fruit
50 ml/2 fl oz/3½ cup soy sauce

Soak the mushrooms in hot water for 30 minutes. Drain and cut into strips. Slash the fleshy parts of the drumsticks and arrange round the edge of a deep 25 cm/10 in diameter dish with the bony ends pointing towards the centre. Cover with clingfilm (plastic wrap) and slit it twice to allow steam to escape. Cook on Full for 12 minutes, turning the dish three times. Mix together the remaining ingredients, including the mushrooms, and spoon over the chicken. Cover as before and cook on Full for 14 minutes. Allow to stand for 5 minutes before serving.

Aristocratic Chicken Wings

SERVES 4

A centuries-old Chinese recipe, favoured by the élite and eaten with egg noodles.

8 Chinese dried mushrooms
6 spring onions (scallions),
coarsely chopped
15 ml/1 tbsp groundnut (peanut)
oil
900 g/2 lb chicken wings
225 g/8 oz canned sliced bamboo
shoots
30 ml/2 tbsp cornflour
(cornstarch)
45 ml/3 tbsp Chinese rice wine or
medium-dry sherry
60 ml/4 tbsp soy sauce
10 ml/2 tsp finely chopped fresh
root ginger

Soak the mushrooms in hot water for 30 minutes. Drain and cut into quarters. Put the onions and oil in a deep 25 cm/10 in diameter dish. Cook, uncovered, on Full for 3 minutes. Stir round. Arrange the chicken wings in the dish, leaving a small hollow in the centre. Cover with clingfilm (plastic wrap) and slit it twice to allow steam to escape. Cook on Full for 12 minutes, turning the dish three times. Uncover. Coat with the bamboo shoots and the liquid from the can and scatter the mushrooms over the top. Blend the cornflour smoothly with the rice wine or sherry. Add the remaining ingredients. Spoon over the chicken and vegetables. Cover as before and cook on Full for 10–12 minutes until the liquid is bubbling. Allow to stand for 5 minutes before serving.

Chicken Chow Mein

SERVES 4

½ cucumber, peeled and cubed
275 g/10 oz/2½ cups cold cooked
chicken, cut into small cubes
450 g/1 lb fresh mixed vegetables
for stir-frying
30 ml/2 tbsp soy sauce
30 ml/2 tbsp medium-dry sherry
5 ml/1 tsp sesame oil
2.5 ml/½ tsp salt
Boiled Chinese noodles, to serve

Place the cucumber and chicken in a 1.75 litre/3 pt/7½ cup dish. Mix in all the remaining ingredients. Cover with a large plate and cook on Full for 10 minutes. Allow to stand for 3 minutes before serving with Chinese noodles.

Chicken Chop Suey

SERVES 4

Prepare as for Chicken Chow Mein, but substitute boiled long-grain rice for the noodles.

Express Marinaded Chinese Chicken

SERVES 3

Authentic tasting but fast as can be. Eat with rice or noodles and Chinese pickles.

6 chunky chicken thighs, about
750 g/1½ lb in all
125 g/4 oz/1 cup sweetcorn
kernels, half thawed if frozen
1 leek, chopped
60 ml/4 tbsp bought Chinese
marinade

Place the chicken in a deep bowl and add the remaining ingredients. Mix well. Cover and chill for 4 hours. Stir. Transfer to a deep 23 cm/9 in diameter dish, arranging the chicken round the edge. Cover with clingfilm (plastic wrap) and slit it twice to allow steam to escape. Cook on Full for 16 minutes, turning the dish four times. Allow to stand for 5 minutes before serving.

Hong Kong Chicken with Mixed Vegetables and Bean Sprouts

SERVES 2–3

4 Chinese dried mushrooms
1 large onion, chopped
1 carrot, grated
15 ml/1 tbsp groundnut (peanut) oil
2 garlic cloves, crushed
225 g/8 oz/2 cups cooked chicken, cut into strips
275 g/10 oz bean sprouts
15 ml/1 tbsp soy sauce
1.5 ml/¼ tsp sesame oil
A good pinch of cayenne pepper
2.5 ml/½ tsp salt
Boiled rice or Chinese noodles, to serve

Soak the mushrooms in hot water for 30 minutes. Drain and cut into strips. Place the onion, carrot and oil in a 1.75 litre/3 pt/7½ cup dish. Cook, uncovered, on Full for 3 minutes. Stir in the remaining ingredients. Cover with clingfilm (plastic wrap) and slit it twice to allow steam to escape. Cook on Full for 5 minutes, turning the dish three times. Allow to stand for 5 minutes before serving with rice or noodles.

Chicken with Golden Dragon Sauce

SERVES 4

4 large fleshy chicken joints, 225 g/8 oz each, skinned
Plain (all-purpose) flour
1 small onion, chopped
2 garlic cloves, crushed
30 ml/2 tbsp soy sauce
30 ml/2 tbsp medium-dry sherry
30 ml/2 tbsp groundnut (peanut) oil
60 ml/4 tbsp lemon juice
60 ml/4 tbsp light soft brown sugar
45 ml/3 tbsp melted and sieved (strained) apricot jam (conserve)
5 ml/1 tsp ground coriander (cilantro)
3–4 drops hot pepper sauce
Bean sprout salad and Chinese noodles, to serve

Slash the thick parts of the chicken joints in several places with a sharp knife, dust with flour, then arrange in a deep 25 cm/10 in diameter dish. Thoroughly stir together the remaining ingredients. Pour over the chicken. Cover the dish loosely with kitchen paper and leave to marinate in the refrigerator for 4–5 hours, turning the joints over twice. Arrange the slashed sides uppermost, then cover the dish with clingfilm (plastic wrap) and slit it twice to allow steam to escape. Cook on Full for 22 minutes, turning the dish four times. Serve on a bed of noodles and coat with juices from dish.

Ginger Chicken Wings with Lettuce

SERVES 4–5

1 large cos (romaine) lettuce,
  shredded
2.5 cm/1 in piece root ginger,
  thinly sliced
2 garlic cloves, crushed
15 ml/1 tbsp groundnut (peanut)
  oil
300 ml/½ pt/1¼ cups boiling
  chicken stock
30 ml/2 tbsp cornflour
  (cornstarch)
2.5 ml/½ tsp five spice powder
60 ml/4 tbsp cold water
5 ml/1 tsp soy sauce
5 ml/1 tsp salt
1 kg/2¼ lb chicken wings
Boiled rice or Chinese noodles, to
  serve

Put the lettuce, ginger, garlic and oil into a fairly large casserole dish (Dutch oven). Cover with a plate and cook on Full for 5 minutes. Uncover and add the boiling stock. Blend the cornflour and five spice powder smoothly with the cold water. Stir in the soy sauce and salt. Mix into the lettuce mixture with the chicken wings, tossing gently until thoroughly combined. Cover with clingfilm (plastic wrap) and slit it twice to allow steam to escape. Cook on Full for 20 minutes, turning the dish four times. Allow to stand for 5 minutes before serving with rice or noodles.

Bangkok Coconut Chicken

SERVES 4

The genuine article, made in my kitchen by a young Thai friend.

4 part-boned chicken breasts,
  175 g/6 oz each
200 ml/7 fl oz/scant 1 cup
  creamed coconut
Juice of 1 lime
30 ml/2 tbsp cold water
2 garlic cloves, crushed
5 ml/1 tsp salt
1 stalk lemon grass, halved
  lengthways, or 6 lemon balm
  leaves
2–6 green chillies or 1.5–2.5 ml/
  ¼–½ tsp dried red chilli powder
4–5 fresh lime leaves
20 ml/4 tsp chopped coriander
  (cilantro)
175 g/6 oz/¾ cup long-grain rice,
  boiled

Arrange the chicken round the edge of a deep 20 cm/8 in diameter dish, leaving a hollow in the centre. Cover with clingfilm (plastic wrap) and slit it twice to allow steam to escape. Cook on Full for 6 minutes, turning the dish twice. Combine the coconut cream, lime juice and water, then stir in the garlic and salt and pour over the chicken. Sprinkle on the lemon grass or lemon balm leaves, chillies to taste and lime leaves. Cover as before and cook on Full for 8 minutes, turning the dish three times. Allow to stand for 5 minutes. Uncover and stir in the coriander, then serve with the rice.

Chicken Satay

SERVES 8 AS A STARTER,
4 AS A MAIN COURSE

For the marinade:
**30 ml/2 tbsp groundnut (peanut)
oil**
30 ml/2 tbsp soy sauce
1 garlic clove, crushed
**900 g/2 lb boned chicken breast,
cubed**
For the satay sauce:
10 ml/2 tsp groundnut oil
1 onion, chopped
**2 green chillies, each about 8
cm/3 in long, seeded and finely
chopped**
2 garlic cloves, crushed
150 ml/¼ pt/⅔ cup boiling water
**60 ml/4 tbsp crunchy peanut
butter**
10 ml/2 tsp wine vinegar
2.5 ml/½ tsp salt
**175 g/6 oz/¾ cup long-grain rice,
boiled (optional)**

To make the marinade, combine the oil, soy sauce and garlic in a mixing bowl and add the chicken, stirring well to coat thoroughly. Cover and chill for 4 hours in winter, 8 in summer.

To make the sauce, pour the oil into a medium-sized dish or bowl and add the onion, chillies and garlic. Before completing the sauce, thread the chicken cubes on eight oiled skewers. Arrange, four at a time, on a large plate like the spokes of a wheel. Cook, uncovered, on Full for 5 minutes, turning over once. Repeat with the remaining four skewers. Keep hot. To finish the sauce, cover the bowl with clingfilm (plastic wrap) and slit it twice to allow steam to escape. Cook on Full for 2 minutes. Stir in the boiling water, peanut butter, vinegar and salt. Cook, uncovered, for 3 minutes, stirring once. Allow to stand for 30 seconds and serve, with the rice if a main course.

Peanut Chicken

SERVES 4

**4 boned chicken breasts, 175 g/
6 oz each**
**125 g/4 oz/½ cup smooth peanut
butter**
2.5 ml/½ tsp ground ginger
2.5 ml/½ tsp garlic salt
10 ml/2 tsp mild curry powder
Chinese hoisin sauce
Boiled Chinese noodles, to serve

Arrange the chicken round the edge of a deep 23 cm/9 in diameter dish, leaving a hollow in the centre. Put the peanut butter, ginger, garlic salt and curry powder in a small dish and heat, uncovered, on Full for 1 minute. Spread evenly over the chicken, then coat lightly with hoisin sauce. Cover with clingfilm (plastic wrap) and slit it twice to allow steam to escape. Cook on Full for 16 minutes, turning the dish four times. Allow to stand for 5 minutes before serving with Chinese noodles.

Indian Chicken with Yoghurt

SERVES 4

A fuss-free curry, fast to put together. It is low in fat so recommended for slimmers, perhaps with a side dish of cauliflower and a slice or two of seedy bread.

**750 g/1½ lb skinned chicken
   thighs
150 ml/¼ pt/⅔ cup plain yoghurt
15 ml/1 tbsp milk
5 ml/1 tsp garam masala
1.5 ml/¼ tsp turmeric
5 ml/1 tsp ground ginger
5 ml/1 tsp ground coriander
   (cilantro)
5 ml/1 tsp ground cumin
15 ml/1 tbsp corn or sunflower oil
45 ml/3 tbsp hot water
60 ml/4 tbsp coarsely chopped
   coriander, to garnish**

Place the chicken in a deep 30 cm/ 12 in diameter dish. Beat together all the remaining ingredients and spoon over the chicken. Cover and marinate in the refrigerator for 6–8 hours. Cover with a plate and warm through on Full for 5 minutes. Stir the chicken round. Cover the dish with clingfilm (plastic wrap) and slit it twice to allow steam to escape. Cook on Full for 15 minutes, turning the dish four times. Allow to stand for 5 minutes. Uncover and sprinkle with the chopped coriander before serving.

Japanese Chicken with Eggs

SERVES 4

**100 ml/3½ fl oz/6½ tbsp hot
   chicken or beef stock
60 ml/4 tbsp medium-dry sherry
30 ml/2 tbsp teriyaki sauce
15 ml/1 tbsp light soft brown
   sugar
250 g/9 oz/1¼ cups cooked
   chicken, cut into strips
4 large eggs, beaten
175 g/6 oz/¾ cup long-grain rice,
   boiled**

Pour the stock, sherry and teriyaki sauce into a shallow 18 cm/7 in diameter dish. Stir in the sugar. Cover with clingfilm (plastic wrap) and slit it twice to allow steam to escape. Cook on Full for 5 minutes. Uncover and stir round. Mix in the chicken and pour the eggs over the top. Cook, uncovered, on Full for 6 minutes, turning the dish three times. To serve, spoon the rice into four warmed bowls and top with the chicken and egg mixture.

Portuguese Chicken Casserole

SERVES 4

25 g/1 oz/2 tbsp butter or
margarine or 25 ml/1½ tbsp
olive oil
2 onions, quartered
2 garlic cloves, crushed
4 chicken joints, 900 g/2 lb in all
125 g/4 oz/1 cup cooked gammon,
cut into small cubes
3 tomatoes, blanched, skinned and
chopped
150 ml/¼ pt/⅔ cup dry white wine
10 ml/2 tsp French mustard
7.5–10 ml/1½–2 tsp salt

Put the butter, margarine or oil into a 20 cm/8 in diameter casserole dish (Dutch oven). Heat, uncovered, on Full for 1 minute. Stir in the onions and garlic. Cook, uncovered, on Full for 3 minutes. Add the chicken. Cover with clingfilm (plastic wrap) and slit it twice to allow steam to escape. Cook on Full for 14 minutes, turning the dish twice. Mix in the remaining ingredients. Cover as before and cook on Full for 6 minutes. Allow to stand for 5 minutes before serving.

English-style Spicy Chicken Casserole

SERVES 4

Prepare as for Portuguese Chicken Casserole, but substitute medium-dry cider for the wine and add 5 quartered pickled walnuts with the other ingredients. Allow an extra 1 minute cooking time.

Compromise Tandoori Chicken

SERVES 8 AS A STARTER,
4 AS A MAIN COURSE

An Indian dish traditionally made in a clay oven or *tandoor*, but this micro-wave version is entirely acceptable.

8 chicken pieces, about
1.25 kg/2¾ lb in all
250 ml/8 fl oz/1 cup thick Greek-
style plain yoghurt
30 ml/2 tbsp tandoori spice mix
10 ml/2 tsp ground coriander
(cilantro)
5 ml/1 tsp paprika
5 ml/1 tsp turmeric
30 ml/2 tbsp lemon juice
2 garlic cloves, crushed
7.5 ml/1½ tsp salt
Indian bread and mixed salad, to
serve

Slash the fleshy parts of the chicken in several places. Lightly whip the yoghurt with all the remaining ingredients. Arrange the chicken in a deep 25 cm/ 10 in diameter dish and coat with the tandoori mix. Cover loosely with kitchen paper and marinate for 6 hours in the refrigerator. Turn over, baste with the marinade and chill for a further 3–4 hours, covered as before. Cover with clingfilm (plastic wrap) and slit it twice to allow steam to escape. Cook on Full for 20 minutes, turning the dish four times. Uncover the dish and turn the chicken. Cover again with clingfilm and cook on Full for a further 7 minutes. Allow to stand for 5 minutes before serving.

Paella

●●●●●●●●●●●●●●●●●●●●●●●●●●●●●●●●
SERVES 6

1 kg/2¼ lb boned chicken breast
30 ml/2 tbsp olive oil
2 onions, chopped
2 garlic cloves, crushed
1 green (bell) pepper, seeded and
chopped
225 g/8 oz/1 cup risotto rice
1 packet saffron powder or 5 ml/
1 tsp turmeric
175 g/6 oz/1½ cups frozen peas
4 tomatoes, blanched and skinned
225 g/8 oz cooked mussels
75 g/3 oz/¾ cup cooked ham,
cubed
125 g/4 oz/1 cup peeled prawns
(shrimp)
600 ml/1 pt/2½ cups boiling water
7.5–10 ml/1½–2 tsp salt
Extra cooked mussels, cooked
prawns and lemon wedges for
garnishing

Arrange the chicken around the edge of a 25 cm/10 in diameter casserole dish (Dutch oven), leaving a hole in the centre. Cover with clingfilm (plastic wrap) and slit it twice to allow steam to escape. Cook on Full for 15 minutes. Drain off the liquid and reserve. Cube the chicken. Wash and dry the dish. Pour the oil into the dish and heat on Full for 1 minute. Stir in the onions, garlic and green pepper. Cook, uncovered, on Full for 4 minutes. Add all the remaining ingredients with the chicken and reserved liquor, stirring in well. Cover as before and cook on Full for 20 minutes, turning the dish three times. Allow to stand inside the oven for 10 minutes, then cook for a further 5 minutes. Uncover and garnish with mussels, prawns and lemon wedges.

Paella with Pimientos

●●●●●●●●●●●●●●●●●●●●●●●●●●●●●●●●
SERVES 6

Prepare as for Paella, but omit the mussels, and other seafood if preferred, and garnish with lemon slices, 200 g/7 oz drained canned pimientos, cut into strips, and extra peas.

Chicken Amandine

●●●●●●●●●●●●●●●●●●●●●●●●●●●●●●●●
SERVES 4

A typically North American short-cut recipe.

4 poussins (chickens), about
450 g/1 lb each
300 ml/10 fl oz/1 can condensed
cream of mushroom soup
150 ml/¼ pt/⅔ cup medium-dry
sherry
1 garlic clove, crushed
90 ml/6 tbsp toasted flaked
(slivered) almonds (page 205)
175 g/6 oz/¾ cup brown rice,
boiled
Broccoli

Put the poussins, breast sides down and in a single layer, in a large, deep dish that will fit into the microwave. Cover with clingfilm (plastic wrap) and slit it twice to allow steam to escape. Cook on Full for 25 minutes, turning the dish four times. Turn the chickens over so that they are now breast sides up. Gently whisk the soup with the sherry and any chicken cooking juices. Mix in the garlic. Pour back over the chickens. Cover as before and cook on Full for 15 minutes, turning the dish three times. Allow to stand for 5 minutes. Transfer the chickens to warmed dinner plates and coat with the sauce. Sprinkle with the almonds and serve with the rice and broccoli.

Chicken Amandine with Tomato and Basil

SERVES 4

Prepare as for Chicken Amandine (page 145), but substitute condensed cream of tomato soup for mushroom and marsala for the sherry. Add 6 torn basil leaves towards the end of the cooking time.

Chicken Divan

SERVES 4

Another easy North American speciality, traditionally made with broccoli.

1 large head of broccoli, cooked
25 g/1 oz/2 tbsp butter or
  margarine
45 ml/3 tbsp plain (all-purpose)
  flour
150 ml/¼ pt/⅔ cup warm chicken
  stock
150 ml/¼ pt/⅔ cup single (light)
  cream
50 g/2 oz/½ cup Red Leicester
  cheese, grated
30 ml/2 tbsp dry white wine
5 ml/1 tsp mild made mustard
225 g/8 oz/2 cups cooked chicken,
  cubed
Salt
Ground nutmeg
45 ml/3 tbsp grated Parmesan
  cheese
Paprika

Separate the broccoli into florets and arrange over the base of a lightly buttered deep 25 cm/10 in diameter dish. In a separate dish, heat the butter or margarine on Full for 45–60 seconds until it sizzles. Stir in the flour and gradually blend in the warm stock and cream. Cook on Full for 4–5 minutes until bubbly and thickened, whisking every minute. Stir

in the Red Leicester, wine, mustard and chicken. Add salt and nutmeg to taste. Spoon the sauce over the broccoli. Sprinkle with Parmesan cheese and paprika. Cover with clingfilm (plastic wrap) and slit it twice to allow steam to escape. Reheat on Defrost for 8–10 minutes until piping hot.

Chicken in Cream Sauce with Celery

SERVES 4

Prepare as for Chicken Divan, but substitute 400 g/14 oz/1 large can celery hearts, drained, for the broccoli. (The liquid from the can may be reserved for other recipes.)

Chicken in Cream Sauce with Crisps

SERVES 4

Prepare as for Chicken Divan, but omit the cheese and paprika topping. Instead, sprinkle with 1 small bag of potato crisps (chips), coarsely crushed.

Turkey à la King

SERVES 4

Prepare as for Chicken à la King (opposite), but substitute cooked turkey for the chicken.

Chicken à la King with Cheese

SERVES 4

Prepare as for Chicken à la King (opposite), but after reheating for 3 minutes, cover with 125 g/4 oz/1 cup grated Red Leicester cheese. Reheat, uncovered, on Full for a further 1–1½ minutes until the cheese melts.

Chicken à la King
●●●●●●●●●●●●●●●●●●●●●●●●●●●●●●
SERVES 4

Another import from the USA and an innovative means of using leftover chicken.

40 g/1½ oz/3 tbsp butter or margarine
40 g/1½ oz/1½ tbsp plain (all-purpose) flour
300 ml/½ pt/1¼ cups warm chicken stock
60 ml/4 tbsp double (heavy) cream
1 canned red pimiento, cut into narrow strips
200 g/7 oz/scant 1 cup canned sliced mushrooms, drained
Salt and freshly ground black pepper
350 g/12 oz/2 cups cooked chicken, diced
15 ml/1 tbsp medium-dry sherry
Freshly made toast, to serve

Put the butter or margarine in a 1.5 litre/2½ pt/6 cup casserole dish (Dutch oven). Heat, uncovered, on Defrost for 1 minute. Stir in the flour, then gradually blend in the stock and cream. Cook, uncovered, on Full for 5–6 minutes until bubbling and thickened, whisking every minute. Stir in all the remaining ingredients and mix well. Cover with a plate and reheat on Full for 3 minutes. Allow to stand for 3 minutes before serving on toast.

Chicken à la King Shortcakes
●●●●●●●●●●●●●●●●●●●●●●●●●●●●●●
SERVES 4

Prepare as for Chicken à la King. Before serving, split open 4 large plain or cheese scones (biscuits) and put the bases on four warmed plates. Cover with the chicken mixture and top with the lids. Eat hot.

Slimmers' Chicken Liver Braise
●●●●●●●●●●●●●●●●●●●●●●●●●●●●●●
SERVES 4

A low-fat, low-starch main course that can be eaten with broccoli or cauliflower instead of potatoes.

15 ml/1 tbsp olive or sunflower oil
1 red (bell) pepper, seeded and thinly sliced
1 large carrot, thinly sliced
1 large onion, thinly sliced
2 large celery stalks, diagonally cut into thin slices
450 g/1 lb chicken livers, cut into bite-sized pieces
10 ml/2 tsp cornflour (cornstarch)
4 large tomatoes, blanched, skinned and coarsely chopped
Salt and freshly ground black pepper

Put the oil in a 1.75 litre/3 pt/7½ cup casserole dish (Dutch oven). Stir in the prepared vegetables and cook, uncovered, on Full for 5 minutes, stirring twice. Mix the liver into the vegetables and cook, uncovered, on Full for 3 minutes, stirring once. Stir in the cornflour, tomatoes and seasoning to taste. Cover with clingfilm (plastic wrap) and slit it twice to allow steam to escape. Cook on Full for 6 minutes, turning once.

Slimmers' Turkey Liver Braise
●●●●●●●●●●●●●●●●●●●●●●●●●●●●●●
SERVES 4

Prepare as for Slimmers' Chicken Liver Braise, but substitute turkey livers for the chicken livers.

Chicken Tetrazzini

•••••••••••••••••••••••••••••••
SERVES 4

175 g/6 oz/1½ cup short-cut
  macaroni
300 ml/10 fl oz/1 can condensed
  cream of chicken or mushroom
  soup
150 ml/¼ pt/⅔ cup milk
225 g/8 oz mushrooms, sliced
350 g/12 oz/2 cups cold cooked
  chicken, diced
15 ml/1 tbsp lemon juice
50 g/2 oz/½ cup flaked (slivered)
  almonds
1.5 ml/¼ tsp ground nutmeg
75 g/3 oz/¾ cup Cheddar cheese,
  finely grated

Cook the macaroni as directed on the packet. Drain. Tip the soup into a buttered 1.75 litre/3 pt/7½ cup dish. Whisk in the milk. Heat, uncovered, on Full for 5–6 minutes until hot and bubbling lightly. Stir in the macaroni and all the remaining ingredients except the cheese. Cover with clingfilm (plastic wrap) and slit it twice to allow steam to escape. Cook on Full for 12 minutes, turning the dish three times. Uncover and sprinkle with the cheese. Brown conventionally under a hot grill (broiler).

Chicken and Mixed Vegetable Layer Casserole

•••••••••••••••••••••••••••••••
SERVES 4

4 large cooked potatoes, thinly
  sliced
3 cooked carrots, thinly sliced
125 g/4 oz/1 cup cooked peas
125 g/4 oz/1 cup cooked sweetcorn
4 portions chicken, 225 g/8 oz
  each, skinned
300 ml/10 fl oz/1 can condensed
  cream of celery soup, or other
  flavour to taste
45 ml/3 tbsp medium-dry sherry
30 ml/2 tbsp single (light) cream
1.5 ml/¼ tsp grated nutmeg
75 g/3 oz/1¼ cups cornflakes,
  coarsely crushed

Cover the base of a buttered deep 25 cm/10 in diameter dish with the potato and carrot slices. Sprinkle with the peas and sweetcorn and top with the chicken. Cover with clingfilm (plastic wrap) and slit it twice to allow steam to escape. Cook on Full for 8 minutes, turning the dish four times. Whisk the soup with all the remaining ingredients except the cornflakes. Spoon over the chicken. Cover as before and cook on Full for 11 minutes, turning the dish twice. Allow to stand for 5 minutes. Uncover and sprinkle with the cornflakes before serving.

Honey Chicken on Rice

SERVES 4

25 g/1 oz/2 tbsp butter or
margarine
1 large onion, chopped
6 streaky bacon rashers (slices),
chopped
75 g/3 oz/⅓ cup easy-cook long-
grain rice
300 ml/½ pt/1¼ cups hot chicken
stock
Freshly ground black pepper
4 boned chicken breasts, 175 g/
6 oz each
Finely grated peel and juice of
1 orange
30 ml/2 tbsp dark clear honey
5 ml/1 tsp paprika
5 ml/1 tsp Worcestershire sauce

Put the butter or margarine in a deep 20 cm/8 in diameter dish. Heat, uncovered, on Full for 1 minute. Stir in the onion, bacon, rice, stock and pepper to taste. Arrange the chicken in a ring on top. Beat together the orange peel and juice, honey, paprika and Worcestershire sauce. Spoon half over the chicken. Cover with clingfilm (plastic wrap) and slit it twice to allow steam to escape. Cook on Full for 9 minutes, turning the dish three times. Uncover. Baste the chicken with the remaining honey mixture. Cook, uncovered, on Full for 5 minutes. Allow to stand for 3 minutes before serving.

Chicken in White Rum Sauce with Lime

SERVES 4

25 g/1 oz/2 tbsp butter or
margarine
10 ml/2 tsp corn or sunflower oil
1 leek, very thinly sliced
1 garlic clove, crushed
75 g/3 oz/¾ cup lean ham,
chopped
675 g/1½ lb boned chicken breast,
cut into bite-sized pieces
3 tomatoes, blanched, skinned and
coarsely chopped
30 ml/2 tbsp white rum
5 cm/2 in strip lime peel
Juice of 1 sweet orange
Salt
150 ml/¼ pt/⅔ cup plain yoghurt
Watercress (optional)

Put the butter or margarine and oil in a 23 cm/9 in diameter casserole dish (Dutch oven). Heat, uncovered, on Full for 1 minute. Stir in the leek, garlic and ham. Cook, uncovered, on Full for 4 minutes, stirring twice. Mix in the chicken. Cover with a plate and cook on Full for 7 minutes, turning the dish twice. Add all remaining ingredients except the yoghurt and watercress, if using. Cover with clingfilm (plastic wrap) and slit it twice to allow steam to escape. Cook on Full for 8 minutes, turning the dish four times. Uncover. Combine the yoghurt with some of the liquid from the dish until smooth and creamy, then pour over the chicken. Reheat, uncovered, on Full for 1½ minutes. Discard the lime peel. Serve garnished with watercress, if liked.

Chicken in Brandy Sauce with Orange

SERVES 4

Prepare as for Chicken in White Rum Sauce with Lime (page 149), but substitute brandy for the rum and orange peel for the lime. Use 60 ml/ 4 tbsp ginger ale instead of the orange juice.

Drumsticks in Barbecue Sauce with Baby Pasta

SERVES 4

900 g/2 lb chicken drumsticks
2 onions, chopped
2 celery stalks, chopped
30 ml/2 tbsp wholegrain mustard
2.5 ml/½ tsp paprika
5 ml/1 tsp Worcestershire sauce
400 g/14 oz/1 large can chopped
    tomatoes in tomato juice
125 g/4 oz/1 cup any small pasta
7.5 ml/1½ tsp salt

Arrange the drumsticks, like the spokes of a wheel, in a deep 25 cm/10 in diameter dish, with the bony ends towards the centre. Cover with clingfilm (plastic wrap) and slit it twice to allow steam to escape. Cook on Full for 8 minutes, turning the dish three times. Meanwhile, place the vegetables in a bowl and stir in the remaining ingredients. Remove the dish of chicken from the microwave, uncover and pour the chicken cooking juices into the vegetable mixture. Mix well. Spoon over the drumsticks. Cover as before and cook on Full for 15 minutes, turning the dish three times. Allow to stand for 5 minutes before serving.

Chicken in Mexican Mole Sauce

SERVES 4

4 boned chicken breasts, 175 g/
    6 oz each, skinned
30 ml/2 tbsp corn oil
1 large onion, finely chopped
1 green (bell) pepper, seeded and
    chopped
1 garlic clove, crushed
30 ml/2 tbsp plain (all-purpose)
    flour
3 whole cloves
1 bay leaf
2.5 ml/½ tsp ground cinnamon
5 ml/1 tsp salt
150 ml/¼ pt/⅔ cup tomato juice
50 g/2 oz/½ cup plain (semi-sweet)
    chocolate, broken into pieces
175 g/6 oz/¾ cup long-grain rice,
    boiled
15 ml/1 tbsp garlic butter

Arrange the chicken round the edge of a deep 20 cm/8 in diameter dish. Cover with clingfilm (plastic wrap) and slit it twice to allow steam to escape. Cook on Full for 6 minutes. Allow to stand while preparing the sauce. In a separate dish, heat the oil, uncovered, on Full for 1 minute. Stir in the onion, green pepper and garlic. Cook, uncovered, on Full for 3 minutes, stirring twice. Stir in the flour, then the cloves, bay leaf, cinnamon, salt and tomato juice. Cook, uncovered, on Full for 4 minutes, stirring every minute. Remove from the microwave. Add the chocolate and stir in thoroughly. Cook, uncovered, on Full for 30 seconds. Uncover the chicken and coat with the hot sauce. Cover as before and cook on Full for 8 minutes. Allow to stand for 5 minutes. Serve with the rice, forked with the garlic butter.

Chicken Wings in Barbecue Sauce with Baby Pasta

SERVES 4

Prepare as for Drumsticks in Barbecue Sauce with Baby Pasta, but substitute chicken wings for the drumsticks.

Chicken Jambalaya

SERVES 3–4

Hotfoot from Louisiana this is a stunning rice and chicken dish, a relative of paella.

2 boned chicken breasts
50 g/2 oz/¼ cup butter or margarine
2 large onions, chopped
1 red (bell) pepper, seeded and chopped
4 celery stalks, chopped
2 garlic cloves, crushed
225 g/8 oz/1 cup easy-cook long-grain rice
400 g/14 oz/1 large can chopped tomatoes in tomato juice
10–15 ml/2–3 tsp salt

Arrange the chicken round the edge of a deep 25 cm/10 in diameter dish. Cover with clingfilm (plastic wrap) and slit it twice to allow steam to escape. Cook on Full for 7 minutes. Allow to stand for 2 minutes. Transfer the chicken to a board and cut into cubes. Pour the chicken cooking juices into a jug and reserve. Wash and dry the dish, add the butter and melt, uncovered, on Full for 1½ minutes. Stir in the reserved liquid, the chicken, prepared vegetables, garlic, rice and tomatoes. Season to taste with the salt. Cover as before and cook on Full for 20–25 minutes until the rice grains are dry and have absorbed all the moisture. Allow to stand for 5 minutes, fluff up with a fork and serve straight away.

Turkey Jambalaya

SERVES 3–4

Prepare as for Chicken Jambalaya, but substitute turkey breast for chicken.

Chicken with Chestnuts

SERVES 4

25 g/1 oz/2 tbsp butter or margarine
2 large onions, peeled and grated
430 g/15 oz/1 large can unsweetened chestnut purée
2.5 ml/½ tsp salt
4 skinned and boned chicken breasts, 175 g/6 oz each
3 tomatoes, blanched, skinned and sliced
30 ml/2 tbsp chopped parsley
Red cabbage and boiled potatoes, to serve

Put the butter or margarine in a deep 20 cm/8 in diameter dish. Melt, uncovered, on Defrost for 1½ minutes. Mix in the onions. Cook, uncovered, on Full for 4 minutes. Spoon in the chestnut purée and salt and mix smoothly, blending well with the onions. Spread in an even layer over the base of the dish and arrange the chicken breasts on top round the edge of the dish. Top with tomato slices and sprinkle with the parsley. Cover with clingfilm (plastic wrap) and slit it twice to allow steam to escape. Cook on Full for 15 minutes, turning the dish three times. Allow to stand for 4 minutes. Serve with red cabbage and potatoes.

Chicken Gumbo

•••••••••••••••••••••••••••••••

SERVES 6

A cross between a soup and a stew, the Gumbo is Southern comfort and one of Louisiana's best exports. Its basis is okra (ladies' fingers) and a brown roux, with the addition of vegetables, spices, stock and chicken.

50 g/2 oz/¼ cup butter
50 g/2 oz/½ cup plain (all-
purpose) flour
900 ml/1½ pts/3¾ cups hot
chicken stock
350 g/12 oz okra (ladies' fingers),
topped and tailed
2 large onions, finely chopped
2 garlic cloves, crushed
2 large celery stalks, thinly sliced
1 green (bell) pepper, seeded and
chopped
15–20 ml/3–4 tsp salt
10 ml/2 tsp ground coriander
(cilantro)
5 ml/1 tsp turmeric
5–10 ml/1–2 tsp ground allspice
30 ml/2 tbsp lemon juice
2 bay leaves
5–10 ml/1–2 tsp hot pepper sauce
450 g/1 lb/4 cups cooked chicken,
chopped
175 g/6 oz/¾ cups long-grain rice,
boiled

Put the butter in a 2.5 litre/4½ pt/ 11 cup casserole dish (Dutch oven). Heat, uncovered, on Full for 2 minutes. Stir in the flour. Cook, uncovered, on Full for 7 minutes, stirring every minute, until the mixture is a light brown roux, the colour of a well-baked biscuit (cookie). Gradually blend in the hot stock. Slice each okra into eight pieces and add to the casserole with all the remaining ingredients except the chicken and rice. Cover with cling-film (plastic wrap) and slit it twice to allow steam to escape. Cook on Full for 15 minutes. Stir in the chicken. Cover as before and cook on Full for 15 minutes. Allow to stand for 5 minutes. Stir round and ladle into soup bowls. Add a mound of rice to each.

Turkey Gumbo

•••••••••••••••••••••••••••••••

SERVES 6

Prepare as for Chicken Gumbo, but substitute cooked turkey for the chicken.

Chicken Breasts with Brown Orange Baste

•••••••••••••••••••••••••••••••

SERVES 4

60 ml/4 tbsp orange jam
(conserve) or fine-cut
marmalade
15 ml/1 tbsp malt vinegar
15 ml/1 tbsp soy sauce
1 garlic clove, crushed
2.5 ml/½ tsp ground ginger
7.5 ml/1½ tsp cornflour
(cornstarch)
4 boned chicken breasts,
200 g/7 oz each, skinned
Chinese noodles, boiled

Combine all the ingredients except the chicken and noodles in a small dish. Heat, uncovered, on Full for 50 seconds. Arrange the chicken breasts round the edge of a deep 20 cm/8 in diameter dish. Spoon over half the baste. Cover with a plate and cook on Full for 8 minutes, turning the dish twice. Turn the breasts over and brush with the remaining baste. Cover as before and cook on Full for a further 8 minutes. Allow to stand for 4 minutes, then serve with Chinese noodles.

Chicken in Creamy Pepper Sauce
••••••••••••••••••••••••••••••••
SERVES 6

25 g/1 oz/2 tbsp butter or margarine
1 small onion, finely chopped
4 boned chicken breasts
15 ml/1 tbsp cornflour (cornstarch)
30 ml/2 tbsp cold water
15 ml/1 tbsp tomato purée (paste)
20–30 ml/4–6 tsp bottled or canned Madagascan green peppercorns
150 ml/¼ pt/⅔ cup soured (dairy sour) cream
5 ml/1 tsp salt
275 g/10 oz/1¼ cup long-grain rice, boiled

Put the butter or margarine in a deep 20 cm/8 in diameter dish. Melt, uncovered, on Full for 45–60 seconds. Add the onion. Cook, uncovered, on Full for 2 minutes. Cut the chicken breasts across the grain into 2.5 cm/1 in wide strips. Mix well into the butter and onions. Cover with clingfilm (plastic wrap) and slit it twice to allow steam to escape. Cook on Full for 6 minutes, turning the dish three times. Meanwhile, mix the cornflour smoothly with the cold water. Stir in all the remaining ingredients except the rice. Combine with the chicken and onion, moving the mixture to the edges of the dish and leaving a small hollow in the centre. Cover as before and cook on Full for 8 minutes, turning the dish four times. Allow to stand for 4 minutes. Stir round before serving with the rice.

Turkey in Creamy Pepper Sauce
••••••••••••••••••••••••••••••••
SERVES 6

Prepare as for Chicken in Creamy Pepper Sauce, but substitute turkey breast for the chicken.

Woodland Chicken
••••••••••••••••••••••••••••••••
SERVES 4

4 skinned chicken quarters, 225 g/8 oz each
30 ml/2 tbsp corn or sunflower oil
175 g/6 oz streaky bacon rashers (slices), chopped
1 onion, chopped
175 g/6 oz button mushrooms, sliced
300 ml/½ pt/1¼ cups sieved tomatoes (passata)
15 ml/1 tbsp brown vinegar
15 ml/1 tbsp lemon juice
30 ml/2 tbsp light soft brown sugar
5 ml/1 tsp prepared mustard
30 ml/2 tbsp Worcestershire sauce
Chopped coriander (cilantro) leaves, to garnish

Arrange the chicken round the edge of a 25 cm/10 in diameter casserole dish (Dutch oven). Cover with clingfilm (plastic wrap) and slit it twice to allow steam to escape. Pour the oil into a separate dish and heat, uncovered, on Full for 1 minute. Add the bacon, onion and mushrooms. Cook, uncovered, on Full for 5 minutes. Mix in all the remaining ingredients. Cook the covered chicken on Full for 9 minutes, turning the dish twice. Uncover and coat with the vegetable mixture. Cover as before and cook on Full for 10 minutes, turning the dish three times. Allow to stand for 5 minutes. Sprinkle with coriander before serving.

Chicken with Apples and Raisins

SERVES 4

25 g/1 oz/2 tbsp butter or margarine
900 g/2 lb chicken joints
2 onions, chopped
3 Cox's apples, peeled and chopped
30 ml/2 tbsp raisins
1 garlic clove, chopped
30 ml/2 tbsp plain (all-purpose) flour
250 ml/8 fl oz/1 cup shandy
2 beef stock cubes
2.5 ml/½ tsp dried thyme
Salt and freshly ground black pepper
30 ml/2 tbsp chopped parsley

Put the butter or margarine in a 25 cm/10 in diameter casserole dish (Dutch oven). Melt, uncovered, on Defrost for 1–1½ minutes. Add the chicken. Cover with clingfilm (plastic wrap) and slit it twice to allow steam to escape. Cook on Full for 8 minutes. Uncover and turn the chicken over. Cover as before and cook on Full for a further 7 minutes. Uncover and sprinkle with the onions, apples, raisins and garlic. Blend the flour smoothly with some of the shandy, then mix in the remaining shandy. Crumble in the gravy cubes, add the thyme and season to taste. Pour over the chicken. Cover as before and cook on Full for 8 minutes until the liquid bubbles and has thickened slightly. Allow to stand for 5 minutes. Uncover and sprinkle with the parsley.

Chicken with Pears and Raisins

SERVES 4

Prepare as for Chicken with Apples and Raisins, but substitute pears for the apples and cider for the shandy.

Grapefruit Chicken

SERVES 4

2 celery stalks
30 ml/2 tbsp butter or margarine
1 large onion, finely grated
4 large chicken joints, 1 kg/2¼ lb in all, skinned
Plain (all-purpose) flour
1 large pink grapefruit
150 ml/¼ pt/⅔ cup white or rosé wine
30 ml/2 tbsp tomato purée (paste)
1.5 ml/¼ tsp dried rosemary
5 ml/1 tsp salt

Cut the celery across the grain into narrow strips. Put the butter or margarine in a deep 25 cm/10 in diameter dish. Melt, uncovered, on Full for 30 seconds. Mix in the onion and celery. Cook, uncovered, on Full for 6 minutes. Dust the chicken lightly with flour, then arrange round the edge of the dish. Cover with clingfilm (plastic wrap) and slit it twice to allow steam to escape. Cook on Full for 10 minutes, turning the dish three times. Meanwhile, peel the grapefruit and separate into segments by cutting between the membranes. Uncover the chicken and scatter the grapefruit segments over. Beat the wine with the tomato purée, rosemary and salt and pour over the chicken. Cover as before and cook on Full for 10 minutes. Allow to stand for 5 minutes before serving.

Hungarian Chicken and Mixed Vegetables

•••••••••••••••••••••••••••••••••••
SERVES 4

25 g/1 oz/2 tbsp butter or lard
2 large onions, chopped
1 small green (bell) pepper
3 small courgettes (zucchini),
thinly sliced
450 g/1 lb boned chicken breast,
cubed
15 ml/1 tbsp paprika
45 ml/3 tbsp tomato purée (paste)
150 ml/¼ pt/⅔ cup soured (dairy
sour) cream
5–7.5 ml/1–1½ tsp salt

Put the butter or lard in a 25 cm/ 10 in diameter casserole dish (Dutch oven). Heat, uncovered, on Defrost for 1–1½ minutes. Stir in the onions. Cook, uncovered, on Full for 3 minutes. Mix in the green pepper, courgettes, chicken, paprika and tomato purée. Cover with clingfilm (plastic wrap) and slit it twice to allow steam to escape. Cook on Full for 5 minutes, turning the dish three times. Uncover. Gradually work in the soured cream and salt. Cover as before and cook on Full for 8 minutes. Allow to stand for 5 minutes, then stir round and serve.

Chicken Bourguignonne

••••••••••••••••••••••••••••••••••••
SERVES 6

A gourmet main course, more traditionally made with beef but lighter with chicken.

25 g/1 oz/2 tbsp butter or
margarine
2 onions, chopped
1 garlic clove, crushed
750 g/1½ lb chicken breast, cubed
30 ml/2 tbsp cornflour
(cornstarch)
5 ml/1 tsp continental mustard
2.5 ml/½ tsp dried mixed herbs
300 ml/½ pt/1¼ cups burgundy
wine
225 g/8 oz mushrooms, thinly
sliced
5–7.5 ml/1–1½ tsp salt
45 ml/3 tbsp chopped parsley

Put the butter or margarine in a 25 cm/10 in diameter casserole dish (Dutch oven). Melt, uncovered, on Defrost for 1½ minutes. Mix in the onions and garlic. Cover with a plate and cook on Full for 3 minutes. Uncover and mix in the chicken. Cover with clingfilm (plastic wrap) and slit it twice to allow steam to escape. Cook on Full for 8 minutes. Mix the cornflour and mustard smoothly with some of the burgundy, then stir in the remainder. Pour over the chicken. Sprinkle with the mushrooms and salt. Cover as before and cook on Full for 8–9 minutes, turning the dish four times, until the sauce has thickened and is beginning to bubble. Allow to stand for 5 minutes, then stir round and sprinkle with the parsley before serving.

Chicken Fricassée

SERVES 6

A revival of a twenties and thirties special-occasion chicken main course, always eaten with white rice fluffed with butter and grilled (broiled) bacon rolls. It needs a large microwave.

1.5 kg/3 lb chicken joints, skinned
1 onion, cut into 8 wedges
2 large celery stalks, thickly sliced
1 small carrot, thinly sliced
2 thick slices lemon
1 small bay leaf
2 whole cloves
Parsley sprigs
10 ml/2 tsp salt
300 ml/½ pt/1¼ cups hot water
150 ml/¼ pt/⅔ cup single (light) cream
40 g/1½ oz/3 tbsp butter or margarine
40 g/1½ oz/1½ tbsp plain (all-purpose) flour
Juice of 1 small lemon
Salt and freshly ground black pepper

Arrange the chicken in a 30 cm/12 in diameter casserole dish (Dutch oven). Add the onion, celery and carrot to the dish with the lemon slices, bay leaf, cloves and 1 parsley sprig. Sprinkle with the salt and add the water. Cover with clingfilm (plastic wrap) and slit it twice to allow steam to escape. Cook on Full for 24 minutes, turning the dish three times. Lift out the chicken. Remove the meat from the bones and cut into bite-sized pieces. Strain the liquid from the dish and reserve 300 ml/½ pt/1¼ cups. Mix in the cream. Place the butter in a large shallow dish. Melt, uncovered, on Full for 1½ minutes. Stir in the flour, then gradually blend in the warm stock and cream mixture. Cook, uncovered, on Full for 5–6 minutes, whisking every minute, until thickened and bubbling. Add the lemon juice, stir in the chicken and season to taste. Cover as before and reheat on Full for 5 minutes, turning the dish twice. Allow to stand for 4 minutes before garnishing with parsley sprigs and serving.

Chicken Fricassée with Wine

SERVES 6

Prepare as for Chicken Fricassée, but use only 150 ml/¼ pt/⅔ cup reserved stock and add 150 ml/¼ pt/⅔ cup dry white wine.

Chicken Supreme

SERVES 6

Prepare as for Chicken Fricassée. After reheating for 5 minutes at the end and then standing, beat in 2 egg yolks mixed with an extra 15 ml/1 tbsp cream. The heat from the mixture will cook the yolks.

Coq au Vin
SERVES 6

50 g/2 oz/¼ cup butter or
  margarine
1.5 kg/3 lb chicken joints, skinned
1 large onion, finely chopped
1 garlic clove, crushed
30 ml/2 tbsp plain (all-purpose)
  flour
300 ml/½ pt/1¼ cups dry red wine
1 beef stock cube
5 ml/1 tsp salt
12 shallots or pickled onions
60 ml/4 tbsp chopped parsley
1.5 ml/¼ tsp dried thyme
Boiled potatoes and Brussels
  sprouts, to serve

Put the butter or margarine in a 30 cm/12 in diameter casserole dish (Dutch oven). Heat, uncovered, on Full for 1 minute. Add the chicken pieces and turn them over once so that all pieces are coated with butter but keep in a single layer. Cover with cling-film (plastic wrap) and slit it twice to allow steam to escape. Cook on Full for 15 minutes, turning the dish three times. Uncover and sprinkle the chicken with the onion and garlic. Gradually mix the flour smoothly with the wine, whisking, if necessary, to remove lumps. Crumble in the stock cube and add the salt. Pour the wine mixture over the chicken. Surround with the shallots or onions and sprinkle with the parsley and thyme. Cover as before and cook on Full for 20 minutes, turning the dish three times. Allow to stand for 6 minutes. Eat with boiled potatoes and Brussels sprouts.

Coq au Vin with Mushrooms
SERVES 6

Prepare as for Coq au Vin, but substitute 125 g/4 oz button mushrooms for the shallots or pickled onions.

Coq au Cola
SERVES 6

Prepare as for Coq au Vin, but substitute cola for the wine to make the dish more suitable for children.

Drumsticks with Devilled Coating
SERVES 4

15 ml/1 tbsp English mustard
  powder
10 ml/2 tsp hot curry powder
10 ml/2 tsp paprika
1.5 ml/¼ tsp hot cayenne pepper
2.5 ml/½ tsp salt
1 kg/2¼ lb chicken drumsticks
  (about 12)
45 ml/3 tbsp garlic butter

Mix together the mustard, curry powder, paprika, cayenne and salt. Use to coat all sides of the drumsticks. Arrange in a deep 25 cm/10 in diameter dish like the spokes of a wheel, with the bony ends towards the centre. Melt the butter, uncovered, on Full for 1 minute. Coat the drumsticks with the melted butter. Cover with clingfilm (plastic wrap) and slit it twice to allow steam to escape. Cook on Full for 16 minutes, turning the dish twice.

Chicken Cacciatore

SERVES 6

An Italian dish, which translates to 'hunter's chicken'.

1.5 kg/3 lb chicken pieces
15 ml/1 tbsp olive oil
1 large onion, finely chopped
1 garlic clove, crushed
30 ml/2 tbsp plain (all-purpose)
flour
5 tomatoes, blanched, skinned and
chopped
150 ml/¼ pt/⅔ cup hot stock
45 ml/3 tbsp tomato purée (paste)
15 ml/1 tbsp brown table sauce
125 g/4 oz mushrooms, sliced
10 ml/2 tsp salt
10 ml/2 tsp dark soft brown sugar
45 ml/3 tbsp marsala or medium-
dry sherry
Creamed potatoes and mixed
salad, to serve

Place the chicken in a 30 cm/12 in diameter casserole dish (Dutch oven). Cover with clingfilm (plastic wrap) and slit it twice to allow steam to escape. Cook on Full for 15 minutes, turning the dish twice. Meanwhile, make the sauce conventionally. Pour the oil into a saucepan and add the onion and garlic. Fry (sauté) gently until lightly golden. Stir in the flour, then add the tomatoes, stock, purée and brown sauce. Cook, stirring, until the sauce comes to the boil and thickens. Stir in all the remaining ingredients and pour over the chicken. Cover as before and cook on Full for 20 minutes, turning the dish three times. Allow to stand for 5 minutes. Serve with creamed potatoes and a mixed salad.

Chicken Chasseur

SERVES 6

Prepare as for Chicken Cacciatore, but substitute dry white wine for the marsala or sherry.

Chicken Marengo

SERVES 6

Invented in about 1800 by Napoleon Bonaparte's personal chef on the battlefields after the Austrian defeat at the Battle of Marengo, near Verona in northern Italy.

Prepare as for Chicken Cacciatore, but use only 50 g/2 oz mushrooms and substitute dry white wine for the marsala or sherry. When stirring in all the remaining ingredients, add 12–16 small stoned (pitted) black olives and 60 ml/4 tbsp chopped parsley.

Sesame Chicken

SERVES 4

50 g/2 oz/¼ cup butter or
margarine, softened
15 ml/1 tbsp mild mustard
5 ml/1 tsp garlic purée (paste)
5 ml/1 tsp tomato purée (paste)
90 ml/6 tbsp sesame seeds, lightly
toasted
4 chicken portions, each
225 g/8 oz, skinned

Cream the butter or margarine with the mustard and the garlic and tomato purées. Stir in the sesame seeds. Spread the mixture evenly over the chicken. Arrange in a deep 25 cm/10 in diameter dish, leaving a hollow in the centre. Cook on Full for 16 minutes, turning the dish four times. Allow to stand for 5 minutes before serving.

Country Captain

SERVES 6

An East Indian mild chicken curry, brought to the southern states of North America long ago by a much-travelled sea captain. It has become a kind of oriental standby in the USA.

50 g/2 oz/¼ cup butter or
margarine
2 onions, chopped
1 celery stalk, chopped
1.5 kg/3 lb chicken joints, skinned
15 ml/1 tbsp plain (all-purpose)
flour
15 ml/1 tbsp mild curry powder
60 ml/4 tbsp almonds, blanched,
skinned, halved and lightly
toasted (page 205)
1 small green (bell) pepper, seeded
and finely chopped
45 ml/3 tbsp sultanas (golden
raisins)
10 ml/2 tsp salt
400 g/14 oz/1 large can chopped
tomatoes
5 ml/1 tsp sugar
275 g/10 oz/1¼ cups long-grain
rice, boiled

Put the butter or margarine in a 30 cm/12 in diameter casserole dish (Dutch oven). Heat, uncovered, on Full for 1½ minutes. Add the onions and celery and stir well. Cook, uncovered, on Full for 3 minutes, stirring twice. Add the chicken joints and toss in the butter and vegetable mixture until well coated. Sprinkle with the flour, curry powder, almonds, pepper and sultanas. Cover with clingfilm (plastic wrap) and slit it twice to allow steam to escape. Cook on Full for 8 minutes. Combine the salt with the tomatoes and sugar. Uncover the chicken and spoon the tomatoes over. Cover as before and cook on Full for 21 minutes, turning the dish twice. Allow to stand for 5 minutes before serving with the rice.

Chicken in Tomato and Caper Sauce

SERVES 6

6 chicken joints, 225 g/8 oz each,
skinned
Plain (all-purpose) flour
50 g/2 oz/¼ cup butter or
margarine
3 rashers (slices) bacon, chopped
2 large onions, chopped
2 garlic cloves, crushed
15 ml/1 tbsp capers, chopped
400 g/14 oz/1 large can chopped
tomatoes
15 ml/1 tbsp dark soft brown
sugar
5 ml/1 tsp dried mixed herbs
15 ml/1 tbsp tomato purée (paste)
15 ml/1 tbsp chopped basil leaves
15 ml/1 tbsp chopped parsley

Dust the chicken joints with flour. Put the butter or margarine in a 30 cm/12 in diameter casserole dish (Dutch oven). Heat, uncovered, on Full for 2 minutes. Stir in the bacon, onions, cloves and capers. Cook, uncovered, on Full for 4 minutes, stirring twice. Add the chicken and toss until well coated with the butter or margarine mixture. Cover with clingfilm (plastic wrap) and slit it twice to allow steam to escape. Cook on Full for 12 minutes, turning the dish three times. Uncover and add the remaining ingredients, mixing in well. Cover as before and cook on Full for 18 minutes. Allow to stand for 6 minutes before serving.

Chicken Paprikas

••••••••••••••••••••••••••••••
SERVES 4

Pronounced paprikash, this chicken fantasy is a relative of *gulas* or goulash, one of Hungary's most renowned dishes.

1.5 kg/3 lb chicken pieces
1 large onion, chopped
1 green (bell) pepper, seeded and
  chopped
1 garlic clove, crushed
30 ml/2 tbsp corn oil or melted lard
45 ml/3 tbsp plain (all-purpose)
  flour
15 ml/1 tbsp paprika
300 ml/½ pt/1¼ cups warm
  chicken stock
30 ml/2 tbsp tomato purée (paste)
5 ml/1 tsp dark soft brown sugar
2.5 ml/½ tsp caraway seeds
5 ml/1 tsp salt
150 ml/5 fl oz/⅔ cup crème fraîche
Small pasta shapes, boiled

Place the chicken pieces in a 30 cm/ 12 in diameter casserole dish (Dutch oven). Cover with clingfilm (plastic wrap) and slit it twice to allow steam to escape. Cook on Full for 15 minutes, turning the dish twice. Meanwhile, make the sauce conventionally. Put the onion, pepper, garlic and oil into a saucepan (skillet) and fry (sauté) gently until the vegetables are soft but not browned. Stir in the flour and paprika, then gradually blend in the stock. Bring to the boil, stirring. Stir in the remaining ingredients except the crème fraîche and pasta. Uncover the chicken and coat with the sauce, working in some of the juices already in the dish. Top with spoonfuls of crème fraîche. Cover as before and cook on Full for 20 minutes, turning the dish three times. Serve with small pasta.

Shades-of-the-East Chicken

•••••••••••••••••••••••••••••••
SERVES 6–8

Indian and Indonesian influences and tastes unite in this outstandingly grand chicken recipe.

15 ml/1 tbsp groundnut (peanut) oil
3 medium onions, chopped
2 garlic cloves, crushed
900 g/2 lb boned chicken breasts,
  skinned and cut into narrow
  strips
15 ml/1 tbsp cornflour
  (cornstarch)
60 ml/4 tbsp crunchy peanut
  butter
150 ml/¼ pt/⅔ cup water
7.5 ml/1½ tsp salt
10 ml/2 tsp mild curry paste
2.5 ml/½ tsp ground coriander
  (cilantro)
2.5 ml/½ tsp ground ginger
Seeds from 5 cardamom pods
60 ml/4 tbsp salted peanuts,
  coarsely-chopped
2 tomatoes, cut into wedges

Heat the oil in a 25 cm/10 in diameter casserole dish (Dutch oven), uncovered, on Full for 1 minute. Add the onions and garlic and cook, uncovered, on Full for 3 minutes, stirring twice. Mix in the chicken and cook, uncovered, on Full for 3 minutes, stirring with a fork every minute to separate. Sprinkle in the cornflour. Work in all the remaining ingredients except the peanuts and tomatoes. Cover with clingfilm (plastic wrap) and slit it twice to allow steam to escape. Cook on Full for 19 minutes, turning the dish four times. Allow to stand for 5 minutes. Stir round and garnish with the peanuts and tomato wedges before serving.

Nasi Goreng

SERVES 6

A Dutch-Indonesian speciality.

175 g/6 oz/¾ cup easy-cook long-
grain rice
50 g/2 oz/¼ cup butter or
margarine
2 onions, chopped
2 leeks, white part only, very
thinly sliced
1 green chilli, seeded and chopped
(optional)
350 g/12 oz/3 cups cold cooked
chicken, coarsely chopped
30 ml/2 tbsp soy sauce
1 Classic Omelette (page 102), cut
into strips
1 large tomato, cut into wedges

Cook the rice as directed on the packet. Allow to cool. Put the butter or margarine in a 25 cm/10 in diameter casserole dish (Dutch oven). Heat, uncovered, on Full for 1 minute. Stir in the onions, leeks and chilli, if using. Cook, uncovered, on Full for 4 minutes. Stir in the rice, chicken and soy sauce. Cover with a plate and cook on Full for 6–7 minutes, stirring three times, until piping hot. Garnish with a criss cross pattern of omelette strips and tomato wedges.

Roast Turkey

SERVES 6

1 turkey, size as required (allow
350 g/12 oz) uncooked weight
per person)
Baste (pages 332–3)

Cover the wing tips and ends of the legs with foil. Stand the turkey, breast side down, in a dish large enough to hold the bird comfortably. Don't worry if the body comes up above the rim. Cover with clingfilm (plastic wrap) and puncture 4 times. Cook on Full for 4 minutes per 450 g/1 lb. Remove from the oven and carefully turn the bird over so that the breast is now uppermost. Brush thickly with a baste (pages 332–3), using a fat-based one if the bird is plain and a non-fat one if the turkey is self-basting. Cover as before and cook on Full for a further 4 minutes per 450 g/1 lb. Transfer to a carving dish and cover with foil. Leave to stand for 15 minutes, then carve.

Spanish Turkey

SERVES 4

30 ml/2 tbsp olive oil
4 pieces boned turkey breast,
175 g/6 oz each
1 onion, chopped
12 stuffed olives, chopped
2 hard-boiled (hard-cooked) eggs
(pages 98–9), shelled and
chopped
30 ml/2 tbsp chopped gherkins
(cornichons)
2 tomatoes, thinly sliced

Heat the oil in a deep 20 cm/8 in diameter dish, uncovered, on Full for 1 minute. Add the turkey and toss well in the oil to coat both sides thoroughly. Combine the onion, olives, eggs and gherkins and spoon equally on to the turkey. Garnish with the tomato slices. Cover with clingfilm (plastic wrap) and slit it twice to allow steam to escape. Cook on Full for 15 minutes, turning the dish five times. Allow to stand for 5 minutes before serving.

Turkey Tacos

SERVES 4

For the tacos:
450 g/1 lb/4 cups minced turkey
1 small onion, chopped
2 garlic cloves, crushed
5 ml/1 tsp cumin seeds, ground if
preferred
2.5–5 ml/½–1 tsp chilli powder
30 ml/2 tbsp chopped coriander
(cilantro) leaves
5 ml/1 tsp salt
60 ml/4 tbsp water
4 large bought tortillas
Shredded lettuce
For the avocado garnish:
1 large ripe avocado
15–20 ml/3–4 tsp bought hot salsa
Juice of 1 lime
Salt
60 ml/4 tbsp soured (dairy sour)
cream

To make the tacos, cover the base of a 20 cm/8 in diameter dish with the turkey. Cover with a plate and cook on Full for 6 minutes. Break down the grains of meat with a fork. Stir in all the remaining ingredients except the tortillas and lettuce. Cover with clingfilm (plastic wrap) and slit it twice to allow steam to escape. Cook on Full for 8 minutes, turning the dish four times. Allow to stand for 4 minutes. Stir thoroughly. Pile equal amounts of the turkey mixture on the tortillas, add some lettuce and roll up. Transfer to a dish and keep warm.

To make the avocado dressing, halve the avocado, scoop out the flesh and mash finely. Stir in the salsa, lime juice and salt. Transfer the tacos to four warmed plates, top each with the avocado mixture and 15 ml/1 tbsp soured cream. Eat straight away.

Pancake Tacos

SERVES 4

Prepare as for Turkey Tacos, but sub-stitute four large home-made pan-cakes for the bought tortillas.

Turkey Loaf

SERVES 4

450 g/1 lb raw minced (ground)
turkey
1 garlic clove, crushed
30 ml/2 tbsp plain (all-purpose)
flour
2 large eggs, beaten
10 ml/2 tsp salt
10 ml/2 tsp dried thyme
5 ml/1 tsp Worcestershire sauce
20 ml/4 tsp ground nutmeg
Jacket Potatoes (page 226)
Cooked cauliflower (page 44)
Cheese Sauce (page 317)

Mix together the turkey, garlic, flour, eggs, salt, thyme, Worcestershire sauce and nutmeg. With damp hands, shape into a 15 cm/6 in loaf. Transfer to a deep dish, cover with clingfilm (plastic wrap) and slit it twice to allow steam to escape. Cook on Full for 9 minutes. Allow to stand for 5 minutes. Slice into four portions and serve with jacket potatoes and cauliflower, coated with cheese sauce and browned conventionally under the grill (broiler).

Anglo-Madras Turkey Curry

SERVES 4

A useful recipe to use up Christmas turkey leftovers.

30 ml/2 tbsp corn or sunflower oil
1 large onion, very thinly sliced
1 garlic clove, crushed
30 ml/2 tbsp raisins
30 ml/2 tbsp desiccated (shredded) coconut
25 ml/1½ tbsp plain (all-purpose) flour
20 ml/4 tsp hot curry powder
300 ml/½ pt/1¼ cups boiling water
30 ml/2 tbsp single (light) cream
2.5 ml/½ tsp salt
Juice of ½ lemon
350 g/12 oz/3 cups cold cooked turkey, cubed
Indian bread, mixed salad and chutney, to serve

Put the oil in a 1.5 litre/2½ pt/6 cup dish with the onion, garlic, raisins and coconut. Mix well. Cook, uncovered, on Full for 3 minutes. Mix in the flour, curry powder, water, cream, salt, lemon juice and turkey. Cover with a plate and cook on Full for 6–7 minutes, stirring twice, until the curry is thickened and bubbling. Allow to stand for 3 minutes. Stir round and serve with Indian bread, salad and chutney.

Fruited Turkey Curry

SERVES 4

30 ml/2 tbsp butter or margarine
10 ml/2 tsp olive oil
2 onions, chopped
15 ml/1 tbsp mild curry powder
30 ml/2 tbsp plain (all-purpose) flour
150 ml/¼ pt/⅔ cup single (light) cream
90 ml/6 tbsp Greek-style plain yoghurt
1 garlic clove, crushed
30 ml/2 tbsp tomato purée (paste)
5 ml/1 tsp garam masala
5 ml/1 tsp salt
Juice of 1 small lime
4 eating (dessert) apples, peeled, cored, quartered and thinly sliced
30 ml/2 tbsp any fruit chutney
450 g/1 lb/4 cups cold cooked turkey, cubed

Put the butter or margarine and oil in a 25 cm/10 in diameter casserole dish (Dutch oven). Heat, uncovered, on Full for 1½ minutes. Mix in the onions. Cook, uncovered, on Full for 3 minutes, stirring twice. Stir in the curry powder, flour, cream and yoghurt. Cook, uncovered, on Full for 2 minutes. Add all the remaining ingredients. Cover with a plate and cook on Full for 12–14 minutes, stirring every 5 minutes, until piping hot.

Bread and Butter Turkey Pie

SERVES 4

75 g/3 oz/⅜ cup butter or
 margarine
60 ml/4 tbsp grated Parmesan
 cheese
2.5 ml/½ tsp dried thyme
1.5 ml/¼ tsp dried sage
5 ml/1 tsp grated lemon peel
4 large slices white or brown
 bread
1 onion, chopped
50 g/2 oz mushrooms, sliced
45 ml/3 tbsp plain (all-purpose)
 flour
300 ml/½ pt/1¼ cups warm
 chicken stock
15 ml/1 tbsp lemon juice
45 ml/3 tbsp single (light) cream
225 g/8 oz/2 cups cold cooked
 chicken, cubed
Salt and freshly ground black
 pepper

Cream half the butter or margarine
with the cheese, thyme, sage and
lemon peel. Spread over the bread,
then cut each slice into four triangles.
Put the remaining butter or margarine
in a deep 20 cm/8 in diameter dish.
Heat, uncovered, on Full for 1½ minutes. Add the onion and mushrooms.
Cook, uncovered, on Full for 3 minutes, stirring twice. Mix in the flour,
then gradually blend in the stock,
lemon juice and cream. Stir in the
chicken and season to taste. Cover
with a plate and heat on Full for 8 minutes, stirring three times, until piping
hot. Remove from the microwave. Top
with the buttered bread triangles and
brown under a hot grill (broiler).

Turkey and Rice Casserole with Stuffing

SERVES 4–5

225 g/8 oz/1 cup easy-cook long-
 grain rice
300 ml/10 fl oz/1 can condensed
 cream of mushroom soup
300 ml/½ pt/1¼ cups boiling water
225 g/8 oz/2 cups sweetcorn
 (corn)
50 g/2 oz/½ cup chopped unsalted
 nuts
175 g/6 oz/1½ cups cooked turkey,
 diced
50 g/2 oz cold stuffing, cubed
Coleslaw, to serve

Put all the ingredients except the
stuffing in a 1.75 litre/3 pt/7½ cup
dish. Mix thoroughly. Cover with clingfilm (plastic wrap) and slit it twice to
allow steam to escape. Cook on Full
for 25 minutes. Uncover and stir with a
fork to fluff up the rice. Top with the
cold stuffing. Cover with a plate and
cook on Full for 2 minutes. Allow to
stand for 4 minutes. Fluff up again and
eat with coleslaw.

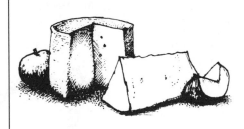

Turkey Breast with Orange Glaze

SERVES 4–6

For small families who want a festive meal with minimal leftovers.

40 g/1½ oz/3 tbsp butter
15 ml/1 tbsp tomato ketchup
  (catsup)
10 ml/2 tsp black treacle
  (molasses)
5 ml/1 tsp paprika
5 ml/1 tsp Worcestershire sauce
Finely grated peel of 1 satsuma or
  clementine
A pinch of ground cloves
1.5 ml/¼ tsp ground cinnamon
1 whole turkey breast, about
  1 kg/2¼ lb

Thoroughly combine all the ingredients except the turkey in a dish. Heat, uncovered, on Defrost for 1 minute. Place the turkey breast in a 25 cm/10 in diameter dish (Dutch oven) and brush with half the baste. Cover with clingfilm (plastic wrap) and slit it twice to allow steam to escape. Cook on Full for 10 minutes. Turn the turkey breast over and brush with the remaining baste. Cover as before and cook on Full for a further 10 minutes, turning the dish three times. Allow to stand for 7–10 minutes before carving.

Sweet and Sour Duck

SERVES 4

1 duck, about 2.25 kg/5 lb,
  washed and dried
45 ml/3 tbsp mango chutney
Bean sprouts
175 g/6 oz/¾ cup brown rice,
  boiled

Stand the duck upside-down on an upturned tea plate standing in a 25 cm/10 in diameter casserole dish (Dutch oven). Cover with clingfilm (plastic wrap) and slit it twice to allow steam to escape. Cook on Full for 20 minutes. Uncover and carefully pour off the fat and juices. Turn the duck over and spread the breast with the chutney. Cover as before and cook on Full for a further 20 minutes. Cut into four portions and serve with bean sprouts and the rice.

Canton Duck

SERVES 4

45 ml/3 tbsp smooth apricot jam
  (conserve)
30 ml/2 tbsp Chinese rice wine
10 ml/2 tsp mild made mustard
5 ml/1 tsp lemon juice
10 ml/2 tsp soy sauce
1 duck, about 2.25 kg/5 lb,
  washed and dried

Put the apricot jam, rice wine, mustard, lemon juice and soy sauce in a small basin. Heat on Full for 1–1½ minutes, stirring twice. Stand the duck upside-down on an upturned tea plate standing in a 25 cm/10 in diameter casserole dish (Dutch oven). Cover with clingfilm (plastic wrap) and slit it twice to allow steam to escape. Cook on Full for 20 minutes. Uncover and carefully pour off the fat and juices. Turn the duck over and spread the breast with the apricot baste. Cover as before and cook on Full for 20 minutes. Cut into four portions and serve.

Duck with Orange Sauce

SERVES 4

A high-class luxury, easily prepared in the microwave in a fraction of the time it would normally take. Garnish with watercress and fresh orange slices for a party centrepiece.

1 duck, about 2.25 kg/5 lb, washed and dried
For the sauce:
Finely grated peel of 1 large orange
Juice of 2 oranges
30 ml/2 tbsp fine-shred lemon marmalade
15 ml/1 tbsp redcurrant jelly (clear conserve)
30 ml/2 tbsp orange liqueur
5 ml/1 tsp soy sauce
10 ml/2 tsp cornflour (cornstarch)

Stand the duck upside-down on an upturned tea plate standing in a 25 cm/10 in diameter casserole dish (Dutch oven). Cover with clingfilm (plastic wrap) and slit it twice to allow steam to escape. Cook on Full for 20 minutes. Uncover and carefully pour off the fat and juices. Turn the duck over. Cover as before and cook on Full for 20 minutes. Cut into four portions, transfer to a serving dish and keep hot. Skim the fat from the cooking juices.

To make the sauce, place all the ingredients except the cornflour in a measuring jug. Add the skimmed cooking juices. Make up to 300 ml/ ½ pt/1¼ cups with hot water. Mix the cornflour to a thin paste with a few spoonfuls of cold water. Add to the jug and mix thoroughly. Cook, uncovered, on Full for 4 minutes, stirring three times. Pour over the duck and serve straight away.

French-style Duck

SERVES 4

1 duck, about 2.25 kg/5 lb, washed and dried
12 stoned (pitted) prunes
1 celery stalk, finely chopped
2 garlic cloves, crushed
For the sauce:
300 ml/½ pt/1¼ cups dry cider
5 ml/1 tsp salt
10 ml/2 tsp tomato purée (paste)
30 ml/2 tbsp crème fraîche
15 ml/1 tbsp cornflour (cornstarch)
Boiled tagliatelle, to serve

Stand the duck upside-down on an upturned tea plate standing in a 25 cm/10 in diameter casserole dish (Dutch oven). Scatter the prunes, celery and garlic around the duck. Cover the dish with clingfilm (plastic wrap) and slit it twice to allow steam to escape. Cook on Full for 20 minutes. Uncover and carefully pour off and reserve the fat and juices. Turn the duck over. Cover as before and cook on Full for 20 minutes. Cut into four portions, transfer to a serving dish and keep hot. Skim the fat from the cooking juices.

To make the sauce, place the cider in a measuring jug. Whisk in the salt, tomato purée, crème fraîche, the skimmed cooking juices and cornflour. Cook, uncovered, on Full for 4–5 minutes until thickened and bubbling, whisking every minute. Pour over the duck and prunes and accompany with tagliatelle.

Meat

Yes, you can cook roast pork with crackling in the microwave – but it also allows you to make superb creations like meat loaves and curries with any minced (ground) meat you care to name. It's great for finishing off Easter and Christmas gammon joints and, if you treat them right, does wonders for casseroles and hotpots.

Roasting Boned and Rolled Joints of Meat

Place the joint, skin side up, on a special microwave trivet standing in a large dish. Cover with a piece of clingfilm (plastic wrap). For every 450 g/1 lb allow the following cooking times:

Pork	–	9 minutes
Ham	–	9 minutes
Lamb	–	9 minutes
Beef	–	6–8 minutes

Turn the dish every 5 minutes for even cooking, protecting your hands with oven gloves. Allow to rest for 5–6 minutes half way through the roasting time. At the end of cooking, transfer the joint to a carving board and cover with a double thickness of foil. Allow to rest for 5–8 minutes, depending on its size, before carving.

Sweet and Sour Pork Chops with Orange and Lime

SERVES 4

4 pork chops, 175 g/6 oz each after trimming
60 ml/4 tbsp tomato ketchup (catsup)
15 ml/1 tbsp teriyaki sauce
20 ml/4 tsp malt vinegar
5 ml/1 tsp finely grated lime peel
Juice of 1 orange
1 garlic clove, crushed (optional)
350 g/12 oz/1½ cups brown rice, boiled

Arrange the chops in a deep 25 cm/10 in diameter dish. Beat together all the remaining ingredients except the rice and spoon over the chops. Cover with clingfilm (plastic wrap) and slit it twice to allow steam to escape. Cook on Full for 12 minutes, turning the dish four times. Allow to stand for 5 minutes before serving with the brown rice.

Meat Loaf

• •
SERVES 8–10

A tried and trusted versatile family terrine. It is excellent when served hot, cut into wedges with gravy or Portugese Sauce or Rustic Tomato Sauce (page 330) and accompanied with Creamed Potatoes (page 225) or macaroni cheese and assorted vegetables. Alternatively, eat it cold with a rich mayonnaise or salad dressing and salad. For sandwiches, slice thinly and use as a filling with lettuce, chopped spring onions (scallions) and tomatoes or, served with baby gherkins (cornichons) and granary bread, it has the makings of a classic French-style starter.

125 g/4¾ oz/3½ slices light-
*   textured white bread*
450 g/1 lb lean minced (ground) beef
450 g/1 lb/4 cups minced (ground)
*   turkey*
10 ml/2 tsp salt
3 garlic cloves, crushed
4 large eggs, beaten
10 ml/2 tsp Worcestershire sauce
10 ml/2 tsp dark soy sauce
10 ml/2 tsp made mustard

Lightly grease a deep 23 cm/9 in diameter dish. Crumb the bread in a food processor. Add all the remaining ingredients and pulse the machine until the mixture is just combined. (Avoid over-mixing as the loaf will be heavy and dense.) Spread into the prepared dish. Push a baby jam (conserve) jar or straight-sided egg cup into the centre so that the meat mixture forms a ring. Cover with clingfilm (plastic wrap) and slit it twice to allow steam to escape. Cook on Full for 18 minutes, turning the dish twice. The loaf will shrink away from sides of dish. Leave to stand for 5 minutes if serving hot.

Turkey and Sausagemeat Terrine

• •
SERVES 8–10

Prepare as for Meat Loaf, but substitute 450 g/1 lb beef or pork sausagemeat for the minced (ground) beef. Cook on Full for 18 minutes instead of 20 minutes.

Pork Satay

• •
SERVES 8 AS A STARTER,
4 AS A MAIN COURSE

Follow the recipe for Chicken Satay (page 142), but substitute pork fillet for the chicken breast.

Japanese Pork with Eggs

• •
SERVES 4

Prepare as for Japanese Chicken with Eggs (page 143), but substitute cooked pork for the chicken.

Pork Chops with Zippy Dressing

• •
SERVES 4

4 pork chops, 175 g/6 oz each
*   after trimming*
30 ml/2 tbsp butter or margarine
5 ml/1 tsp paprika
5 ml/1 tsp soy sauce
5 ml/1 tsp Worcestershire sauce

Arrange the chops in a deep 25 cm/ 10 in diameter dish. Melt the butter or margarine on Defrost for 1½ minutes. Beat in the remaining ingredients and pour over the chops. Cover with clingfilm (plastic wrap) and slit it twice to allow steam to escape. Cook on Full for 9 minutes, turning the dish four times. Allow to stand for 4 minutes.

Hawaiian Pork and Pineapple Casserole
························

SERVES 6

Delicacy, tenderness and a fine flavour characterise this meat and fruit recipe from the tropical island of Hawaii.

15 ml/1 tbsp groundnut (peanut)
*   oil*
1 onion, finely chopped
2 garlic cloves, crushed
900 g/2 lb pork fillet, cubed
15 ml/1 tbsp cornflour
*   (cornstarch)*
400 g/14 oz/3½ cups canned
*   crushed pineapple in natural*
*   juice*
45 ml/3 tbsp soy sauce
5 ml//1 tsp ground ginger
Freshly ground black pepper

Brush the oil over the base and sides of a deep 23 cm/9 in diameter dish. Add the onion and garlic and cook, uncovered, on Full for 3 minutes. Stir in the pork, cornflour, pineapple and juice, soy sauce and ginger. Season to taste with pepper. Arrange in a ring round the inside edge of the dish, leaving a small hollow in the centre. Cover with clingfilm (plastic wrap) and slit it twice to allow steam to escape. Cook on Full for 16 minutes, turning the dish four times. Allow to stand for 5 minutes, then stir before serving.

Hawaiian Gammon and Pineapple Casserole
························

SERVES 6

Prepare as for Hawaiian Pork and Pineapple Casserole, but substitute unsmoked and mild gammon cubes for the pork.

Festive Gammon
·······························

SERVES 10–12

Ideal for a Christmas or New Year buffet, gammon cooked in the microwave is moist and succulent and carves beautifully. This is the maximum size for a satisfactory result.

Gammon joint, maximum weight
*   2.5 kg/5½ lb*
50 g/2 oz/1 cup browned
*   breadcrumbs*
Whole cloves

The joint is first boiled conventionally to decrease saltiness. Place the gammon in a large saucepan, cover with cold water, bring to the boil and drain. Repeat. Weigh the drained joint and allow 8 minutes cooking time on Full per 450 g/1 lb. Either stand the joint directly on the glass tray inside the microwave or put it in a large shallow dish. If there is a narrow end, wrap it in a piece of foil to prevent overcooking. Cover the gammon with kitchen paper and cook for half the cooking time. Allow to stand in the microwave for 30 minutes. Remove the foil, if used, turn the joint over and cover with kitchen paper. Complete the cooking and leave to stand for a further 30 minutes. Transfer to a board. Strip off the skin, score the fat into diamonds, then sprinkle with the crumbs. Stud each diamond with a clove.

169

Glazed Gala Gammon

SERVES 10–12

*Gammon joint, maximum weight
2.5 kg/5½ lb*
*50 g/2 oz/1 cup browned
breadcrumbs*
Whole cloves
60 ml/4 tbsp demerara sugar
10 ml/2 tsp mustard powder
*60 ml/4 tbsp butter or margarine,
melted*
5 ml/1 tsp Worcestershire sauce
30 ml/2 tbsp white grape juice
Cocktail cherries

Prepare as for Festive Gammon (page 169), but stud each alternate diamond with a clove. To make the glaze, mix together the sugar, mustard, butter or margarine, Worcestershire sauce and grape juice. Transfer the gammon to a roasting tin and cover the fat with the glaze. Cook the joint conventionally at 190°C/375°F/gas mark 5 for 25–30 minutes until the fat is golden brown. Stud the remaining diamonds of fat with cocktail cherries speared on to cocktail sticks (toothpicks).

Paella with Spanish Salami

SERVES 6

Prepare as for Paella (page 145), but substitute coarsely chopped salami for the chicken.

Swedish-style Meatballs

SERVES 4

Known as *kottbullar*, this is one of Sweden's national dishes, where it is served with boiled potatoes, cranberry sauce, gravy and a mixed salad.

*75 g/3 oz/1½ cups fresh white
breadcrumbs*
1 onion, finely chopped
*225 g/8 oz/2 cups lean minced
(ground) pork*
*225 g/8 oz/2 cups minced (ground)
beef*
1 large egg
2.5 ml/½ tsp salt
*175 ml/6 fl oz/1 small can
evaporated milk*
2.5 ml/½ tsp ground allspice
25 g/1 oz/2 tbsp margarine

Thoroughly combine all the ingredients except the margarine. Shape into 12 even-sized balls. Heat a microwave browning dish as directed either on page 14 or in the instruction book supplied with your dish or microwave. Add the margarine and, with hands protected by oven gloves, swirl the dish until the base is completely covered. At this point it will also sizzle. Add the meatballs and turn immediately to brown all over. Cover with clingfilm (plastic wrap) and slit it twice to allow steam to escape. Cook on Full for 9½ minutes, turning the dish four times. Allow to stand for 3 minutes before serving.

Roast Pork with Crackling

A surprisingly crisp skin on the pork, due to the meat's long cooking time.

Choose a piece of leg, allowing 175 g/6 oz per person. Score the skin deeply with a knife and sprinkle thickly with salt and more lightly with paprika. Place the joint, skin side up, on a special microwave trivet standing in a large dish. Cover with a piece of baking parchment. Open roast like this, allowing 9 minutes for every 450 g/1 lb. Turn the dish every 5 minutes for even cooking, protecting your hands with oven gloves. Allow to rest for 6 minutes half-way through the cooking time. At the end of cooking, transfer the joint to a carving board and cover with a double thickness of foil. Allow to stand for 8 minutes before carving and serve with vegetables and Sage and Onion Stuffing (page 240).

Roast Pork with Honey

Prepare as for Roast Pork with Crackling, but brush with a baste made from 90 ml/6 tbsp dark clear honey mixed with a 20 ml/generous 1 tbsp made mustard and 10 ml/2 tsp Worcestershire sauce before sprinkling with salt and paprika.

Pork Chops with Red Cabbage

SERVES 4

A winter affair, when jars and cans of red cabbage fill the shelves for Christmas. Eat with Creamed Potatoes (page 225) and mashed parsnip.

450 g/1 lb cooked red cabbage
4 tomatoes, blanched, skinned and
chopped
10 ml/2 tsp salt
4 pork chops, 175 g/6 oz each
after trimming
10 ml/2 tsp soy sauce
2.5 ml/½ tsp garlic salt
2.5 ml/½ tsp paprika
15 ml/1 tbsp dark soft brown
sugar

Arrange the cabbage over the base of a 20 cm/8 in diameter casserole dish (Dutch oven). Mix in the tomatoes and salt and place the chops on top. Pour the soy sauce over and sprinkle with the remaining ingredients. Cover with clingfilm (plastic wrap) and slit it twice to allow steam to escape. Cook on Full for 15 minutes, turning the dish four times. Allow to stand for 4 minutes before serving.

Roman-style Pork Fillets

SERVES 4

15 ml/1 tbsp olive oil
1 small onion, chopped
1 garlic clove, crushed
4 slices pork fillet, 125 g/4 oz
  each, beaten until very thin
60 ml/4 tbsp tomato juice
5 ml/1 tsp dried oregano
125 g/4 oz Mozzarella cheese,
  sliced
30 ml/2 tbsp capers
Polenta (page 212)

Pour the oil into a deep 25 cm/10 in diameter dish. Heat on Full for 1 minute. Stir in the onion and garlic. Cook, uncovered, on Full for 4 minutes, stirring twice. Add the pork to the dish in single layer. Cook, uncovered, on Full for 2 minutes. Turn over and cook for a further 2 minutes. Sprinkle with the tomato juice and oregano, top with the Mozzarella slices, then stud with the capers. Cover with clingfilm (plastic wrap) and slit it twice to allow steam to escape. Cook on Full for 2–3 minutes or until the cheese is just melting. Allow to stand for 1 minute before serving with polenta.

Pork Fillet and Vegetable Casserole

SERVES 6–8

15 ml/1 tbsp sunflower or corn oil
1 onion, grated
2 garlic cloves, crushed
675 g/1½ lb pork fillet, cut into
  1.5 cm/¾ in slices
30 ml/2 tbsp plain (all-purpose)
  flour
5 ml/1 tsp dried marjoram
5 ml/1 tsp finely grated orange
  peel
200 g/7 oz/1¾ cups canned or
  thawed frozen mixed peas and
  carrots
200 g/7 oz/1½ cups sweetcorn
  (corn)
300 ml/½ pt/1¼ cups rosé wine
150 ml/¼ pt/⅔ cup hot water
5 ml/1 tsp salt

Pour the oil into a 2 litre/3½ pt/8½ cup casserole dish (Dutch oven). Heat, uncovered, on Full for 1 minute. Mix in the onion and garlic. Cook, uncovered, on Full for 4 minutes, stirring twice. Add the pork. Cover the dish with a plate and cook on Full for 4 minutes. Mix in the flour, making sure the pieces of meat are well coated. Add all remaining ingredients except the salt. Cover with clingfilm (plastic wrap) and slit it twice to allow steam to escape. Cook on Full for 17 minutes, turning the dish four times. Allow to stand for 5 minutes before seasoning with the salt and serving.

Chilli Pork Chops

SERVES 4

4 pork spare rib chops, 225 g/8 oz each, fat removed
10 ml/2 tsp chilli or Cajun seasoning
5 ml/1 tsp garlic powder
400 g/14 oz/1 large can red kidney beans, drained
400 g/14 oz/1 large can chopped tomatoes
30 ml/2 tbsp chopped fresh coriander (cilantro)
2.5 ml/½ tsp salt

Arrange the chops in a deep 30 cm/12 in diameter dish. Sprinkle with the seasoning and garlic powder. Cover with clingfilm (plastic wrap) and slit it twice to allow steam to escape. Cook on Full for 8 minutes, turning the dish twice. Uncover and spread with the beans and tomatoes with their juice. Sprinkle with the coriander and salt. Cover as before and cook on Full for 15 minutes, turning 3 times. Allow to stand for 5 minutes before serving.

Pork with Chutney and Mandarins

SERVES 4

4 pork spare rib chops, 225 g/8 oz each, fat removed
350 g/12 oz/1 large can mandarin segments in light syrup
5 ml/1 tsp paprika
20 ml/4 tsp soy sauce
45 ml/3 tbsp fruit chutney, chopped if necessary
2 garlic cloves, crushed
Curried Rice (page 213)

Arrange the chops in a deep 30 cm/12 in diameter dish. Drain the mandarins, reserving 30 ml/2 tbsp of the syrup, and divide the fruit over the chops. Beat the reserved syrup with the remaining ingredients except the rice and spoon over the mandarins. Cover with clingfilm (plastic wrap) and slit it twice to allow steam to escape. Cook on Full for 20 minutes, turning the dish four times. Allow to stand for 5 minutes, then serve with the rice.

'Barbecued' Ribs

SERVES 4

1 kg/2¼ lb meaty pork sheet ribs or spare ribs
50 g/2 oz/¼ cup butter or margarine
15 ml/1 tbsp tomato ketchup (catsup)
10 ml/2 tsp soy sauce
5 ml/1 tsp paprika
1 garlic clove, crushed
5 ml/1 tsp hot chilli sauce

Wash and dry the pork and separate into individual ribs. Arrange in the largest round shallow dish that will fit comfortably in the microwave, with the narrow part of each rib pointing towards the centre. Cover with clingfilm (plastic wrap) and slit it twice to allow steam to escape. Cook on Full for 10 minutes, turning the dish three times. To make the baste, combine the remaining ingredients in a bowl and warm, uncovered, on Defrost for 2 minutes. Uncover the ribs and carefully pour off the fat. Brush with about half the the baste. Cook, uncovered, on Full for 3 minutes. Turn over with tongs and brush with the remaining baste. Cook, uncovered, on Full for 2 minutes. Allow to stand for 3 minutes before serving.

Ham-wrapped Chicory in Cheese Sauce

••••••••••••••••••••••••••••••••
SERVES 4

Called *chicorées au jambon* in Belgium, its country of origin. The silvery-white vegetable wrapped in ham and enveloped in a simple cheese sauce is a gastonomic masterpiece.

8 heads chicory (Belgian endive),
  about 1 kg/2¼ lb in all
150 ml/¼ pt/⅔ cup boiling water
15 ml/1 tbsp lemon juice
8 large slices cooked ham
600 ml/1 pt/2½ cups milk
50 g/2 oz/¼ cup butter or
  margarine
45 ml/3 tbsp plain (all-purpose)
  flour
175 g/6 oz/1½ cups Edam cheese,
  grated
Salt and freshly ground pepper
Chips (fries), to serve

Trim the chicory, removing any bruised or damaged outer leaves, and cut out a cone-shaped piece from the base of each to prevent a bitter taste. Arrange the heads like spokes of a wheel in a deep 30 cm/12 in diameter dish. Coat with the water and lemon juice. Cover with clingfilm (plastic wrap) and slit it twice to allow steam to escape. Cook on Full for 14 minutes, turning the dish twice. Allow to stand for 5 minutes, then drain thoroughly. Wash and dry the dish. When the chicory is lukewarm, wrap a ham slice round each and return to the dish. Place the milk in a jug and heat, uncovered, on Full for 3 minutes. Put butter or margarine into a 1.2 litre/ 2 pt/5 cup dish and melt on Full for 1 minute. Stir in the flour, then gradually whisk in the hot milk. Cook, uncovered, on Full for 5–6 minutes, whisking every minute to ensure smoothness, until the sauce is bubbly and thickened. Mix in the cheese and season to taste. Pour evenly over the chicory and ham. Cover with a plate and reheat on Full for 3 minutes. Allow to stand for 3 minutes. Brown conventionally under a hot grill (broiler), if liked, then serve with chips.

Pork Ribs in Sticky Orange Barbecue Sauce

••••••••••••••••••••••••••••••••
SERVES 4

1 kg/2¼ lb meaty pork sheet ribs
  or spare ribs
30 ml/2 tbsp lemon juice
30 ml/2 tbsp soy sauce
5 ml/1 tsp Japanese wasabi
  powder
15 ml/1 tbsp Worcestershire sauce
300 ml/½ pt/1¼ cups freshly
  squeezed orange juice
30 ml/2 tbsp dark orange
  marmalade
10 ml/2 tsp made mustard
1 garlic clove, crushed
Chinese noodles, boiled, to serve
A few orange wedges, to garnish

Place the ribs in a large shallow dish. Cover with clingfilm (plastic wrap) and slit it twice to allow steam to escape. Cook on Full for 7 minutes, turning the dish twice. Uncover and carefully pour off the fat. Beat together the remaining ingredients except the noodles and pour over the ribs. Cover loosely with kitchen paper and cook on Full for 20 minutes, turning the dish four times and basting with sauce each time. Eat with boiled Chinese noodles and orange wedges served separately.

Steak and Mushroom Pudding

SERVES 4

This old English treasure works like a dream in the microwave, with the suet crust pastry (paste) behaving exactly as it should. The trick is to use precooked meat, such as a home-made stew or canned meat, because cubes of raw meat have a tendency to toughen in the microwave when cooked with liquid.

For the pastry:
175 g/6 oz/1½ cups self-raising (self-rising) flour
2.5 ml/½ tsp salt
50 g/2 oz/½ cup shredded beef or vegetarian suet
90 ml/6 tbsp cold water
For the filling:
450 g/1 lb stewed meat with gravy
125 g/4 oz button mushrooms

To make the pastry, sift the flour and salt into bowl and toss in the suet. Using a fork, stir in enough of the water to make a soft but pliable dough. Knead lightly until smooth, then roll out on a floured surface to a 30 cm/12 in round. Cut out a wedge-shaped quarter and reserve for the lid. Throughly grease a 900 ml/1½ pt/ 3¾ cup pudding basin and line with the pastry, easing it over the base and sides until it reaches the inner rim at the top of the basin and pressing out any wrinkles with your fingertips. Seal the joins by pinching them together with dampened fingers.

To make the filling, heat together the stewed meat and mushrooms, either in the microwave or conventionally. Allow to cool. Spoon into the pastry-lined basin. Roll out the reserved pastry to make a lid, dampen the edge and place on the lining pastry, pinching them together to seal. Cover with clingfilm (plastic wrap) and slit it twice to allow steam to escape. Cook on Full for 7 minutes until the pastry is well risen. Allow to stand for 3 minutes, then spoon out on to plates to serve.

Steak and Kidney Pudding

SERVES 4

Prepare as for Steak and Mushroom Pudding, but use 450 g/1 lb mixed stewed steak and kidney.

Steak and Chestnut Pudding

SERVES 4

Prepare as for Steak and Mushroom Pudding, but substitute whole chestnuts for the button mushrooms.

Steak and Pickled Walnut Pudding with Prunes

SERVES 4

Prepare as for Steak and Mushroom Pudding, but substitute 4 pickled walnuts, quartered, and 8 stoned (pitted) prunes for the mushrooms.

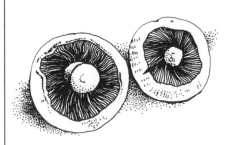

South American 'Chopped' Meat

SERVES 4

2 onions, finely chopped or grated
275 g/10 oz peeled pumpkin,
butternut squash or unpeeled
courgettes (zucchini), diced
1 large tomato, blanched, skinned
and chopped
450 g/1 lb/4 cups coarsely minced
(ground) beef
5–10 ml/1–2 tsp salt
Brazilian Rice (page 215)

Put the vegetables and mince in a 20 cm/8 inch diameter casserole dish (Dutch oven). Cover with clingfilm (plastic wrap) and slit it twice to allow steam to escape. Cook on Full for 10 minutes, turning the dish three times. Uncover and mash thoroughly to break up the meat. Cover with a plate and cook on Full for 5 minutes, stirring once. Allow to stand for 3 minutes and season with the salt. The meat will be a fairly loose consistency in its unthickened gravy. Serve with Brazilian rice.

Brazilian 'Chopped' Meat with Eggs and Olives

SERVES 4

Prepare as for South American Chopped Meat, but omit the pumpkin, squash or courgettes (zucchini). Add 60 ml/4 tbsp stock to the meat mixture. Reduce the initial cooking time to 7 minutes. After standing, stir in 3 hard-boiled (hard-cooked) egg (pages 98–9) wedges and 12 stoned (pitted) green olives.

The Reuben Sandwich

SERVES 2

As any North American will testify, the open Reuben Sandwich is a feast of a meal, produced by delis from New York to California.

2 large slices brown or rye bread
Mayonnaise
175 g/6 oz salt beef, pastrami or
brisket, thinly sliced
175 g/6 oz drained sauerkraut
4 large thin slices Gruyère (Swiss)
or Emmental cheese

Spread the bread with mayonnaise and place the slices side by side on a large plate. Heat, uncovered, on Defrost for 1½ minutes. Cover each evenly with the beef and top with the sauerkraut, pressing it down lightly with a spatula. Cover with the cheese. Cook on Full for 1½ –2 minutes until the cheese melts. Eat straight away.

Beef Chow Mein

SERVES 4

Prepare as for Chicken Chow Mein (page 139), but substitute beef for the chicken.

Beef Chop Suey

SERVES 4

Prepare as for Chicken Chop Suey (page 139), but substitute beef for the chicken.

Aubergine and Beef Casserole

SERVES 6

This Louisiana speciality is a treat for one and all and is relished by the locals.

4 aubergines (eggplants)
10 ml/2 tsp salt
45 ml/3 tbsp boiling water
1 onion, finely grated
450 g/1 lb/4 cups lean minced (ground) beef
75 g/3 oz/1½ cups fresh white breadcrumbs
1.5–2.5 ml/¼–½ tsp hot pepper sauce
Salt and freshly ground pepper
25 g/1 oz/2 tbsp butter
250 g/8 oz/2¼ cups American long-grain rice, boiled

Top, tail and peel the aubergines and cube the flesh. Put into a large bowl or dish and mix in the salt and boiling water. Cover with clingfilm (plastic wrap) and slit it twice to allow steam to escape. Cook on Full for 14 minutes. Allow to stand for 2 minutes. Drain thoroughly, then place in a blender or food processor and process to a purée. Thoroughly grease a shallow dish. Mix together the aubergine purée, onion, beef, half the breadcrumbs, the pepper sauce and salt and freshly ground black pepper to taste. Spread into the casserole. Sprinkle with the remaining breadcrumbs, then dot with flakes of butter. Cook, uncovered, on Full for 10 minutes. Flash briefly under a hot grill (broiler) before serving, if liked, to crisp the top. Serve with the rice.

Meatball Curry

SERVES 8

675 g/1½ lb/6 cups lean minced (ground) beef
50 g/2 oz/1 cup fresh white breadcrumbs
1 garlic clove, crushed
1 large egg, beaten
300 ml/10 fl oz/1 can condensed tomato soup
6 tomatoes
10 ml/2 tsp soy sauce
15–30 ml/1–2 tbsp mild curry powder
15 ml/1 tbsp tomato purée (paste)
1 beef stock cube
75 ml/5 tbsp mango chutney
Boiled rice or mashed potato, to serve

Mix together the beef, breadcrumbs, garlic and egg. Shape into 16 balls and arrange round the edge of a deep 25 cm/10 in diameter dish. Mix together the remaining ingredients and spoon over the meatballs. Cover with clingfilm (plastic wrap) and slit it twice to allow steam to escape. Cook on Full for 18 minutes, turning the dish four times. Allow to stand for 5 minutes. Uncover and baste the meatballs with the sauce. Leave uncovered and reheat on Full for a further 1½–2 minutes. Serve with boiled rice or mashed potato.

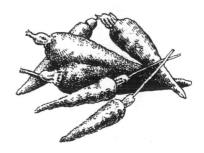

Italian Meatballs

SERVES 4

15 ml/2 tbsp olive oil
1 onion, grated
2 garlic cloves, crushed
450 g/1 lb/4 cups lean minced
(ground) beef
75 ml/5 tbsp fresh white
breadcrumbs
1 egg, beaten
10 ml/2 tsp salt
400 g/14 oz/1¾ cups passata
(sieved tomatoes)
10 ml/2 tsp dark soft brown sugar
5 ml/1 tsp dried basil or oregano

Pour the oil into a deep 20 cm/8 in diameter dish. Add the onion and garlic. Cook, uncovered, on Full for 4 minutes. Combine the meat with the breadcrumbs, egg and half the salt. Shape into 12 small balls. Add to the dish and cook, uncovered, on Full for 5 minutes, turning the meatballs halfway through the cooking time. Stand while mixing together the passata, sugar, oregano and remaining salt. Pour over the meatballs. Cover with clingfilm (plastic wrap) and slit it twice to allow steam to escape. Cook on Full for 10 minutes, turning the dish three times. Allow to stand for 3 minutes before serving.

Speedy Paprika Meatballs

SERVES 4–6

This is good with plain boiled potatoes, or microwaved chips (fries) if you're really in a hurry!

450 g/1 lb/4 cups lean minced
(ground) beef
50 g/2 oz/1 cup fresh white
breadcrumbs
1 garlic clove, crushed
1 large egg, beaten
300 ml/½ pt/1¼ cups passata
(sieved tomatoes)
300 ml/½ pt/1¼ cups boiling water
30 ml/2 tbsp dried red and green
(bell) pepper flakes
10 ml/2 tsp paprika
5 ml/1 tsp caraway seeds
(optional)
10 ml/2 tsp dark soft brown sugar
5 ml/1 tsp salt
150 ml/5 oz/⅔ cup soured (dairy
sour) cream

Mix together the meat, breadcrumbs, garlic and egg. Shape into 12 balls. Arrange round the edge of a deep 20 cm/8 in diameter dish. Combine the passata with the water. Stir in the pepper flakes, paprika, caraway seeds, if using, and sugar. Spoon over the meatballs. Cover with clingfilm (plastic wrap) and slit it twice to allow steam to escape. Cook on Full for 15 minutes, turning the dish three times. Allow to stand for 5 minutes, then uncover and stir in the salt and soured cream. Reheat, uncovered, on Full for 2 minutes.

Herbed Beef Buffet Slice

SERVES 8

900 g/2 lb/8 cups minced (ground)
beef
2 large eggs, beaten
1 beef stock cube
1 small onion, finely grated
60 ml/4 tbsp plain (all-purpose)
flour
45 ml/3 tbsp tomato ketchup
(catsup)
10 ml/2 tsp dried mixed herbs
10 ml/2 tsp soy sauce
Mint leaves and peeled orange
slices, to garnish

Thoroughly combine all the ingredients except the soy sauce. Spread into a 1¼ litre/2 pt/5 cup greased rectangular dish shaped like a loaf tin (pan). Brush the top with the soy sauce. Cover with clingfilm (plastic wrap) and slit it twice to allow steam to escape. Cook on Full for 10 minutes, then allow to stand in the microwave for 5 minutes. Cook on Defrost for a further 12 minutes, turning the dish four times. Allow to stand for 5 minutes, then uncover and carefully drain off the surplus fat and juices, which can be used for sauces and gravies. Leave until cold, then carefully transfer to a serving dish and garnish with the mint leaves and orange slices. Serve sliced.

Malaysian-style Peanut Beef with Coconut

SERVES 4

2 onions, finely chopped
1 garlic clove, crushed
450 g/1 lb/4 cups extra lean
minced (ground) beef
125 g/4 oz/½ cup crunchy peanut
butter
45 ml/3 tbsp desiccated (shredded)
coconut
2.5 ml/½ tsp hot pepper sauce
15 ml/1 tbsp soy sauce
2.5 ml/½ tsp salt
300 ml/½ pt/1¼ cups boiling water
175 g/6 oz/1½ cups rice, boiled
Oriental pickles, to garnish
(optional)

Place the onions, garlic and beef into a 1.5 litre/2½ pt/6 cup casserole dish (Dutch oven). Mix together well with a fork, making sure the beef is thoroughly broken up. Cover with clingfilm (plastic wrap) and slit it twice to allow steam to escape. Cook on Full for 8 minutes, turning the dish twice. Uncover and stir in all the remaining ingredients except the rice. Cover as before and cook on Full for a further 8 minutes, turning the dish three times. Allow to stand for 3 minutes. Uncover and stir, then serve with the boiled rice and oriental pickles, if wished.

Speedy Beef and Mayonnaise Loaf

SERVES 6

A super dinner party main course, more luxurious than you would expect from a dish so quick to prepare.

750 g/1½ lb/6 cups lean minced (ground) beef
15 ml/1 tbsp dried red and green (bell) pepper flakes
15 ml/1 tbsp finely chopped parsley
7.5 ml/1½ tsp onion salt
30 ml/2 tbsp plain (all-purpose) flour
60 ml/4 tbsp thick mayonnaise
7.5 ml/1½ tsp mustard powder
5 ml/1 tsp soy sauce

Thoroughly grease a deep 20 cm/8 in diameter dish. Combine the beef with all the remaining ingredients and spread smoothly into the dish. Cover with clingfilm (plastic wrap) and slit it twice to allow steam to escape. Cook on Full for 12 minutes, turning the dish four times. Allow to stand for 5 minutes, then lift the loaf out of the dish with two spatulas, leaving the fat behind. Transfer to a warmed serving plate and cut into six wedges to serve.

Beef Cooked in Red Wine

SERVES 4

A smart and stylish dish, especially when served with Classic Macaroni Cheese (page 196) or Savoyard Potatoes (page 228) and perhaps canned artichoke hearts, warmed through in a little butter.

30 ml/2 tbsp butter or margarine
2 large onions, grated
1 garlic clove, crushed
125 g/4 oz button mushrooms, thinly sliced
450 g/1 lb rump (tip) steak, cut into small cubes
15 ml/1 tbsp tomato purée (paste)
15 ml/1 tbsp chopped parsley
15 ml/1 tbsp cornflour (cornstarch)
5 ml/1 tsp strong made mustard
300 ml/½ pt/1¼ cups dry red wine
5 ml/1 tsp salt

Put the butter or margarine in a 20 cm/8 in diameter casserole dish (Dutch oven). Melt, uncovered, on Defrost for 1–1½ minutes. Stir in the onions, garlic and mushrooms. Cook, uncovered, on Full for 5 minutes. Stir in the steak, then move the mixture to the edge of the dish to form a ring, leaving a small hollow in the centre. Cover with a plate and cook on Full for 5 minutes. Meanwhile, mix together the tomato purée, parsley, cornflour and mustard. Blend smoothly with a little of the red wine, then stir in the remainder. Mix gently into the steak mixture. Cover with a plate and cook on Full for 5 minutes, stirring twice. Allow to stand for 3 minutes. Stir in the salt, then serve.

Belgian-style Beef in Beer

SERVES 4

Prepare as for Beef Cooked in Red Wine, but substitute strong beer for the wine. Add 15 ml/1 tbsp dark soft brown sugar to the cornflour (cornstarch) mixture and stir in 45 ml/3 tbsp soft white breadcrumbs just before serving.

Braised Beef and Vegetables

SERVES 4

30 ml/2 tbsp butter or margarine, at kitchen temperature
1 large onion, grated
3 carrots, thinly sliced
75 g/3 oz mushrooms, thinly sliced
450 g/1 lb rump (tip) steak, cut into small cubes
1 beef stock cube
15 ml/1 tbsp plain (all-purpose) flour
300 ml/½ pt/1¼ cups hot water or beef stock
Freshly ground black pepper
5 ml/1 tsp salt

Put the butter or margarine into a 20 cm/8 in diameter casserole dish (Dutch oven). Melt on Defrost for 45 seconds. Add the vegetables and steak and mix well. Cook, uncovered, on Full for 3 minutes. Crumble in the stock cube and stir in the flour and hot water or stock. Move the mixture to the edge of the dish to form a ring, leaving a small hollow in the centre. Sprinkle with pepper. Cover with clingfilm (plastic wrap) and slit it twice to allow steam to escape. Cook on Full for 9 minutes, turning the dish once. Allow to stand for 5 minutes, then season with the salt and serve.

Beef Stew

SERVES 4

450 g/1 lb lean stewing steak, cut into small cubes
15 ml/1 tbsp plain (all-purpose) flour
250 g/9 oz unthawed frozen vegetable stewpack
300 ml/½ pt/1¼ cups boiling water
1 beef stock cube
Freshly ground pepper
2.5–5 ml/½–1 tsp salt

Put the steak in a 23 cm/9 in diameter casserole dish (Dutch oven), not too deep. Sprinkle with the flour, then toss well to coat. Spread out loosely into a single layer. Break up the vegetables, then arrange round the meat. Cover with clingfilm (plastic wrap) and slit it twice to allow steam to escape. Cook on Full for 15 minutes, turning the dish four times. Pour the water over the meat and crumble in the stock cube. Season to taste with pepper and stir thoroughly. Cover as before, then cook on Full for 10 minutes, turning the dish three times. Allow to stand for 5 minutes, then stir round, season with the salt and serve.

Beef and Vegetable Hot-pot

SERVES 4

450 g/1 lb potatoes
2 carrots
1 large onion
450 g/1 lb lean stewing steak, cut into small cubes
1 beef stock cube
150 ml/¼ pt/⅔ cup hot beef or vegetable stock
30 ml/2 tbsp butter or margarine

Cut the potatoes, carrots and the onion into transparent wafer-thin slices. Separate the onion slices into rings. Thoroughly grease a 1.75 litre/3 pt/7½ cup dish. Fill with alternate layers of the vegetables and meat, beginning and ending with the potatoes. Cover with clingfilm (plastic wrap) and slit it twice to allow steam to escape. Cook on Full for 15 minutes, turning the dish three times. Crumble the stock cube into the hot stock and stir until dissolved. Pour gently down the side of the dish so it flows through the meat and vegetables. Top with flakes of the butter or margarine. Cover as before and cook on Full for 15 minutes, turning the dish three times. Allow to stand for 5 minutes. Brown under a hot grill (broiler), if liked.

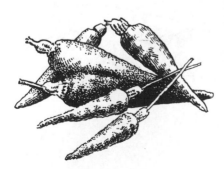

Beef Curry

SERVES 4–5

An Anglicised version of a medium-hot curry. Serve with basmati rice and *sambals* (side dishes) of plain yoghurt, sliced cucumber sprinkled with chopped fresh coriander (cilantro), and chutney.

450 g/1 lb lean stewing beef, cut into small cubes
2 onions, chopped
2 garlic cloves, crushed
15 ml/1 tbsp sunflower or corn oil
30 ml/2 tbsp hot curry powder
30 ml/2 tbsp tomato purée (paste)
15 ml/1 tbsp plain (all-purpose) flour
4 green cardamom pods
15 ml/1 tbsp garam masala
450 ml/¾ pt/2 cups hot water
5 ml/1 tsp salt

Arrange the meat in a single layer in a deep 25 cm/10 in diameter dish. Cover with a plate and cook on Full for 15 minutes, stirring twice. Meanwhile, fry (sauté) the onions and garlic conventionally in the oil in a frying pan (skillet) over a medium heat until pale golden. Stir in the curry powder, tomato purée, flour, cardamom pods and garam masala, then gradually blend in the hot water. Cook, stirring, until the mixture comes to the boil and thickens. Remove the dish of meat from the microwave and stir in the contents of the frying pan. Cover with clingfilm (plastic wrap) and slit it twice to allow steam to escape. Cook on Full for 10 minutes, turning the dish twice. Allow to stand for 5 minutes before serving.

Basic Mince

SERVES 4

450 g/1 lb/4 cups lean minced
    (ground) beef
1 onion, grated
30 ml/2 tbsp plain (all-purpose)
    flour
450 ml/¾ pt/2 cups hot water
1 beef stock cube
5 ml/1 tsp salt

Place the meat in a deep 20 cm/8 in
diameter dish. Thoroughly mix in
the onion and flour with a fork. Cook,
uncovered, on Full for 5 minutes.
Break up the meat with a fork. Add the
water and crumble in the stock cube.
Stir well to mix. Cover with clingfilm
(plastic wrap) and slit it twice to allow
steam to escape. Cook on Full for 15
minutes, turning the dish four times.
Allow to stand for 4 minutes. Add the
salt and stir round before serving.

Cottage Pie

SERVES 4

1 quantity Basic Mince
675 g/1½ lb freshly cooked
    potatoes
30 ml/2 tbsp butter or margarine
60–90 ml/4–6 tbsp hot milk

Cool the Basic Mince to lukewarm
and transfer to a greased 1 litre/
1¾ pt/4¼ cup pie dish. Cream the potatoes with the butter or margarine and
enough of the milk to make a light and
fluffy mash. Pipe over the meat mixture or spread smoothly then rough up
with a fork. Reheat, uncovered, on Full
for 3 minutes. Alternatively, brown
under a hot grill (broiler).

Cottage Pie with Cheese

SERVES 4

Prepare as for Cottage Pie, but add
50–75 g/2–3 oz/½–¾ cup grated
Cheddar cheese to the potatoes after
creaming with the butter and hot milk.

Mince with Oats

SERVES 4

Prepare as for Basic Mince, but add
1 carrot, grated, with the onion.
Substitute 25 g/1 oz/½ cup porridge
oats for the flour. Cook for the first
time for 7 minutes.

Chilli con Carne

SERVES 4–5

450 g/1 lb/4 cups lean minced
    (ground) beef
1 onion, grated
2 garlic cloves, crushed
5–20 ml/1–4 tsp chilli seasoning
400 g/14 oz/1 large can chopped
    tomatoes
5 ml/1 tsp Worcestershire sauce
400 g/14 oz/1 large can red kidney
    beans, drained
5 ml/1 tsp salt
Jacket Potatoes (page 226) or
    boiled rice, to serve

Put the beef into a 23 cm/9 in diameter casserole dish (Dutch oven).
Stir in the onion and garlic with a fork.
Cook, uncovered, on Full for 5 minutes. Break up the meat with a fork.
Work in all the remaining ingredients
except the salt. Cover with clingfilm
(plastic wrap) and slit it twice to allow
steam to escape. Cook on Full for 15
minutes, turning the dish three times.
Allow to stand for 4 minutes. Season
with the salt before serving with
jacket potatoes or boiled rice.

Curried Mince

SERVES 4

2 onions, grated
2 garlic cloves, crushed
450 g/1 lb/4 cups lean minced
  (ground) beef
15 ml/1 tbsp plain (all-purpose)
  flour
5–10 ml/1–2 tbsp mild curry
  powder
30 ml/2 tbsp fruity chutney
60 ml/4 tbsp tomato purée (paste)
300 ml/½ pt/1¼ cups boiling water
1 beef stock cube
Salt and freshly ground black
  pepper

Mash together the onions, garlic and beef. Spread into a 20 cm/ 8 in diameter casserole dish (Dutch oven). Form into a ring round the edge of the dish, leaving small hollow in the centre. Cover with plate and cook on Full for 5 minutes. Break up with fork. Work in the flour, curry powder, chutney and tomato purée. Gradually stir in the water, then crumble in the stock cube. Cover with clingfilm (plastic wrap) and slit it twice to allow steam to escape. Cook on Full for 15 minutes, turning the dish three times. Allow to stand for 4 minutes. Season to taste, then stir round and serve.

Beef Goulash

SERVES 6

40 g/1½ oz/3 tbsp butter,
  margarine or lard
675 g/1½ lb stewing steak, cut
  into small cubes
2 large onions, grated
1 medium green (bell) pepper,
  seeded and finely diced
2 garlic cloves, crushed
4 tomatoes, blanched, skinned and
  chopped
45 ml/3 tbsp tomato purée (paste)
15 ml/1 tbsp paprika
5 ml/1 tsp caraway seeds
5 ml/1 tsp salt
300 ml/½ pt/1¼ cups boiling water
150 ml/¼ pt/⅔ cup soured (dairy
  sour) cream

Put the fat in a 1.75 litre/3 pt/7½ cup dish. Melt, uncovered, on Full for 1 minute. Mix in the meat, onions, peppers and garlic. Cover with clingfilm (plastic wrap) and slit it twice to allow steam to escape. Cook on Full for 15 minutes, turning the dish four times. Uncover and stir in the tomatoes, tomato purée, paprika and caraway seeds. Cover as before and cook on Full for 15 minutes, turning the dish four times. Season with the salt and gently mix in the boiling water. Ladle into deep plates and top each generously with the cream.

Beef Goulash with Boiled Potatoes

SERVES 6

Prepare as for Beef Goulash, but omit the cream and add 2–3 whole boiled potatoes to each serving.

Butter Bean and Beef Stew with Tomatoes

••••••••••••••••••••••••••••••••••
SERVES 6

425 g/15 oz/1 large can butter beans
275 g/10 oz/1 can tomato soup
30 ml/2 tbsp dried onions
6 slices braising steak, about
*   125 g/4 oz each, beaten flat*
Salt and freshly ground black
*   pepper*

Combine the beans, soup and onions in a 20 cm/8 in diameter casserole dish (Dutch oven). Cover with a plate and cook on Full for 6 minutes, stirring three times. Arrange the steaks round the edge of the dish. Cover with clingfilm (plastic wrap) and slit it twice to allow steam to escape. Cook on Full for 17 minutes, turning the dish three times. Allow to stand for 5 minutes. Uncover and season to taste before serving.

Beef and Tomato Cake

••••••••••••••••••••••••••••••••••
SERVES 2–3

275 g/10 oz/2½ cups minced
*   (ground) beef*
30 ml/2 tbsp plain (all-purpose)
*   flour*
1 egg
5 ml/1 tsp onion powder
150 ml/¼ pt/⅔ cup tomato juice
5 ml/1 tsp soy sauce
5 ml/1 tsp dried oregano
Boiled pasta, to serve

Thoroughly grease a 900 ml/1½ pt/ 3¾ cup oval pie dish. Mix the beef with all remaining ingredients and spread smoothly into the dish. Cover with clingfilm (plastic wrap) and slit it twice to allow steam to escape. Cook on Full for 7 minutes, turning the dish twice. Allow to stand for 5 minutes. Cut into two or three portions and serve hot with pasta.

Beef and Mushroom Kebabs

••••••••••••••••••••••••••••••••••
SERVES 4

24 fresh or dried bay leaves
½ red (bell) pepper, cut into small
*   squares*
½ green (bell) pepper, cut into
*   small squares*
750 g/1½ lb grilling (broiling)
*   steak, trimmed and cut into*
*   2.5 cm/1 in cubes*
175 g/6 oz button mushrooms
50 g/2 oz/¼ cup butter or
*   margarine, at kitchen*
*   temperature*
5 ml/1 tsp paprika
5 ml/1 tsp Worcestershire sauce
1 garlic clove, crushed
175 g/6 oz/1½ cups rice, boiled

If using dried bay leaves, place in a small dish, add 90 ml/6 tbsp water and cover with a saucer. Heat on Full for 2 minutes to soften. Put the pepper squares into a dish and just cover with water. Cover with a plate and heat on Full for 1 minute to soften. Drain the peppers and bay leaves. Thread the beef, mushrooms, pepper squares and bay leaves on to twelve 10 cm/4 in wooden skewers. Arrange the kebabs like the spokes of a wheel in a deep 25 cm/10 in diameter dish. Put the butter or margarine, paprika, Worcestershire sauce and garlic in a small dish and heat, uncovered, on Full for 1 minute. Brush over the kebabs. Cook, uncovered, on Full for 8 minutes, turning the dish four times. Carefully turn the kebabs over and brush with the rest of the butter mixture. Cook on Full for a further 4 minutes, turning the dish twice. Arrange on a bed of rice and coat with the juices from the dish. Allow three kebabs per person.

Stuffed Lamb

SERVES 4

A slightly Middle Eastern approach here. Serve the lamb with warm pitta bread and a green salad dotted with olives and capers.

4 pieces neck of lamb fillet, about 15 cm/6 in long and 675 g/½ lb each
3 large slices white bread with crusts, cubed
1 onion, cut into 6 wedges
45 ml/3 tbsp toasted pine nuts (page 205)
30 ml/2 tbsp currants
2.5 ml/½ tsp salt
150 g/5 oz/⅔ cup thick Greek plain yoghurt
Ground cinnamon
8 button mushrooms
15 ml/1 tbsp olive oil

Trim the fat from the lamb. Make a lengthways slit in each piece, taking care not to cut right through the meat. Grind up the bread cubes and onion pieces together in a food processor or blender. Scrape out into a bowl and mix in the pine nuts, currants and salt. Spread equal amounts into the lamb pieces and secure with wooden cocktail sticks (toothpicks). Arrange in a square in a deep 25 cm/ 10 in diameter dish. Smear with all the yoghurt and dust lightly with cinnamon. Stud randomly with the mushrooms and coat thinly with the oil. Cover with clingfilm (plastic wrap) and slit it twice to allow steam to escape. Cook on Full for 16 minutes, turning the dish four times. Allow to stand for 5 minutes, then serve.

Minted Lamb Kebabs

SERVES 6

900 g/2 lb neck of lamb fillet, trimmed
12 large mint leaves
60 ml/4 tbsp thick plain yoghurt
60 ml/4 tbsp tomato ketchup (catsup)
1 garlic clove, crushed
5 ml/1 tsp Worcestershire sauce
6 pitta breads, warmed
Lettuce leaves, tomato and cucumber slices

Cut the meat into 2.5 cm/1 in cubes. Thread on to six wooden skewers alternately with the mint leaves. Arrange like the spokes of a wheel in a deep 25 cm/10 in diameter dish. Thoroughly combine the yoghurt, ketchup, garlic and Worcestershire sauce and brush half the mixture over the kebabs. Cook, uncovered, on Full for 8 minutes, turning the dish twice. Turn the kebabs over and brush with the remaining baste. Cook on Full for a further 8 minutes, turning the dish twice. Allow to stand for 5 minutes. Warm the pitta breads briefly under the grill (broiler) until they puff up, then slice along the long edge to make a pocket. Remove the meat from the skewers and discard the bay leaves. Pack the lamb into the pittas, then add a good helping of the salad to each.

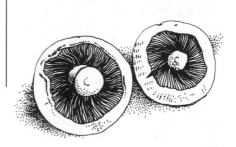

Classic Lamb Kebabs

SERVES 6

900 g/2 lb neck of lamb fillet,
trimmed
12 large mint leaves
30 ml/2 tbsp butter or margarine
5 ml/1 tsp garlic salt
5 ml/1 tsp Worcestershire sauce
5 ml/1 tsp soy sauce
2.5 ml/½ tsp paprika
6 pitta breads, warmed
Lettuce leaves, tomato and
cucumber slices

Cut the meat into 2.5 cm/1 in cubes. Thread on to six wooden skewers alternately with the mint leaves. Arrange like the spokes of a wheel in a deep 25 cm/10 in diameter dish. Melt the butter or margarine on Full for 1 minute, then add the garlic salt, Worcestershire sauce, soy sauce and paprika and mix together thoroughly. Brush half the mixture over the kebabs. Cook, uncovered, on Full for 8 minutes, turning the dish twice. Turn the kebabs over and brush with the remaining baste. Cook on Full for a further 8 minutes, turning the dish twice. Allow to stand for 5 minutes. Warm the pitta breads briefly under the grill (broiler) until they puff up, then slice along the long edge to make a pocket. Remove the meat from the skewers and discard the bay leaves. Pack the lamb into the pittas, then add a good helping of the salad to each.

Middle Eastern Lamb with Fruit

SERVES 4–6

This delicately spiced and fruited lamb dish is understated elegance, enhanced by its coating of toasted pine nuts and flaked almonds. Serve with yoghurt and buttery rice.

675 g/1½ lb boned lamb, as lean
as possible
5 ml/1 tsp ground cinnamon
2.5 ml/½ tsp ground cloves
30 ml/2 tbsp light soft brown
sugar
1 onion, chopped
30 ml/2 tbsp lemon juice
10 ml/2 tsp cornflour (cornstarch)
15 ml/1 tbsp cold water
7.5–10 ml/1½–2 tsp salt
400 g/14 oz/1 large can peach
slices in natural or apple juice,
drained
30 ml/2 tbsp toasted pine nuts
(page 205)
30 ml/2 tbsp flaked (slivered)
almonds

Cut the lamb into small cubes. Place in a 1.75 litre/3 pt/7½ cup casserole dish (Dutch oven). Mix together the spices, sugar, onion and lemon juice and add to the dish. Cover with a plate and cook on Full for 5 minutes, then allow to stand for 5 minutes. Repeat three times, stirring well each time. Mix together the cornflour and water to make a smooth paste. Drain the liquid from the lamb and add the cornflour mixture and salt. Pour over the lamb and stir well to mix. Cook, uncovered, on Full for 2 minutes. Stir in the peach slices and cook, uncovered, on Full for a further 1½ minutes. Sprinkle with the pine nuts and almonds and and serve.

Mock Irish Stew

•••••••••••••••••••••••••••••••••
SERVES 4

675 g/1½ lb cubed stewing lamb
2 large onions, coarsely grated
450 g/1 lb potatoes, finely diced
300 ml/½ pt/1¼ cups boiling water
5 ml/1 tsp salt
45 ml/3 tbsp chopped parsley

Trim away any excess fat from the lamb. Place the meat and vegetables in a single layer in a deep 25 cm/10 in diameter dish. Cover with clingfilm (plastic wrap) and slit it twice to allow steam to escape. Cook on Full for 15 minutes, turning the dish twice. Mix the water and salt and pour over the meat and vegetables, stirring thoroughly to combine. Cover as before and cook on Full for 20 minutes, turning the dish three times. Allow to stand for 10 minutes. Uncover and sprinkle with the parsley before serving.

Farmer's Wife Lamb Chops

•••••••••••••••••••••••••••••••••
SERVES 4

3 cold cooked potatoes, thinly
*   sliced*
3 cold cooked carrots, thinly sliced
4 lean lamb chops, 150 g/5 oz
*   each*
1 small onion, grated
1 cooking (tart) apple, peeled and
*   grated*
30 ml/2 tbsp apple juice
Salt and freshly ground black
*   pepper*
15 ml/1 tbsp butter or margarine

Arrange the potato and carrot slices in a single layer over the base of a deep 20 cm/8 in diameter dish. Arrange the chops on top. Sprinkle with the onion and apple and pour the juice over. Season to taste and dot with flakes of the butter or margarine. Cover with clingfilm (plastic wrap) and slit it twice to allow steam to escape. Cook on Full for 15 minutes, turning the dish twice. Allow to stand for 5 minutes before serving.

Lamb Hot-pot

•••••••••••••••••••••••••••••••••
SERVES 4

675 g/1½ lb potatoes, very thinly
*   sliced*
2 onions, very thinly sliced
3 carrots, very thinly sliced
2 large celery stalks, cut
*   diagonally into thin strips*
8 best end of neck lamb chops,
*   about 1 kg/2 lb in all*
1 beef stock cube
300 ml/½ pt/1¼ cups boiling water
5 ml/1 tsp salt
25 ml/1½ tbsp melted butter or
*   margarine*

Arrange half the prepared vegetables in layers in a lightly greased 2.25 litre/4 pt/10 cup casserole dish (Dutch oven). Place the chops on top and cover with the remaining vegetables. Cover with clingfilm (plastic wrap) and slit it twice to allow steam to escape. Cook on Full for 15 minutes, turning the dish three times. Remove from the microwave and uncover. Crumble the stock cube into the water and add the salt. Pour gently down the side of the casserole. Trickle the butter or margarine over the top. Cover as before and cook on Full for 15 minutes. Allow to stand for 6 minutes before serving.

Lamb Loaf with Mint and Rosemary

SERVES 4

450 g/1 lb/4 cups minced (ground) lamb
1 garlic clove, crushed
2.5 ml/½ tsp dried crumbled rosemary
2.5 ml/½ tsp dried mint
30 ml/2 tbsp plain (all-purpose) flour
2 large eggs, beaten
2.5 ml/½ tsp salt
5 ml/1 tsp brown table sauce
Grated nutmeg

Lightly grease a 900 ml/1½ pt/3¾ cup oval pie dish. Mix together all the ingredients except the nutmeg and spread smoothly into the dish. Cover with clingfilm (plastic wrap) and slit it twice to allow steam to escape. Cook on Full for 8 minutes, turning the dish twice. Allow to stand for 4 minutes, then uncover and sprinkle with nutmeg. Cut into portions to serve.

Lamb Bredie with Tomatoes

SERVES 6

Prepare as for Chicken Bredie with Tomatoes (page 137), but substitute boned and coarsely chopped lamb for the chicken.

Lamb Biriani

SERVES 4–6

5 cardamom pods
30 ml/2 tbsp sunflower oil
450 g/1 lb trimmed neck of lamb fillet, cut into small cubes
2 garlic cloves, crushed
20 ml/4 tsp garam masala
225 g/8 oz/1¼ cups easy-cook long-grain rice
600 ml/1 pt/2½ cups hot chicken stock
10 ml/2 tsp salt
125 g/4 oz/1 cup flaked (slivered) almonds, toasted (page 205)

Split the cardamom pods to remove the seeds, then crush the seeds with a pestle and mortar. Heat the oil in a 1.5 litre/3 pt/7½ cup casserole dish (Dutch oven) on Full for 1½ minutes. Add the lamb, garlic, cardamom seeds and garam masala. Mix well, then arrange round the edge of the dish, leaving a small hollow in the centre. Cover with clingfilm (plastic wrap) and slit it twice to allow steam to escape. Cook on Full for 10 minutes. Uncover and mix in the rice, stock and salt. Cover as before and cook on Full for 15 minutes. Allow to stand for 3 minutes, then spoon out on to warmed plates and sprinkle each portion with the almonds.

Ornate Biriani

SERVES 4–6

Prepare as for Lamb Biriani, but arrange the biriani on a warmed serving dish and garnish with chopped hard-boiled (hard-cooked) eggs (page 98–9), tomato wedges, coriander (cilantro) leaves and fried (sautéed) chopped onion.

Moussaka
••••••••••••••••••••••••••••••••••
SERVES 6–8

You require a little patience to prepare this multi-layered lamb-based Greek classic but the results are well worth the effort. Poached aubergine (eggplant) slices makes this less rich and easier to digest than some versions.

For the aubergine layers:
675 g/1½ lb aubergines
75 ml/5 tbsp hot water
5 ml/1 tsp salt
15 ml/1 tbsp fresh lemon juice
For the meat layers:
40 g/1½ oz/3 tbsp butter,
margarine or olive oil
2 onions, finely chopped
1 garlic clove, crushed
350 g/12 oz/3 cups cold cooked
minced (ground) lamb
125 g/4 oz/2 cups fresh white
breadcrumbs
Salt and freshly ground black
pepper
4 tomatoes, blanched, skinned and
sliced
For the sauce:
425 ml/¾ pt/scant 2 cups full-
cream milk
40 g/1½ oz/3 tbsp butter or
margarine
45 ml/3 tbsp plain (all-purpose)
flour
75 g/3 oz/¾ cup Cheddar cheese,
grated
1 egg yolk
Salt and freshly ground black
pepper

To make the aubergine layer, wash and dry the aubergines, top and tail them, then slice thinly. Transfer to a large bowl and add the water, salt and lemon juice. Cover with clingfilm (plastic wrap) and slit it twice to allow steam to escape. Cook on Full for 12

minutes. Remove from the microwave and allow to stand for 20 minutes, then drain thoroughly.

To make the meat layer, put the butter, margarine or oil into a deep 2.25 litre/4 pt/10 cup dish. Heat, uncovered, on Full for 1 minute. Stir in the onions and garlic. Cook, uncovered, on Full for 3 minutes. Add the meat and breadcrumbs and stir in gently with a fork. Season to taste. Brush a deep 25 cm/10 in diameter dish with a little oil. Fill with alternate layers of aubergine slices and the meat mixture. Cover with the tomato slices.

To make the sauce, warm the milk and butter or margarine in a jug on Full for 4–4½ minutes. Put the flour into a medium-sized basin and gradually stir in the warm milk and butter mixture. Cook, uncovered, on Full for 4–5 minutes until thickened and bubbling, whisking every minute to ensure smoothness. Mix in the cheese and egg yolk and season to taste. Spoon over the tomatoes. Cover with clingfilm and slit it twice to allow steam to escape. Cook on Full for 12 minutes, turning the dish four times. Allow to stand for 8 minutes before serving.

Moussaka with Potatoes
••••••••••••••••••••••••••••••••••
SERVES 6–8

Prepare as for Moussaka, but substitute sliced cooked potatoes for the aubergines (eggplants).

Quick Moussaka

SERVES 3–4

A quick alternative with an acceptable flavour and texture.

*1 aubergine (eggplant), about
    225 g/8 oz
15 ml/1 tbsp cold water
300 ml/½ pt/1¼ cups cold milk
300 ml/½ pt/1¼ cups water
1 packet instant mashed potato to
    serve 4
225 g/8 oz/2 cups cold cooked
    minced (ground) lamb
5 ml/1 tsp dried marjoram
5 ml/1 tsp salt
2 garlic cloves, crushed
3 tomatoes, blanched, skinned and
    sliced
150 ml/¼ pt/⅔ cup thick Greek
    plain yoghurt
1 egg
Salt and freshly ground black
    pepper
50 g/2 oz/½ cup Cheddar cheese,
    grated*

Top and tail the aubergine and halve it lengthways. Place in a shallow dish, cut sides uppermost and sprinkle with the cold water. Cover with clingfilm (plastic wrap) and slit it twice to allow steam to escape. Cook on Full for 5½–6 minutes until tender. Allow to stand for 2 minutes, then drain. Pour the milk and water into a bowl and stir in the dried potato. Cover with a plate and cook on Full for 6 minutes. Stir well, then mix in the lamb, marjoram, salt and garlic. Slice the unpeeled aubergine. Arrange alternate layers of aubergine slices and the potato mixture in a 2.25 litre/4 pt/10 cup greased casserole dish (Dutch oven), using half the tomato slices to form a 'sandwich filling' in the centre. Cover with the remaining tomato slices. Beat together the yoghurt and egg and season to taste. Spoon over the tomatoes and sprinkle with the cheese. Cover with clingfilm as before. Cook on Full for 7 minutes. Uncover and brown under a hot grill (broiler) before serving.

Lamb Mince

SERVES 4

Prepare as for Basic Mince (page 183), but substitute minced (ground) lamb for the minced beef.

Shepherd's Pie

SERVES 4

Prepare as for Basic Mince (page 183), but substitute lamb mince for beef. Cool to lukewarm, then transfer to a 1 litre/1¾ pt/4½ cup greased pie dish. Top with 750 g/1½ lb hot mashed potato creamed with 15–30 ml/1–2 tbsp butter or margarine and 60 ml/4 tbsp hot milk. Season well with salt and freshly ground black pepper. Spread over the meat mixture, then rough up with a fork. Reheat, uncovered, on Full for 2–3 minutes or brown under a hot grill (broiler).

191

Country Liver in Red Wine

SERVES 4

25 g/1 oz/2 tbsp butter or
  margarine
2 onions, grated
450 g/1 lb lambs' liver, cut into
  narrow strips
15 ml/1 tbsp plain (all-purpose)
  flour
300 ml/½ pt/1¼ cups red wine
15 ml/1 tbsp dark soft brown
  sugar
1 beef stock cube, crumbled
30 ml/2 tbsp chopped parsley
Salt and freshly ground black
  pepper
Buttered boiled potatoes and
  lightly cooked shredded
  cabbage, to serve

Put the butter or margarine in a
deep 25 cm/10 in diameter dish.
Melt, uncovered, on Defrost for 2 minutes. Stir in the onions and liver. Cover
with a plate and cook on Full for 5
minutes. Mix in all the remaining
ingredients except the salt and pepper.
Cover with a plate and cook on Full
for 6 minutes, stirring twice. Allow
to stand for 3 minutes. Season to taste
and serve with buttered boiled potatoes and cabbage.

Liver and Bacon

SERVES 4–6

2 onions, grated
8 bacon rashers (slices), coarsely
  chopped
450 g/1 lb lambs' liver, cut into
  small cubes
45 ml/3 tbsp cornflour
  (cornstarch)
60 ml/4 tbsp cold water
150 ml/¼ pt/⅔ cup boiling water
Salt and freshly ground black
  pepper

Put the onions and bacon in a
1.75 litre/3 pt/7½ cup casserole dish
(Dutch oven). Cook, uncovered, on
Full for 7 minutes, stirring twice. Mix
in the liver. Cover with a plate and
cook on Full for 8 minutes, stirring
three times. Mix the cornflour with the
cold water to make a smooth paste.
Stir into the liver and onions, then
gradually blend in the boiling water.
Cover with a plate and cook on Full for
6 minutes, stirring three times. Allow
to stand for 4 minutes. Season to taste
and serve.

Liver and Bacon with Apple

SERVES 4–6

Prepare as for Liver and Bacon, but
substitute 1 eating (dessert) apple,
peeled and grated, for one of the
onions. Substitute apple juice at room
temperature for half the boiling water.

Kidneys in Red Wine with Brandy

SERVES 4

6 lambs' kidneys
30 ml/2 tbsp butter or margarine
1 onion, finely chopped
30 ml/2 tbsp plain (all-purpose)
    flour
150 ml/¼ pt/⅔ cup dry red wine
2 beef stock cubes
50 g/2 oz mushrooms, sliced
10 ml/2 tsp tomato purée (paste)
2.5 ml/½ tsp paprika
2.5 ml/½ tsp mustard powder
30 ml/2 tbsp chopped parsley
30 ml/2 tbsp brandy

Skin and halve the kidneys, then cut out and discard the cores with a sharp knife. Slice very thinly. Melt half the butter, uncovered, on Defrost for 1 minute. Stir in the kidneys and set aside. Put the remaining butter and the onion in a 1.5 litre/2½ pt/6 cup dish. Cook, uncovered, on Full for 2 minutes, stirring once. Mix in the flour, then the wine. Cook, uncovered, on Full for 3 minutes, stirring briskly every minute. Crumble in the stock cubes, then stir in the mushrooms, tomato purée, paprika, mustard and the kidneys with the butter or margarine. Mix thoroughly. Cover with clingfilm (plastic wrap) and slit it twice to allow steam to escape. Cook on Full for 5 minutes, turning the dish once. Allow to stand for 3 minutes, then uncover and sprinkle with the parsley. Warm the brandy in a cup on Full for 10–15 seconds. Pour over the kidney mixture and ignite. Serve when the flames have subsided.

Venison Steaks with Oyster Mushrooms and Blue Cheese

SERVES 4

Salt and freshly ground black
    pepper
8 small venison steaks
5 ml/1 tsp juniper berries, crushed
5 ml/1 tsp herbes de Provence
30 ml/2 tbsp olive oil
300 ml/½ pt/1¼ cups dry red wine
60 ml/4 tbsp rich beef stock
60 ml/4 tbsp gin
1 onion, chopped
225 g/8 oz oyster mushrooms,
    trimmed and sliced
250 ml/8 fl oz/1 cup single (light)
    cream
30 ml/2 tbsp redcurrant jelly
    (clear conserve)
60 ml/4 tbsp blue cheese,
    crumbled
30 ml/2 tbsp chopped parsley

Season the venison to taste, then work in the juniper berries and herbes de Provence. Heat the oil in a browning dish on Full for 2 minutes. Add the steaks and cook, uncovered, on Full for 3 minutes, turning once. Add the wine, stock, gin, onion, mushrooms, cream and redcurrant jelly. Cover with clingfilm (plastic wrap) and slit it twice to allow steam to escape. Cook on Medium for 25 minutes, turning the dish four times. Mix in the cheese. Cover with a heatproof plate and cook on Full for 2 minutes. Allow to stand for 3 minutes, then uncover and serve garnished with the parsley.

Pasta and Pizza

If you are looking at pasta, you have my assurance that the microwave treats it with the respect it deserves and gives you ample opportunity to try out some delicious combinations, from old favourites like Spaghetti Bolognese and Lasagne to new ideas like Pasta Matriciana. The pizzas included are made from real dough – moist, juicy and tender.

Quantity

Allow 75–100 g/3–4 oz per person if the pasta is to be eaten as a main course. Halve this weight for a starter. For small pasta, usually eaten in soup, allow about 25 g/1 oz for every two people.

Cooking Large Pasta

The following technique is highly successful for long pasta, such as macaroni, spaghetti and wide noodles, and any other large pasta, regardless of shape. Put the amount of pasta required into a sufficiently large and roomy bowl. Add salt to taste or as recommended on the packet and a tiny splash of oil. Add enough boiling water to come 5 cm/2 in above the level of the pasta. Stir round. Cook, uncovered, on Full for about 10 minutes for dried pasta and 5–6 minutes for fresh or until the pasta is tender but still *al dente* - a little bit firm to the bite. Cover with a plate and stand inside the microwave for 3–4 minutes for dried and 2–3 minutes for fresh pasta. Drain and serve.

Cooking Small Pasta

Follow the directions for cooking large pasta but cook for only 4–5 minutes. Cover and stand for 3 minutes, then drain and serve.

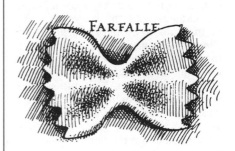

FARFALLE

Chinese Noodle and Mushroom Salad with Walnuts

SERVES 6

30 ml/2 tbsp sesame oil
175 g/6 oz mushrooms, sliced
250 g/9 oz thread egg noodles
7.5 ml/1½ tsp salt
75 g/3 oz/¾ cup chopped walnuts
5 spring onions (scallions),
*   chopped*
30 ml/2 tbsp soy sauce

Heat the oil, uncovered, on Defrost for 2½ minutes. Add the mushrooms. Cover with a plate and cook on Full for 3 minutes, stirring twice. Set aside. Put the noodles in a large bowl and add enough boiling water to come 5 cm/2 in above the level of the pasta. Stir in the salt. Cook, uncovered, on Full for 4–5 minutes until the noodles swell and are just tender. Drain and allow to cool. Mix in the remaining ingredients including the mushrooms and toss well to mix.

Pepper Macaroni

SERVES 2

300 ml/½ pt/1¼ cups tomato juice
125 g/4 oz/1 cup elbow macaroni
5 ml/1 tsp salt
30 ml/2 tbsp white wine, heated
1 small red or green (bell) pepper,
*   seeded and chopped*
45 ml/3 tbsp olive oil
75 g/3 oz/¾ cup Gruyère (Swiss) or
*   Emmental cheese, grated*
30 ml/2 tbsp chopped parsley

Pour the tomato juice into a 1.25 litre/2¼ pt/5½ cup dish. Cover with a plate and heat on Full for 3½–4 minutes until very hot and bubbling. Stir in all the remaining ingredients except the cheese and parsley. Cover as before and cook on Full for 10 minutes, stirring twice. Allow to stand for 5 minutes. Sprinkle with the cheese and parsley. Reheat, uncovered, on Full for about 1 minute until the cheese melts.

Family Macaroni Cheese

SERVES 6–7

For convenience, this recipe is for a large family-sized meal, but any leftovers can be reheated in portions in the microwave.

350 g/12 oz/3 cups elbow macaroni
10 ml/2 tsp salt
30 ml/2 tbsp cornflour (cornstarch)
600 ml/1 pt/2½ cups cold milk
1 egg, beaten
10 ml/2 tsp made mustard
Freshly ground black pepper
275 g/10 oz/2½ cups Cheddar cheese, grated

Put the macaroni in a deep dish. Stir in the salt and sufficient boiling water to come 5 cm/2 in above the level of the pasta. Cook, uncovered, on Full for about 10 minutes until just tender, stirring three times. Drain if necessary, then leave to stand while preparing the sauce. In a separate large bowl, mix the cornflour smoothly with some of the cold milk, then mix in the remainder. Cook, uncovered, on Full for 6–7 minutes until smoothly thickened, whisking every minute. Mix in the egg, mustard and pepper followed by two-thirds of the cheese and all the macaroni. Mix thoroughly with a fork. Spread evenly into a buttered 30 cm/12 in diameter dish. Sprinkle the remaining cheese over the top. Reheat, uncovered, on Full for 4–5 minutes. If liked, brown quickly under a hot grill (broiler) before serving.

Classic Macaroni Cheese

SERVES 4–5

This version is slightly richer than Family Macaroni Cheese and lends itself to a number of variations.

225 g/8 oz/2 cups elbow macaroni
7.5 ml/1½ tsp salt
30 ml/2 tbsp butter or margarine
30 ml/2 tbsp plain (all-purpose) flour
300 ml/½ pt/1¼ cups milk
225 g/8 oz/2 cups Cheddar cheese, grated
5–10 ml/1–2 tsp made mustard
Salt and freshly ground black pepper

Put the macaroni in a deep dish. Stir in the salt and sufficient boiling water to come 5 cm/2 in above the level of the pasta. Cook, uncovered, on Full for 8–10 minutes until just tender, stirring two or three times. Stand for 3–4 minutes inside the microwave. Drain if necessary, then leave to stand while preparing the sauce. Melt the butter or margarine, uncovered, on Defrost for 1–1½ minutes. Stir in the flour, then gradually blend in the milk. Cook, uncovered, on Full for 6–7 minutes until smoothly thickened, whisking every minute. Mix in two-thirds of the cheese, followed by the mustard and seasoning, then the macaroni. Spread evenly in a 20 cm/8 in diameter dish. Sprinkle with the remaining cheese. Reheat, uncovered, on Full for 3–4 minutes. If liked, brown quickly under a hot grill (broiler) before serving.

Macaroni Cheese with Stilton

SERVES 4–5

Prepare as for Classic Macaroni Cheese, but substitute 100 g/3½ oz/ 1 cup crumbled Stilton for half the Cheddar cheese.

Macaroni Cheese with Bacon

SERVES 4–5

Prepare as for Classic Macaroni Cheese, but stir in 6 rashers (slices) streaky bacon, grilled (broiled) until crisp then crumbled, with the mustard and seasoning.

Macaroni Cheese with Tomatoes

SERVES 4–5

Prepare as for Classic Macaroni Cheese, but place a layer of tomato slices from about 3 skinned tomatoes on top of the pasta before sprinkling with the remaining cheese.

Spaghetti Carbonara

SERVES 4

75 ml/5 tbsp double (heavy) cream
2 large eggs
100 g/4 oz/1 cup Parma ham, chopped
175 g/6 oz/1½ cups grated Parmesan cheese
350 g/12 oz spaghetti or other large pasta

Beat together the cream and eggs. Stir in the ham and 90 ml/6 tbsp of the Parmesan. Cook the spaghetti as directed (page 194). Drain and place in a serving dish. Add the cream mixture and toss all together with two wooden forks or spoons. Cover with kitchen paper and reheat on Full for 1½ minutes. Serve each portion topped with the remaining Parmesan.

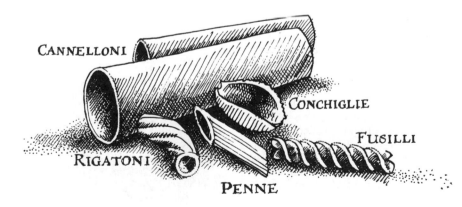

CANNELLONI

CONCHIGLIE

FUSILLI

RIGATONI

PENNE

Pizza-style Macaroni Cheese

•••••••••••••••••••••••••••••••••••
SERVES 4-5

225 g/8 oz/2 cups elbow macaroni
7.5 ml/1½ tsp salt
30 ml/2 tbsp butter or margarine
30 ml/2 tbsp plain (all-purpose) flour
300 ml/½ pt/1¼ cups milk
125 g/4 oz/1 cup Cheddar cheese, grated
125 g/4 oz/1 cup Mozzarella cheese, grated
5–10 ml/1–2 tsp made mustard
Salt and freshly ground black pepper
212 g/7 oz/1 small can tuna in oil, drained and oil reserved
12 stoned (pitted) black olives, sliced
1 canned pimiento, sliced
2 tomatoes, blanched, skinned and coarsely chopped
5–10 ml/1–2 tsp red or green pesto (optional)
Basil leaves, to garnish

Put the macaroni in a deep dish. Stir in the salt and sufficient boiling water to come 5 cm/2 in above the level of the pasta. Cook, uncovered, on Full for 8–10 minutes until just tender, stirring two or three times. Stand for 3–4 minutes inside the microwave. Drain if necessary, then leave to stand while preparing the sauce. Melt the butter or margarine, uncovered, on Defrost for 1–1½ minutes. Stir in the flour, then gradually blend in the milk. Cook, uncovered, on Full for 6–7 minutes until smoothly thickened, whisking every minute. Mix in two-thirds of each cheese, followed by the mustard and seasoning. Stir in the macaroni, tuna, 15 ml/1 tbsp of the tuna oil, the olives, pimiento, tomatoes and pesto, if using. Spread evenly in a 20 cm/8 in diameter dish. Sprinkle with the remaining cheeses. Reheat, uncovered, on Full for 3–4 minutes. If liked, brown quickly under a hot grill (broiler) before serving garnished with basil leaves.

Spaghetti Cream with Spring Onions

•••••••••••••••••••••••••••••••••••
SERVES 4

150 ml/¼ pt/⅔ cup double (heavy) cream
1 egg yolk
150 g/5 oz/1¼ cups grated Parmesan cheese
8 spring onions (scallions), finely chopped
Salt and freshly ground black pepper
350 g/12 oz spaghetti or other large pasta

Beat together the cream, egg yolk, 45 ml/3 tbsp of the Parmesan and the spring onions. Season well to taste. Cook the spaghetti as directed (page 195). Drain and place in a serving dish. Add the cream mixture and toss all together with two wooden forks or spoons. Cover with kitchen paper and reheat on Full for 1½ minutes. Offer the remaining Parmesan cheese separately.

Spaghetti Bolognese

SERVES 4–6

*450 g/1 lb/4 cups lean minced
(ground) beef*
1 garlic clove, crushed
1 large onion, grated
*1 green (bell) pepper, seeded and
finely chopped*
*5 ml/1 tsp Italian seasoning or
dried mixed herbs*
*400 g/14 oz/1 large can chopped
tomatoes*
45 ml/3 tbsp tomato purée (paste)
1 beef stock cube
75 ml/5 tbsp red wine or water
*15 ml/1 tbsp dark soft brown
sugar*
5 ml/1 tsp salt
Freshly ground black pepper
*350 g/12 oz freshly cooked and
drained spaghetti or other pasta
(page 195)*
Grated Parmesan cheese

Combine the beef with the garlic in a
1.75 litre/3 pt/7½ cup dish. Cook,
uncovered, on Full for 5 minutes. Mix
in all the remaining ingredients except
the salt, pepper and spaghetti. Cover
with a plate and cook on Full for 15
minutes, stirring four times with a fork
to break up the meat. Allow to stand
for 4 minutes. Season with the salt and
pepper to taste and serve with the
spaghetti. Offer the Parmesan cheese
separately.

Spaghetti with Turkey Bolognese Sauce

SERVES 4

Prepare as for Spaghetti Bolognese,
but substitute minced (ground)
turkey for the beef.

Spaghetti with Ragu Sauce

SERVES 4

A traditional and economical sauce,
first used in England in Soho trattorias
shortly after World War Two.

20 ml/4 tsp olive oil
1 large onion, finely chopped
1 garlic clove, crushed
1 small carrot, grated
*250 g/8 oz/2 cups lean minced
(ground) beef*
*10 ml/2 tsp plain (all-purpose)
flour*
15 ml/1 tbsp tomato purée (paste)
300 ml/½ pt/1¼ cups beef stock
45 ml/3 tbsp dry white wine
1.5 ml/¼ tsp dried basil
1 small bay leaf
*175 g/6 oz mushrooms, coarsely
chopped*
*Salt and freshly ground black
pepper*
*350 g/12 oz freshly cooked and
drained spaghetti or other pasta
(page 195)*
Grated Parmesan cheese

Place the oil, onion, garlic and carrot
in a 1.75 litre/3 pt/7½ cup dish.
Heat, uncovered, on Full for 6 minutes.
Add all the remaining ingredients
except the salt, pepper and spaghetti.
Cover with a plate and cook on Full for
11 minutes, stirring three times. Allow
to stand for 4 minutes. Season with
salt and pepper, remove the bay leaf
and serve with the spaghetti. Offer the
Parmesan cheese separately.

Spaghetti with Butter

SERVES 4

350 g/12 oz pasta
60 ml/4 tbsp butter or olive oil
Grated Parmesan cheese

Cook the pasta as directed (page 195). Drain and place in a large dish with the butter or olive oil. Toss with two spoons until the pasta is well coated. Spoon on to four warmed plates and heap grated Parmesan cheese on each.

Pasta with Garlic

SERVES 4

350 g/12 oz pasta
2 cloves garlic, crushed
50 g/2 oz butter
10 ml/2 tsp olive oil
30 ml/2 tbsp chopped parsley
Grated Parmesan cheese
Rocket or radicchio leaves,
*   shredded*

Cook the pasta as directed (page 195). Heat the garlic, butter and oil on Full for 1½ minutes. Stir in the parsley. Drain the pasta and place in a serving dish. Add the garlic mixture and toss all together with two wooden spoons. Serve straight away sprinkled with Parmesan and garnished with shredded rocket or radicchio leaves.

Spaghetti with Beef and Mixed Vegetable Bolognese Sauce

SERVES 4

30 ml/2 tbsp olive oil
1 large onion, finely chopped
2 garlic cloves, crushed
4 rashers (slices) streaky bacon,
*   chopped*
1 celery stalk, chopped
1 carrot, grated
125 g/4 oz button mushrooms,
*   thinly sliced*
225 g/8 oz/2 cups lean minced
*   (ground) beef*
30 ml/2 tbsp plain (all-purpose)
*   flour*
1 wine glass dry red wine
150 ml/¼ pt/⅔ cup passata (sieved
*   tomatoes)*
60 ml/4 tbsp beef stock
2 large tomatoes, blanched,
*   skinned and chopped*
15 ml/1 tbsp dark soft brown
*   sugar*
1.5 ml/¼ tsp grated nutmeg
15 ml/1 tbsp chopped basil leaves
Salt and freshly ground black
*   pepper*
350 g/12 oz freshly cooked and
*   drained spaghetti (page 195)*
Grated Parmesan cheese

Put the oil, onion, garlic, bacon, celery and carrot in a 2 litre/3½ pt/8½ cup dish. Add the mushrooms and meat. Cook, uncovered, on Full for 6 minutes, stirring twice with a fork to break up the meat. Mix in all the remaining ingredients except the salt, pepper and spaghetti. Cover with a plate and cook on Full for 13–15 minutes, stirring three times. Allow to stand for 4 minutes. Season with salt and pepper and serve with the pasta. Offer the Parmesan cheese separately.

Spaghetti with Meat Sauce and Cream

SERVES 4

Prepare as for Spaghetti with Beef and Mixed Vegetable Bolognese Sauce, but stir in 30–45 ml/2–3 tbsp double (heavy) cream at the end.

Spaghetti with Marsala Meat Sauce

SERVES 4

Prepare as for Spaghetti with Beef and Mixed Vegetable Bolognese Sauce, but substitute marsala for the wine and add 45 ml/3 tbsp Marscapone cheese at the end.

Pasta alla Marinara

SERVES 4

This means 'sailor style' and comes from Naples.

30 ml/2 tbsp olive oil
3–4 garlic cloves, crushed
8 large tomatoes, blanched, skinned and chopped
5 ml/1 tsp finely chopped mint
15 ml/1 tbsp finely chopped basil leaves
Salt and freshly ground black pepper
350 g/12 oz freshly cooked and drained pasta (page 195)
Grated Pecorino or Parmesan cheese, to serve

Put all the ingredients except the pasta in a 1.25 litre/2¼ pt/5½ cup dish. Cover with a plate and cook on Full for 6–7 minutes, stirring three times. Serve with the pasta and offer the Pecorino or Parmesan cheese separately.

Pasta Matriciana

SERVES 4

A rustic pasta sauce from the central Abruzzo region in Italy.

30 ml/2 tbsp olive oil
1 onion, chopped
5 rashers (slices) unsmoked streaky bacon, coarsely chopped
8 tomatoes, blanched, skinned and chopped
2–3 garlic cloves, crushed
350 g/12 oz freshly cooked and drained pasta (page 195)
Grated Pecorino or Parmesan cheese, to serve

Put all the ingredients except the pasta in a 1.25 litre/2¼ pt/5½ cup dish. Cover with a plate and cook on Full for 6 minutes, stirring twice. Serve with the pasta and offer the Pecorino or Parmesan cheese separately.

Pasta with Tuna and Capers

SERVES 4

15 ml/1 tbsp butter
200 g/7 oz/1 small can tuna in oil
60 ml/4 tbsp vegetable stock or white wine
15 ml/1 tbsp capers, chopped
30 ml/2 tbsp chopped parsley
350 g/12 oz freshly cooked and drained pasta (page 195)
Grated Parmesan cheese

Put the butter in a 600 ml/1 pt/ 2½ cup dish and melt, uncovered, on Defrost for 1½ minutes. Add the contents of the can of tuna and flake the fish. Stir in the stock or wine, capers and parsley. Cover with a plate and heat on Full for 3–4 minutes. Serve with the pasta and offer the Parmesan cheese separately.

Pasta Napoletana

SERVES 4

This flamboyant tomato sauce from Naples, with a warm and colourful flavour, is best made in summer when tomatoes are at their most abundant.

8 large ripe tomatoes, blanched, skinned and coarsely chopped
30 ml/2 tbsp olive oil
1 onion, chopped
2–4 garlic cloves, crushed
1 celery stalk, finely chopped
15 ml/1 tbsp chopped basil leaves
10 ml/2 tsp light soft brown sugar
60 ml/4 tbsp water or red wine
Salt and freshly ground black pepper
30 ml/2 tbsp chopped parsley
350 g/12 oz freshly cooked and drained pasta (page 195)
Grated Parmesan cheese

Put the tomatoes, oil, onion, garlic, celery, basil, sugar and water or wine in a 1.25 litre/2¼ pt/5½ cup dish. Mix well. Cover with a plate and cook on Full for 7 minutes, stirring twice. Season to taste, then stir in the parsley. Serve straight away with the pasta and offer the Parmesan cheese separately.

Pasta Pizzaiola

SERVES 4

Prepare as for Pasta Napoletana, but increase the tomatoes to 10, omit the onion, celery and water and use double the amount of parsley. Add 15 ml/1 tbsp fresh or 2.5 ml/½ tsp dried oregano with the parsley.

Pasta with Peas

SERVES 4

Prepare as for Pasta Napoletana, but add 125 g/4 oz/1 cup coarsely chopped ham and 175 g/6 oz/1½ cups fresh peas to the tomatoes with the other ingredients. Cook for 9–10 minutes.

Pasta with Chicken Liver Sauce

SERVES 4

225 g/8 oz chicken livers
30 ml/2 tbsp plain (all-purpose) flour
15 ml/1 tbsp butter
15 ml/1 tbsp olive oil
1–2 garlic cloves, crushed
125 g/4 oz mushrooms, sliced
150 ml/¼ pt/⅔ cup hot water
150 ml/¼ pt/⅔ cup dry red wine
Salt and freshly ground black pepper
350 g/12 oz pasta, freshly cooked and drained
Grated Parmesan cheese

Cut the livers into small pieces and coat with the flour. Put the butter, oil and garlic in a 1.25 litre/2¼ pt/ 5½ cup dish. Heat, uncovered, on Full for 1 minute. Add the mushrooms. Cover with a plate and cook on Full for 4 minutes, stirring twice. Mix in the livers, hot water and wine. Season to taste. Cover as before and cook on Full for 4–5 minutes, stirring twice. Toss with the pasta and serve with Parmesan offered separately.

Pasta with Anchovies

SERVES 4

30 ml/2 tbsp olive oil
15 ml/1 tbsp butter
2 garlic cloves, crushed
50 g/2 oz/1 small can anchovy
  fillets in oil
45 ml/3 tbsp chopped parsley
2.5 ml/½ tsp dried basil
Freshly ground black pepper
350 g/12 oz freshly cooked and
  drained pasta (page 195)

Put the oil, butter and garlic in a 600 ml/1 pt/2½ cup dish. Chop the anchovies and add with the oil from the can. Mix in the parsley, basil and pepper to taste. Cover with a plate and cook on Full for 3–3½ minutes. Serve straight away with the pasta.

Ravioli with Sauce

SERVES 4

350 g/12 oz/3 cups ravioli

Cook as for large pasta (page 195), then serve with any of the tomato-based pasta sauces above.

Tortellini

SERVES 4

Allow about 250 g/9 oz bought tortellini and cook as for large fresh or dried pasta (page 195). Drain thoroughly, add 25 g/1 oz/2 tbsp unsalted (sweet) butter and toss thoroughly. Serve each portion dusted with grated Parmesan cheese.

Lasagne

SERVES 4–6

45 ml/3 tbsp hot water
Spaghetti Bolognese sauce (page
  199)
9–10 sheets no-need-to-precook
  plain, green (verdi) or brown
  (wholewheat) lasagne
Cheese Sauce (page 317)
25 g/1 oz/¼ cup grated Parmesan
  cheese
30 ml/2 tbsp butter
Grated nutmeg

Oil or butter a 20 cm/8 in square dish. Add the hot water to the Bolognese sauce. Place a layer of lasagne sheets in the bottom of the dish, then a layer of Bolognese sauce, then a layer of cheese sauce. Continue with the layers, finishing with the cheese sauce. Sprinkle with the Parmesan cheese, dot with the butter and dust with nutmeg. Cook, uncovered, for 15 minutes, turning the dish twice. Allow to stand for 5 minutes, then continue to cook for a further 15 minutes or until the lasagne feels soft when a knife is pushed through the centre. (The cooking time will vary depending on the initial temperature of the two sauces.)

Pizza Napoletana

MAKES 4

The microwave does a great job on pizzas, reminiscent of the ones you can find all over Italy and in Naples in particular.

30 ml/2 tbsp olive oil
2 onions, peeled and finely chopped
1 garlic clove, crushed
150 g/5 oz/⅔ cup tomato purée (paste)
Basic White or Brown Bread Dough (page 278)
350 g/12 oz/3 cups Mozzarella cheese, grated
10 ml/2 tsp dried oregano
50 g/2 oz/1 small can anchovy fillets in oil

Cook the oil, onions and garlic, uncovered, on Full for 5 minutes, stirring twice. Mix in the tomato purée and set aside. Divide the dough equally into four pieces. Roll each into a round large enough to cover an oiled and floured 20 cm/8 in flat plate. Cover with kitchen paper and leave to stand for 30 minutes. Spread each with the tomato mixture. Mix the cheese with the oregano and sprinkle equally over each pizza. Garnish with the anchovies. Bake individually, covered with kitchen paper, on Full for 5 minutes, turning twice. Eat straight away.

Pizza Margherita

MAKES 4

Prepare as for Pizza Napoletana, but substitute dried basil for the oregano and omit the anchovies.

Seafood Pizza

MAKES 4

Prepare as for Pizza Napoletana. When cooked, stud with prawns (shrimp), mussels, clams etc.

Pizza Siciliana

MAKES 4

Prepare as for Pizza Napoletana. When cooked, stud with 18 small black olives between the anchovies.

Mushroom Pizza

MAKES 4

Prepare as for Pizza Napoletana, but sprinkle 100 g/3½ oz thinly sliced mushrooms over the tomato mixture before adding the cheese and herbs. Cook for an extra 30 seconds.

Ham and Pineapple Pizza

MAKES 4

Prepare as for Pizza Napoletana, but sprinkle 125 g/4 oz/1 cup chopped ham over the tomato mixture before adding the cheese and herbs. Chop 2 canned pineapple rings and scatter over the top of the pizza. Cook for an extra 45 seconds.

Pepperoni Pizzas

MAKES 4

Prepare as for Pizza Napoletana, but top each pizza with 6 thin slices of pepperoni sausage.

Grains, Nuts and Cereals

A steam-free, cool kitchen is one of the advantages of cooking grains in the microwave and another is the choice of dishes before you from Italy's golden and creamy semolina gnocchi to Russia's buckwheat, bulgar from the Middle East, couscous, millet, polenta and rice of all kinds.

Toasting Cereals, Nuts and Seeds

For the most part, microwaves are not known for their ability to brown foods in the same way as a conventional oven or grill (broiler); nevertheless, they do have a marvellous effect on nuts, toasting them to perfection. The type of plate used will govern the cooking time, and nuts on a pottery plate will take a little longer than those on a glass (Pyrex) dish or plate.

Whole Almonds: blanch, skin and halve 125 g/4 oz/1 cup almonds. Spread in a single layer on a fairly large pottery plate or in a shallow glass dish. Toast, uncovered, on Full for 6–7 minutes, moving the nuts around with a wooden spoon every minute so that they brown evenly. Remove from microwave but leave the nuts on the plate or dish until cold so that they continue to cook gently and crispen. Store in an airtight container when cold.

Flaked (Slivered) Almonds: as for whole almonds.

Brazil Nuts: as for whole almonds, but toast for only 5 minutes, stirring often. Do not skin.

Pine Nuts: as for whole almonds.

Cashew Nuts: as for whole almonds.

Walnut Halves: as for whole almonds, but do not skin and toast for only 5 minutes, stirring often.

Hazelnuts: as for whole almonds, but cook, uncovered, on Full for 10 minutes and move the nuts around with a wooden spoon every 1½ minutes. Cool completely, then rub off the skins in a clean tea towel (dish cloth).

Desiccated (Shredded) Coconut: as for whole almonds, but cook on Full for 5 minutes.

Coconut Curls: these are curly coconut strips, which look a bit like short and narrow noodles and make an attractive garnish or unusual nibble. Follow the directions for whole almonds but use 125 g/4 oz/1½–2 cups coconut strands (coarse shredded coconut) and cook on Full for 5½–6 minutes.

Peanuts: peanuts contain natural sodium and cooking in the microwave makes them taste slightly salted. As rubbing off the skins can be messy and people tend to eat peanuts by the handful, it makes sense to toast them in a larger quantity than other nuts. Spread 450 g/1 lb/4 cups shelled peanuts over the turntable or put into a large round or square dish that fits comfortably into the microwave. Cook, uncovered, on Full for 15–17 minutes, turning and moving about with a wooden spoon every 5 minutes to ensure even browning. If the nuts have brown skins, rub them off between the palms of your hands or in a clean tea towel (dish cloth). Store in an airtight container when cold.

Sesame Seeds: the seeds can brown suddenly and burn, so use a pottery plate rather than glass in this instance as it will slow down the cooking process. Follow the directions for whole almonds but cook on Full for 10–12 minutes, moving and turning the seeds with a wooden spoon every 2 minutes. Cool and store in an airtight container.

Sunflower Seeds: as for sesame seeds.

Porridge (Rolled) Oats: as for whole almonds but cook, uncovered, on Full for 6½–7 minutes. Use to sprinkle over savoury dishes before cooking.

Buttered Flaked Almonds

A splendid topping for sweet and savoury dishes.

15 ml/1 tbsp unsalted (sweet)
*   butter*
50 g/2 oz/½ cup flaked (slivered)
*   almonds*
Plain or flavoured salt or caster
*   (superfine) sugar*

Put the butter in a shallow 20 cm/ 8 in diameter dish. Melt, un- covered, on Full for 45–60 seconds. Add the almonds and cook, uncovered, on Full for 5–6 minutes until golden brown, stirring and turning every minute. Sprinkle with salt for topping savoury dishes, caster sugar for sweet.

Flaked Almonds in Garlic Butter

Prepare as for Buttered Flaked Almonds, but use bought garlic butter. This makes a smart topping for dishes like mashed potato and can also be added to creamy soups.

Dried Chestnuts

•••••••••••••••••••••••••••••••••••

The microwave enables dried chestnuts to be cooked and usable in under 2 hours without soaking overnight followed by prolonged cooking. Also the hard job of peeling has already been done for you.

Wash 250 g/8 oz/2 cups dried chestnuts. Put into a 1.75 litre/3 pt/ 7½ cup dish. Stir in 600 ml/1 pt/ 2½ cups boiling water. Cover with a plate and cook on Full for 15 minutes, turning the dish three times. Stand in the microwave for 15 minutes. Repeat with the same cooking and standing times. Uncover, add a further 150 ml/ ¼ pt/⅔ cup boiling water and stir round. Cover as before and cook on Full for 10 minutes, stirring twice. Allow to stand for 15 minutes before using.

Drying Herbs

•••••••••••••••••••••••••••••••••••

If you grow your own herbs but find it difficult to dry them in a damp and unpredictable climate, the microwave will do the job for you effectively, efficiently and cleanly in next to no time, so your annual crop can be savoured through the winter months. Each variety of herb should be dried by itself to keep the flavour intact. If you want to later on, you can make up your own blends by mixing several dried herbs together.

Start by cutting the herbs off their shrubs with secateurs or scissors. Pull the leaves (needles in the case of rosemary) off the stalks and pack them loosely into a 300 ml/½ pt/1¼ cup measuring jug, filling it almost to overflowing. Tip into a colander (strainer) and rinse them quickly and gently under cold running water. Drain thoroughly, then dry between the folds of a clean, dry tea towel (dish cloth). Put on top of a double thickness of kitchen paper placed directly on the microwave turntable. Heat, uncovered, on Full for 5–6 minutes, carefully moving the herbs about on the paper two or three times. As soon as they sound like autumn leaves rustling and have lost their bright green colour, you can assume the herbs are dried through. If not, continue to heat for 1–1½ minutes. Remove from the oven and allow to cool. Crush the dried herbs by rubbing them between your hands. Transfer to airtight jars with stoppers and label. Store away from bright light.

Crisping Breadcrumbs

•••••••••••••••••••••••••••••••••••

High-quality pale breadcrumbs – as opposed to marigold-yellow packet ones – are made perfectly in the microwave and turn crisp and brittle without browning. The bread can be fresh or stale but fresh will take a little longer to dry. Crumble 3½ large slices of white or brown bread with crusts into fine crumbs. Spread the crumbs into a shallow 25 cm/10 in diameter dish. Cook, uncovered, on Full for 5–6 minutes, stirring four times, until you can feel in your fingers that the crumbs are dry and crisp. Allow to cool, stirring round from time to time, then store in an airtight container. They will keep almost indefinitely in a cool place.

Nut Burgers

MAKES 12

These are by no means new, particularly to vegetarians and vegans, but the combination of nuts gives these burgers an outstanding flavour, and the crunchy texture is equally appetising. They can be served hot with a sauce (pages 316–332), cold with salad and mayonnaise, halved horizontally and used as a sandwich filling, or eaten just as they are for a snack.

30 ml/2 tbsp butter or margarine
125 g/4 oz/1 cup unskinned whole
*   almonds*
125 g/4 oz/1 cup pecan nut pieces
125 g/4 oz/1 cup cashew nut
*   pieces, toasted (page 205)*
125 g/4 oz/2 cups fresh soft brown
*   breadcrumbs*
1 medium onion, grated
2.5 ml/½ tsp salt
5 ml/1 tsp made mustard
30 ml/2 tbsp cold milk

Melt the butter or margarine, uncovered, on Full for 1–1½ minutes. Grind the nuts fairly finely in a blender or food processor. Tip out and combine with the remaining ingredients including the butter or margarine. Divide into 12 equal pieces and shape into ovals. Arrange round the edge of a large greased plate. Cook, uncovered, on Full for 4 minutes, turning once. Allow to stand for 2 minutes.

Nutkin Cake

SERVES 6–8

Prepare as for Nut Burgers, but substitute 350 g/12 oz/3 cups ground mixed nuts of your choice for the almonds, pecans and cashews. Shape into a 20 cm/8 in round and put on a greased plate. Cook, uncovered, on Full for 3 minutes. Allow to stand for 5 minutes, then cook on Full for a further 2½ minutes. Allow to stand for 2 minutes. Serve hot or cold, cut into wedges.

Buckwheat

SERVES 4

Also known as Saracen corn and native to Russia, buckwheat is related to no other grain. It is the small fruit of a sweetly perfumed pink-flowering plant which is a member of the dock family. The basis of blinis (or Russian pancakes), the grain is a hearty, earthy staple and is a healthy substitute for potatoes with meat and poultry.

175 g/6 oz/1 cup buckwheat
1 egg, beaten
5 ml/1 tsp salt
750 ml/1¼ pts/3 cups boiling
*   water*

Mix the buckwheat and egg in a 2 litre/3½ pt/8½ cup dish. Toast, uncovered, on Full for 4 minutes, stirring and breaking up with a fork every minute. Add the salt and water. Stand on a plate in the microwave in case of spillage and cook, uncovered, on Full for 22 minutes, stirring four times. Cover with a plate and allow to stand for 4 minutes. Fork round before serving.

Bulgar

SERVES 6–8

Also called burghal, burghul or cracked wheat, this grain is one of the staples of the Middle East. It is now widely available from supermarkets and health food shops.

225 g/8 oz/1¼ cups bulgar
600 ml/1 pt/2½ cups boiling water
5–7.5 ml/1–1½ tsp salt

Put the bulgar in a 1.75 litre/3 pt/ 7½ cup dish. Toast, uncovered, on Full for 3 minutes, stirring every minute. Stir in the boiling water and salt. Cover with a plate and allow to stand for 6–15 minutes, depending on the variety of bulgar used, until the grain is *al dente*, like pasta. Fluff up with a fork and eat hot or cold.

Bulgar with Fried Onion

SERVES 4

1 onion, grated
15 ml/1 tbsp olive or sunflower
1 quantity Bulgar

Put the onion and oil in a small dish. Cook, uncovered, on Full for 4 minutes, stirring three times. Add to the cooked bulgar at the same time as the water and salt.

Tabbouleh

SERVES 4

Coloured deep green by the parsley, this dish evokes the Lebanon and is one of the most appetising salads imaginable, a perfect accompaniment to many dishes from vegetarian nut cutlets to roast lamb. It also makes an attractive starter, arranged over salad greens on individual plates.

1 quantity Bulgar
120–150 ml/4–5 fl oz/½–⅔ cup
finely chopped flatleaf parsley
30 ml/2 tbsp chopped mint leaves
1 medium onion, finely grated
15 ml/1 tbsp olive oil
Salt and freshly ground black
pepper
Salad leaves
Diced tomatoes, diced cucumber
and black olives, to garnish

Cook the bulgar as directed. Transfer half the quantity to a bowl and mix in the parsley, mint, onion, oil and plenty of salt and pepper to taste. When cold, arrange on salad leaves and decorate attractively with the garnish. Use the remaining bulgar in any way you wish.

Sultan's Salad

SERVES 4

A personal favourite and, topped with pieces of Feta cheese and served with pitta bread, it makes a complete meal.

1 quantity Bulgar (page 209)
1–2 garlic cloves, crushed
1 carrot, grated
15 ml/1 tbsp chopped mint leaves
60 ml/4 tbsp chopped parsley
Juice of 1 large lemon, strained
45 ml/3 tbsp olive or sunflower
oil, or a mixture of both
Salad greens
Toasted almonds (page 205) and
green olives, to garnish

Cook the bulgar as directed, then stir in the garlic, carrot, mint, parsley, lemon juice and oil. Arrange on a plate lined with salad greens and stud with toasted almonds and green olives.

Couscous

SERVES 4

Couscous is both a grain and the name of a North African meat or vegetable stew. Made from durum wheat semolina (cream of wheat), it looks like tiny, perfectly rounded pearls. It used to be hand-made by dedicated and talented home cooks but is now available in packets and can be cooked in a flash, thanks to a French technique that does away with the laborious and slow task of steaming. You can substitute cous-cous for any of the dishes made with bulgar (pages 209–10).

250 g/9 oz/1½ cups bought
couscous
300 ml/½ pt/1¼ cups boiling water
5–10 ml/1–2 tsp salt

Put the couscous in a 1.75 litre/ 3 pt/7½ cup dish and toast, uncovered, on Full for 3 minutes, stirring every minute. Add the water and salt and fork round. Cover with a plate and cook on Full for 1 minute. Allow to stand in the microwave for 5 minutes. Fluff up with a fork before serving.

Grits

SERVES 4

Grits (hominy grits) is a an almost-white North American cereal based on maize (corn). It is eaten with hot milk and sugar or with butter and salt and pepper. It is available from speciality food shops like Harrods in London.

150 g/5 oz/scant 1 cup grits
150 ml/¼ pt/⅔ cup cold water
600 ml/1 pt/2½ cups boiling water
5 ml/1 tsp salt

Put the grits in a 2.5 litre/4½ pt/ 11 cup bowl. Mix smoothly with the cold water, then stir in the boiling water and salt. Cook, uncovered, on Full for 8 minutes, stirring four times. Cover with a plate and allow to stand for 3 minutes before serving.

Gnocchi alla Romana

SERVES 4

Gnocchi is often to be found in Italian restaurants, where it is well liked. It makes a substantial and wholesome lunch or supper dish with salad and uses economical ingredients.

600 ml/1 pt/2½ cups cold milk
150 g/5 oz/¾ cup semolina (cream of wheat)
5 ml/1 tsp salt
50 g/2 oz/¼ cup butter or margarine
75 g/3 oz/¾ cup grated Parmesan cheese
2.5 ml/½ tsp continental made mustard
1.5 ml/¼ tsp grated nutmeg
1 large egg, beaten
Mixed salad
Tomato ketchup (catsup)

Mix half the cold milk smoothly with the semolina in a 1.5 litre/2½ pt/6 cup dish. Heat the remaining milk, uncovered, on Full for 3 minutes. Stir into the semolina with the salt. Cook, uncovered, on Full for 7 minutes until very thick, stirring four or five times to keep the mixture smooth. Remove from the microwave and mix in half the butter, half the cheese and all the mustard, nutmeg and egg. Cook, uncovered, on Full for 1 minute. Cover with a plate and allow to stand for 1 minute. Spread in an oiled or buttered shallow 23 cm/9 in square dish. Cover loosely with kitchen paper and leave in the cool until firm and set. Cut into 2.5 cm/1 in squares. Arrange in a 23 cm/9 in buttered round dish in overlapping rings. Sprinkle with the remaining cheese, dot with flakes of the remaining butter and reheat in a hot oven for 15 minutes until golden brown. Serve very hot with salad and tomato sauce.

Ham Gnocchi

SERVES 4

Prepare as for Gnocchi alla Romana, but add 75 g/3 oz/¾ cup chopped Parma ham with the warm milk.

Millet

SERVES 4–6

A pleasing and delicate grain, related to sorghum, which is an off-beat substitute for rice. If eaten with pulses (peas, beans and lentils), it makes a well-balanced, protein-rich meal.

175 g/6 oz/1 cup millet
750 ml/1¼ pts/3 cups boiling water or stock
5 ml/1 tsp salt

Put the millet in a 2 litre/3½ pt/8½ cup dish. Toast, uncovered, on Full for 4 minutes, stirring twice. Mix in the water and salt. Stand on a plate in case of spillage. Cook, uncovered, on Full for 20–25 minutes until all the water has been absorbed. Fluff up with a fork and eat straight away.

Polenta

SERVES 6

A bright yellow grain made from corn, similar to semolina (cream of wheat) but coarser. It is a staple starch food in Italy and Romania, where it is much respected and often eaten as a side dish with meat, poultry, egg and vegetable dishes. In recent years it has become a trendy restaurant speciality, often cut into squares and served grilled (broiled) or fried (sautéed) with the sauces similar to those used for spaghetti (pages 197–203).

150 g/5 oz/³⁄₄ cup polenta
5 ml/1 tsp salt
125 ml/¼ pt/²⁄₃ cup cold water
600 ml/1 pt/2½ cups boiling water
*   or stock*

Put the polenta and salt in a 2 litre/ 3½ pt/8½ cup dish. Blend smoothly with the cold water. Gradually mix in the boiling water or stock. Stand on a plate in case of spillage. Cook, uncovered, on Full for 7–8 minutes until very thick, stirring four times. Cover with a plate and allow to stand for 3 minutes before serving.

Grilled Polenta

SERVES 6

Prepare as for Polenta. When cooked, spread in a buttered or oiled 23 cm/9 in square dish. Smooth the top with a knife dipped in and out of hot water. Cover loosely with kitchen paper and allow to cool completely. Cut into squares, brush with olive or corn oil and grill (broil) or fry (sauté) conventionally until golden brown.

Polenta with Pesto

SERVES 6

Prepare as for Polenta, but add 20 ml/4 tsp red or green pesto with the boiling water.

Polenta with Sun-dried Tomato or Olive Paste

SERVES 6

Prepare as for Polenta, but add 45 ml/3 tbsp sun-dried tomato or olive paste with the boiling water.

Quinoa

SERVES 2–3

A fairly new-on-the-scene high-protein grain from Peru with a curiously crunchy texture and slightly smoky flavour. It goes with all foods and makes a novel substitute for rice.

125 g/4 oz/²⁄₃ cup quinoa
2.5 ml/½ tsp salt
550 ml/18 fl oz/2⅓ cups boiling
*   water*

Put the quinoa in a 1.75 litre/3 pt/ 7½ cup bowl. Toast, uncovered, on Full for 3 minutes, stirring once. Add the salt and water and mix in thoroughly. Cook on Full for 15 minutes, stirring four times. Cover and allow to stand for 2 minutes.

Romanian Polenta

SERVES 4

Romania's notoriously rich national dish – *mamaliga*.

1 quantity Polenta
75 g/3 oz/⅓ cup butter
4 freshly poached large eggs
(page 99)
100 g/4 oz/1 cup Feta cheese,
crumbled
150 ml/¼ pt/⅔ cup soured (dairy
sour) cream

Prepare the polenta and leave in the dish in which it was cooked. Beat in half the butter. Spoon equal mounds on to four warmed plates and make an indentation in each. Fill with the eggs, sprinkle with the cheese and top with the remaining butter and the cream. Eat straight away.

Cooking Rice

Whether the rice is basmati, white long-grain, easy-cook, brown, wild, oriental or Italian, all that is necessary is to follow the directions and timings on the packet exactly, but to cook the rice in a deep dish on Full. Boiling liquid should always be used and the dish covered with clingfilm (plastic wrap), slit twice to allow steam to escape. Although there is no saving in time, the energy cost is lower and there is no pan to wash, no steamy kitchen and the rice retains its flavour and shape perfectly.

Curried Rice

SERVES 4

Suitable as an accompaniment for most oriental and Asiatic foods, especially Indian.

30 ml/2 tbsp groundnut (peanut)
oil
2 onions, finely chopped
225 g/8 oz/1 cup basmati rice
2 small bay leaves
2 whole cloves
Seeds from 4 cardamom pods
30–45 ml/2–3 tbsp mild curry
powder
5 ml/1 tsp salt
600 ml/1 pt/2½ cups boiling water
or vegetable stock

Put the oil in a 2.25 litre/4 pt/10 cup dish. Heat, uncovered, on Full for 1 minute. Mix in the onions. Cook, uncovered, on Full for 5 minutes. Stir in all the remaining ingredients. Cover with clingfilm (plastic wrap) and slit it twice to allow steam to escape. Cook on Full for 15 minutes, turning the dish four times. Allow to stand for 2 minutes. Fork round lightly and serve.

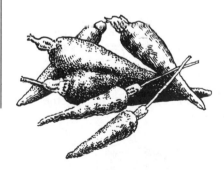

Cottage Cheese and Rice Casserole

••••••••••••••••••••••••••••
SERVES 3–4

A great amalgam of tastes and textures brought back from North America some years ago.

225 g/8 oz/1 cup brown rice
50 g/2 oz/¼ cup wild rice
1.25 litre/2¼ pts/5½ cups boiling water
10 ml/2 tsp salt
4 spring onions (scallions), coarsely chopped
1 small green chilli, seeded and chopped
4 tomatoes, blanched, skinned and sliced
125 g/4 oz button mushrooms, sliced
225 g/8 oz/1 cup cottage cheese
75 g/3 oz/¾ cup Cheddar cheese, grated

Put the brown and wild rice in a 2.25 litre/4 pt/10 cup dish. Stir in the water and salt. Cover with cling-film (plastic wrap) and slit it twice to allow steam to escape. Cook on Full for 40–45 minutes until the rice is plump and tender. Drain, if necessary, and set aside. Fill a 1.75 litre/3 pt/7½ cup casserole dish (Dutch oven) with alternate layers of rice, onions, chilli, tomatoes, mushrooms and cottage cheese. Sprinkle thickly with the grated Cheddar. Cook, uncovered, on Full for 7 minutes, turning the dish twice.

Italian Risotto

••••••••••••••••••••••••••••
SERVES 2–3

2.5–5 ml/½–1 tsp saffron powder or 5 ml/1 tsp saffron strands
50 g/2 oz/¼ cup butter
5 ml/1 tsp olive oil
1 large onion, peeled and grated
225 g/8 oz/1 cup easy-cook risotto rice
600 ml/1 pt/2½ cups boiling water or chicken stock
150 ml/¼ pt/⅔ cup dry white wine
5 ml/1 tsp salt
50 g/2 oz/½ cup grated Parmesan cheese

If using saffron strands, crumble them between your fingers into an egg cup of hot water and allow to stand for 10–15 minutes. Put half the butter and the oil in a 1.75 litre/3 pt/7½ cup dish. Heat, uncovered, on Defrost for 1 minute. Stir in the onion. Cook, uncovered, on Full for 5 minutes. Stir in the rice, water or stock and wine and either the saffron strands with the water, or the saffron powder. Cover with clingfilm (plastic wrap) and slit it twice to allow steam to escape. Cook on Full for 14 minutes, turning the dish three times. Gently fork in the remaining butter, followed by the salt and half the Parmesan cheese. Cook, uncovered, on Full for 4–8 minutes, stirring gently with a fork every 2 minutes, until the rice has absorbed all the liquid. The cooking time will depend on the rice used. Spoon into dishes and sprinkle the remaining cheese on top.

Mushroom Risotto

SERVES 2–3

Break 20 g/1 oz dried mushrooms, porcini for preference, into smallish pieces, wash thoroughly under cold running water and then soak them for 10 minutes in the boiling water or chicken stock used in the Italian Risotto recipe. Proceed as for Italian Risotto.

Brazilian Rice

SERVES 3–4

15 ml/1 tbsp olive or corn oil
30 ml/2 tbsp dried onion
225 g/8 oz/ 1 cup American long-
grain or basmati rice
5–10 ml/1–2 tsp salt
600 ml/1 pt/2½ cups boiling water
2 large tomatoes, blanched,
skinned and chopped

Pour the oil in a 2 litre/3½ pt/8½ cup dish. Add the dried onion. Cook, uncovered, on Full for 1¼ minutes. Stir in all the remaining ingredients. Cover with clingfilm (plastic wrap) and slit it twice to allow steam to escape. Cook on Full for 15 minutes, turning the dish four times. Allow to stand for 2 minutes. Fork round lightly and serve.

Spanish Rice

SERVES 6

A North American special that has little to do with Spain other than the addition of peppers and tomatoes! Eat with poultry and egg dishes.

225 g/8 oz/1 cup easy-cook long-
grain rice
600 ml/1 pt/2½ cups boiling water
10 ml/2 tsp salt
30 ml/2 tbsp corn or sunflower oil
2 onions, finely chopped
1 green (bell) pepper, seeded and
coarsely chopped
400 g/14 oz/1 large can chopped
tomatoes

Cook the rice in the water with half the salt as directed (page 213). Keep hot. Pour the oil into a 1.75 litre/3 pt/7½ cup bowl. Heat, uncovered, on Full for 1 minute. Stir in the onions and pepper. Cook, uncovered, on Full for 5 minutes, stirring twice. Mix in the tomatoes. Heat, uncovered, on Full for 3½ minutes. Fork in the hot rice with the remaining salt and serve straight away.

Plain Turkish Pilaf

SERVES 4

225 g/8 oz/1 cup easy-cook risotto
rice
Boiling water or vegetable stock
5 ml/1 tsp salt
40 g/1½ oz/3 tbsp butter

Cook the rice in the boiling water or stock with the salt added as directed (page 213). Add the butter to the dish or bowl. Allow to stand for 10 minutes. Uncover and fork round. Cover with a plate and reheat on Full for 3 minutes.

215

Rich Turkish Pilaf

SERVES 4

*225 g/8 oz/1 cup easy-cook risotto
rice*
Boiling water
5 ml/1 tsp salt
5 cm/2 in piece cinnamon stick
40 g/1½ oz/3 tbsp butter
15 ml/1 tbsp olive oil
2 onions, finely chopped
*60 ml/4 tbsp toasted pine nuts
(page 205)*
*25 g/1 oz lambs' or chicken liver,
cut into small pieces*
30 ml/2 tbsp currants or raisins
*2 tomatoes, blanched, skinned and
chopped*

Cook the rice in the water and salt, in a large dish or bowl, as directed (page 213) with the cinnamon stick added. Set aside. Put the butter and oil in a 1.25 litre/2¼ pt/5½ cup bowl and heat, uncovered, on Full for 1 minute. Mix in all the remaining ingredients. Cover with a plate and cook on Full for 5 minutes, stirring twice. Stir gently into the hot rice with a fork. Cover as before and reheat on Full for 2 minutes.

Thai Rice with Lemon Grass, Lime Leaves and Coconut

SERVES 4

A marvel of exquisite delicacy, appropriate for all Thai-style chicken and fish dishes.

*250 g/9 oz/generous 1 cup Thai
rice*
*400 ml/14 fl oz/1¾ cups canned
coconut milk*
2 fresh lime leaves
*1 blade lemon grass, split
lengthways, or 15 ml/1 tbsp
chopped lemon balm leaves*
7.5 ml/1½ tsp salt

Tip the rice into a 1.5 litre/2½ pt/6 cup dish. Pour the coconut milk into a measuring jug and make up to 600 ml/1 pt/2½ cups with cold water. Heat, uncovered, on Full for 7 minutes until it begins to bubble and boil. Stir gently into the rice with all the remaining ingredients. Cover with clingfilm (plastic wrap) and slit it twice to allow steam to escape. Cook on Full for 14 minutes. Allow to stand for 5 minutes. Uncover and remove the lemon grass, if used. Fork round gently and eat the slightly soft and sticky rice straight away.

Vegetables and Salads

The microwave is simply brilliant with vegetables and easily tackles jacket potatoes and its family of variations, off-beats like okra (ladies' fingers) and cabbage, sour cabbage from Norway and red cabbage from Central Europe. There are also hot beetroot dishes, France's cheesy Dauphine Potatoes, Ratatouille and a veritable vegetable feast of hot-pots, braises, casseroles and curries. Vegetarians should find plenty to write home about and slimmers have a healthy choice as well, making this a useful section for quality main courses and side dishes. As with fish, vegetables in the microwave 'steam' in a small quantity of liquid and most nutrients are therefore retained.

Okra with Cabbage
SERVES 6

A curiosity from the Gabon, mild or hot depending on the amount of chilli included.

30 ml/2 tbsp groundnut (peanut) oil
450 g/1 lb Savoy cabbage or spring greens (collard greens), finely shredded
200 g/7 oz okra (ladies' fingers), topped, tailed and cut into chunks
1 onion, grated
300 ml/½ pt/1¼ cups boiling water
10 ml/2 tsp salt
45 ml/3 tbsp pine nuts, lightly toasted under the grill (broiler)
2.5–20 ml/¼–4 tsp chilli powder

Pour the oil into a 2.25 litre/4 pt/10 cup casserole dish (Dutch oven). Stir in the greens and okra followed by the remaining ingredients. Mix well. Cover with clingfilm (plastic wrap) and slit it twice to allow steam to escape. Cook on Full for 7 minutes. Allow to stand for for 5 minutes. Cook on Full for a further 3 minutes. Drain if necessary and serve.

Red Cabbage with Apple
SERVES 8

Magnificent with hot gammon, goose and duck, red cabbage is of Scandinavian and North European descent, a sweet-sour and now quite smart side dish, on its best behaviour in the microwave where it stays a deep rosy colour.

900 g/2 lb red cabbage
450 ml/¾ pt/2 cups boiling water
7.5 ml/1½ tsp salt
3 onions, finely chopped
3 cooking (tart) apples, peeled and
** grated**
30 ml/2 tbsp light soft brown
** sugar**
2.5 ml/½ tsp caraway seeds
30 ml/2 tbsp cornflour
** (cornstarch)**
45 ml/3 tbsp malt vinegar
15 ml/1 tbsp cold water

Trim the cabbage, removing any bruised or damaged outer leaves. Cut into quarters and remove the hard central stalk, then shred as finely as possible. Put into a 2.25 litre/4 pt/10 cup dish. Add half the boiling water and 5 ml/1 tsp of the salt. Cover with a plate and cook on Full for 10 minutes, turning the dish four times. Stir well, then mix in the remaining boiling water and remaining salt, the onions, apples, sugar and caraway seeds. Cover with clingfilm (plastic wrap) and slit it twice to allow steam to escape. Cook on Full for 20 minutes, turning the dish four times. Remove from the microwave. Mix the cornflour smoothly with the vinegar and cold water. Add to the hot cabbage and mix well. Cook, uncovered, on Full for 10 minutes, stirring three times. Leave until cold before chilling overnight. To serve, re-cover with fresh clingfilm and slit it twice to allow steam to escape, then heat on Full for 5–6 minutes before serving. Alternatively, transfer portions to side plates and cover each with kitchen paper, then reheat individually on Full for 1 minute each.

Red Cabbage with Wine
SERVES 8

Prepare as for Red Cabbage with Apples, but substitute 250 ml/8 fl oz/1 cup red wine for half the boiling water.

Norwegian Sour Cabbage
SERVES 8

900 g/2 lb white cabbage
90 ml/6 tbsp water
60 ml/4 tbsp malt vinegar
60 ml/4 tbsp granulated sugar
10 ml/2 tsp caraway seeds
7.5–10 ml/1½–2 tsp salt

Trim the cabbage, removing any bruised or damaged outer leaves. Cut into quarters and remove the hard central stalk, then shred as finely as possible. Put into a 2.25 litre/4 pt/10 cup dish with all the remaining ingredients. Mix thoroughly with two spoons. Cover with clingfilm (plastic wrap) and slit it twice to allow steam to escape. Cook on Defrost for 45 minutes, turning the dish four times. Leave at kitchen temperature overnight for the flavours to mature. To serve, put individual servings on to side plates and cover each with kitchen paper. Reheat individually on Full, allowing about 1 minute each. Securely cover and then refrigerate any leftovers.

Greek-style Stewed Okra with Tomatoes

SERVES 6–8

Very marginally Eastern in character, this slightly off-beat vegetable dish has become a viable proposition now that okra (ladies' fingers) is more widely available. This recipe is excellent with lamb or as a dish in its own right, served with rice.

900 g/2 lb okra, topped and tailed
Salt and freshly ground black pepper
90 ml/6 tbsp malt vinegar
45 ml/3 tbsp olive oil
2 onions, peeled and finely chopped
6 tomatoes, blanched, skinned and coarsely chopped
15 ml/1 tbsp light soft brown sugar

Spread out the okra on a large flat plate. To reduce the chances of the okra splitting and taking on a slimy feel, sprinkle with salt and the vinegar. Allow to stand for for 30 minutes. Wash and wipe dry on kitchen paper. Pour the oil into a 2.5 litre/4½ pt/11 cup dish and add the onions. Cook, uncovered, on Full for 7 minutes, stirring three times. Stir in all the remaining ingredients including the okra and season to taste. Cover with a plate and cook on Full for 9–10 minutes, stirring three or four times, until the okra is tender. Allow to stand for 3 minutes before serving.

Greens with Tomatoes, Onions and Peanut Butter

SERVES 4–6

Try this Malawi speciality with sliced white bread as a vegetarian main course or serve as a side dish with chicken.

450 g/1 lb spring greens (collard greens), finely shredded
150 ml/¼ pt/⅔ cup boiling water
5–7.5 ml/1–1½ tsp salt
4 tomatoes, blanched, skinned and sliced
1 large onion, finely chopped
60 ml/4 tbsp crunchy peanut butter

Place the greens in a 2.25 litre/4 pt/10 cup dish. Mix in the water and salt. Cover with clingfilm (plastic wrap) and slit it twice to allow steam to escape. Cook on Full for 20 minutes. Uncover and stir in the tomatoes, onion and peanut butter. Cover as before and cook on Full for 5 minutes.

The Reuben Veggie Sandwich

SERVES 2

Prepare as for The Reuben Sandwich (page 176), but substitute 2 sliced hard-boiled (hard-cooked) eggs (pages 98–9) or bought vegetable pâté for the meat.

Sweet-sour Creamed Beetroot

SERVES 4

This attractive way of presenting beetroot dates back to 1890, but it's currently back in fashion.

450 g/1 lb cooked beetroot (red beets), coarsely grated
150 ml/¼ pt/⅔ cup double (heavy) cream
Salt
15 ml/1 tbsp vinegar
30 ml/2 tbsp demerara sugar

Put the beetroot in a 900 ml/1½ pt/3¾ cup dish with the cream and salt to taste. Cover with a plate and heat through on Full for 3 minutes, stirring once. Stir in the vinegar and sugar and serve straight away.

Beetroot in Orange

SERVES 4–6

A lively and original accompaniment to Christmas meats and poultry.

450 g/1 lb cooked beetroot (red beets), peeled and sliced
75 ml/5 tbsp freshly squeezed orange juice
15 ml/1 tbsp malt vinegar
2.5 ml/½ tsp salt
1 garlic clove, peeled and crushed

Place the beetroot in a shallow 18 cm/7 in diameter dish. Beat together the remaining ingredients and pour over the beetroot. Cover with clingfilm (plastic wrap) and slit it twice to allow steam to escape. Cook on Full for 6 minutes, turning the dish three times. Allow to stand for 1 minute.

Scalloped Celeriac

SERVES 6

A handsome and gourmet-style winter side dish that teams happily with fish and poultry.

4 lean rashers (slices) bacon, chopped
900 g/2 lb celeriac (celery root)
300 ml/½ pt/1¼ cups cold water
15 ml/1 tbsp lemon juice
7.5 ml/1½ tsp salt
300 ml/½ pt/1¼ cups single (light) cream
1 small bag potato crisps (chips), crushed in the bag

Put the bacon on a plate and cover with kitchen paper. Cook on Full for 3 minutes. Peel the celeriac thickly, wash well and cut each head into eight pieces. Place in a 2.25 litre/4 pt/10 cup dish with the water, lemon juice and salt. Cover with clingfilm (plastic wrap) and slit it twice to allow steam to escape. Cook on Full for 20 minutes, turning the dish four times. Drain. Slice the celeriac and return to the dish. Stir in the bacon and cream and sprinkle with the crisps. Cook, uncovered, on Full for 4 minutes, turning the dish twice. Allow to stand for 5 minutes before serving.

Celeriac with Orange Hollandaise Sauce

SERVES 6

Celeriac with a gloriously golden, gleaming topping of citrus Hollandaise sauce to try with duck and game.

900 g/2 lb celeriac (celery root)
300 ml/½ pt/1¼ cups cold water
15 ml/1 tbsp lemon juice
7.5 ml/1½ tsp salt
Maltese Sauce (page 319)
1 very sweet orange, peeled and
*   segmented*

Peel the celeriac thickly, wash well and cut each head into eight pieces. Place in a 2.25 litre/4 pt/10 cup dish with the water, lemon juice and salt. Cover with clingfilm (plastic wrap) and slit it twice to allow steam to escape. Cook on Full for 20 minutes, turning the dish four times. Drain. Slice the celeriac and return to the dish. Keep hot. Make the Maltese Sauce and spoon over the celeriac. Garnish with the orange segments.

Slimmers' Vegetable Pot

SERVES 2

Prepare as for Slimmer's Fish Pot (page 133) but omit the fish. Add the diced flesh of 2 avocados to the cooked vegetables with the spices and herbs. Cover and reheat on Full for 1½ minutes.

Slimmers' Vegetable Pot with Eggs

SERVES 2

Prepare as for Slimmer's Vegetable Pot, but sprinkle each portion with 1 chopped hard-boiled (hard-cooked) egg (page 98).

Ratatouille

SERVES 6–8

An explosion of Mediterranean flavours and colours is part and parcel of this glorious vegetable pot-pourri. Hot, cold or warm – it seems to go with everything.

60 ml/4 tbsp olive oil
3 onions, peeled and coarsely
*   chopped*
1–3 garlic cloves, crushed
225 g/8 oz courgettes (zucchini),
*   thinly sliced*
350 g/12 oz/3 cups cubed
*   aubergine (eggplant)*
1 large red or green (bell) pepper,
*   seeded and chopped*
3 ripe tomatoes, skinned,
*   blanched and chopped*
30 ml/2 tbsp tomato purée (paste)
20 ml/4 tsp light soft brown sugar
10 ml/2 tsp salt
45–60 ml/3–4 tbsp chopped
*   parsley*

Pour the oil into a 2.5 litre/4½ pt/ 11 cup dish. Heat, uncovered, on Full for 1 minute. Mix in the onions and garlic. Cook, uncovered, on Full for 4 minutes. Stir in all the remaining ingredients except half the parsley. Cover with a plate and cook on Full for 20 minutes, stirring three or four times. Uncover and cook on Full for 8–10 minutes, stirring four times, until most of the liquid has evaporated. Mix in the remaining parsley. Serve straight away or cool, cover and chill if to be eaten later.

Caramelised Parsnips

•••••••••••••••••••••••••••••••••
SERVES 4

Ideal with all poultry and beef roasts, choose baby parsnips no bigger than large carrots for this.

450 g/1 lb small parsnips, thinly sliced
45 ml/3 tbsp water
25 g/1 oz/2 tbsp butter
7.5 ml/1½ tbsp dark soft brown sugar
Salt

Put the parsnips in a 1.25 litre/ 2¼ pt/5½ cup dish with the water. Cover with clingfilm (plastic wrap) and slit it twice to allow steam to escape. Cook on Full for 8–10 minutes, turning the dish and gently shaking the contents twice, until tender. Drain off the water. Add the butter and sugar and toss the parsnips to coat them thoroughly. Heat, uncovered, on Full for 1–1½ minutes until glazed. Sprinkle with salt and eat straight away.

Parsnips with Egg and Butter Crumb Sauce

•••••••••••••••••••••••••••••••••
SERVES 4

450 g/1 lb parsnips, diced
45 ml/3 tbsp water
75 g/3 oz/⅓ cup unsalted (sweet) butter
4 spring onions (scallions), finely chopped
45 ml/3 tbsp light-coloured toasted breadcrumbs
1 hard-boiled (hard-cooked) egg (page 98), grated
30 ml/2 tbsp finely chopped parsley
Juice of ½ small lemon

Place the parsnips in a 1.5 litre/ 2½ pt/6 cup dish with the water. Cover with clingfilm (plastic wrap) and slit it twice to allow steam to escape. Cook on Full for 8–10 minutes. Allow to stand while preparing the sauce. Put the butter in a measuring jug and melt, uncovered, on Defrost for 2–2½ minutes. Stir in the onions and cook, uncovered, on Defrost for 3 minutes, stirring twice. Mix in all the remaining ingredients and heat on Defrost for 30 seconds. Drain the parsnips and transfer to a warmed serving dish. Coat with the crumb sauce and serve straight away.

Broccoli with Cheese Supreme

•••••••••••••••••••••••••••••••••
SERVES 4–6

450 g/1 lb broccoli
60 ml/4 tbsp water
5 ml/1 tsp salt
150 ml/¼ pt/⅔ cup soured (dairy sour) cream
125 g/4 oz/1 cup Cheddar or Jarlsberg cheese, grated
1 egg
5 ml/1 tsp mild made mustard
2.5 ml/½ tsp paprika
1.5 ml/¼ tsp grated nutmeg

Wash the broccoli, separate into small florets and put into a deep 20 cm/8 in diameter dish with the water and salt. Cover with clingfilm (plastic wrap) and slit it twice to allow steam to escape. Cook on Full for 12 minutes. Drain thoroughly. Beat together the remaining ingredients and spoon over the broccoli. Cover with a plate and cook on Full for 3 minutes. Allow to stand for 2 minutes.

Guvetch

SERVES 6–8

A vibrantly coloured and flavour-packed Bulgarian relation of ratatouille. Serve on its own with rice, pasta or polenta or as an accompaniment to egg, meat and poultry dishes.

450 g/1 lb French or Kenya (green) beans, topped and tailed
4 onions, very thinly sliced
3 garlic cloves, crushed
60 ml/4 tbsp olive oil
6 (bell) peppers in mixed colours, seeded and cut into strips
6 tomatoes, blanched, skinned and chopped
1 green chilli, seeded and finely chopped (optional)
10–15 ml/2–3 tsp salt
15 ml/1 tbsp caster (superfine) sugar

Cut each bean into three pieces. Put the onions and garlic in a 2.5 litre/4½ pt/11 cup dish with the oil. Stir well to mix. Cook, uncovered, on Full for 4 minutes. Thoroughly mix in all the remaining ingredients including the beans. Cover with a plate and cook on Full for 20 minutes, stirring three times. Uncover and cook on Full for a further 8–10 minutes, stirring four times, until most of the liquid has evaporated. Serve straight away or cool, cover and chill if to be eaten later.

Celery Cheese with Bacon

SERVES 4

6 rashers (slices) streaky bacon
350 g/12 oz celery, diced
30 ml/2 tbsp boiling water
30 ml/2 tbsp butter or margarine
30 ml/2 tbsp plain (all-purpose) flour
300 ml/½ pt/1¼ cups warm full-cream milk
5 ml/1 tsp English made mustard
225 g/8 oz/2 cups Cheddar cheese, grated
Salt and freshly ground black pepper
Paprika
Fried (sautéed) bread, to serve

Put the bacon on a plate and cover with kitchen paper. Cook on Full for 4–4½ minutes, turning the plate once. Drain off the fat, then coarsely chop the bacon. Put the celery in a separate dish with the boiling water. Cover with a plate and cook on Full for 10 minutes, turning the dish twice. Drain and reserve the liquid. Put the butter in a 1.5 litre/2½ pt/6 cup dish. Melt, uncovered, on Defrost for 1–1½ minutes. Stir in the flour and cook on Full for 1 minute. Gradually blend in the milk. Cook, uncovered, on Full for 4–5 minutes until smoothly thickened, whisking every minute. Mix in the celery water, celery, bacon, mustard and two-thirds of the cheese. Season to taste. Transfer the mixture to a clean dish. Sprinkle the remaining cheese on top and dust with paprika. Reheat, uncovered, on Full for 2 minutes. Serve with fried bread.

Artichoke Cheese with Bacon

SERVES 4

Prepare as for Celery Cheese with Bacon (page 223), but omit the celery. Put 350 g/12 oz Jerusalem artichokes in a bowl with 15 ml/1 tbsp lemon juice and 90 ml/6 tbsp boiling water. Cover with clingfilm (plastic wrap) and slit it twice to allow steam to escape. Cook on Full for 12–14 minutes until tender. Drain, reserving 45 ml/3 tbsp of the water. Add the artichokes and the water to the sauce with the mustard, bacon and cheese.

Karelian Potatoes

SERVES 4

A recipe from eastern Finland for springtime potatoes.

450 g/1 lb new potatoes, washed but unpeeled
30 ml/2 tbsp boiling water
125 g/4 oz/½ cup butter, at kitchen temperature
2 hard-boiled (hard-cooked) eggs (pages 98–99), chopped

Put the potatoes in a 900 ml/ 1½ pt/3¾ cup dish with the boiling water. Cover with a plate and cook on Full for 11 minutes, stirring twice. Meanwhile, beat the butter to a smooth cream and stir in the eggs. Drain the potatoes and stir in the egg mixture while the potatoes are still very hot. Serve straight away.

Dutch Potato and Gouda Casserole with Tomatoes

SERVES 4

A filling and warming vegetarian casserole that can be served with cooked green vegetables or a crunchy salad.

750 g/1½ lb cooked potatoes, thickly sliced
3 large tomatoes, blanched, skinned and thinly sliced
1 large red onion, coarsely grated
30 ml/2 tbsp finely chopped parsley
175 g/6 oz/1½ cups Gouda cheese, grated
Salt and freshly ground black pepper
30 ml/2 tbsp cornflour (cornstarch)
30 ml/2 tbsp cold milk
150 ml/¼ pt/⅔ cup hot water or vegetable stock
Paprika

Fill a buttered 1.5 litre/2½ pt/6 cup dish with alternate layers of potatoes, tomatoes, onion, parsley and two-thirds of the cheese, sprinkling salt and pepper between the layers. Mix the cornflour smoothly with the cold milk, then gradually whisk in the hot water or stock. Pour down the side of the dish. Sprinkle the remaining cheese on top and dust with paprika. Cover with kitchen paper and heat through on Full for 12–15 minutes. Allow to stand for 5 minutes before serving.

Buttered and Fluffed Sweet Potatoes with Cream

SERVES 4

450 g/1 lb sweet pink-skinned and
yellow-fleshed potatoes (not
yams), peeled and diced
60 ml/4 tbsp boiling water
45 ml/3 tbsp butter or margarine
60 ml/4 tbsp whipped cream,
warmed
Salt and freshly ground black
pepper

Put the potatoes in a 1.25 litre/
2¼ pt/5½ cup dish. Add the water.
Cover with clingfilm (plastic wrap) and
slit it twice to allow steam to escape.
Cook on Full for 10 minutes, turning
the dish three times. Allow to stand for
3 minutes. Drain and finely mash.
Thoroughly beat in the butter and
cream. Season well to taste. Transfer
to a serving dish, cover with a plate
and reheat on Full for 1½ –2 minutes.

Maître d'Hôtel Sweet Potatoes

SERVES 4

450 g/1 lb sweet pink-skinned and
yellow-fleshed potatoes (not
yams), peeled and diced
60 ml/4 tbsp boiling water
45 ml/3 tbsp butter or margarine
45 ml/3 tbsp chopped parsley

Put the potatoes in a 1.25 litre/
2¼ pt/5½ cup dish. Add the water.
Cover with clingfilm (plastic wrap) and
slit it twice to allow steam to escape.
Cook on Full for 10 minutes, turning
the dish three times. Allow to stand for
3 minutes, then drain. Add the butter
and toss to coat the potatoes, then
sprinkle with the parsley.

Creamed Potatoes

SERVES 4–6

Potatoes cooked in the microwave
retain their flavour and colour and
have an excellent texture. Their
nutrients are conserved because the
amount of water used for cooking is
minimal. Fuel is saved and there is no
pan to wash – you can even cook the
potatoes in their own serving dish.
Peel potatoes as thinly as possible to
retain the vitamins.

900 g/2 lb peeled potatoes, cut
into chunks
90 ml/6 tbsp boiling water
30–60 ml/2–4 tbsp butter or
margarine
90 ml/6 tbsp warm milk
Salt and freshly ground black
pepper

Put the potato chunks in a 1.75 litre/
3 pt/7½ cup with the water. Cover
with clingfilm (plastic wrap) and slit it
twice to allow steam to escape. Cook
on Full for 15–16 minutes, turning the
dish four times, until tender. Drain if
necessary, then mash finely, beating in
the butter or margarine and milk alternately. Season. When light and fluffy,
rough up with a fork and reheat,
uncovered, on Full for 2–2½ minutes.

Creamed Potatoes with Parsley

SERVES 4–6

Prepare as for Creamed Potatoes,
but mix in 45–60 ml/3–4 tbsp
chopped parsley with the seasoning.
Reheat for an extra 30 seconds.

Creamed Potatoes with Cheese

••••••••••••••••••••••••••••••
SERVES 4–6

Prepare as for Creamed Potatoes (page 225), but mix in 125 g/4 oz/ 1 cup grated hard cheese with the seasoning. Reheat for an extra 1½ minutes.

Jacket Potatoes

••••••••••••••••••••••••••••••
Although the skin is softer and less crusty than on potatoes baked conventionally, the fluffy and tender inside makes up for it.

Wash and scrub the potatoes thoroughly. Slit or prick in several places. Stand on a plate or kitchen paper on the microwave turntable and cover with kitchen paper. The cooking time will vary according to the variety of potato and the following guide is a minimum:

1 medium potato: 5–6 minutes
2 medium potatoes: 6½–8 minutes
3 medium potatoes: 9–11 minutes, arranged in a triangle
4 medium potatoes: 12–14 minutes, arranged in a square
5–8 medium potatoes: 20–25 minutes, arranged in a ring round the edge of a large plate

The cooked potatoes should feel soft when gently squeezed. Wrap them in foil or a tea towel (dish cloth) and allow to stand for 5 minutes.

Filled Jacket Potatoes

••••••••••••••••••••••••••••••
Classic Jackets: halve each baked potato horizontally and fill with butter and/or soured (dairy sour) cream.

Cheese Jackets: halve each baked potato horizontally and fill with a knob of butter and 30–45 ml/2–3 tbsp grated Cheddar cheese.

Blue Cheese and Cream Jackets: halve each baked potato horizontally and fill with 30–45 ml/2–3 tbsp crumbled blue cheese and 15 ml/ 1 tbsp double (heavy) cream.

Brie and Cranberry Sauce Jackets: halve each baked potato horizontally and fill with a large rinded piece of ripe Brie and 15 ml/1 tbsp cranberry sauce.

Chilli Jackets: halve each baked potato horizontally and fill with hot home-made or bought chilli con carne.

Coleslaw Jackets: halve each baked potato horizontally and fill with coleslaw.

Baked Bean Jackets: halve each baked potato horizontally and fill with hot baked beans.

Cheese-stuffed Potatoes

••••••••••••••••••••••••••••••
Halve each baked potato horizontally and scoop the insides into a bowl. Mash finely, then beat until light with milk and 25 g/1 oz/2 tbsp cream cheese with garlic and herbs, or cream cheese with crushed pepper. Return the mixture to the potato shells, put on a plate and cover with a kitchen paper. Reheat two halves on Full for 1½–1¾ minutes, four halves on Full for 2¾–3¼ minutes.

226

Rarebit-stuffed Potatoes

Halve each baked potato horizontally and scoop the insides into a bowl. Mash finely, then beat until light with a knob of butter or margarine, 15–30 ml/1–2 tbsp cold milk, 5 ml/ 1 tsp made mustard and seasoning to taste. Mix in 30–45 ml/2–3 tbsp grated Cheddar, Gouda, Emmental or Edam cheese. Return the mixture to the potato shells, put on a plate and cover with kitchen paper. Reheat two halves on Full for 1½ –2 minutes, four halves on Full for 3–4 minutes.

Rarebit-stuffed Potatoes with Bacon

Prepare as for Rarebit-stuffed Potatoes, but substitute 15–25 ml/ 1–1½ tbsp crisply cooked crumbled bacon for half the cheese.

Hummous-stuffed Potatoes

Halve each baked potato horizontally and scoop the insides into a bowl. Mash finely, then beat in 30 ml/ 2 tbsp hummous, 30 ml/2 tbsp finely grated carrot and 5 ml/1 tsp chopped coriander (cilantro) leaves. Season well to taste with salt and pepper. Continue as for Rarebit-stuffed Potatoes.

Taramasalata-stuffed Potatoes

Halve each baked potato horizontally and scoop the insides into a bowl. Mash finely, then beat in 15 ml/ 1 tbsp taramasalata, 10 ml/2 tsp finely chopped parsley and plenty of freshly ground black pepper. Continue as for Rarebit-stuffed Potatoes.

Tzatziki-stuffed Potatoes

Halve each baked potato horizontally and scoop the insides into a bowl. Mash finely, then beat in 30 ml/ 2 tbsp tzatziki and 15 ml/1 tbsp grated Feta cheese. Season to taste with freshly ground black pepper. Continue as for Rarebit-stuffed Potatoes.

Hungarian Potatoes with Paprika

SERVES 4

50 g/2 oz/¼ cup margarine or lard
1 large onion, finely chopped
750 g/1½ lb potatoes, cut into
    small chunks
45 ml/3 tbsp dried pepper flakes
10 ml/2 tsp paprika
5 ml/1 tsp salt
300 ml/½ pt/1¼ cups boiling water
60 ml/4 tbsp soured (dairy sour)
    cream

Put the margarine or lard in a 1.75 litre/3 pt/7½ cup dish. Heat, uncovered, on Full for 2 minutes until sizzling. Add the onion. Cook, uncovered, on Full for 2 minutes. Stir in the potatoes, pepper flakes, paprika, salt and boiling water. Cover with clingfilm (plastic wrap) and slit it twice to allow steam to escape. Cook on Full for 20 minutes, turning the dish four times. Allow to stand for 5 minutes. Spoon out on to warmed plates and top each with 15 ml/1 tbsp soured cream.

Dauphine Potatoes

•••••••••••••••••••••••••••••••
SERVES 6

Gratin dauphinoise – one of the French greats and an experience to be relished. Serve with a leafy salad or baked tomatoes, or as an accompaniment to meat, poultry, fish and eggs.

900 g/2 lb waxy potatoes, very thinly sliced
1–2 garlic cloves, crushed
75 ml/5 tbsp melted butter or margarine
175 g/6 oz/1½ cups Emmental or Gruyère (Swiss) cheese
Salt and freshly ground black pepper
300 ml/½ pt/1¼ cups full-cream milk
Paprika

To tenderise the potatoes, place in a large bowl and cover with boiling water. Leave for 10 minutes, then drain. Combine the garlic with the butter or margarine. Butter a deep 25 cm/10 in diameter dish. Beginning and ending with potatoes, fill the dish with alternate layers of potato slices, two-thirds of the cheese and two-thirds of the butter mixture, sprinkling salt and pepper between the layers. Pour the milk carefully down the side of the dish, then scatter over the remaining cheese and garlic butter. Sprinkle with paprika. Cover with clingfilm (plastic wrap) and slit it twice to allow steam to escape. Cook on Full for 20 minutes, turning the dish four times. The potatoes should be slightly *al dente*, like pasta, but if you would prefer them softer, cook on Full for an extra 3–5 minutes. Allow to stand for 5 minutes, then uncover and serve.

Savoyard Potatoes

•••••••••••••••••••••••••••••••
SERVES 6

Prepare as for Dauphine Potatoes, but substitute stock, or half white wine and half stock, for the milk.

Château Potatoes

•••••••••••••••••••••••••••••••
SERVES 6

Prepare as for Dauphine Potatoes, but substitute medium cider for the milk.

Potatoes with Almond Butter Sauce

•••••••••••••••••••••••••••••••
SERVES 4–5

450 g/1 lb new potatoes, unpeeled and scrubbed
30 ml/2 tbsp water
75 g/3 oz/⅓ cup unsalted (sweet) butter
75 g/3 oz/¾ cup flaked (slivered) almonds, toasted (page 205) and crumbled
15 ml/1 tbsp fresh lime juice

Place the potatoes in a 1.5 litre/2½ pt/6 cup dish with the water. Cover with clingfilm (plastic wrap) and slit it twice to allow steam to escape. Cook on Full for 11–12 minutes until tender. Allow to stand while preparing the sauce. Put the butter in a measuring jug and melt, uncovered, on Defrost for 2–2½ minutes. Stir in the remaining ingredients. Toss with the drained potatoes and serve.

Mustard and Lime Tomatoes

SERVES 4

A fresh zestiness makes the tomatoes attractive as a dish on the side with lamb and poultry, and also with salmon and mackerel.

4 large tomatoes, halved
horizontally
Salt and freshly ground black
pepper
5 ml/1 tsp finely grated lime peel
30 ml/2 tbsp wholegrain mustard
Juice of 1 lime

Stand the tomatoes, in a circle, cut sides up, round the edge of a large plate. Sprinkle with salt and pepper. Thoroughly combine the remaining ingredients and spread over the tomatoes. Cook, uncovered, on Full for 6 minutes, turning the plate three times. Allow to stand for 1 minute.

Braised Cucumber

SERVES 4

1 cucumber, peeled
30 ml/2 tbsp butter or margarine,
at kitchen temperature
2.5–5 ml/½–1 tsp salt
30 ml/2 tbsp finely chopped
parsley or coriander (cilantro)
leaves

Slice the cucumber very thinly, leave to stand for 30 minutes, then wring dry in a clean tea towel (dish cloth). Put the butter or margarine in a 1.25 litre/2¼ pt/5½ cup dish and melt, uncovered, on Defrost for 1–1½ minutes. Stir in the cucumber and salt, tossing gently until well coated with butter. Cover with a plate and cook on Full for 6 minutes, stirring twice. Uncover and stir in the parsley or coriander.

Braised Cucumber with Pernod

SERVES 4

Prepare as for Braised Cucumber, but add 15 ml/1 tbsp Pernod with the cucumber.

Marrow Espagnole

SERVES 4

A summer side dish to complement poultry and fish.

15 ml/1 tbsp olive oil
1 large onion, peeled and chopped
3 large tomatoes, blanched,
skinned and chopped
450 g/1 lb marrow (squash),
peeled and cubed
15 ml/1 tbsp marjoram or
oregano, chopped
5 ml/1 tsp salt
Freshly ground black pepper

Heat the oil in a 1.75 litre/3 pt/ 7½ cup dish, uncovered, on Full for 1 minute. Stir in the onion and tomatoes. Cover with a plate and cook on Full for 3 minutes. Mix in all remaining ingredients, adding pepper to taste. Cover with a plate and cook on Full for 8–9 minutes until the marrow is tender. Allow to stand for 3 minutes.

Gratin of Courgettes and Tomatoes

••••••••••••••••••••••••••••••
SERVES 4

3 tomatoes, blanched, skinned and
coarsely chopped
4 courgettes (zucchini), topped,
tailed and thinly sliced
1 onion, chopped
15 ml/1 tbsp malt or rice vinegar
30 ml/2 tbsp chopped flatleaf
parsley
1 garlic clove, crushed
Salt and freshly ground black
pepper
75 ml/5 tbsp Cheddar or
Emmental cheese, grated

Put the tomatoes, courgettes, onion, vinegar, parsley and garlic in a deep 20 cm/8 in diameter dish. Season to taste and toss well to mix. Cover with clingfilm (plastic wrap) and slit it twice to allow steam to escape. Cook on Full for 15 minutes, turning the dish three times. Uncover and sprinkle with the cheese. Either brown conventionally under the grill (broiler) or, to save time, return to the microwave and heat on Full for 1–2 minutes until the cheese bubbles and melts.

Courgettes with Juniper Berries

••••••••••••••••••••••••••••••
SERVES 4–5

8 juniper berries
30 ml/2 tbsp butter or margarine
450 g/1 lb courgettes (zucchini),
topped, tailed and thinly sliced
2.5 ml/½ tsp salt
30 ml/2 tbsp finely chopped
parsley

Crush the juniper berries lightly with the back of a wooden spoon. Put the butter or margarine in a deep 20 cm/8 in diameter dish. Melt, uncovered, on Defrost for 1–1½ minutes. Mix in the juniper berries, courgettes and salt and spread in an even layer to cover the base of the dish. Cover with clingfilm (plastic wrap) and slit it twice to allow steam to escape. Cook on Full for 10 minutes, turning the dish four times. Allow to stand for 2 minutes. Uncover and sprinkle with the parsley.

Buttered Chinese Leaves with Pernod

••••••••••••••••••••••••••••••
SERVES 4

A cross in texture and flavour between white cabbage and firm lettuce, Chinese leaves make a highly presentable cooked vegetable and are greatly enhanced by the addition of Pernod, which adds a delicate and subtle hint of aniseed.

675 g/1½ lb Chinese leaves,
shredded
50 g/2 oz/¼ cup butter or
margarine
15 ml/1 tbsp Pernod
2.5–5 ml/½–1 tsp salt

Put the shredded leaves in a 2 litre/ 3½ pt/8½ cup dish. In a separate dish, melt the butter or margarine on Defrost for 2 minutes. Add to the cabbage with the Pernod and salt and toss gently to mix. Cover with a plate and cook on Full for 12 minutes, stirring twice. Allow to stand for 5 minutes before serving.

Chinese-style Bean Sprouts

SERVES 4

450 g/1 lb fresh bean sprouts
10 ml/2 tsp dark soy sauce
5 ml/1 tsp Worcestershire sauce
5 ml/1 tsp onion salt

Toss all the ingredients together in a large mixing bowl. Transfer to a deep 20 cm/8 in diameter casserole dish (Dutch oven). Cover with a plate and cook on Full for 5 minutes. Allow to stand for 2 minutes, then stir round and serve.

Carrots with Orange

SERVES 4–6

50 g/2 oz/¼ cup butter or
**   margarine**
450 g/1 lb carrots, grated
1 onion, grated
15 ml/1 tbsp fresh orange juice
5 ml/1 tsp finely grated orange
**   peel**
5 ml/1 tsp salt

Put the butter or margarine in a deep 20 cm/8 in diameter dish. Melt, uncovered, on Defrost for 1½ minutes. Stir in all the remaining ingredients and mix thoroughly. Cover with clingfilm (plastic wrap) and slit it twice to allow steam to escape. Cook on Full for 15 minutes, turning the dish twice. Allow to stand for 2–3 minutes before serving.

Braised Chicory

SERVES 4

An unusual vegetable side dish that tastes faintly of asparagus. Serve with egg and poultry dishes.

4 heads chicory (Belgian endive)
30 ml/2 tbsp butter or margarine
1 vegetable stock cube
15 ml/1 tbsp boiling water
2.5 ml/½ tsp onion salt
30 ml/2 tbsp lemon juice

Trim the chicory, discarding any bruised or damaged outer leaves. Remove a cone-shaped core from the base of each to reduce bitterness. Cut the chicory into 1.5 cm/½ in thick slices and put in a 1.25 litre/2¼ pt/ 5½ cup casserole dish (Dutch oven). Melt the butter or margarine separately on Defrost for 1½ minutes. Pour over the chicory. Crumble the stock cube into the boiling water, then add the salt and lemon juice. Spoon over the chicory. Cover with clingfilm (plastic wrap) and slit it twice to allow steam to escape. Cook on Full for 9 minutes, turning the dish three times. Allow to stand for 1 minute before serving with the juices from the dish.

Braised Carrots with Lime
SERVES 4

An intensely orange-coloured carrot dish, designed for meat stews and game.

450 g/1 lb carrots, thinly sliced
60 ml/4 tbsp boling water
30 ml/2 tbsp butter
1.5 ml/¼ tsp turmeric
5 ml/1 tsp finely grated lime peel

Place the carrots in a 1.25 litre/ 2¼ pt/5½ cup dish with the boiling water. Cover with clingfilm (plastic wrap) and slit it twice to allow steam to escape. Cook on Full for 9 minutes, turning the dish three times. Allow to stand for 2 minutes. Drain. Immediately toss in the butter, turmeric and lime peel. Eat straight away.

Fennel in Sherry
SERVES 4

900 g/2 lb fennel
50 g/2 oz/¼ cup butter or
margarine
2.5 ml/½ tsp salt
7.5 ml/1½ tsp French mustard
30 ml/2 tbsp medium-dry sherry
2.5 ml/½ tsp dried or 5 ml/1 tsp
chopped fresh tarragon

Wash and dry the fennel. Discard any brown areas but leave on the 'fingers' and green fronds. Melt the butter or margarine, uncovered, on Defrost for 1½ –2 minutes. Gently beat in the remaining ingredients. Quarter each head of fennel and place in a deep 25 cm/10 in diameter dish. Coat with the butter mixture. Cover with a plate and cook on Full for 20 minutes, turning the dish four times. Allow to stand for 7 minutes before serving.

Wine-braised Leeks with Ham
SERVES 4

5 narrow leeks, about 450g/1 lb in
all
30 ml/2 tbsp butter or margarine,
at kitchen temperature
225 g/8 oz/2 cups cooked ham,
chopped
60 ml/4 tbsp red wine
Salt and freshly ground black
pepper

Trim off the whiskery ends of the leeks, then cut off all but 10 cm/4 in of green 'skirt' from each. Carefully halve the leeks lengthways almost to the top. Wash thoroughly between the leaves under cold running water to remove any earth or grit. Put the butter or margarine in a 25 × 20 cm/ 10 × 8 in dish. Melt on Defrost for 1–1½ minutes, then brush over the base and sides. Arrange the leeks, in a single layer, over the base. Sprinkle with the ham and wine and season. Cover with clingfilm (plastic wrap) and slit it twice to allow steam to escape. Cook on Full for 15 minutes, turning the dish twice. Allow to stand for 5 minutes.

Casseroled Leeks

SERVES 4

5 narrow leeks, about 450g/1 lb in
all
30 ml/2 tbsp butter or margarine
60 ml/4 tbsp vegetable stock
Salt and freshly ground black
pepper

Trim off the whiskery ends of the leeks, then cut off all but 10 cm/4 in of green 'skirt' from each. Carefully halve the leeks lengthways almost to the top. Wash thoroughly between the leaves under cold running water to remove any earth or grit. Cut into 1.5 cm/ ½ in thick slices. Place in a 1.75 litre/3 pt/7½ cup casserole dish (Dutch oven). In a separate bowl, melt the butter or margarine on Defrost for 1½ minutes. Add the stock and season well to taste. Spoon over the leeks. Cover with a plate and cook on Full for 10 minutes, stirring twice.

Casseroled Leeks with Chestnuts

SERVES 4

Rehydrate and cook 225 g/8 oz dried chestnuts as described on page 207. Break into large pieces. Follow the recipe for Casseroled Leeks and add the chestnuts after cooking. Cover with a plate and reheat on Full for 3 minutes.

Casseroled Celery

SERVES 4

Prepare as for Casseroled Leeks, but substitute 450 g/1 lb washed celery for the leeks. If liked, add a small chopped onion and cook for an extra 1½ minutes.

Meat-stuffed Peppers

SERVES 4

4 green (bell) peppers
30 ml/2 tbsp butter or margarine
1 onion, finely chopped
225 g/8 oz/2 cups lean minced
(ground) beef
30 ml/2 tbsp long-grain rice
5 ml/1 tsp dried mixed herbs
5 ml/1 tsp salt
120 ml/4 fl oz/¼ cup hot water

Cut the tops off the peppers and reserve. Discard the inside fibres and seeds from each pepper. Cut a thin sliver off each base so that they stand upright without toppling over. Put the butter or margarine in a dish and heat on Full for 1 minute. Add the onion. Cook, uncovered, on Full for 3 minutes. Mix in the meat, breaking it up with a fork. Cook, uncovered, on Full for 3 minutes. Stir in the rice, herbs, salt and 60 ml/4 tbsp of the water. Spoon the mixture into the peppers. Arrange upright and close together in a clean deep dish. Replace the lids and pour the rest of the water into the dish around the peppers for gravy. Cover with clingfilm (plastic wrap) and slit it twice to allow steam to escape. Cook on Full for 15 minutes, turning the dish twice. Allow to stand for 10 minutes before serving.

Meat-stuffed Peppers with Tomato

SERVES 4

Prepare as for Meat-stuffed Peppers, but substitute tomato juice sweetened with 10 ml/2 tsp caster (superfine) sugar for the water.

Turkey-stuffed Peppers with Lemon and Thyme

SERVES 4

Prepare as for Meat-stuffed Peppers (page 233), but substitute minced (ground) turkey for the beef and 2.5 ml/½ tsp thyme for the mixed herbs. Add 5 ml/1 tsp finely grated lemon peel.

Polish-style Creamed Mushrooms

SERVES 6

Commonplace in Poland and Russia where mushrooms take pride of place on any table. Eat with new potatoes and boiled eggs.

30 ml/2 tbsp butter or margarine
450 g/1 lb button mushrooms
30 ml/2 tbsp cornflour
  (cornstarch)
30 ml/2 tbsp cold water
300 ml/½ pt/1¼ cups soured (dairy
  sour) cream
10 ml/2 tsp salt

Put the butter or margarine in a deep 2.25 litre/4 pt/10 cup dish. Melt, uncovered, on Defrost for 1½ minutes. Mix in the mushrooms. Cover with a plate and cook on Full for 5 minutes, stirring twice. Blend the cornflour smoothly with the water and stir in the cream. Gently stir into the mushrooms. Cover as before and cook on Full for 7–8 minutes, stirring three times, until thick and creamy. Fold in the salt and eat straight away.

Paprika Mushrooms

SERVES 6

Prepare as for Polish-style Creamed Mushrooms, but add 1 crushed garlic clove to the butter or margarine before melting. Mix in 15 ml/1 tbsp each tomato purée (paste) and paprika with the mushrooms. Serve with small pasta.

Curried Mushrooms

SERVES 6

Prepare as for Polish-style Creamed Mushrooms, but add 15–30 ml/ 1–2 tbsp mild curry paste and one crushed garlic clove to the butter or margarine before melting. Substitute thick plain yoghurt for the cream and fold in 10 ml/2 tsp caster (superfine) sugar with the salt. Serve with rice.

Lentil Dhal

SERVES 6–7

Distinctively Oriental with its roots in India, this Lentil Dhal is graciously flavoured with a myriad spices and can be served either as an accompaniment to curries or by itself with rice as a nutritious and complete meal.

*50 g/2 oz/¼ cup ghee, butter or
  margarine*
4 onions, chopped
1–2 garlic cloves, crushed
*225 g/8 oz/1⅓ cups orange lentils,
  thoroughly rinsed*
5 ml/1 tsp turmeric
5 ml/1 tsp paprika
2.5 ml/½ tsp ground ginger
20 ml/4 tsp garam masala
1.5 ml/¼ tsp cayenne pepper
*Seeds from 4 green cardamom
  pods*
15 ml/1 tbsp tomato purée (paste)
*750 ml/1¼ pts/3 cups boiling
  water*
7.5 ml/1½ tsp salt
*Chopped coriander (cilantro)
  leaves, to garnish*

Put the ghee, butter or margarine in a 1.75 litre/3 pt/7½ cup casserole dish (Dutch oven). Heat, uncovered, on Full for 1 minute. Mix in the onions and garlic. Cover with a plate and cook on Full for 3 minutes. Stir in all the remaining ingredients Cover with a plate and cook on Full for 15 minutes, stirring four times. Allow to stand for 3 minutes. If too thick for personal taste, thin down with a little extra boiling water. Fluff up with fork before serving garnished with the coriander.

Dhal with Onions and Tomatoes

SERVES 6–7

3 onions
*50 g/2 oz/¼ cup ghee, butter or
  margarine*
1–2 garlic cloves, crushed
*225 g/8 oz/1⅓ cups orange lentils,
  thoroughly rinsed*
*3 tomatoes, blanched, skinned and
  chopped*
5 ml/1 tsp turmeric
5 ml/1 tsp paprika
2.5 ml/½ tsp ground ginger
20 ml/4 tsp garam masala
1.5 ml/¼ tsp cayenne pepper
*Seeds from 4 green cardamom
  pods*
15 ml/1 tbsp tomato purée (paste)
750 ml/1¼ pts/3 cups boiling water
7.5 ml/1½ tsp salt
1 large onion, thinly sliced
10 ml/2 tsp sunflower or corn oil

Thinly slice 1 onion and chop the remainder. Put the ghee, butter or margarine in a 1.75 litre/3 pt/7½ cup casserole dish (Dutch oven). Heat, uncovered, on Full for 1 minute. Mix in the chopped onions and garlic. Cover with a plate and cook on Full for 3 minutes. Stir in all the remaining ingredients. Cover with a plate and cook on Full for 15 minutes, stirring four times. Allow to stand for 3 minutes. If too thick for personal taste, thin down with a little extra boiling water. Separate the sliced onion into rings and fry (sauté) conventionally in the oil until lightly golden and crisp. Fluff up the dhal with a fork before serving garnished with the onion rings. (Alternatively, omit the sliced onion and instead garnish with ready-prepared fried onions available from supermarkets.)

Vegetable Madras

SERVES 4

25 g/1 oz/2 tbsp ghee or 15 ml/
  1 tbsp groundnut (peanut) oil
1 onion, peeled and chopped
1 leek, trimmed and chopped
2 garlic cloves, crushed
15 ml/1 tbsp hot curry powder
5 ml/1 tsp ground cumin
5 ml/1 tsp garam masala
2.5 ml/½ tsp turmeric
Juice of 1 small lemon
150 ml/¼ pt/⅔ cup vegetable stock
30 ml/2 tbsp tomato purée (paste)
30 ml/2 tbsp toasted cashew nuts
  (page 205)
450 g/1 lb mixed cooked root
  vegetables, diced
175 g/6 oz/¾ cup brown rice,
  boiled
Popadoms, to serve

Put the ghee or oil in a 2.5 litre/
4½ pt/11 cup dish. Heat, uncovered,
on Full for 1 minute. Add the onion,
leek and garlic and mix in thoroughly.
Cook, uncovered, on Full for 3 minutes. Add the curry powder, cumin,
garam masala, turmeric and lemon
juice. Cook, uncovered, on Full for 3
minutes, stirring twice. Add the stock,
tomato purée and cashew nuts. Cover
with an inverted plate and cook on Full
for 5 minutes. Stir in the vegetables.
Cover as before and heat through on
Full for 4 minutes. Serve with the
brown rice and popadoms.

Mixed Vegetable Curry

SERVES 6

1.6 kg/3½ lb mixed vegetables,
  such as red or green (bell)
  peppers; courgettes (zucchini);
  unpeeled aubergines
  (eggplants); carrots; potatoes;
  Brussels sprouts or broccoli;
  onions; leeks
30 ml/2 tbsp groundnut (peanut)
  or corn oil
2 garlic cloves, crushed
60 ml/4 tbsp tomato purée (paste)
45 ml/3 tbsp garam masala
30 ml/2 tbsp mild, medium or hot
  curry powder
5 ml/1 tsp ground coriander
  (cilantro)
5 ml/1 tsp ground cumin
15 ml/1 tbsp salt
1 large bay leaf
400 g/14 oz/1 large can chopped
  tomatoes
15 ml/1 tbsp caster (superfine)
  sugar
150 ml/¼ pt/⅔ cup boiling water
250 g/9 oz/generous 1 cup basmati
  or long-grain rice, boiled
Thick plain yoghurt, to serve

Prepare all the vegetables according
to type. Cut into small cubes or
slice where appropriate. Place in a
2.75 litre/5 pt/12 cup deep dish. Mix in
all the remaining ingredients except
the boiling water and rice. Cover with
a large plate and cook on Full for
25–30 minutes, stirring four times,
until the vegetables are tender but still
firm to the bite. Remove the bay leaf,
blend in the water and adjust the
seasonings to taste – the curry may
need some extra salt. Serve with the
rice and a bowl of thick plain yoghurt.

Jellied Mediterranean Salad

SERVES 6

*300 ml/½ pt/1¼ cups cold
vegetable stock or vegetable
cooking water*
15 ml/1 tbsp powdered gelatine
45 ml/3 tbsp tomato juice
45 ml/3 tbsp red wine
*1 green (bell) pepper, seeded and
cut into strips*
*2 tomatoes, blanched, skinned and
chopped*
30 ml/2 tbsp drained capers
*50g /2 oz/¼ cup chopped gherkins
(cornichons)*
12 stuffed olives, sliced
10 ml/2 tsp anchovy sauce

Pour 45 ml/3 tbsp of the stock or vegetable cooking water in a bowl. Stir in the gelatine. Allow to stand for 5 minutes to soften. Melt, uncovered, on Defrost for 2–2½ minutes. Stir in the remaining stock with the tomato juice and wine. Cover when cold, then chill until just beginning to thicken and set. Place the pepper strips in a bowl and cover with boiling water. Leave for 5 minutes to soften, then drain. Stir the tomatoes and pepper strips into the setting jelly with all the remaining ingredients. Transfer to a 1.25 litre/2¼ pt/5½ cup wetted jelly mould or basin. Cover and chill for several hours until firm. To serve, dip the mould or basin in and out of bowl of hot water to loosen, then run a hot wet knife gently round the sides. Invert on to a wetted plate before serving. (The wetting stops the jelly sticking.)

Jellied Greek Salad

SERVES 6

Prepare as for Jellied Mediterranean Salad, but omit the capers and gherkins (cornichons). Add 125 g/4 oz/ 1 cup finely diced Feta cheese and 1 small chopped onion. Substitute stoned (pitted) black olives for stuffed.

Jellied Russian Salad

SERVES 6

Prepare as for Jellied Mediterranean Salad, but substitute 90 ml/6 tbsp mayonnaise for the tomato juice and wine and 225 g/8 oz/2 cups diced carrots and potatoes for the tomatoes and (bell) pepper. Add 30 ml/2 tbsp cooked peas.

Kohlrabi Salad with Mustardy Mayonnaise

SERVES 6

900 g/2 lb kohlrabi
75 ml/5 tbsp boiling water
5 ml/1 tsp salt
10 ml/2 tsp lemon juice
*60–120 ml/4–6 tbsp thick
mayonnaise*
10–20 ml/2–4 tsp wholegrain mustard
Sliced radishes, to garnish

Peel the kohlrabi thickly, wash well and cut each head into eight pieces Place in a 1.25 litre/3 pt/7½ cup dish with the water, salt and lemon juice. Cover with clingfilm (plastic wrap) and slit it twice to allow steam to escape. Cook on Full for 10–15 minutes, turning the dish three times, until tender. Drain and slice or dice and put in a mixing bowl. Mix together the mayonnaise and mustard and toss the kohlrabi in this mixture until the pieces are thoroughly coated. Transfer to a serving dish and garnish with the radish slices.

Beetroot, Celery and Apple Cups

SERVES 6

60 ml/4 tbsp cold water
15 ml/1 tbsp powdered gelatine
225 ml/8 fl oz/1 cup apple juice
30 ml/2 tbsp raspberry vinegar
5 ml/1 tsp salt
225 g/8 oz cooked (not pickled)
    beetroot (red beets), coarsely
    grated
1 eating (dessert) apple, peeled
    and coarsely grated
1 celery stalk, cut into thin
    matchsticks
1 small onion, chopped

Pour 45 ml/3 tbsp of the cold water in a small bowl and stir in the gelatine. Leave to stand for 5 minutes to soften. Melt, uncovered, on Defrost for 2–2½ minutes. Stir in the remaining cold water with the apple juice, vinegar and salt. Cover when cold, then chill until just beginning to thicken and set. Add the beetroot, apple, celery and onion to the part-set jelly and stir gently until thoroughly combined. Transfer to six small wetted cups, then cover and chill until firm and set. Turn out on to individual plates.

Mock Waldorf Cups

SERVES 6

Prepare as for Beetroot, Celery and Apple Cups, but add 30 ml/2 tbsp chopped walnuts with the vegetables and apple.

Celeriac Salad with Garlic, Mayonnaise and Pistachios

SERVES 6

900 g/2 lb celeriac (celery root)
300 ml/½ pt/1¼ cups cold water
15 ml/1 tbsp lemon juice
7.5 ml/1½ tsp salt
1 garlic clove, crushed
45 ml/3 tbsp coarsely chopped
    pistachio nuts
60–120 ml/4–8 tbsp thick
    mayonnaise
Radicchio leaves and whole
    pistachio nuts, to garnish

Peel the celeriac thickly, wash well and cut each head into eight pieces. Place in a 2.25 litre/4 pt/10 cup dish with the water, lemon juice and salt. Cover with clingfilm (plastic wrap) and slit it twice to allow steam to escape. Cook on Full for 20 minutes, turning the dish four times. Drain and slice and put in a mixing bowl. Add the garlic and chopped pistachio nuts. While still warm, toss with the mayonnaise until the pieces of celeriac are thoroughly coated. Transfer to a serving dish. Garnish with radicchio leaves and pistachios before serving, if possible while still slightly warm.

Continental Celeriac Salad

SERVES 4

An assembly of fine and complementary flavours makes this a suitable Christmas salad to go with cold turkey and gammon.

750 g/1½ lb celeriac (celery root)
75 ml/5 tbsp boiling water
5 ml/1 tsp salt
10 ml/2 tsp lemon juice
For the dressing:
30 ml/2 tbsp corn or sunflower oil
15 ml/1 tbsp malt or cider vinegar
15 ml/1 tbsp made mustard
2.5–5 ml/½–1 tsp caraway seeds
1.5 ml/¼ tsp tsp salt
5 ml/1 tsp caster (superfine) sugar
Freshly ground black pepper

Peel the celeriac thickly and cut it into small cubes. Place in a 1.75 litre/3 pt/7½ cup dish. Add the boiling water, salt and lemon juice. Cover with clingfilm (plastic wrap) and slit it twice to allow steam to escape. Cook on Full for 10–15 minutes, turning the dish three times, until tender. Drain. Thoroughly beat together all the remaining ingredients. Add to the hot celeriac and toss thoroughly. Cover and allow to cool. Serve at room temperature.

Celeriac Salad with Bacon

SERVES 4

Prepare as for Continental Celeriac Salad, but add 4 rashers (slices) bacon, crisply grilled (broiled) and crumbled, at the same time as the dressing.

Artichoke Salad with Peppers and Eggs in Warm Dressing

SERVES 6

400 g/14 oz/1 large can artichoke
*   hearts, drained*
400 g/14 oz/1 large can red
*   pimientos, drained*
10 ml/2 tsp red wine vinegar
60 ml/4 tbsp lemon juice
125 ml/4 fl oz/½ cup olive oil
1 garlic clove, crushed
5 ml/1 tsp continental mustard
5 ml/1 tsp salt
5 ml/1 tsp caster (superfine) sugar
4 large hard-boiled (hard-cooked)
*   eggs (pages 98–9), shelled and*
*   grated*
225 g/8 oz/2 cups Feta cheese,
*   diced*

Halve the artichokes and cut the pimientos into strips. Arrange alternately round a large plate, leaving a hollow in the centre. Put the vinegar, lemon juice, oil, garlic, mustard, salt and sugar in small bowl. Heat, uncovered, on Full for 1 minute, beating twice. Pile the eggs and cheese in a mound in the centre of the salad and gently spoon over the warm dresssing.

Stuffings

For successful results, stuffings (dressings) should be on the loose and crumbly side but still firm enough to hold together when gathered up with the fingertips. Stuffings can be cooked separately in a dish of their own or placed round a bird or joint of meat. If to be used for meat, fish and poultry, allow 50–75 g/2–3 oz prepared stuffing for every 450 g/1 lb. It is important to note that because of the danger of salmonella, only the neck hollows of poultry should be stuffed and the body cavities left empty except for things like fruit – say an orange or lemon – or a portion of butter or margarine.

Sage and Onion Stuffing

MAKES 225–275 G/8–10 OZ/1⅓–1⅔ CUPS

For pork.

25 g/1 oz/2 tbsp butter or margarine
2 onions, pre-boiled (see table page 45), chopped
125 g/4 oz/2 cups white or brown breadcrumbs
5 ml/1 tsp dried sage
A little water or milk
Salt and freshly ground black pepper

Put the butter or margarine in a 1 litre/1¾ pt/4¼ cup dish. Heat, uncovered, on Full for 1 minute. Stir in the onions. Cook, uncovered, on Full for 3 minutes, stirring every minute. Mix in the breadcrumbs and sage and sufficient water or milk to bind to a crumbly consistency. Season to taste. Use when cold.

Celery and Pesto Stuffing

MAKES 225–275 G/8–10 OZ/1⅓–1⅔ CUPS

For fish and poultry.

Prepare as for Sage and Onion Stuffing, but substitute 2 finely chopped celery stalks for the onions. Before seasoning, stir in 10 ml/2 tsp green pesto.

Leek and Tomato Stuffing

MAKES 225–275 G/8–10 OZ/1⅓–1⅔ CUPS

For meat and poultry.

25 g/1 oz/2 tbsp butter or
margarine
2 leeks, white part only, cut into
very thin slices
2 tomatoes, blanched, skinned and
chopped
125 g/4 oz/2 cups fresh white
breadcrumbs
Salt and freshly ground black
pepper
Chicken stock, if necessary

Put the butter or margarine in a 1 litre/1¾ pt/4¼ cup dish. Heat, uncovered, on Full for 1 minute. Stir in the leeks. Cook, uncovered, on Full for 3 minutes, stirring three times. Mix in the tomatoes and breadcrumbs and season to taste. Bind with stock if necessary. Use when cold.

Bacon Stuffing

MAKES 225–275 G/8–10 OZ/1⅓–1⅔ CUPS

For meat, poultry and strong-tasting fish.

4 rashers (slices) streaky bacon,
chopped into small pieces
25 g/1 oz/2 tbsp butter, margarine
or lard
125 g/4 oz/2 cups fresh white
breadcrumbs
5 ml/1 tsp Worcestershire sauce
5 ml/1 tsp made mustard
2.5 ml/½ tsp dried mixed herbs
Salt and freshly ground black
pepper
Milk, if necessary

Put the bacon in a 1 litre/1¾ pt/4¼ cup dish with the butter, margarine or lard. Cook, uncovered, on Full for 2 minutes, stirring once. Mix in the breadcrumbs, Worcestershire sauce, mustard and herbs and season to taste. Bind with milk if necessary.

Bacon and Apricot Stuffing

MAKES 225–275 G/8–10 OZ/1⅓–1⅔ CUPS

For poultry and game

Prepare as for Bacon Stuffing, but add 6 well-washed and coarsely chopped apricot halves with the herbs.

Mushroom, Lemon and Thyme Stuffing

MAKES 225–275 G/8–10 OZ/1⅓–1⅔ CUPS

For poultry.

25 g/1 oz/2 tbsp butter or
margarine
125 g/4 oz button mushrooms,
sliced
5 ml/1 tsp finely grated lemon peel
2.5 ml/½ tsp dried thyme
1 garlic clove, crushed
125 g/4 oz/2 cups fresh white
breadcrumbs
Salt and freshly ground black
pepper
Milk, if necessary

Put the butter or margarine in a 1 litre/1¾ pt/4¼ cup dish. Heat, uncovered, on Full for 1 minute. Stir in the mushrooms. Cook, uncovered, on Full for 3 minutes, stirring twice. Mix in the lemon peel, thyme, garlic and breadcrumbs and season to taste. Bind with milk only if the stuffing remains on the dry side. Use when cold.

Mushroom and Leek Stuffing

MAKES 225–275 G/8–10 OZ/1⅓–1⅔ CUPS

For poultry, vegetables and fish.

25 g/1 oz/2 tbsp butter or
margarine
1 leek, white part only, very thinly
sliced
125 g/4 oz mushrooms, sliced
125 g/4 oz/2 cups fresh brown
breadcrumbs
30 ml/2 tbsp chopped parsley
Salt and freshly ground black
pepper
Milk, if necessary

Put the butter or margarine in a 1.25 litre/2¼ pt/5½ cup dish. Heat, uncovered, on Full for 1 minute. Stir in the leek. Cook, uncovered, on Full for 2 minutes, stirring once. Mix in the mushrooms. Cook, uncovered, on Full for 2 minutes, stirring twice. Mix in the breadcrumbs and parsley and season to taste. Bind with milk only if the stuffing remains on the dry side. Use when cold.

Ham and Pineapple Stuffing

MAKES 225–275 G/8–10 OZ/1⅓–1⅔ CUPS

For poultry.

25 g/1 oz/2 tbsp butter or
margarine
1 onion, finely chopped
1 fresh pineapple ring, skin
removed and flesh chopped
75 g/3 oz/¾ cup cooked ham,
chopped
125 g/4 oz/2 cups fresh white
breadcrumbs
Salt and freshly ground black
pepper

Put the butter or margarine in a 1 litre/1¾ pt/4¼ cup dish. Heat, uncovered, on Full for 1 minute. Stir in the onion. Cook, uncovered, on Full for 2 minutes, stirring once. Mix in the pineapple and ham. Cook, uncovered, on Full for 2 minutes, stirring twice. Fork in the breadcrumbs and season to taste. Use when cold.

Asian Mushroom and Cashew Nut Stuffing

MAKES 225–275 G/8–10 OZ/1⅓–1⅔ CUPS

For poultry and fish.

25 g/1 oz/2 tbsp butter or
margarine
6 spring onions (scallions),
chopped
125 g/4 oz mushrooms, sliced
125 g/4 oz/2 cups fresh brown
breadcrumbs
45 ml/3 tbsp cashew nuts, toasted
(page 205)
30 ml/2 tbsp coriander (cilantro)
leaves
Salt and freshly ground black
pepper
Soy sauce, if necessary

Put the butter or margarine in a 1.25 litre/2¼ pt/5½ cup dish. Heat, uncovered, on Full for 1 minute. Stir in the onions. Cook, uncovered, on Full for 2 minutes, stirring once. Mix in the mushrooms. Cook, uncovered, on Full for 2 minutes, stirring twice. Mix in the breadcrumbs, cashew nuts and coriander and season to taste. Bind with soy sauce only if the stuffing remains on the dry side. Use when cold.

Ham and Carrot Stuffing

MAKES 225–275 G/8–10 OZ/1⅓–1⅔ CUPS

For poultry, lamb and game.

Prepare as for Ham and Pineapple Stuffing, but substitute 2 grated carrots for the pineapple.

Ham, Banana and Sweetcorn Stuffing

MAKES 225–275 G/8–10 OZ/1⅓–1⅔ CUPS

For poultry.

Prepare as for Ham and Pineapple Stuffing, but substitute 1 small coarsely mashed banana for the pineapple. Add 30 ml/2 tbsp sweetcorn (corn) with the breadcrumbs.

Italian Stuffing

MAKES 225–275 G/8–10 OZ/1⅓–1⅔ CUPS

For lamb, poultry and fish.

30 ml/2 tbsp olive oil
1 garlic clove
1 celery stalk, finely chopped
2 tomatoes, blanched, skinned and coarsely chopped
12 stoned (pitted) black olives, halved
10 ml/2 tsp chopped basil leaves
125 g/4 oz/2 cups fresh crumbs made from Italian bread such as ciabatta
Salt and freshly ground black pepper

Put the olive oil in a 1 litre/1¾ pt/4¼ cup dish. Heat, uncovered, on Full for 1 minute. Stir in the garlic and celery. Cook, uncovered, on Full for 2½ minutes, stirring once. Mix in all the remaining ingredients. Use when cold.

Spanish Stuffing

MAKES 225–275 G/8–10 OZ/1⅓–1⅔ CUPS

For strong fish and poultry.

Prepare as for Italian Stuffing, but substitute halved stuffed olives for the stoned (pitted) black olives. Use ordinary white breadcrumbs instead of crumbs from Italian bread and add 30 ml/2 tbsp flaked (slivered) and toasted almonds (page 205).

Orange and Coriander Stuffing

MAKES 175 G/6 OZ/1 CUP

For meat and poultry.

25 g/1 oz/2 tbsp butter or margarine
1 small onion, finely chopped
125 g/4 oz/2 cups fresh white breadcrumbs
Finely grated peel and juice of 1 orange
45 ml/3 tbsp finely chopped coriander (cilantro) leaves
Salt and freshly ground black pepper
Milk, if necessary

Put the butter or margarine in a 1 litre/1¾ pt/4¼ cup dish. Heat, uncovered, on Full for 1 minute. Stir in the onion. Cook, uncovered, on Full for 3 minutes, stirring once. Mix in the crumbs, orange peel and juice and the coriander (cilantro) and season to taste. Bind with milk only if the stuffing remains on the dry side. Use when cold.

Lime and Coriander Stuffing

MAKES 175 G/6 OZ/1 CUP

For fish.

Prepare as for Orange and Coriander Stuffing (page 243), but substitute the grated peel and juice of 1 lime for the orange.

Orange and Apricot Stuffing

MAKES 275 G/10 OZ/1⅔ CUPS

For rich meats and poultry.

125 g/4 oz dried apricots, washed
Warm black tea
25 g/1 oz/2 tbsp butter or margarine
1 small onion, chopped
5 ml/1 tsp finely grated orange peel
Juice of 1 orange
125 g/4 oz/2 cups fresh white breadcrumbs
Salt and freshly ground black pepper

Soak the apricots in warm tea for at least 2 hours. Drain and snip into small pieces with scissors. Put the butter or margarine in a 1.25 litre/2¼ pt/5½ cup dish. Heat, uncovered, on Full for 1 minute. Add the onion. Cook, uncovered, on Full for 2 minutes, stirring once. Mix in all the remaining ingredients including the apricots. Use when cold.

Apple, Raisin and Walnut Stuffing

MAKES 275 G/10 OZ/1⅔ CUPS

For pork, lamb, duck and goose.

25 g/1 oz/ 2 tbsp butter or margarine
1 eating (dessert) apple, peeled, quartered, cored and chopped
1 small onion, chopped
30 ml/2 tbsp raisins
30 ml/2 tbsp chopped walnuts
5 ml/1 tsp caster (superfine) sugar
125 g/4 oz/2 cups fresh white breadcrumbs
Salt and freshly ground black pepper

Put the butter or margarine in a 1.25 litre/2¼ pt/5½ cup dish. Heat, uncovered, on Full for 1 minute. Stir in the apple and onion. Cook, uncovered, on Full for 2 minutes, stirring once. Mix in all the remaining ingredients. Use when cold.

Apple, Prune and Brazil Nut Stuffing

MAKES 275 G/10 OZ/1⅔ CUPS

For lamb and turkey.

Prepare as for Apple, Raisin and Walnut Stuffing, but substitute 8 stoned (pitted) and chopped prunes for the raisins and 30 ml/2 tbsp thinly sliced Brazil nuts for the walnuts.

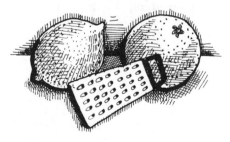

Apple, Date and Hazelnut Stuffing

MAKES 275 G/10 OZ/1⅔ CUPS

For lamb and game.

Prepare as for Apple, Raisin and Walnut Stuffing, but substitute 45 ml/3 tbsp chopped dates for the raisins and 30 ml/2 tbsp toasted (page 205) and chopped hazelnuts for the walnuts.

Garlic, Rosemary and Lemon Stuffing

MAKES 175 G/6 OZ/1 CUP

For lamb and pork.

25 g/1 oz/2 tbsp butter or margarine
2 garlic cloves, crushed
Grated peel of 1 small lemon
5 ml/1 tsp dried rosemary, crushed
15 ml/1 tbsp chopped parsley
125 g/4 oz/2 cups fresh white or brown breadcrumbs
Salt and freshly ground black pepper
Milk or dry red wine, if necessary

Put the butter or margarine in a 1 litre/1¾ pt/4¼ cup dish. Heat, uncovered, on Full for 1 minute. Stir in the garlic and lemon peel. Heat, uncovered, on Full for 30 seconds. Mix round and stir in the rosemary, parsley and breadcrumbs. Season to taste. Bind with milk or wine only if the stuffing remains on the dry side. Use when cold.

Garlic, Rosemary and Lemon Stuffing with Parmesan Cheese

MAKES 175 G/6 OZ/1 CUP.

For beef.

Prepare as for Garlic, Rosemary and Lemon Stuffing, but add 45 ml/3 tbsp grated Parmesan cheese with the breadcrumbs.

Seafood Stuffing

MAKES 275 G/10 OZ/1⅔ CUPS

For fish and vegetables.

25 g/1 oz/2 tbsp butter or margarine
125 g/4 oz/1 cup whole peeled prawns (shrimp)
5 ml/1 tsp finely grated lemon peel
125 g/4 oz/2 cups fresh white breadcrumbs
1 egg, beaten
Salt and freshly ground black pepper
Milk, if necessary

Put the butter or margarine in a 1 litre/1¾ pt/4¼ cup dish. Heat, uncovered, on Full for 1 minute. Stir in the prawns, lemon peel, breadcrumbs and egg and season to taste. Bind with milk only if the stuffing remains on the dry side. Use when cold.

Parma Ham Stuffing

MAKES 275 G/10 OZ/1⅔ CUPS

For poultry.

Prepare as for Seafood Stuffing, but substitute 75 g/3 oz/¾ cup coarsely chopped Parma ham for the prawns (shrimp).

Sausagemeat Stuffing

MAKES 275 G/10 OZ/1⅔ CUPS

For poultry and pork.

25 g/1 oz/2 tbsp butter or margarine
225 g/8 oz/1 cup pork or beef sausagemeat
1 small onion, grated
30 ml/2 tbsp finely chopped parsley
2.5 ml/½ tsp mustard powder
1 egg, beaten

Put the butter or margarine in a 1 litre/1¾ pt/4¼ cup dish. Heat, uncovered, on Full for 1 minute. Mix in the sausagemeat and onion. Cook, uncovered, on Full for 4 minutes, stirring every minute to ensure the sausagemeat is thoroughly broken up. Mix in all the remaining ingredients. Use when cold.

Sausagemeat and Liver Stuffing

MAKES 275 G/10 OZ/1⅔ CUPS

For poultry.

Prepare as for Sausagemeat Stuffing, but reduce the sausagemeat to 175 g/6 oz/¾ cup. Add 50 g/2 oz/½ cup coarsely chopped chicken livers with the sausagemeat and onion.

Sausagemeat and Sweetcorn Stuffing

MAKES 275 G/10 OZ/1⅔ CUPS

For poultry.

Prepare as for Sausagemeat Stuffing, but stir in 30–45 ml/2–3 tbsp cooked sweetcorn (corn) at the end of the cooking time.

Sausagemeat and Orange Stuffing

MAKES 275 G/10 OZ/1⅔ CUPS

For poultry.

Prepare as for Sausagemeat Stuffing, but add 5–10 ml/1–2 tsp finely grated orange peel at the end of the cooking time

Chestnut Stuffing with Egg

MAKES 350 G/12 OZ/2 CUPS

For poultry.

125 g/4 oz/1 cup dried chestnuts, soaked overnight in water, then drained
25 g/1 oz/2 tbsp butter or margarine
1 small onion, grated
1.5 ml/¼ tsp ground nutmeg
125 g/4 oz/2 cups fresh brown breadcrumbs
5 ml/1 tsp salt
1 large egg, beaten
15 ml/1 tbsp double (heavy) cream

Put the chestnuts in a 1.25 litre/2¼ pt/5½ cup casserole dish (Dutch oven) and cover with boiling water. Allow to stand for 5 minutes. Cover with clingfilm (plastic wrap) and slit it twice to allow steam to escape. Cook on Full for 30 minutes until the chestnuts are tender. Drain and allow to cool. Break up into small pieces. Put the butter or margarine in a 1.25 litre/2¼ pt/5½ cup dish. Heat, uncovered, on Full for 1 minute. Add the onion. Cook, uncovered, on Full for 2 minutes, stirring once. Mix in the chestnuts, nutmeg, breadcrumbs, salt and egg. Bind together with the cream. Use when cold.

Chestnut and Cranberry Stuffing

••••••••••••••••••••••••••••••••••
MAKES 350 G/12 OZ/2 CUPS

For poultry.

Prepare as for Chestnut Stuffing with Egg, but instead of egg, bind the stuffing with 30–45 ml/2–3 tbsp cranberry sauce. Add a little cream if the stuffing remains on the dry side.

Creamy Chestnut Stuffing

••••••••••••••••••••••••••••••••••
MAKES 900 G/2 LB/5 CUPS

For poultry and fish.

50 g/2 oz/¼ cup butter, margarine or bacon dripping
1 onion, grated
500 g/1lb 2 oz/2¼ cups canned unsweetened chestnut purée
225 g/8 oz/4 cups fresh white breadcrumbs
Salt and freshly ground black pepper
2 eggs, beaten
Milk, if necessary

Put the butter, margarine or dripping in a 1¾ litre/3 pt/7½ cup dish. Heat, uncovered, on Full for 1½ minutes. Add the onion. Cook, uncovered, on Full for 2 minutes, stirring once. Thoroughly mix in the chestnut purée, breadcrumbs, salt and pepper to taste, and the eggs. Bind with milk only if the stuffing remains on the dry side. Use when cold.

Creamy Chestnut and Sausagement Stuffing

••••••••••••••••••••••••••••••••••
MAKES 900 G/2 LB/5 CUPS

For poultry and game.

Prepare as for Creamy Chestnut Stuffing, but substitute 250 g/9 oz/generous 1 cup sausagemeat for half the chestnut purée.

Creamy Chestnut Stuffing with Whole Chestnuts

••••••••••••••••••••••••••••••••••
MAKES 900 G/2 LB/5 CUPS

For poultry.

Prepare as for Creamy Chestnut Stuffing, but add 12 cooked and broken up chestnuts with the breadcrumbs.

247

Chestnut Stuffing with Parsley and Thyme

MAKES 675 G/1½ LB/4 CUPS

For turkey and chicken.

15 ml/1 tbsp butter or margarine
5 ml/1 tsp sunflower oil
1 small onion, finely chopped
1 garlic clove, crushed
50 g/2 oz/1 cup parsley and thyme
  dry stuffing mix
440 g/15½ oz/2 cups canned
  unsweetened chestnut purée
150 ml/¼ pt/⅔ cup hot water
Finely grated peel of 1 lemon
1.5–2.5 ml/¼–½ tsp salt

Put the butter or margarine and oil in a 1.25 litre/2¼ pt/5½ cup bowl. Heat, uncovered, on Full for 25 seconds. Add the onion and garlic. Cook, uncovered, on Full for 3 minutes. Add the dry stuffing mix and stir in well. Cook, uncovered, on Full for 2 minutes, stirring twice. Remove from the microwave. Gradually stir in the chestnut purée alternately with the hot water until smoothly combined. Stir in the lemon peel and salt to taste. Use when cold.

Chestnut Stuffing with Gammon

MAKES 675 G/1½ LB/4 CUPS

For turkey and chicken.

Prepare as for Chestnut Stuffing with Parsley and Thyme, but add 75 g/ 3 oz/¾ cup chopped gammon with the lemon peel and salt.

Chicken Liver Stuffing

MAKES 350 G/12 OZ/2 CUPS

For poultry and game.

125 g/4 oz/⅔ cup chicken livers
25 g/1 oz/2 tbsp butter or
  margarine
1 onion, grated
30 ml/2 tbsp finely chopped
  parsley
1.5 ml/¼ tsp ground allspice
125 g/4 oz/2 cups fresh white or
  brown breadcrumbs
Salt and freshly ground black
  pepper
Chicken stock, if necessary

Wash the livers and dry on kitchen paper. Cut into small pieces. Put the butter or margarine in a 1.25 litre/ 2¼ pt/5½ cup dish. Heat, uncovered, on Full for 1 minute. Add the onion. Cook, uncovered, on Full for 2 minutes, stirring once. Add the livers. Cook, uncovered, on Defrost for 3 minutes, stirring 3 times. Mix in the parsley, allspice and breadcrumbs and season to taste. Bind with a little stock only if the stuffing remains on the dry side. Use when cold.

Chicken Liver Stuffing with Pecans and Orange

MAKES 350 G/12 OZ/2 CUPS

For poultry and game.

Prepare as for Chicken Liver Stuffing, but add 30 ml/2 tbsp broken pecan nuts and 5 ml/1 tsp finely grated orange peel with the breadcrumbs.

Triple Nut Stuffing

••••••••••••••••••••••••••••••••

MAKES 350 G/12 OZ/2 CUPS

For poultry and meat.

15 ml/1 tbsp sesame oil
1 garlic clove, crushed
125 g/4 oz/⅔ cup finely ground
hazelnuts
125 g/4 oz/⅔ cup finely ground
walnuts
125 g/4 oz/⅔ cup finely ground
almonds
Salt and freshly ground black
pepper
1 egg, beaten

Pour the oil into a fairly large dish. Heat, uncovered, on Full for 1 minute. Add the garlic. Cook, uncovered, on Full for 1 minute. Stir in all the nuts and season to taste. Bind with the egg. Use when cold.

Potato and Turkey Liver Stuffing

••••••••••••••••••••••••••••••••

MAKES 675 G/1½ LB/4 CUPS

For poultry.

450 g/1 lb floury potatoes
25 g/1 oz/2 tbsp butter or
margarine
1 onion, chopped
2 rashers (slices) streaky bacon,
chopped
5 ml/1 tsp dried mixed herbs
45 ml/3 tbsp finely chopped
parsley
2.5 ml/½ tsp ground cinnamon
2.5 ml/½ tsp ground ginger
1 egg, beaten
Salt and freshly ground black
pepper

Cook the potatoes as directed for Creamed Potatoes (page 225), but using only 60 ml/4 tbsp water. Drain and mash. Put the butter or margarine in a 1.25 litre/2¼ pt/5½ cup dish. Heat, uncovered, on Full for 1 minute. Stir in the onion and bacon. Cook, uncovered, on Full for 3 minutes, stirring twice. Mix in all the remaining ingredients including the potatoes, seasoning to taste. Use when cold.

Rice Stuffing with Herbs

••••••••••••••••••••••••••••••••

MAKES 450 G/1 LB/2⅔ CUPS

For poultry.

125 g/4 oz/⅔ cup easy-cook long-
grain rice
250 ml/8 fl oz/1 cup boiling water
2.5 ml/½ tsp salt
25 g/1 oz/2 tbsp butter or
margarine
1 small onion, grated
5 ml/1 tsp chopped parsley
5 ml/1 tsp coriander (cilantro)
leaves
5 ml/1 tsp sage
5 ml/1 tsp basil leaves

Cook the rice with the water and salt as directed (page 213). Put the butter or margarine in a 1.25 litre/2¼ pt/ 5½ cup dish. Heat, uncovered, on Full for 1 minute. Stir in the onion. Cook, uncovered, on Full for 1 minute, stirring once. Mix in the rice and herbs. Use when cold.

Spanish Rice Stuffing with Tomato

••••••••••••••••••••••••••••••••
MAKES 450 G/1 LB/2⅔ CUPS

For poultry.

125 g/4 oz/²⁄₃ cup easy-cook long-grain rice
250 ml/8 fl oz/1 cup boiling water
2.5 ml/½ tsp salt
25 g/1 oz/2 tbsp butter or margarine
1 small onion, grated
30 ml/2 tbsp chopped green (bell) pepper
1 tomato, chopped
30 ml/2 tbsp chopped stuffed olives

Cook the rice with the water and salt as directed (page 213). Put the butter or margarine in a 1.25 litre/2¼ pt/5½ cup dish. Heat, uncovered, on Full for 1 minute. Stir in the onion, green pepper, tomato and olives. Cook, uncovered, on Full for 2 minute, stirring once. Mix in the rice. Use when cold.

Fruited Rice Stuffing

••••••••••••••••••••••••••••••••
MAKES 450 G/1 LB/2⅔ CUPS

For poultry.

125 g/4 oz/²⁄₃ cup easy-cook long-grain rice
250 ml/8 fl oz/1 cup boiling water
2.5 ml/½ tsp salt
25 g/1 oz/2 tbsp butter or margarine
1 small onion, grated
5 ml/1 tsp chopped parsley
6 dried apricot halves, chopped
6 stoned (pitted) prunes, chopped
5 ml/1 tsp finely grated clementine or satsuma peel

Cook the rice with the water and salt as directed (page 213). Put the butter or margarine in a 1.25 litre/2¼ pt/5½ cup dish. Heat, uncovered, on Full for 1 minute. Stir in the onion, parsley, apricots, prunes and peel. Cook, uncovered, on Full for 1 minute, stirring once. Mix in the rice. Use when cold.

Far East Rice Stuffing

••••••••••••••••••••••••••••••••
MAKES 450 G/1 LB/2⅔ CUPS

For poultry.

Prepare as for Rice Stuffing with Herbs (page 249), but use only the coriander (cilantro). Add 6 canned and sliced water chestnuts and 30 ml/2 tbsp coarsely chopped toasted cashew nuts (page 205) with the onion.

Savoury Rice Stuffing with Nuts

••••••••••••••••••••••••••••••••
MAKES 450 G/1 LB/2⅔ CUPS

For poultry.

Prepare as for Rice Stuffing with Herbs (page 249), but use only the parsley. Add 30 ml/2 tbsp flaked (slivered) and toasted almonds (page 205) and 30 ml/2 tbsp salted peanuts with the onion.

Cakes and Breads

Cakes and bread cooked in the microwave turn out light and delicate with a tender crumb and take a fraction of the time one would normally allow for traditional oven baking. Christmas cakes are moist and succulent and a good colour, sponges brilliant, cheesecakes a dream. All the tortes, gâteaux, chocolate cakes, brownies, flapjacks and family cakes you can think of work a treat and there are no complaints either where gingerbreads, carrot cake or fruit-packed health bars are concerned. You can even microwave crumbly shortbread, create hitherto-difficult brandy snaps and produce enviable breads and buns, some with a foreign slant. The answer to all microwaved cakes and breads is to camouflage their pale tops and you'll find instructions for this where it applies throughout the section.

Cakes

Cake Mixes
••••••••••••••••••••••••••••••••••••
Make up shop-bought cake mixes as directed on the packet but whisking for only half the time recommended in the recipe, otherwise the cake will rise too much and then collapse on itself. Add an extra 15 ml/1 tbsp when adding the second amount of water. Divide the mixture between two 20 cm/8 in round shallow dishes, lined with clingfilm (plastic wrap). Cover loosely with kitchen paper and cook singly, allowing 2½ minutes on Full. Allow to cool in the dishes for 5 minutes. Invert on to a wire rack when almost cold, then peel away the clingfilm. Fill as directed, then decorate.

Chocolate Crispies
••••••••••••••••••••••••••••••••••••
MAKES 16

75 g/3 oz/⅓ cup butter or margarine
30 ml/2 tbsp golden (light corn) syrup, melted
15 ml/1 tbsp cocoa (unsweetened chocolate) powder, sifted
45 ml/3 tbsp caster (superfine) sugar
75 g/3 oz/1½ cups cornflakes

Melt the butter or margarine and syrup, uncovered, on Defrost for 2–3 minutes. Stir in the cocoa and sugar. Fold in the cornflakes with a large metal spoon, tossing until well coated. Spoon into paper cake cases (cupcake papers), stand on a board or tray and chill until set.

Devil's Food Cake
••••••••••••••••••••••••••••••••
SERVES 8

A dream of a North American food processor cake, with a light and fluffy texture and deep chocolatey flavour.

100 g/4 oz/1 cup plain (semi-sweet) chocolate, broken into pieces

225 g/8 oz/2 cups self-raising (self-rising) flour

25 g/1 oz/2 tbsp cocoa (unsweetened chocolate) powder

1.5 ml/¼ tsp bicarbonate of soda (baking soda)

200 g/7 oz/scant 1 cup dark soft brown sugar

150 g/5 oz/⅔ cup butter or soft margarine, at kitchen temperature

5 ml/1 tsp vanilla essence (extract)

2 large eggs, at kitchen temperature

120 ml/4 fl oz/½ cup buttermilk or 60 ml/4 tbsp each skimmed milk and plain yoghurt

Icing (confectioners') sugar, for dusting

Closely line the base and sides of a straight-sided deep 20 cm/8 in diameter soufflé dish with clingfilm (plastic wrap). Melt the chocolate in a small bowl on Defrost for 3–4 minutes, stirring twice. Sift the flour, cocoa and bicarbonate of soda directly into a food processor bowl. Add the melted chocolate with all the remaining ingredients and process for about 1 minute or until the ingredients are well combined and the mixture resembles a thick batter. Spoon into the prepared dish and cover loosely with kitchen paper. Cook on Full for 9–10 minutes, turning the dish twice, until the cake has risen to the rim of the dish and the top is covered with small, broken bubbles and looks fairly dry. If any sticky patches remain, cook on Full for a further 20–30 seconds. Allow to stand in the microwave for about 15 minutes (the cake will fall slightly), then take it out and leave to cool until just warm. Carefully lift out of dish by holding the clingfilm and transfer to a wire rack to cool completely. Peel away the clingfilm and dust the top with sifted icing sugar before serving. Store in an airtight container.

Mocha Torte
••••••••••••••••••••••••••••••••
SERVES 8

Prepare as for Devil's Food Cake, but when cold cut the cake horizontally into three layers. Beat 450 ml/¾ pt/2 cups double (heavy) or whipping cream until thick. Sweeten to taste with a little sifted icing (confectioners') sugar, then flavour quite strongly with cold black coffee. Use some of the cream to sandwich the cake layers together, then swirl the remainder over the top and sides. Chill lightly before serving.

Multi-layer Cake
••••••••••••••••••••••••••••••••
SERVES 8

Prepare as for Devil's Food Cake, but when cold cut the cake horizontally into three layers. Sandwich together with apricot jam, whipped cream and grated chocolate or chocolate spread.

Black Forest Cherry Torte

SERVES 8

Prepare as for Devil's Food Cake, but when cold cut the cake horizontally into three layers and moisten each with cherry liqueur. Sandwich together with cherry jam (conserve) or cherry fruit filling. Beat 300 ml/½ pt/1¼ cups double (heavy) or whipping cream until thick. Spread over the top and sides of the cake. Press a crushed chocolate flake bar or grated chocolate against the sides, then decorate the top with halved glacé (candied) cherries.

Chocolate Orange Gateau

SERVES 8

Prepare as for Devil's Food Cake, but when cold cut the cake horizontally into three layers and moisten each with orange liqueur. Sandwich together with fine-shred orange marmalade and a thin round of marzipan (almond paste). Beat 300 ml/½ pt/ 1¼ cups double (heavy) or whipping cream until thick. Colour and sweeten lightly with 10–15 ml/2–3 tsp black treacle (molasses), then stir in 10 ml/2 tsp grated orange peel. Spread over the top and sides of the cake.

Chocolate Butter Cream Layer Cake

SERVES 8–10

30 ml/2 tbsp cocoa (unsweetened chocolate) powder
60 ml/4 tbsp boiling water
175 g/6 oz/¾ cup butter or margarine, at kitchen temperature
175 g/6 oz/¾ cup dark soft brown sugar
5 ml/1 tsp vanilla essence (extract)
3 eggs, at kitchen temperature
175 g/6 oz/1½ cups self-raising (self-rising) flour
15 ml/1 tbsp black treacle (molasses)
Butter Cream Icing (page 274)
Icing (confectioners') sugar, for dusting (optional)

Closely line the base and sides of an 18 × 9 cm/7 × 3½ in diameter soufflé dish with clingfilm (plastic wrap), allowing it to hang slightly over the edge. Mix the cocoa smoothly with the boiling water. Cream together the butter or margarine, sugar and vanilla essence until light and fluffy. Beat in the eggs one at a time, adding 15 ml/ 1 tbsp flour with each one. Fold in the remaining flour with the black treacle until evenly combined. Spread smoothly into the prepared dish and cover loosely with kitchen paper. Cook on Full for 6–6½ minutes until the cake is well risen and no longer damp-looking on top. Do not overcook or the cake will shrink and toughen. Allow to stand for 5 minutes, then ease the cake out of its dish by holding the clingfilm (plastic wrap) and transfer to a wire rack. Gently peel away the wrap and leave to cool. Cut the cake horizontally into three layers and sandwich together with the icing (frosting). Dust the top with sifted icing sugar before cutting, if liked.

Chocolate Mocha Cake

SERVES 8–10

Prepare as for Chocolate Butter Cream Layer Cake (page 253), but flavour the Butter Cream Icing (frosting) with 15 ml/1 tbsp very strong black coffee. For a more intense flavour, add 5 ml/1 tsp ground coffee with the liquid coffee.

Orange-choc Layer Cake

SERVES 8–10

Prepare as for Chocolate Butter Cream Layer Cake (page 253), but add 10 ml/2 tsp finely grated orange peel to the cake ingredients.

Double Chocolate Cake

SERVES 8–10

Prepare as for Chocolate Butter Cream Layer Cake (page 253), but add 100 g/4 oz/1 cup melted and cooled plain (semi-sweet) chocolate to the Butter Cream Icing (frosting). Allow to firm up before using.

Whipped Cream and Walnut Torte

SERVES 8–10

1 Chocolate Butter Cream Layer Cake (see page 253)
300 ml/½ pt/1¼ cups double (heavy) cream
150 ml/¼ pt/⅔ cup whipping cream
45 ml/3 tbsp icing (confectioners') sugar, sifted
Any flavouring essence (extract), such as vanilla, rose, coffee, lemon, orange, almond, ratafia
Nuts, chocolate shavings, silver dragees, crystallised flower petals or glacé (candied) fruits, to decorate

Cut the cake horizontally into three layers. Beat together the creams until thick. Fold in the icing sugar and flavouring to taste. Sandwich the cake layers together with the cream and decorate the top as wished.

Christmas Gâteau

SERVES 8–10

1 Chocolate Butter Cream Layer Cake (see page 253)
45 ml/3 tbsp seedless raspberry jam (conserve)
Marzipan (almond paste)
300 ml/½ pt/1¼ cups double (heavy) cream
150 ml/¼ pt/⅔ cup whipping cream
60 ml/4 tbsp caster (superfine) sugar
Glacé (candied) cherries and edible holly sprigs, to decorate

Cut the cake into three layers and sandwich together with the jam topped with thinly rolled out rounds of marzipan. Beat together the creams and caster sugar until thick and use to cover the top and sides of the cake. Decorate the top with cherries and holly.

American Brownies

MAKES 12

50 g/2 oz/½ cup plain (semi-sweet) chocolate, broken into pieces
75 g/3 oz/⅓ cup butter or margarine
175 g/6 oz/¾ cup dark soft brown sugar
2 eggs, at kitchen temperature, beaten
150 g/5 oz/1¼ cups plain (all-purpose) flour
1.5 ml/¼ tsp baking powder
5 ml/1 tsp vanilla essence (extract)
30 ml/2 tbsp cold milk
Icing (confectioners') sugar, for dusting

Butter and base line a 25 × 16 × 5 cm/ 10 × 6½ × 2 in dish. Melt the chocolate and butter or margarine on Full for 2 minutes, stirring until well mixed. Beat in the sugar and eggs until well combined. Sift together the flour and baking powder, then lightly stir into the chocolate mixture with the vanilla essence and milk. Spread evenly into the prepared dish and cover loosely with kitchen paper. Cook on Full for 7 minutes until the cake is well risen and the top is peppered with small broken air holes. Allow to cool in the dish for 10 minutes. Cut into squares, dust the tops fairly thickly with icing sugar, then leave to cool completely on a wire rack. Store in an airtight container.

Chocolate Nut Brownies

MAKES 12

Prepare as for American Brownies, but add 90 ml/6 tbsp coarsely chopped walnuts with the sugar. Cook for 1 minute extra.

Oaten Toffee Triangles

MAKES 8

125 g/4 oz/½ cup butter or margarine
50 g/2 oz/3 tbsp golden (light corn) syrup
25 ml/1½ tbsp black treacle (molasses)
100 g/4 oz/½ cup dark soft brown sugar
225 g/8 oz/2 cups porridge oats

Thoroughly grease a deep 20 cm/8 in diameter dish. Melt together the butter, syrup, treacle and sugar, uncovered, on Defrost for 5 minutes. Stir in the oats and spread the mixture into the dish. Cook, uncovered, on Full for 4 minutes, turning the dish once. Allow to stand for 3 minutes. Cook for a further 1½ minutes. Allow to cool to lukewarm, then cut into eight triangles. Remove from the dish when cold and store in an airtight container.

Muesli Triangles

MAKES 8

Prepare as for Oaten Toffee Triangles, but substitute unsweetened muesli for the porridge oats.

Chocolate Queenies

MAKES 12

125 g/4 oz/1 cup self-raising (self-rising) flour
30 ml/2 tbsp cocoa (unsweetened chocolate) powder
50 g/2 oz/¼ cup butter or margarine, at kitchen temperature
50 g/2 oz/¼ cup light soft brown sugar
1 egg
5 ml/1 tsp vanilla essence (extract)
30 ml/2 tbsp cold milk
Icing (confectioners') sugar or chocolate spread, to decorate (optional)

Sift together the flour and cocoa. In a separate bowl, cream together the butter or margarine and sugar until soft and fluffy. Beat in the egg and vanilla essence. Fold in the flour mixture alternately with the milk, stirring briskly with a fork without beating. Divide between 12 paper cake cases (cupcake papers). Place six at a time on the glass or plastic turntable, cover loosely with kitchen paper and cook on Full for 2 minutes. Cool on a wire rack. Dust with sifted icing sugar or cover with chocolate spread, if wished. Store in an airtight container.

Flaky Chocolate Queenies

MAKES 12

Prepare as for Chocolate Queenies, but crush a small chocolate flake bar and gently stir it into the cake mixture after the egg and vanilla essence have been added.

Breakfast Bran and Pineapple Cake

MAKES ABOUT 12 PIECES

A fairly dense cake and a useful snack breakfast served with yoghurt and a drink.

100 g/3½ oz/1 cup All Bran cereal
50 g/2 oz/¼ cup dark soft brown sugar
175 g/6 oz canned crushed pineapple
20 ml/4 tsp thick honey
1 egg, beaten
300 ml/½ pt/1¼ cups skimmed milk
150 g/5 oz/1¼ cups self-raising (self-rising) wholemeal flour

Closely line the base and sides of an 18 cm/7 in diameter soufflé dish with clingfilm (plastic wrap), allowing it to hang very slightly over the edge. Put the cereal, sugar, pineapple and honey into a bowl. Cover with a plate and warm on Defrost for 5 minutes. Mix in the remaining ingredients, stirring briskly without beating. Transfer to the prepared dish. Cover loosely with kitchen paper and cook on Defrost for 20 minutes, turning the dish four times. Leave until cooled to just warm, then transfer to a wire rack by holding the clingfilm. When completely cold, store in an airtight container for 1 day before cutting.

Fruited Chocolate Biscuit Crunch Cake

MAKES 10–12

200 g/7 oz/scant 1 cup plain (semi-sweet) chocolate, broken into squares
225 g/8 oz/1 cup unsalted (sweet) butter (not margarine)
2 large eggs, at kitchen temperature, beaten
5 ml/1 tsp vanilla essence (extract)
75 g/ 3 oz/¾ cup coarsely chopped mixed nuts
75 g/3 oz/¾ cup chopped crystallised pineapple or papaya
75 g/3 oz/¾ cup chopped crystallised ginger
25 ml/1½ tbsp icing (confectioners') sugar, sifted
15 ml/1 tbsp fruit liqueur, such as Grand Marnier or Cointreau
225 g/8 oz plain sweet biscuits (cookies) such as digestives (Graham crackers), each snapped into 8 pieces

Closely line the base and sides of a 20 cm/8 in diameter dish or sponge sandwich tin (pan) with clingfilm (plastic wrap). Melt the chocolate pieces in a large bowl, uncovered, on Defrost for 4–5 minutes until very soft but still holding their original shape. Cut the butter into large cubes and melt, uncovered, on Defrost for 2–3 minutes. Stir thoroughly into the melted chocolate with the eggs and vanilla essence. Mix in all the remaining ingredients. When well combined, spread into the prepared tin and cover with foil or clingfilm (plastic wrap). Chill for 24 hours, then carefully lift out and peel away the clingfilm. Cut into wedges to serve. Keep refrigerated between servings as the cake softens at room temperature.

Fruited Mocha Biscuit Crunch Cake

MAKES 10–12

Prepare as for Fruited Chocolate Biscuit Crunch Cake, but melt 20 ml/4 tsp instant coffee powder or granules with the chocolate and substitute coffee liqueur for the fruit liqueur.

Fruited Rum and Raisin Biscuit Crunch Cake

MAKES 10–12

Prepare as for Fruited Chocolate Biscuit Crunch Cake, but substitute 100 g/3½ oz/¾ cup raisins for the crystallised fruit and substitute dark rum for the liqueur.

Fruited Whisky and Orange Biscuit Crunch Cake

MAKES 10–12

Prepare as for Fruited Chocolate Biscuit Crunch Cake, but stir the finely grated peel of 1 orange into the chocolate and butter and substitute whisky for the liqueur.

White Chocolate Fruited Crunch Cake

MAKES 10–12

Prepare as for Fruited Chocolate Biscuit Crunch Cake, but substitute white chocolate for dark.

Two-layer Apricot and Raspberry Cheesecake

••••••••••••••••••••••••••••••••••
SERVES 12

For the base:
100 g/3½ oz/½ cup butter
225 g/8 oz/2 cups chocolate digestive biscuit (Graham cracker) crumbs
5 ml/1 tsp mixed (apple-pie) spice
For the apricot layer:
60 ml/4 tbsp cold water
30 ml/2 tbsp powdered gelatine
500 g/1 lb 2 oz/2¼ cups curd (smooth cottage) cheese
250 g/9 oz/1¼ cups fromage frais or quark
60 ml/4 tbsp smooth apricot jam (conserve)
75 g/3 oz/⅓ cup caster (superfine) sugar
3 eggs, separated
A pinch of salt
For the raspberry layer:
45 ml/3 tbsp cold water
15 ml/1 tbsp powdered gelatine
225 g/8 oz fresh raspberries, crushed and sieved (strained)
30 ml/2 tbsp caster (superfine) sugar
150 ml/¼ pt/⅔ cup double (heavy) cream
For decoration:
Fresh raspberries, strawberries and strings of redcurrants

To make the base, melt the butter, uncovered, on Defrost for 3–3½ minutes. Stir in the biscuit crumbs and mixed spice. Spread evenly over the base of a 25 cm/10 in diameter spring-form cake tin (pan). Chill for 30 minutes until firm.

To make the apricot layer, put the water and gelatine into a basin and stir well to mix. Stand for 5 minutes until softened. Melt, uncovered, on Defrost for 2½–3 minutes. Put in a food processor with the curd cheese, fromage frais or quark, jam, sugar and egg yolks and run the machine until the ingredients are thoroughly combined. Scrape out into a large bowl, cover with a plate and chill until just beginning to thicken and set round the edge. Whisk the egg whites and salt to stiff peaks. Beat one-third into the cheese mixture, then fold in the remainder with a metal spoon or spatula. Spread evenly over the biscuit base. Cover loosely with kitchen paper and chill for at least 1 hour until firm.

To make the raspberry layer, put the water and gelatine into a basin and stir well to mix. Stand for 5 minutes until softened. Melt, uncovered, on Defrost for 1½–2 minutes. Combine with the raspberry purée and sugar. Cover with foil or clingfilm (plastic wrap) and chill until just beginning to thicken and set round the edge. Beat the cream until softly thickened. Beat one-third into the fruit mixture, then fold in the remainder with a metal spoon or spatula. Spread evenly over the cheesecake mixture. Cover loosely and chill for several hours until firm. To serve, run a knife dipped in hot water round the inside edge to loosen the cheesecake. Unclip the tin and remove the side. Decorate the top with fruits. Cut into portions with a knife dipped in hot water.

Peanut Butter Cheesecake

SERVES 10

For the base:
100 g/3½ oz/½ cup butter
225 g/8 oz/2 cups ginger biscuit
(cookie) crumbs
For the topping:
90 ml/6 tbsp cold water
45 ml/3 tbsp powdered gelatine
750 g/1½ lb/3 cups curd (smooth
cottage) cheese
4 eggs, separated
5 ml/1 tsp vanilla essence (extract)
150 g/5 oz/⅔ cup caster (superfine)
sugar
A pinch of salt
150 ml/¼ pt/⅔ cup double (heavy)
cream
60 ml/4 tbsp smooth peanut
butter, at kitchen temperature
Chopped lightly salted or plain
peanuts (optional)

To make the base, melt the butter, uncovered, on Defrost for 3–3½ minutes. Stir in the biscuit crumbs. Spread over the base of a 20 cm/8 in diameter springform tin (pan) and chill for 20–30 minutes until firm.

To make the topping, put the water and gelatine into a basin and stir well to mix. Stand for 5 minutes to soften. Melt, uncovered, on Defrost for 3–3½ minutes. Put in a food processor with the cheese, egg yolks, vanilla essence and sugar and run the machine until smooth. Scrape out into a large bowl. Whisk the egg whites and salt to stiff peaks. Whip the cream until softly thickened. Fold the egg whites and cream alternately into the cheese mixture. Finally, swirl in the peanut butter. Spread evenly into the prepared tin, cover securely and chill for at least 12 hours. To serve, run a knife dipped in hot water round the side to loosen. Unclip the tin and remove the sides.

Decorate with chopped peanuts, if liked. Cut into portions with a knife dipped in hot water.

Lemon Curd Cheesecake

SERVES 10

Prepare as for Peanut Butter Cheesecake, but substitute lemon curd for the peanut butter.

Chocolate Cheesecake

SERVES 10

Prepare as for Peanut Butter Cheesecake, but substitute chocolate spread for the peanut butter.

Sharon Fruit Cheesecake
SERVES 10

A recipe, sent to me by a New Zealand lady, based on the tomato-like fruit tamarillo. As they are not always easy to obtain, winter sharon fruit make an admirable substitute, or even the look-alike persimmon as long as they are very ripe.

For the base:
175 g/6 oz/¾ cup butter
**100 g/3½ oz/½ cup light soft
brown sugar**
**225 g/8 oz malt biscuit (cookie)
crumbs**
For the filling:
4 sharon fruit, chopped
**100 g/4 oz/½ cup light soft brown
sugar**
30 ml/2 tbsp powdered gelatine
30 ml/2 tbsp cold water
300 g/10 oz/1¼ cups cream cheese
3 large eggs, separated
Juice of ½ lemon

Thoroughly rinse a 25 cm/10 in diameter springform tin (pan) and leave wet. Melt the butter or mar-garine, uncovered, on Defrost for 3–3½ minutes. Stir in the sugar and biscuit crumbs. Press evenly over the base of the tin. Chill while preparing the cake filling.

To make the filling, put the sharon fruit into a dish and sprinkle with half the sugar. Put the gelatine into a basin and stir in the water. Stand for 5 minutes until softened. Melt, uncovered, on Defrost for 3–3½ minutes. In separate bowl, beat the cheese until soft and fluffy, then work in the gelatine, egg yolks, lemon juice and remaining sugar. Whisk the egg whites to stiff peaks. Fold into the cheese mixture alternatively with the sharon fruit. Spoon over the biscuit base and chill overnight. To serve, run a knife dipped in hot water round the side to loosen, then unclip the tin and remove the sides.

Blueberry Cheesecake
SERVES 10

Prepare as for Sharon Fruit Cheesecake, but substitute 350 g/ 12 oz blueberries for the sharon fruit.

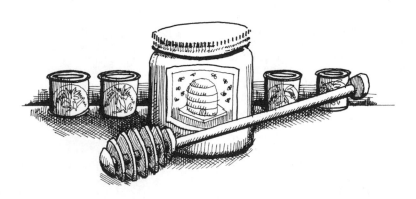

Baked Lemon Cheesecake

SERVES 10

For the base:
75 g/3 oz/⅓ cup butter, at kitchen temperature
175 g/6 oz/1½ cups digestive biscuit (Graham cracker) crumbs
30 ml/2 tbsp caster (superfine) sugar
For the filling:
450 g/1 lb/2 cups medium-fat curd (smooth cottage) cheese, at kitchen temperature
75 g/3 oz/⅓ cup caster (superfine) sugar
2 large eggs, at kitchen temperature
5 ml/1 tsp vanilla essence (extract)
15 ml/1 tbsp cornflour (cornstarch)
Finely grated peel and juice of 1 lemon
150 ml/¼ pt/⅔ cup double (heavy) cream
150 ml/5 oz/⅔ cup soured (dairy sour) cream

To make the base, melt the butter, uncovered, on Defrost for 2–2½ minutes. Stir in the biscuit crumbs and sugar. Line the base and side of a 20 cm/8 in diameter dish with clingfilm (plastic wrap), allowing it to hang very slightly over the edge. Cover the base and sides with the biscuit mixture. Cook, uncovered, on Full for 2½ minutes.

To make the filling, beat the cheese until soft, then blend in the remaining ingredients except the soured cream. Pour into the crumb case and cover loosely with kitchen paper. Cook on Full for 12 minutes, turning the dish twice. The cake is ready when there is some movement to be seen in the middle. and the top has risen slightly and is just beginning to crack. Allow to stand for 5 minutes. Remove from the microwave and gently spread with the soured cream, which will set on top and even out as the cake cools.

Baked Lime Cheesecake

SERVES 10

Prepare as for Baked Lemon Cheesecake, but substitute the peel and juice of 1 lime for the lemon.

Baked Blackcurrant Cheesecake

SERVES 10

Prepare as for Baked Lemon Cheesecake, but when completely cold spread the top with either good-quality blackcurrant jam (conserve) or canned blackcurrant fruit filling.

Baked Raspberry Cheesecake

SERVES 10

Prepare as for Baked Lemon Cheesecake, but substitute raspberry blancmange powder for the cornflour (cornstarch). Decorate the top with fresh raspberries,

Fruit and Nut Butter Cheesecake

•••••••••••••••••••••••••••••••••
SERVES 8–10

A continental-style cheesecake, the sort you'd find in a quality patisserie.

45 ml/3 tbsp flaked (slivered) almonds
75 g/3 oz/⅓ cup butter
175 g/6 oz/1½ cups oaten biscuit (cookie) or digestive biscuit (Graham cracker) crumbs
450 g/1 lb/2 cups curd (smooth cottage) cheese, at kitchen temperature
125 g/4 oz/½ cup caster (superfine) sugar
15 ml/1 tbsp cornflour (cornstarch)
3 eggs, at kitchen temperature, beaten
Juice of ½ fresh lime or lemon
30 ml/2 tbsp raisins

Put the almonds on a plate and toast, uncovered, on Full for 2–3 minutes. Melt the butter, uncovered, on Defrost for 2–2½ minutes. Thoroughly butter a 20 cm/8 in diameter dish and cover the base and side with the biscuit crumbs. Beat the cheese with all the remaining ingredients and stir in the almonds and melted butter. Spread evenly over the biscuit crumbs and cover loosely with kitchen paper. Cook on Defrost for 24 minutes, turning the dish four times. Remove from the microwave and leave to cool. Chill for at least 6 hours before cutting.

Preserved Ginger Cake

•••••••••••••••••••••••••••••••••
SERVES 8

225 g/8 oz/2 cups self-raising (self-rising) flour
10 ml/2 tsp mixed (apple-pie) spice
125 g/4 oz/½ cup butter or margarine, at kitchen temperature
125 g/4 oz/½ cup light soft brown sugar
100 g/4 oz/1 cup chopped preserved ginger in syrup
2 eggs, beaten
75 ml/5 tbsp cold milk
Icing (confectioners') sugar, for dusting

Closely line a 20 cm/8 in diameter soufflé or similar straight-sided dish with clingfilm (plastic wrap), allowing it to hang very slightly over the edge. Sift the flour and spice into a bowl. Finely rub in the butter or margarine. Fork in the sugar and ginger, making sure they are evenly distributed. Stir to a soft consistency with the eggs and milk. When smoothly combined, spoon into the prepared dish and cover lightly with kitchen paper. Cook on Full for 6½–7½ minutes until the cake is well risen and beginning to shrink away from the side. Allow to stand for 15 minutes. Transfer to a wire rack by holding the clingfilm. Peel away the wrap when cold and store the cake in an airtight container. Dust with icing sugar before serving.

Preserved Ginger Cake with Orange

•••••••••••••••••••••••••••••••••
SERVES 8

Prepare as for Preserved Ginger Cake, but add the coarsely grated peel of 1 small orange with the eggs and milk.

Honey Cake with Nuts
·······························
SERVES 8–10

A star of a cake, full of sweetness and light. It is Greek in origin, where it is known as *karithopitta*. Serve it with coffee at the end of a meal.

For the base:
100 g/3½ oz/½ cup butter, at kitchen temperature
175 g/6 oz/¾ cup light soft brown sugar
4 eggs, at kitchen temperature
5 ml/1 tsp vanilla essence (extract)
10 ml/2 tsp bicarbonate of soda (baking soda)
10 ml/2 tsp baking powder
5 ml/1 tsp ground cinnamon
75 g/3 oz/¾ cup plain (all-purpose) flour
75 g/3 oz/¾ cup cornflour (cornstarch)
100 g/3½ oz/1 cup flaked (slivered) almonds
For the syrup:
200 ml/7 fl oz/scant 1 cup warm water
60 ml/4 tbsp dark soft brown sugar
5 cm/2 in piece cinnamon stick
5 ml/1 tsp lemon juice
150 g/5 oz/⅔ cup clear dark honey
For decoration:
60 ml/4 tbsp chopped mixed nuts
30 ml/2 tbsp clear dark honey

To make the base, closely line the base and side of an 18 cm/7 in diameter soufflé dish with clingfilm (plastic wrap), allowing it to hang very slightly over the edge. Put all the ingredients except the almonds in a food processor bowl and run the machine until smooth and evenly combined. Pulse in the almonds briefly to stop them breaking up too much. Spread the mixture into the prepared dish and cover lightly with kitchen paper. Cook on Full for 8 minutes, turning the dish twice, until the cake has risen appreciably and the top is peppered with small air pockets. Allow to stand for 5 minutes, then invert into a shallow serving dish and peel away the clingfilm.

To make the syrup, place all the ingredients in a jug and cook, uncovered, on Full for 5–6 minutes or until the mixture just begins to bubble. Watch closely in case it starts to boil over. Allow to stand for 2 minutes, then gently stir round with a wooden spoon to mix the ingredients smoothly. Spoon slowly over the cake until all the liquid is absorbed. Combine the nuts and honey in small dish. Warm through, uncovered, on Full for 1½ minutes. Spread or spoon over the top of the cake.

Gingered Honey Cake

SERVES 10–12

45 ml/3 tbsp orange marmalade
225 g/8 oz/1 cup clear dark honey
2 eggs
125 ml/4 fl oz/½ cup corn or
 sunflower oil
150 ml/¼ pt/⅔ cup warm water
250 g/9 oz/generous 2 cups self-
 raising (self-rising) flour
5 ml/1 tsp bicarbonate of soda
 (baking soda)
3 tsp ground ginger
10 ml/2 tsp ground allspice
5 ml/1 tsp ground cinnamon

Closely line a deep 1.75 litre/3 pt/7½ cup soufflé dish with cling-film (plastic wrap), allowing it to hang very slightly over the edge. Put the marmalade, honey, eggs, oil and water in a food processor and blend until smooth, then switch off. Sift together all the remaining ingredients and spoon into the processor bowl. Run the machine until the mixture is well combined. Spoon into the prepared dish and cover lightly with kitchen paper. Cook on Full for 10–10½ minutes until the cake is well risen and the top is covered with tiny air holes. Allow to cool almost completely in the dish, then transfer to a wire rack by holding the clingfilm. Carefully peel away the clingfilm and leave until completely cold. Store in an airtight container for 1 day before cutting.

Gingered Syrup Cake

SERVES 10–12

Prepare as for Gingered Honey Cake, but substitute golden (light corn) syrup for the honey.

Traditional Gingerbread

SERVES 8–10

A winter's tale of the best kind, essential for Hallowe'en and Guy Fawkes night.

175 g/6 oz/1½ cups plain (all-
 purpose) flour
15 ml/1 tbsp ground ginger
5 ml/1 tsp ground allspice
10 ml/2 tsp bicarbonate of soda
 (baking soda)
125 g/4 oz/⅓ cup golden (light
 corn) syrup
25 ml/1½ tbsp black treacle
 (molasses)
30 ml/2 tbsp dark soft brown
 sugar
45 ml/3 tbsp lard or white cooking
 fat (shortening)
1 large egg, beaten
60 ml/4 tbsp cold milk

Closely line the base and side of a 15 cm/6 in diameter soufflé dish with clingfilm (plastic wrap), allowing it to hang very slightly over the edge. Sift the flour, ginger, allspice and bicarbonate of soda into a mixing bowl. Put the syrup, treacle, sugar and fat in another bowl and heat, un-covered, on Full for 2½–3 minutes until the fat has just melted. Stir well to blend. Mix with a fork into the dry ingredients with the egg and milk. When well combined, transfer to the prepared dish and cover lightly with kitchen paper. Cook on Full for 3–4 minutes until the gingerbread is well risen with a hint of a shine across the top. Allow to stand 10 minutes. Transfer to a wire rack by holding the clingfilm. Peel away the clingfilm and store the gingerbread in an airtight container for 1–2 days before cutting.

Orange Gingerbread

•••••••••••• SERVES 8–10 ••••••••••••

Prepare as for Traditional Gingerbread, but add the finely grated peel of 1 small orange with the egg and milk.

Coffee Apricot Torte

••••••••••••• SERVES 8 •••••••••••••

4 digestive biscuits (Graham crackers), finely crushed
225 g/8 oz/1 cup butter or margarine, at kitchen temperature
225 g/8 oz/1 cup dark soft brown sugar
4 eggs, at kitchen temperature
225 g/8 oz/2 cups self-raising (self-rising) flour
75 ml/5 tbsp coffee and chicory essence (extract)
425 g/14 oz/1 large can apricot halves, drained
300 ml/½ pt/1¼ cups double (heavy) cream
90 ml/6 tbsp flaked (slivered) almonds, toasted (page 205)

Brush two shallow 20 cm/8 inch diameter dishes with melted butter, then line the bases and sides with the biscuit crumbs. Cream together the butter or margarine and sugar until light and fluffy. Beat in the eggs one at a time, adding 15 ml/1 tbsp flour with each. Fold in the remaining flour alternately with 45 ml/3 tbsp of the coffee essence. Spread equally into the prepared dishes and cover loosely with kitchen paper. Cook, one at a time, on Full for 5 minutes. Allow to cool in the dishes for 5 minutes, then invert on to a wire rack. Chop three of the apricots and set aside the remainder. Whip the cream with the remaining coffee essence until thick. Take out about a quarter of the cream and stir in the chopped apricots. Use to sandwich the cakes together. Cover the top and sides with the remaining cream. Press the almonds against the side and decorate the top with the reserved apricots, cut sides down.

Rum Pineapple Torte

••••••••••••• SERVES 8 •••••••••••••

Prepare as for Coffee Apricot Torte, but omit the apricots. Flavour the cream with 30 ml/2 tbsp dark rum instead of the coffee essence (extract). Stir 2 chopped canned pineapple rings into three-quarters of the cream and use to sandwich the cakes together. Cover the top and sides with the remaining cream and decorate with halved pineapple rings. Stud with green and yellow glacé (candied) cherries, if wished.

Rich Christmas Cake

MAKES 1 LARGE FAMILY CAKE

A luxurious cake, full of the splendours of Christmas and well endowed with alcohol. Keep it plain or coat it with marzipan (almond paste) and white icing (frosting).

200 ml/7 fl oz/scant 1 cup sweet sherry
75 ml/5 tbsp brandy
5 ml/1 tsp mixed (apple-pie) spice
5 ml/1 tsp vanilla essence (extract)
10 ml/2 tsp dark soft brown sugar
350 g/12 oz/2 cups mixed dried fruit (fruit cake mix)
15 ml/1 tbsp chopped mixed peel
15 ml/1 tbsp red glacé (candied) cherries
50 g/2 oz/⅓ cup dried apricots
50 g/2 oz/⅓ cup chopped dates
Finely grated peel of 1 small orange
50 g/2 oz/½ cup chopped walnuts
125 g/4 oz/½ cup unsalted (sweet) butter, melted
175 g/6 oz/¾ cup dark soft brown sugar
125 g/4 oz/1 cup self-raising (self-rising) flour
3 small eggs

Put the sherry and brandy in a large mixing bowl. Cover with a plate and cook on Full for 3–4 minutes until the mixture just begins to bubble. Add the spice, vanilla, the 10 ml/2 tsp brown sugar, the dried fruit, mixed peel, cherries, apricots, dates, orange peel and walnuts. Mix thoroughly. Cover with a plate and warm through on Defrost for 15 minutes, stirring four times. Leave overnight for the flavours to mature. Closely line a 20 cm/8 in diameter soufflé dish with clingfilm (plastic wrap), allowing it to hang very slightly over the edge. Stir the butter, brown sugar, flour and eggs into the cake mixture. Spoon into the prepared dish and cover loosely with kitchen paper. Cook on Defrost for 30 minutes, turning four times. Allow to stand in the microwave for 10 minutes. Cool to lukewarm, then carefully transfer to a wire rack by holding the clingfilm. Peel away the clingfilm when the cake is cold. To store, wrap in a double thickness of greaseproof (waxed) paper, then wrap again in foil. Store in a cool place for about 2 weeks before covering and icing.

Fast Simnel Cake

MAKES 1 LARGE FAMILY CAKE

Follow the recipe for Rich Christmas Cake and store for 2 weeks. The day before serving, cut the cake in half to make two layers. Brush both cut sides with melted apricot jam (conserve) and sandwich together with 225–300 g/8–11 oz marzipan (almond paste) rolled out to a thick round. Decorate the top with shop-bought miniature Easter eggs and chicks.

Seed Cake

SERVES 8

A reminder of old times, known in Wales as shearing cake.

225 g/8 oz/2 cups self-raising (self-rising) flour
125 g/4 oz/½ cup butter or margarine
175 g/6 oz/¾ cup light soft brown sugar
Finely grated peel of 1 lemon
10–20 ml/2–4 tsp caraway seeds
10 ml/2 tsp grated nutmeg
2 eggs, beaten
150 ml/¼ pt/⅔ cup cold milk
75 ml/5 tbsp icing (confectioners') sugar, sifted
10–15 ml/2–3 tsp lemon juice

Closely line the base and side of a 20 cm/8 in diameter soufflé dish with clingfilm (plastic wrap), allowing it to hang very slightly over the edge. Sift the flour into a bowl and rub in the butter or margarine. Add the brown sugar, lemon peel, caraway seeds and nutmeg and mix in the eggs and milk with a fork to form a smooth, fairly soft batter. Transfer to the prepared dish and cover loosely with kitchen paper. Cook on Full for 7–8 minutes, turning the dish twice until the cake has risen to the top of the dish and the surface is peppered with small holes. Allow to stand for 6 minutes, then invert on to a wire rack. When completely cold, peel away the clingfilm, then turn the cake the right way up. Combine the icing sugar and lemon juice to make a thickish paste. Spread over the top of the cake.

Simple Fruit Cake

SERVES 8

225 g/8 oz/2 cups self-raising (self-rising) flour
10 ml/2 tsp mixed (apple-pie) spice
125 g/4 oz/½ cup butter or margarine
125 g/4 oz/½ cup light soft brown sugar
175 g/6 oz/1 cup mixed dried fruit (fruit cake mix)
2 eggs
75 ml/5 tbsp cold milk
75 ml/5 tbsp icing (confectioners') sugar

Closely line an 18 cm/7 in diameter soufflé dish with clingfilm (plastic wrap), allowing it to hang very slightly over the edge. Sift the flour and spice into a bowl and rub in the butter or margarine. Add the sugar and dried fruit. Beat together the eggs and milk and pour into the dry ingredients, stirring to a smooth soft consistency with a fork. Spoon into the prepared dish and cover loosely with kitchen paper. Cook on Full for 6½–7 minutes until the cake is well risen and just beginning to shrink away from the side of the dish. Remove from the microwave and allow to stand for 10 minutes. Transfer to a wire rack by holding the clingfilm. When completely cold, peel away the clingfilm and dust the top with sifted icing sugar.

Date and Walnut Cake

SERVES 8

Prepare as for Simple Fruit Cake, but substitute a mixture of chopped dates and walnuts for the dried fruit.

Carrot Cake

SERVES 8

Once called paradise cake, this transatlantic import has been with us for a good many years and never loses its appeal.

For the cake:
3–4 carrots, cut into chunks
50 g/2 oz/½ cup walnut pieces
50 g/2 oz/½ cup packeted chopped dates, rolled in sugar
175 g/6 oz/¾ cup light soft brown sugar
2 large eggs, at kitchen temperature
175 ml/6 fl oz/¾ cup sunflower oil
5 ml/1 tsp vanilla essence (extract)
30 ml/2 tbsp cold milk
150 g/5 oz/1¼ cups plain (all-purpose) flour
5 ml/1 tsp baking powder
4 ml/¾ tsp bicarbonate of soda (baking soda)
5 ml/1 tsp mixed (apple-pie) spice
For the cream cheese frosting:
175 g/6 oz/¾ cup full-fat cream cheese, at kitchen temperature
5 ml/1 tsp vanilla essence (extract)
75 g/3 oz/½ cup icing (confectioners') sugar, sifted
15 ml/1 tbsp freshly squeezed lemon juice

To make the cake, brush a 20 cm/8 in diameter microwave ring mould with oil and line the base with non-stick parchment paper. Put the carrots and walnut pieces into a blender or food processor and run the machine until both are coarsely chopped. Transfer to a bowl and work in the dates, sugar, eggs, oil, vanilla essence and milk. Sift together the dry ingredients, then stir into the carrot mixture with a fork. Transfer to the prepared mould. Cover with clingfilm (plastic wrap) and slit it twice to allow steam to escape. Cook on Full for 6 minutes, turning three times. Allow to stand for 15 minutes, then turn out on to a wire rack. Remove the paper. Invert on to a plate when cooled completely.

To make the cream cheese frosting, beat the cheese until smooth. Add the rest of the ingredients and beat lightly until smooth. Spread thickly over the top of the cake.

Parsnip Cake

SERVES 8

Prepare as for Carrot Cake, but substitute 3 small parsnips for the carrots.

Pumpkin Cake

SERVES 8

Prepare as for Carrot Cake, but substitute peeled pumpkin for the carrots, allowing a medium wedge which should yield about 175 g/6 oz seeded flesh. Substitute dark soft brown sugar for light and allspice for the mixed (apple-pie) spice.

Scandinavian Cardamom Cake

• •
SERVES 8

Cardamom is much used in Scandinavian baking and this cake is a typical example of northern hemisphere exotica. Try your local ethnic food shop if you have any trouble getting the ground cardamom.

For the cake:
175 g/6 oz/1½ cups self-raising (self-rising) flour
2.5 ml/½ tsp baking powder
75 g/3 oz/⅓ cup butter or margarine, at kitchen temperature
75 g/3 oz/⅓ cup light soft brown sugar
10 ml/2 tsp ground cardamom
1 egg
Cold milk
For the topping:
30 ml/2 tbsp flaked (slivered) almonds, toasted (page 205)
30 ml/2 tbsp light soft brown sugar
5 ml/1 tsp ground cinnamon

Line a deep 16.5 cm/6½ in diameter dish with clingfilm (plastic wrap), allowing it to hang very slightly over the edge. Sift the flour and baking powder into a bowl and rub in the butter or margarine finely. Add the sugar and cardamom. Beat the egg in a measuring jug and make up to 150 ml/ ¼ pt/⅔ cup with milk. Stir into the dry ingredients with a fork until well mixed but avoid beating. Pour into the prepared dish. Combine the topping ingredients and sprinkle over the cake. Cover with clingfilm and slit it twice to allow steam to escape. Cook on Full for 4 minutes, turning twice. Allow to stand for 10 minutes, then carefully transfer to a wire rack by holding the clingfilm. Carefully peel away the clingfilm when the cake is cold.

Fruited Tea Bread

• •
MAKES 8 SLICES

225 g/8 oz/1⅓ cups mixed dried fruit (fruit cake mix)
100 g/3½ oz/½ cup dark soft brown sugar
30 ml/2 tbsp cold strong black tea
100 g/4 oz/1 cup self-raising (self-rising) wholemeal flour
5 ml/1 tsp ground allspice
1 egg, at kitchen temperature, beaten
8 whole almonds, blanched
30 ml/2 tbsp golden (light corn) syrup
Butter, for spreading

Closely line the base and side of a 15 cm/6 in diameter soufflé dish with clingfilm (plastic wrap), allowing it to hang very slightly over the side. Put the fruit, sugar and tea into a bowl, cover with a plate and cook on Full for 5 minutes. Stir in the flour, allspice and egg with a fork, then transfer to the prepared dish. Arrange the almonds on top. Cover loosely with kitchen paper and cook on Defrost for 8–9 minutes until the cake is well risen and beginning to shrink away from the side of the dish. Allow to stand for 10 minutes, then transfer to a wire rack by holding the clingfilm. Warm the syrup in a cup on Defrost for 1½ minutes. Peel the clingfilm off the cake and brush the top with the warmed syrup. Serve sliced and buttered.

Victoria Sandwich Cake

SERVES 8

175 g/6 oz/1½ cups self-raising (self-rising) flour
175 g/6 oz/¾ cup butter or margarine, at kitchen temperature
175 g/6 oz/¾ cup caster (superfine) sugar
3 eggs, at kitchen temperature
45 ml/3 tbsp cold milk
45 ml/3 tbsp jam (conserve)
120 ml/4 fl oz/½ cup double (heavy) or whipping cream, whipped
Icing (confectioners') sugar, sifted, for dusting

Line the bases and sides of two shallow 20 cm/8 in diameter dishes with clingfilm (plastic wrap), allowing it to hang very slightly over the edge. Sift the flour on to a plate. Cream together the butter or margarine and sugar until the mixture is light and fluffy and the consistency of whipped cream. Beat in the eggs one at a time, adding 15 ml/1 tbsp flour with each. Fold in the remaining flour alternately with the milk using a large metal spoon. Spread equally into the prepared dishes. Cover loosely with kitchen paper. Cook one at a time on Full for 4 minutes. Allow to cool to lukewarm, then invert on to a wire rack. Peel away the clingfilm and leave until completely cold. Sandwich together with the jam and whipped cream and dust the top with icing sugar before serving.

Walnut Cake

SERVES 8

175 g/6 oz/1½ cups self-raising (self-rising) flour
175 g/6 oz/¾ cup butter or margarine, at kitchen temperature
5 ml/1 tsp vanilla essence (extract)
175 g/6 oz/¾ cup caster (superfine) sugar
3 eggs, at kitchen temperature
50 g/2 oz/½ cup walnuts, finely chopped
45 ml/3 tbsp cold milk
2 quantities Butter Cream Icing (page 274)
16 walnut halves, to decorate

Line the bases and sides of two shallow 20 cm/8 in diameter dishes with clingfilm (plastic wrap), allowing it to hang very slightly over the edge. Sift the flour on to a plate. Cream together the butter or margarine, vanilla essence and sugar until the mixture is light and fluffy and the consistency of whipped cream. Beat in the eggs one at a time, adding 15 ml/1 tbsp flour with each. Using a large metal spoon, fold in the walnuts with the remaining flour alternately with the milk. Spread equally into the prepared dishes. Cover loosely with kitchen paper. Cook one at a time on Full for 4½ minutes. Allow to cool to lukewarm, then invert on to a wire rack. Peel away the clingfilm and leave until completely cold. Sandwich together with half the icing (frosting) and top the cake with the remainder. Arrange a border of walnut halves on the top of the cake to decorate.

Carob Cake
SERVES 8

Prepare as for Victoria Sandwich Cake but substitute 25 g/1 oz/¼ cup cornflour (cornstarch) and 25 g/1 oz/ ¼ cup carob powder for 50 g/2 oz/ ½ cup of the flour. Sandwich together with cream and/or canned or fresh fruit. Add 5 ml/1 tsp vanilla essence (extract) to the creamed ingredients, if wished.

Easy Chocolate Cake
SERVES 8

Prepare as for Victoria Sandwich Cake, but substitute 25 g/1 oz/ ¼ cup cornflour (cornstarch) and 25 g/ 1 oz/¼ cup cocoa (unsweetened chocolate) powder for 50 g/2 oz/½ cup of the flour. Sandwich together with cream and/or chocolate spread

Almond Cake
SERVES 8

Prepare as for Victoria Sandwich Cake, but substitute 40 g/1½ oz/ 3 tbsp ground almonds for the same amount of flour. Flavour the creamed ingredients with 2.5–5 ml/½–1 tsp almond essence (extract). Sandwich together with smooth apricot jam (conserve) and a thin round of marzipan (almond paste).

Victoria Sandwich Gâteau
SERVES 8

Prepare as for Victoria Sandwich Cake or any of the variations. Sandwich together with cream or Butter Cream Icing (frosting) (page 274) and/or jam (conserve), chocolate spread, peanut butter, orange or lemon curd, orange marmalade, canned fruit filling, honey or marzipan

(almond paste). Coat the top and side with cream or Butter Cream Icing. Decorate with fresh or preserved fruits, nuts or dragees. For an even richer cake, halve each baked layer to make total of four layers before filling.

Nursery Tea Sponge Cake
MAKES 6 SLICES

75 g/3 oz/⅔ cup caster (superfine) sugar
3 eggs, at kitchen temperature
75 g/3 oz/¾ cup plain (all-purpose) flour
90 ml/6 tbsp double (heavy) or whipping cream, whipped
45 ml/3 tbsp jam (conserve)
Caster (superfine) sugar, for sprinkling

Line the base and side of a 18 cm/ 7 in diameter soufflé dish with clingfilm (plastic wrap), allowing it to hang very slightly over the edge. Put the sugar in a bowl and warm, uncovered, on Defrost for 30 seconds. Add the eggs and beat until the mixture froths up and thickens to the consistency of whipped cream. Gently and lightly cut and fold in the flour using a metal spoon. Do not beat or stir. When the ingredients are well combined, transfer to the prepared dish. Cover loosely with kitchen paper and cook on Full for 4 minutes. Allow to stand for 10 minutes, then transfer to a wire rack by holding the clingfilm. When cold, peel away the clingfilm. Split in half and sandwich together with the cream and jam. Sprinkle the top with caster sugar before serving.

Lemon Sponge Cake
•••••••••••••••••••••••••••••••
MAKES 6 SLICES

Prepare as for Nursery Tea Sponge Cake (page 271), but add 10 ml/ 2 tsp finely grated lemon peel to the warmed egg and sugar mixture immediately before adding the flour. Sandwich together with lemon curd and thick cream.

Orange Sponge Cake
•••••••••••••••••••••••••••••••
MAKES 6 SLICES

Prepare as for Nursery Tea Sponge Cake (page 271), but add 10 ml/ 2 tsp finely grated orange peel to the warmed egg and sugar mixture immediately before adding the flour. Sandwich together with chocolate spread and thick cream.

Espresso Coffee Cake
•••••••••••••••••••••••••••••••
SERVES 8

250 g/8 oz/2 cups self-raising (self-rising) flour
15 ml/1 tbsp/2 sachets instant espresso coffee powder
125 g/4 oz/½ cup butter or margarine
125 g/4 oz/½ cup dark soft brown sugar
2 eggs, at kitchen temperature
75 ml/5 tbsp cold milk

Line the base and side of an 18 cm/ 7 in diameter soufflé dish with clingfilm (plastic wrap), allowing it to hang very slightly over the edge. Sift the flour and coffee powder into a bowl and rub in the butter or margarine. Add the sugar. Thoroughly beat together the eggs and milk, then mix evenly into the dry ingredients with a fork. Spoon into the prepared dish and cover loosely with kitchen paper. Cook on Full for 6½–7 minutes until the cake is well risen and just beginning to shrink away from the side of the dish. Allow to stand for 10 minutes. Transfer to a wire rack by holding the clingfilm. When completely cold, peel away the clingfilm and store the cake in an airtight container.

Orange-iced Espresso Coffee Cake
•••••••••••••••••••••••••••••••
SERVES 8

Make the Espresso Coffee Cake. About 2 hours before serving, make up a thick glacé icing (frosting) by mixing 175 g/6 oz/1 cup icing (confectioners') sugar with enough orange juice to form a paste-like icing. Spread over the top of the cake, then decorate with grated chocolate, chopped nuts, hundreds and thousands etc.

Espresso Coffee Cream Torte
•••••••••••••••••••••••••••••••
SERVES 8

Make the Espresso Coffee Cake and cut into two layers. Whip 300 ml/½ pt/1¼ cups double (heavy) cream with 60 ml/4 tbsp cold milk until thick. Sweeten with 45 ml/3 tbsp caster (superfine) sugar and flavour to taste with espresso coffee powder. Use some to sandwich the layers together, then spread the remainder thickly over the top and side of the cake. Stud the top with hazelnuts.

Raisin Cup Cakes

MAKES 12

125 g/4 oz/1 cup self-raising (self-
rising) flour
50 g/2 oz/¼ cup butter or
margarine
50 g/2 oz/¼ cup caster (superfine)
sugar
30 ml/2 tbsp raisins
1 egg
30 ml/2 tbsp cold milk
2.5 ml/½ tsp vanilla essence
(extract)
Icing (confectioner's) sugar, for
dusting

Sift the flour into bowl and rub in the butter or margarine finely. Add the sugar and raisins. Beat the egg with the milk and vanilla essence and stir into the dry ingredients with a fork, mixing to a soft batter without beating. Divide between 12 paper cake cases (cupcake papers) and place six at a time on the microwave turntable. Cover loosely with kitchen paper. Cook on Full for 2 minutes. Transfer to a wire rack to cool. Dust with sifted icing sugar when cold. Store in an airtight container.

Coconut Cup Cakes

MAKES 12

Prepare as for Raisin Cup Cakes, but substitute 25 ml/1½ tbsp desiccated (shredded) coconut for the raisins and increase the milk to 25 ml/1½ tbsp.

Chocolate Chip Cakes

MAKES 12

Prepare as for Raisin Cup Cakes, but substitute 30 ml/2 tbsp chocolate chips for the raisins.

Banana Spice Cake

SERVES 8

3 large ripe bananas
175 g/6 oz/¾ cup mixture of
margarine and white cooking
fat (shortening), at kitchen
temperature
175 g/6 oz/¾ cup dark soft brown
sugar
10 ml/2 tsp baking powder
5 ml/1 tsp ground allspice
225 g/8 oz/2 cups malted brown
flour, such as granary
1 large egg, beaten
15 ml/1 tbsp chopped pecan nuts
100 g/4 oz/⅔ cup chopped dates

Closely line the base and side of a 20 cm/8 in diameter soufflé dish with clingfilm (plastic wrap), allowing it to hang very slightly over the edge. Peel the bananas and thoroughly mash in a bowl. Beat in both fats. Mix in the sugar. Toss the baking powder and allspice with the flour. Stir into the banana mixture with the egg, nuts and dates using a fork. Spread smoothly into the prepared dish. Cover loosely with kitchen paper and cook on Full for 11 minutes, turning the dish three times. Allow to stand for 10 minutes. Transfer to a wire rack by holding the clingfilm. Cool completely, then peel away the clingfilm and store the cake in an airtight container.

Banana Spice Cake with Pineapple Icing

SERVES 8

Make the Banana Spice Cake. About 2 hours before serving, cover the cake with a thick glacé icing (frosting) made by sifting 175 g/6 oz/1 cup icing (confectioners') sugar into a bowl and mixing to a paste-like icing with a few drops of pineapple juice. When set, decorate with dried banana chips.

Butter Cream Icing

MAKES 225 G/8 OZ/1 CUP

75 g/3 oz/⅓ cup butter, at kitchen
temperature
175 g/6 oz/1 cup icing
(confectioners') sugar, sifted
10 ml/2 tsp cold milk
5 ml/1 tsp vanilla essence (extract)
Icing (confectioners') sugar, for
dusting (optional)

Beat the butter until light, then gradually beat in the sugar until light, fluffy and doubled in volume. Mix in the milk and vanilla essence and beat the icing (frosting) until smooth and thick.

Chocolate Fudge Frosting

MAKES 350 G/12 OZ/1½ CUPS

An American-style icing (frosting) which is useful for topping any plain cake.

30 ml/2 tbsp butter or margarine
60 ml/4 tbsp milk
30 ml/2 tbsp cocoa (unsweetened
chocolate) powder
5 ml/1 tsp vanilla essence (extract)
300 g/10 oz/1⅔ cups icing
(confectioners') sugar, sifted

Put the butter or margarine, milk, cocoa and vanilla essence in a bowl. Cook, uncovered, on Defrost for 4 minutes until hot and the fat has melted. Beat in the sifted icing sugar until the frosting is smooth and quite thick. Use straight away.

Fruited Health Wedges

MAKES 8

100 g/3½ oz dried apple rings
75 g/3 oz/¾ cup self-raising (self-
rising) wholemeal flour
75 g/3 oz/¾ cup oatmeal
75 g/3 oz/⅔ cup margarine
75 g/3 oz/⅔ cup dark soft brown
sugar
6 California prunes, chopped

Soak the apple rings in water overnight. Closely line the base and side of a shallow 18 cm/7 in diameter dish with clingfilm (plastic wrap), allowing it to hang very slightly over the edge. Put the flour and oatmeal into a bowl, add the margarine and rub in finely with the fingertips. Mix in the sugar to make a crumbly mixture. Spread half over the base of the prepared dish. Drain and chop the apple rings. Gently press with the prunes over the oatmeal mixture. Sprinkle the rest of the oatmeal mixture evenly on top. Cook, uncovered, on Full for 5½–6 minutes. Allow to cool completely in the dish. Lift out by holding the clingfilm, then peel away the clingfilm and cut into wedges. Store in an airtight container.

Fruited Health Wedges with Apricots

MAKES 8

Prepare as for Fruited Health Wedges, but substitute 6 dried apricots, well washed, for the prunes.

Shortbread

MAKES 12 WEDGES

225 g/8 oz/1 cup unsalted (sweet)
butter, at kitchen temperature
125 g/4 oz/½ cup caster (superfine)
sugar, plus extra for sprinkling
350 g/12 oz/3 cups plain (all-
purpose) flour

Grease and base line a 20 cm/8 in diameter deep dish. Cream together the butter and sugar until light and fluffy, then mix in the flour until smooth and evenly combined. Spread smoothly into the prepared dish and prick all over with a fork. Cook, uncovered, on Defrost for 20 minutes. Remove from the microwave and sprinkle with 15 ml/1 tbsp caster sugar. Cut into 12 wedges when still slightly warm. Carefully transfer to a wire rack and allow to cool completely. Store in an airtight container.

Extra Crunchy Shortbread

MAKES 12 WEDGES

Prepare as for Shortbread, but substitute 25 g/1 oz/¼ cup semolina (cream of wheat) for 25 g/1 oz/¼ cup of the flour.

Extra Smooth Shortbread

MAKES 12 WEDGES

Prepare as for Shortbread, but substitute 25 g/1 oz/¼ cup cornflour (cornstarch) for 25 g/1 oz/¼ cup of the flour.

Spicy Shortbread

MAKES 12 WEDGES

Prepare as for Shortbread, but sift in 10 ml/2 tsp mixed (apple-pie) spice with the flour.

Dutch-style Shortbread

MAKES 12 WEDGES

Prepare as for Shortbread, but substitute self-raising (self-rising) flour for the plain flour and sift 10 ml/2 tsp ground cinnamon with the flour. Before cooking, brush the top with 15–30 ml/1–2 tbsp cream, then gently press on lightly toasted flaked (slivered) almonds (page 205).

Cinnamon Balls

MAKES 20

A Passover Festival speciality, a cross between a biscuit (cookie) and a cake, which seems to behave better in the microwave than it does when baked conventionally.

2 large egg whites
125 g/4 oz/½ cup caster (superfine)
sugar
30 ml/2 tbsp ground cinnamon
225 g/8 oz/2 cups ground almonds
Sifted icing (confectioners') sugar

Whip the egg whites until they just begin to foam, then stir in the sugar, cinnamon and almonds. Using damp hands, roll into 20 balls. Arrange in two rings, one just inside the other, round the edge of a large flat plate. Cook, uncovered, on Full for 8 minutes, turning the plate four times. Cool to just warm, then roll in icing sugar until each one is heavily coated. Allow to cool completely and store in an airtight container.

Golden Brandy Snaps
••••••••••••••••••••••••••••••
MAKES 14

Quite difficult to make conventionally, these work like a dream in the microwave.

50 g/2 oz/¼ cup butter
50 g/2 oz/⅙ cup golden (light corn) syrup
40 g/1½ oz/3 tbsp golden granulated sugar
40 g/1½ oz/1½ tbsp malted brown flour, such as granary
2.5 ml/½ tsp ground ginger
150 ml/¼ pt/⅔ cup double (heavy) or whipping cream, whipped

Put the butter in a dish and melt, uncovered, on Defrost for 2–2½ minutes. Add the syrup and sugar and stir in well. Cook, uncovered, on Full for 1 minute. Stir in the flour and ginger. Place four 5 ml/1 tsp sized spoonfuls of the mixture very well apart directly on to the microwave glass or plastic turntable. Cook on Full for 1½–1¾ minutes until the brandy snaps begin to brown and look lacy on top. Carefully lift the turntable out of the microwave and allow the biscuits (cookies) to stand for 5 minutes. Lift off each one in turn with the help of a palette knife. Roll round the handle of a large wooden spoon. Press the joins together with the fingertips and slide up to the bowl end of the spoon. Repeat with the remaining three biscuits. When they are set, remove from the handle and transfer to a wire cooling rack. Repeat until the remaining mixture is used up. Store in an airtight tin. Before eating, pipe thick cream into both ends of each brandy snap and eat the same day as they soften on standing.

Chocolate Brandy Snaps
••••••••••••••••••••••••••••••
MAKES 14

Prepare as for Golden Brandy Snaps. Before filling with cream, arrange on a baking sheet and brush the uppermost surface with melted dark or white chocolate. Leave to set, then add the cream.

Bun Scones

A cross between a bun and a scone, these are exceptionally light and make a delicious treat eaten while still warm, spread with butter and a choice of jam (conserve) or heather honey.

225 g/8 oz/2 cups wholemeal flour
5 ml/1 tsp cream of tartar
5 ml/1 tsp bicarbonate of soda (baking soda)
1.5 ml/¼ tsp salt
20 ml/4 tsp caster (superfine) sugar
25 g/1 oz/2 tbsp butter or margarine
150 ml/¼ pt/⅔ cup buttermilk, or substitute a mixture of half plain yoghurt and half skimmed milk if unavailable
Beaten egg, for brushing
Extra 5 ml/1 tsp sugar mixed with 2.5 ml/½ tsp ground cinnamon, for sprinkling

Sift together the flour, cream of tartar, bicarbonate of soda and salt into a bowl. Toss in the sugar and finely rub in the butter or margarine. Add the buttermilk (or substitute) and mix with a fork to form a fairly soft dough. Turn out on to a floured surface and knead quickly and lightly until smooth. Pat out evenly to 1 cm/½ in thick, then cut into rounds with a 5 cm/2 in biscuit (cookie) cutter. Re-roll the trimmings and continue cutting into rounds. Place round the edge of a buttered 25 cm/10 in flat plate. Brush with egg and sprinkle with the sugar and cinnamon mixture. Cook, uncovered, on Full for 4 minutes, turning the plate four times. Allow to stand for 4 minutes, then transfer to a wire rack. Eat while still warm.

Raisin Bun Scones

Prepare as for Bun Scones, but add 15 ml/1 tbsp raisins with the sugar.

Breads

Any liquid used in yeasted breads must be lukewarm – not hot or cold. The best way to achieve the correct temperature is to mix half boiling liquid with half cold liquid. If it still feels hot when you dip in the second knuckle of your little finger, cool it down slightly before use. Over-hot liquid is more of a problem than too cold liquid as it can kill off the yeast and stop the bread rising.

Basic White Bread Dough

MAKES 1 LOAF

A speedy bread dough for those who enjoy baking but are short of time.

450 g/1 lb/4 cups strong plain (bread) flour
5 ml/1 tsp salt
1 sachet easy-blend dried yeast
30 ml/2 tbsp butter, margarine, white cooking fat (shortening) or lard
300 ml/½ pt/1¼ cups lukewarm water

Sift the flour and salt into a bowl. Warm, uncovered, on Defrost for 1 minute. Add the yeast and rub in the fat. Mix to a dough with the water. Knead on a floured surface until smooth, elastic and no longer sticky. Return to the cleaned and dried but now lightly greased bowl. Cover the bowl itself, not the dough, with cling-film (plastic wrap) and slit it twice to allow steam to escape. Warm on Defrost for 1 minute. Rest in the microwave for 5 minutes. Repeat three or four times until the dough has doubled in size. Quickly re-knead, then use as in conventional recipes or in the microwave recipes below.

Basic Brown Bread Dough

MAKES 1 LOAF

Follow the recipe for Basic White Bread Dough, but in place of the strong bread (plain) flour use one of the following:
● half white and half wholemeal flour
● all wholemeal flour
● half malted wholemeal and half white flour

Basic Milk Bread Dough

MAKES 1 LOAF

Follow the recipe for Basic White Bread Dough, but in place of the water use one of the following:
● all skimmed milk
● half full-cream milk and half water

Bap Loaf

MAKES 1 LOAF

A soft crusted and pale loaf, eaten more in the north of Britain than the south.

Make up either the Basic White Bread Dough, Basic Brown Bread Dough or Basic Milk Bread Dough. Knead quickly and lightly after the first rising, then shape into a round about 5 cm/2 in thick. Stand on a greased and floured round flat plate. Cover with kitchen paper and warm on Defrost for 1 minute. Allow to rest for 4 minutes. Repeat three or four times until the dough has doubled in size. Sprinkle with white or brown flour. Cook, uncovered, on Full for 4 minutes. Cool on a wire rack.

Bap Rolls

MAKES 16

Make up either the Basic White Bread Dough, Basic Brown Bread Dough or Basic Milk Bread Dough. Knead quickly and lightly after the first rising, then divide equally into 16 pieces. Shape into flattish rounds. Arrange eight baps round the edge of each of two greased and floured plates. Cover with kitchen paper and cook, one plate at a time, on Defrost for 1 minute, then rest for 4 minutes, and repeat three or four times until the rolls have doubled in size. Sprinkle with white or brown flour. Cook, uncovered, on Full for 4 minutes. Cool on a wire rack.

Hamburger Buns

MAKES 12

Prepare as for Bap Rolls, but divide the dough into 12 pieces instead of 16. Put six buns round the edge of each of two plates and cook as directed.

Fruited Sweet Bap Rolls

MAKES 16

Prepare as for Bap Rolls, but add 60 ml/4 tbsp raisins and 30 ml/ 2 tbsp caster (superfine) sugar to the dry ingredients before mixing in the liquid.

Cornish Splits

MAKES 16

Prepare as for Bap Rolls, but do not sprinkle the tops with flour before cooking. Halve when cold and fill with thick cream or clotted cream and strawberry or raspberry jam (conserve). Dust the tops heavily with sifted icing (confectioners') sugar. Eat the same day.

Fancy Rolls

MAKES 16

Make up either the Basic White Bread Dough, Basic Brown Bread Dough or Basic Milk Bread Dough. Knead quickly and lightly after the first rising, then divide equally into 16 pieces. Shape four pieces into round rolls and cut a slit across the top of each. Roll four pieces into ropes, each 20 cm/8 in long, and tie in a knot. Shape four pieces into baby Vienna loaves and make three diagonal slits on top of each. Divide each of the remaining four pieces into three, roll into narrow ropes and plait together. Arrange all the rolls on a greased and floured baking tray and leave in the warm until doubled in size. Brush the tops with egg and bake conventionally at 230°C/450°F/gas mark 8 for 15–20 minutes. Remove from the oven and transfer the rolls to a wire rack. Store in an airtight container when cold.

Rolls with Toppings

MAKES 16

Prepare as for Fancy Rolls. After brushing the tops of the rolls with egg, sprinkle with any of the following: poppy seeds, toasted sesame seeds (page 206), fennel seeds, porridge oats, cracked wheat, grated hard cheese, coarse sea salt, flavoured seasoning salts.

Caraway Seed Bread

MAKES 1 LOAF

Make up the Basic Brown Bread Dough (page 278), adding 10-15 ml/2–3 tsp caraway seeds to the dry ingredients before mixing in the liquid. Knead lightly after the first rising, then shape into a ball. Put into a 450 ml/¾ pt/2 cup straight-sided greased round dish. Cover with kitchen paper and warm on Defrost for 1 minute. Allow to rest for 4 minutes. Repeat three or four times until the dough has doubled in size. Brush with beaten egg and sprinkle with coarse salt and/or extra caraway seeds. Cover with kitchen paper and cook on Full for 5 minutes, turning the dish once. Cook on Full for a further 2 minutes. Leave for 15 minutes, then carefully turn out on to a wire rack.

Rye Bread

MAKES 1 LOAF

Make up the Basic Brown Bread Dough (page 278), using half wholemeal and half rye flour. Bake as for Bap Loaf (page 278).

Oil Bread

MAKES 1 LOAF

Make up either the Basic White Bread Dough or Basic Brown Bread Dough (page 278), but substitute olive, walnut or hazelnut oil for the other fats. If the dough remains on the sticky side, work in a little extra flour. Cook as for Bap Loaf (page 278).

Italian Bread

MAKES 1 LOAF

Make up the Basic White Bread Dough (page 278), but substitute olive oil for the other fats and add 15 ml/1 tbsp red pesto and 10 ml/2 tsp sun-dried tomato purée (paste) to the dry ingredients before mixing in the liquid. Cook as for Bap Loaf (page 278), allowing an extra 30 seconds.

Spanish Bread

MAKES 1 LOAF

Make up the Basic White Bread Dough (page 278), but substitute olive oil for the other fats and add 30 ml/2 tbsp dried onions (in their dry state) and 12 chopped stuffed olives to the dry ingredients before mixing in the liquid. Cook as for Bap Loaf (page 278), allowing an extra 30 seconds.

Tikka Masala Bread

MAKES 1 LOAF

Make up the Basic White Bread Dough (page 278), but substitute melted ghee or corn oil for the other fats and add 15 ml/1 tbsp tikka spice blend and the seeds from 5 green cardamom pods to the dry ingredients before mixing in the liquid. Cook as for Bap Loaf (page 278), allowing an extra 30 seconds.

Fruited Malt Bread

••••••••••••••••••••••••••••••••••
MAKES 2 LOAVES

450 g/1 lb/4 cups strong plain
  (bread) flour
10 ml/2 tsp salt
1 sachet easy-blend dried yeast
60 ml/4 tbsp mixed currants and
  raisins
60 ml/4 tbsp malt extract
15 ml/1 tbsp black treacle
  (molasses)
25 g/1 oz/2 tbsp butter or margarine
45 ml/3 tbsp lukewarm skimmed
  milk
150 ml/¼ pt/⅔ cup lukewarm water
Butter, for spreading

Sift the flour and salt into a bowl.
Toss in the yeast and dried fruit. Put
the malt extract, treacle and butter or
margarine into a small basin. Melt,
uncovered, on Defrost for 3 minutes.
Add to the flour with the milk and
enough water to make a soft but not
sticky dough. Knead on a floured surface until smooth, elastic and no
longer sticky. Divide into two equal
pieces. Shape each to fit a greased
900 ml/1½ pt/3¾ cup round or rectangular dish. Cover the dishes, not
the dough, with clingfilm (plastic
wrap) and slit it twice to allow steam
to escape. Warm together on Defrost
for 1 minute. Allow to stand for 5
minutes. Repeat three or four times
until the dough has doubled in size.
Remove the clingfilm. Place the dishes
side by side in the microwave and
cook, uncovered, on Full for 2 minutes.
Reverse the position of the dishes and
cook for a further 2 minutes. Repeat
once more. Allow to stand for 10 minutes. Invert on to a wire rack. Store in
an airtight container when completely
cold. Leave for 1 day before slicing
and spreading with butter.

Irish Soda Bread

••••••••••••••••••••••••••••••••••
MAKES 4 SMALL LOAVES

200 ml/7 fl oz/scant 1 cup
  buttermilk or 60 ml/4 tbsp each
  skimmed milk and plain
  yoghurt
75 ml/5 tbsp full-cream milk
350 g/12 oz/3 cups wholemeal
  flour
125 g/4 oz/1 cup plain (all-
  purpose) flour
10 ml/2 tsp bicarbonate of soda
  (baking soda)
5 ml/1 tsp cream of tartar
5 ml/1 tsp salt
50 g/2 oz/¼ cup butter, margarine
  or white cooking fat
  (shortening)

Thoroughly grease a 25 cm/10 in
dinner plate. Mix together the buttermilk or substitute and milk. Tip the
wholemeal flour into a bowl and sift in
the plain flour, bicarbonate of soda,
cream of tartar and salt. Rub the fat in
finely. Add the liquid in one go and stir
to a soft dough with a fork. Knead
quickly with floured hands until
smooth. Shape into an 18 cm/7 in
round. Transfer to the centre of the
plate. Cut a deepish cross on the top
with the back of a knife, then dust
lightly with flour. Cover loosely with
kitchen paper and cook on Full for 7
minutes. The bread will rise and
spread. Allow to stand for 10 minutes.
Lift off the plate with the help of a fish
slice and place on a wire rack. Divide
into four portions when cold. Store in
an airtight container for up to only 2
days as this type of bread is best eaten
fresh.

Soda Bread with Bran

MAKES 4 SMALL LOAVES

Prepare as for Irish Soda Bread (page 281), but add 60 ml/4 tbsp coarse bran before mixing in the liquid.

To Freshen Stale Bread

Put the bread or rolls in a brown paper bag or place between the folds of a clean tea towel (dish cloth) or table napkin. Heat on Defrost until the bread feels slightly warm on the surface. Eat straight away and don't repeat with leftovers of the same bread.

Greek Pittas

MAKES 4 LOAVES

Make up the Basic White Bread Dough (page 278). Divide into four equal pieces and knead each lightly into a ball. Roll into ovals, each 30 cm/12 in long down the centre. Dust lightly with flour. Dampen the edges with water. Fold each in half by bringing the top edge over the bottom. Press the edges well together to seal. Place on a greased and floured baking sheet. Bake straight away in a conventional oven at 230°C/450°F/gas mark 8 for 20–25 minutes until the loaves are well risen and a deep golden brown. Cool on a wire rack. Leave until just cold, then split open and eat with Greek-style dips and other foods.

Desserts

Take a cold day, one microwave oven and a handful of ingredients and you can cook a large range of stunning puddings: lovely, heart-warming goodies like mulled fruits, sweet and friendly crumbles, delicate soufflé omelettes snow-capped with sugar, exotics from abroad, tarts, flans, pies and old favourites like bread and butter pudding, egg custards, milk and steamed puddings, plus some delicious sweet fondues. And here are elegant cool desserts, all made swiftly and with minimal effort in the microwave. The magnificent royal chocolate mousse was given to me by a top chef, and there's also a charmer of a crème caramel, fruits with alcohol, trifles with home-made custard, an airy apricot snow, whips, foams, froths and jellies. When there's something to celebrate, turn to the microwave for lucious home-made cream dishes or even banana splits

Jellied Cherries in Port

SERVES 6

750 g/1½ lb canned stoned (pitted) morello cherries in light syrup, drained and syrup reserved
15 ml/1 tbsp powdered gelatine
45 ml/3 tbsp caster (superfine) sugar
2.5 ml/½ tsp ground cinnamon
Tawny port
Double (heavy) cream, whipped, and mixed (apple-pie) spice, to decorate

Pour 30 ml/2 tbsp of the syrup into a large measuring jug. Stir in the gelatine and leave for 2 minutes to soften. Cover with a saucer and melt on Defrost for 2 minutes. Stir to ensure the gelatine has melted. Mix in the remaining cherry syrup, the sugar and cinnamon. Make up to 450 ml/ ¾ pt/2 cups with port. Cover as before and heat on Full for 2 minutes, stirring three times, until the liquid is warm and the sugar has dissolved. Transfer to a 1.25 litre/2¼ pt/5½ cup basin and allow to cool. Cover and chill until the jelly mixture is beginning to thicken and set slightly round the side of the basin. Fold in the cherries and divide between six dessert dishes. Chill until completely set. Decorate with thick cream and a dusting of mixed spice before serving.

Jellied Cherries in Cider

SERVES 6

Prepare as for Jellied Cherries in Port, but substitute strong dry cider for the port and 5 ml/1 tsp grated orange peel for the cinnamon.

Mulled Pineapple
SERVES 8

225 g/8 oz/1 cup caster (superfine)
 sugar
150 ml/¼ pt/⅔ cup cold water
1 large fresh pineapple
6 whole cloves
5 cm/2 in piece cinnamon stick
1.5 ml/¼ tsp grated nutmeg
60 ml/4 tbsp medium-dry sherry
15 ml/1 tbsp dark rum
Biscuits (cookies), to serve

Put the sugar and water in a 2.5 litre/4½ pt/11 cup dish and stir well. Cover with a large inverted plate and cook on Full for 8 minutes to make a syrup. Meanwhile, peel and core the pineapple and remove the 'eyes' with the tip of a potato peeler. Cut into slices, then cut the slices into chunks. Add to the syrup with the remaining ingredients. Cover with clingfilm (plastic wrap) and slit it twice to allow steam to escape. Cook on Full for 10 minutes, turning the dish three times. Allow to stand for 8 minutes before spooning into dishes and eating with crisp, buttery biscuits.

Mulled Sharon Fruit
SERVES 8

Prepare as for Mulled Pineapple, but substitute 8 quartered sharon fruit for the pineapple. After adding to the syrup with the other ingredients, cook on Full for only 5 minutes. Flavour with brandy instead of rum.

Mulled Peaches
SERVES 8

Prepare as for Mulled Pineapple, but substitute 8 large halved and stoned (pitted) peaches for the pineapple. After adding to the syrup with the other ingredients, cook on Full for only 5 minutes. Flavour with an orange liqueur instead of rum.

Pink Pears
SERVES 6

450 ml/¾ pt/2 cups rosé wine
75 g/3 oz/⅓ cup caster (superfine)
 sugar
6 dessert pears, stalks left on
30 ml/2 tbsp cornflour
 (cornstarch)
45 ml/3 tbsp cold water
45 ml/3 tbsp tawny port

Pour the wine into a deep dish large enough to hold all the pears on their sides in a single layer. Add the sugar and stir in well. Cook, uncovered, on Full for 3 minutes. Meanwhile, peel the pears, taking care not to lose the stalks. Arrange on their sides in the wine and sugar mixture. Cover with clingfilm (plastic wrap) and slit it twice to allow steam to escape. Cook on Full for 4 minutes. Turn the pears over with two spoons. Cover as before and cook on Full for a further 4 minutes. Allow to stand for 5 minutes. Rearrange upright in the serving dish. To thicken the sauce, mix the cornflour smoothly with the water and stir in the port. Blend into the wine mixture. Cook, uncovered, on Full for 5 minutes, stirring briskly every minute until lightly thickened and clear. Pour over the pears and serve warm or chilled.

Christmas Pudding

MAKES 2 PUDDINGS, EACH SERVING 6–8

65 g/2½ oz plain (all-purpose) flour
15 ml/1 tbsp cocoa (unsweetened chocolate) powder
10 ml/2 tsp mixed (apple-pie) spice or ground allspice
5 ml/1 tsp grated orange or tangerine peel
75 g/3 oz/1½ cups fresh brown breadcrumbs
125 g/4 oz/½ cup dark soft brown sugar
450 g/1 lb/4 cups mixed dried fruit (fruit cake mix) with peel
125 g/4 oz/1 cup shredded suet (vegetarian if preferred)
2 large eggs, at kitchen temperature
15 ml/1 tbsp black treacle (molasses)
60 ml/4 tbsp Guinness
15 ml/1 tbsp milk

Thoroughly grease two 900 ml/ 1½ pt/3¾ cup pudding basins. Sift the flour, cocoa and spice into a large bowl. Toss in the peel, breadcrumbs, sugar, fruit and suet. In a separate bowl, beat together the eggs, treacle, Guinness and milk. Stir into the dry ingredients with a fork to make a soft-ish mixture. Divide equally between the prepared basins. Cover each loosely with kitchen paper. Cook, one at a time, on Full for 4 minutes. Allow to stand for 3 minutes inside the microwave. Cook each pudding on Full for a further 2 minutes. Turn out of the basins when cool. When cold, wrap with a double thickness of greaseproof (waxed) paper and freeze until needed. To serve, defrost completely, cut into portions and reheat individually on plates for 50–60 seconds.

Butter Plum Pudding

MAKES 2 PUDDINGS, EACH SERVING 6–8

Prepare as for Christmas Pudding, but substitute 125 g/4 oz/½ cup melted butter for the suet.

Plum Pudding with Oil

MAKES 2 PUDDINGS, EACH SERVING 6–8

Prepare as for Christmas Pudding, but substitute 75 ml/5 tbsp sun-flower or corn oil for the suet. Add an extra 15 ml/1 tbsp milk.

Fruit Soufflé in Glasses

SERVES 6

400 g/14 oz/1 large can any fruit filling
3 eggs, separated
90 ml/6 tbsp unbeaten whipping cream

Spoon the fruit filling into a bowl and stir in the egg yolks. Beat the whites to stiff peaks and fold lightly into the fruit mixture until thoroughly combined. Spoon the mixture equally into six stemmed wine glasses (not crystal) until half-filled. Cook in pairs on Defrost for 3 minutes. The mixture should rise to the top of each glass, but will drop slightly when removed from the oven. Make a slit in top of each with a knife. Spoon 15 ml/1 tbsp of the cream on to each. It will flow down the sides of the glasses to the bases. Serve straight away.

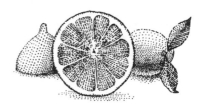

Almost Instant Christmas Pudding

••••••••••••••••••••••••••••••••••••••
MAKES 2 PUDDINGS, EACH SERVING 8

Absolutely superb, amazingly rich-tasting, deep-toned, fruity and quick to mature so they don't have to be made weeks ahead. Canned fruit filling is the prime mover here and accounts for the unfailing success of the puddings.

225 g/8 oz/4 cups fresh white breadcrumbs
125 g/4 oz/1 cup plain (all-purpose) flour
12.5 ml/2½ tsp ground allspice
175 g/6 oz/¾ cup dark soft brown sugar
275 g/10 oz/2¼ cups finely shredded suet (vegetarian if preferred)
675 g/1½ lb/4 cups mixed dried fruit (fruit cake mix)
3 eggs, thoroughly beaten
400 g/14 oz/1 large can cherry fruit filling
30 ml/2 tbsp black treacle (molasses)
Dutch Butter Blender Cream (page 333) or whipped cream, to serve.

Thoroughly grease two 900 ml/ 1½ pt/3¾ cup pudding basins. Place the breadcrumbs into a bowl and sift in the flour and allspice. Add the sugar, suet and dried fruit. Mix to a fairly soft mixture with the eggs, fruit filling and treacle. Divide between the prepared basins and cover each loosely with kitchen paper. Cook, one at a time, on Full for 6 minutes. Allow to stand for 5 minutes inside the microwave. Cook each pudding on Full for a further 3 minutes, turning the basin twice. Turn out of the basins when cool. When cold, wrap in greaseproof (waxed) paper and refrigerate until needed. Cut into portions and reheat as directed in the Convenience Foods table (page 65). Serve with the blender cream or whipped cream.

Ultra-fruity Christmas Pudding

••••••••••••••••••••••••••••••••••••••
SERVES 8–10

An oldie from Billington's Sugar, with butter or margarine replacing sugar.

75 g/3 oz/¾ cup plain (all-purpose) flour
7.5 ml/1½ tsp ground allspice
40 g/1½ oz/¾ cup wholemeal breadcrumbs
75 g/3 oz/⅓ cup demerara sugar
75 g/3 oz/⅓ molasses sugar
125 g/4 oz/⅔ cup currants
125 g/4 oz/⅔ cup sultanas (golden raisins)
125 g/4 oz/⅔ cup dried apricots, snipped into small pieces
45 ml/3 tbsp chopped roasted hazelnuts (page 205)
1 small eating (dessert) apple, peeled and grated
Finely grated peel and juice of 1 small orange
50 ml/2 fl oz/3½ tbsp cold milk
75 g/3 oz/⅓ cup butter or margarine
50 g/2 oz plain (semi-sweet) chocolate, broken into pieces
1 large egg, beaten
Brandy Sauce (page 336)

Thoroughly butter a 900 ml/1½ pt/ 3¾ cup pudding basin. Sift the flour and spice into a large bowl. Add the breadcrumbs and sugars and toss to ensure any lumps are broken down. Mix in the dried currants, sultanas, apricots, nuts, apple and orange peel. Pour the orange juice into a jug. Add the milk, butter or margarine and the chocolate. Heat on Defrost for 2½–3 ıııınuutes until the butter and chocolate have melted. Fork into the dry ingredients with the beaten egg. Spoon into the prepared basin. Cover loosely with a round of parchment or greaseproof (waxed) paper. Cook on Full for 5 minutes, turning the basin twice. Allow to stand for 5 minutes. Cook on Full for a further 5 minutes, turning the basin twice. Allow to stand for 5 minutes before inverting on to a plate and serving with Brandy Sauce.

Plum Crumble
SERVES 4

450 g/1 lb stoned (pitted) plums
125 g/4 oz/½ cup soft brown sugar
175 g/6 oz/1½ cups plain (all-
*   purpose) wholemeal flour*
125 g/4 oz/½ cup butter or
*   margarine*
75 g/3 oz/⅓ cup demerara sugar
2.5 ml/½ tsp ground allspice
*   (optional)*

Place the plums in a buttered 1 litre/ 1¾ pt/4¼ cup pie dish. Mix in the sugar. Tip the flour into bowl and rub in the butter or margarine finely. Add the sugar and spice and toss together. Sprinkle the mixture thickly over the fruit. Cook, uncovered, on Full for 10 minutes, turning the dish twice. Allow to stand for 5 minutes. Eat hot or warm.

Plum and Apple Crumble
SERVES 4

Prepare as for Plum Crumble, but substitute 225 g/ 8 oz peeled and sliced apples for half the plums. Add 5 ml/1 tsp grated lemon peel to the fruit with the sugar.

Apricot Crumble
SERVES 4

Prepare as for Plum Crumble, but substitute stoned (pitted) fresh apricots for the plums.

Berry Fruit Crumble with Almonds
SERVES 4

Prepare as for Plum Crumble, but substitute prepared mixed berry fruits for the plums. Add 30 ml/2 tbsp toasted flaked (slivered) almonds (page 205) to the crumble mixture.

Pear and Rhubarb Crumble
SERVES 4

Prepare as for Plum Crumble, but substitute a mixture of peeled and chopped pears and chopped rhubarb for the plums.

Nectarine and Blueberry Crumble
SERVES 4

Prepare as for Plum Crumble, but substitute a mixture of stoned (pitted) and sliced nectarines and blueberries for the plums

Apple Betty

SERVES 4–6

50 g/2 oz/¼ cup butter or
margarine
125 g/4 oz/2 cups crisp
breadcrumbs, bought or made
from toast
175 g/6 oz/¾ cup light soft brown
sugar
750 g/1½ lb cooking (tart) apples,
peeled, cored and thinly sliced
30 ml/2 tbsp lemon juice
Grated zest of 1 small lemon
2.5 ml/½ tsp ground cinnamon
75 ml/5 tbsp cold water
Double (heavy) cream, whipped, or
ice cream, to serve

Butter a 600 ml/1 pt/2½ cup pie dish. Melt the butter or margarine on Full for 45 seconds. Stir in the breadcrumbs and two-thirds of the sugar. Combine the apple slices, lemon juice, lemon zest, cinnamon, water and remaining sugar. Fill the prepared pie dish with alternate layers of the breadcrumb and apple mixtures, beginning and ending with breadcrumbs. Cook, uncovered, on Full for 7 minutes, turning the dish twice. Allow to stand for 5 minutes before eating with thick cream or ice cream.

Nectarine or Peach Betty

SERVES 4–6

Prepare as for Apple Betty, but substitute sliced stoned (pitted) nectarines or peaches for the apples.

Middle Eastern Shred Pudding with Nuts

SERVES 6

This is a fine pudding from what was once known as Arabia. The orange flower water is available from some supermarkets and pharmacies.

6 large Shredded Wheats
100 g/3½ oz/1 cup toasted pine
nuts (page 205)
125 g/4 oz/½ cup caster (superfine)
sugar
150 ml/¼ pt/⅔ cup full-cream milk
50 g/2 oz/¼ cup butter (not
margarine)
45 ml/3 tbsp orange flower water

Butter a deep 20 cm/8 in diameter dish and crumble 3 of the Shredded Wheats across the base. Combine the nuts and sugar and sprinkle evenly on top. Crush over the remaining Shredded Wheats. Heat the milk and butter in a jug, uncovered, on Full for 1½ minutes. Mix in the orange flower water. Spoon gently over the ingredients in the dish. Cook, uncovered, on Full for 6 minutes. Allow to stand for 2 minutes before serving.

Cocktail of Summer Fruits

SERVES 8

**225 g/8 oz/2 cups gooseberries,
topped and tailed**
225 g/8 oz rhubarb, chopped
30 ml/2 tbsp cold water
**250 g/8 oz/1 cup caster (superfine)
sugar**
450 g/1 lb strawberries, sliced
125 g/4 oz raspberries
**125 g/4 oz redcurrants, stalks
removed**
**30 ml/2 tbsp Cassis or orange
liqueur (optional)**

Put the gooseberries and rhubarb into a deep dish with the water. Cover with clingfilm (plastic wrap) and slit it twice to allow steam to escape. Cook on Full for 6 minutes, turning the dish once. Uncover. Add the sugar and stir until dissolved. Mix in the remaining fruit. Cover when cold and chill thoroughly. Add the Cassis or liqueur, if using, just before serving.

Middle Eastern Date and Banana Compôte

SERVES 6

Fresh dates, usually from Israel, are readily available in the winter.

450 g/1 lb fresh dates
450 g/1 lb bananas
Juice of ½ lemon
Juice of ½ orange
**45 ml/3 tbsp orange or apricot
brandy**
15 ml/1 tbsp rose water
30 ml/2 tbsp demerara sugar
Sponge cake, to serve

Skin the dates and slit in half to remove the stones (pits). Place in a 1.75 litre/3 pt/7½ cup serving bowl. Peel the bananas and slice directly on to the top. Add all the remaining ingredients and toss gently to mix. Cover with clingfilm (plastic wrap) and slit it twice to allow steam to escape. Cook on Full for 6 minutes, turning the dish twice. Eat warm with sponge cake.

Mixed Dried Fruit Salad

SERVES 4

**225 g/8 oz mixed dried fruits such
as apple rings, apricots,
peaches, pears, prunes**
300 ml/½ pt/1¼ cups boiling water
50 g/2 oz/¼ cup granulated sugar
**10 ml/2 tsp finely grated lemon
peel**
Thick plain yoghurt, to serve

Wash the fruit thoroughly and place in a 1.25 litre/2¼ pt/5½ cup bowl. Stir in the water and sugar. Cover with a plate and leave to soak for 4 hours. Transfer to the microwave and cook on Full for about 20 minutes until the fruit is tender. Stir in the lemon peel and serve warm with thick yoghurt.

Stodgy Apple and Blackberry Pudding

SERVES 6

A little melted butter
275 g/10 oz/2¼ cups self-raising (self-rising) flour
150 g/5 oz/⅔ cup butter or margarine, at kitchen temperature
125 g/4 oz/½ cup soft brown sugar
2 eggs, beaten
400 g/14 oz/1 large can apple and blackberry fruit filling
45 ml/3 tbsp cold milk
Cream or custard, to serve

Brush a 1.25 litre/2¼ pt/5½ cup round soufflé dish with the melted butter. Sift the flour into a bowl and rub in the butter or margarine finely. Add the sugar and mix to a soft consistency with the eggs, fruit filling and milk, stirring briskly without beating. Spread evenly into the prepared dish. Cook, uncovered, on Full for 9 minutes, turning the dish three times. Allow to stand for 5 minutes. Turn out into a warmed shallow dish. Spoon on to plates to serve with cream or custard.

Lemony Bramble Pudding

SERVES 4

A little melted butter
225g/8 oz/2 cups blackberries, crushed
Finely grated peel and juice of 1 lemon
225 g/8 oz/2 cups self-raising (self-rising) flour
125 g/4 oz/½ cup butter or margarine
100 g/3½ oz/scant ½ cup dark soft brown sugar
2 eggs, beaten
60 ml/4 tbsp cold milk
Cream, ice cream or lemon sorbet, to serve

Brush a deep 18 cm/7 in diameter dish with melted butter. Combine the blackberries with the lemon peel and juice and set aside. Sift the flour into a bowl. Rub in the butter and sugar. Mix to a softish consistency with the crushed fruit, eggs and milk. Spread smoothly into the prepared dish. Cook, uncovered, on Full for 7–8 minutes until the pudding has risen to the top of the dish and the top has no shiny patches. Allow to stand for 5 minutes during which time the pudding will drop slightly. Loosen edges with a knife and turn out on to a warmed plate. Eat warm with cream, ice cream or lemon sorbet.

Lemony Raspberry Pudding

SERVES 4

Prepare as for Lemony Bramble Pudding, but substitute raspberries for the blackberries.

Apricot and Walnut Upside-down Pudding

SERVES 8

For the pudding:
50 g/2 oz/¼ cup butter or margarine
50 g/2 oz/¼ cup light soft brown sugar
400 g/14 oz canned apricot halves in syrup, drained and syrup reserved
50 g/2 oz/½ cup walnut halves
For the topping:
225 g/8 oz/2 cups self-raising (self-rising) flour
125 g/4 oz/½ cup butter or margarine
125 g/4 oz/½ cup caster (superfine) sugar
Finely grated peel of 1 orange
2 eggs
75 ml/5 tbsp cold milk
2.5–5 ml/½–1 tsp almond essence (extract)
Coffee ice cream, to serve

To make the pudding, butter the base and sides of a deep 25 cm/10 in diameter dish. Add the butter or margarine. Melt, uncovered, on Defrost for 2 minutes. Sprinkle the brown sugar over the butter so that it almost covers the base of the dish. Arrange the apricot halves attractively on top of the sugar, cut sides facing, and intersperse them with the walnut halves.

To make the topping, sift the flour into a bowl. Finely rub in the butter or margarine. Add the sugar and orange peel and toss to combine. Thoroughly beat together the remaining ingredients, then fork into the dry ingredients until evenly mixed. Spread smoothly over the fruit and nuts. Cook, uncovered, on Full for 10 minutes. Allow to stand for 5 minutes, then turn out carefully into a shallow dish. Heat the reserved syrup on Full for 25 seconds. Serve the pudding with coffee ice cream and the warm syrup.

Bananas Foster

SERVES 4

From New Orleans and named after Dick Foster, who was in charge of cleaning up the city's morals in the 1950s. Or so the story goes.

25 g/1 oz/2 tbsp butter or sunflower margarine
4 bananas
45 ml/3 tbsp dark soft brown sugar
1.5 ml/¼ tsp ground cinnamon
5 ml/1 tsp finely grated orange peel
60 ml/4 tbsp dark rum
Vanilla ice cream, to serve

Place the butter in a deep 23 cm/9 in diameter dish. Melt on Defrost for 1½ minutes. Peel the bananas, halve lengthways, then cut each half into two pieces. Arrange in the dish and sprinkle with the sugar, cinnamon and orange peel. Cover with clingfilm (plastic wrap) and slit it twice to allow steam to escape. Cook on Full for 3 minutes. Allow to stand for 1 minute. Heat the rum on Defrost until just warm. Ignite the rum with a match and pour over the uncovered bananas. Serve with rich vanilla ice cream.

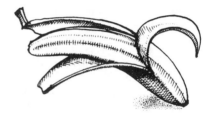

Mississippi Spice Pie

SERVES 8

For the flan case (pie shell):
225 g/8 oz ready-prepared shortcrust pastry (basic pie crust)
1 egg yolk
For the filling:
450 g/1 lb yellow-fleshed pink-skinned sweet potatoes, peeled and cubed
60 ml/4 tbsp boiling water
75 g/3 oz/⅓ cup caster (superfine) sugar
10 ml/2 tsp ground allspice
3 large eggs
150 ml/¼ pt/⅔ cup cold milk
30 ml/2 tbsp melted butter
Whipped cream or vanilla ice cream, to serve

To make the flan case, roll out the pastry thinly and use to line a lightly buttered 23 cm/9 in diameter fluted flan dish. Prick well all over with a fork, especially where the side joins the base. Cook, uncovered, on Full for 6 minutes, turning the dish three times. If bulges appear, gently press down with fingers protected by oven gloves. Brush all over with the egg yolk to seal holes. Cook, uncovered, on Full for a further 1 minute. Set aside.

To make the filling, put the potatoes in a 1 litre/1¾ pt/4¼ cup dish. Add the boiling water. Cover with clingfilm (plastic wrap) and slit it twice to allow steam to escape. Cook on Full for 10 minutes, turning the dish twice. Allow to stand for 5 minutes. Drain. Put into a food processor or blender and add the remaining ingredients. Work to a smooth purée. Spread evenly in the baked pastry case. Cook, uncovered, on Defrost for 20–25 minutes until the filling has set, turning the dish four times. Cool to lukewarm. Cut into portions and serve with softly whipped cream or vanilla ice cream.

Jamaica Pudding

SERVES 4–5

225 g/8 oz/2 cups self-raising (self-rising) flour
125 g/4 oz/½ cup mixture white cooking fat (shortening) and margarine
125 g/4 oz/½ cup caster (superfine) sugar
2 large eggs, beaten
50 g/2 oz/¼ cup canned crushed pineapple with syrup
15 ml/1 tbsp coffee and chicory essence (extract) or coffee liqueur
Clotted cream, to serve

Butter a 1.75 litre/3 pt/7½ cup soufflé dish. Sift the flour into a bowl and rub in the fats finely. Mix in the sugar. Mix with a fork to a soft consistency with the eggs, pineapple with syrup and coffee essence or liqueur. Spread smoothly into the dish. Cook, uncovered, on Full for 6 minutes, turning the dish once. Invert on to a serving plate and leave to stand for 5 minutes. Return to the microwave. Cook on Full for a further 1–1½ minutes. Serve with clotted cream.

Pumpkin Pie

SERVES 8

Eaten in North America on the last Thursday of every November to celebrate Thanksgiving.

For the flan case (pie shell):
225 g/8 oz ready-prepared
  shortcrust pastry (basic pie
  crust)
1 egg yolk
For the filling:
½ small pumpkin or a 1.75 kg/
  4 lb portion, seeded
30 ml/2 tbsp black treacle
  (molasses)
175 g/6 oz/¾ cup light soft brown
  sugar
15 ml/1 tbsp cornflour
  (cornstarch)
10 ml/2 tsp ground allspice
150 ml/¼ pt/⅔ cup double (heavy)
  cream
3 eggs, beaten
Whipped cream, to serve

To make the flan case, roll out the pastry thinly and use to line a lightly buttered 23 cm/9 in diameter fluted flan dish. Prick well all over with a fork, especially where the side joins the base. Cook, uncovered, on Full for 6 minutes, turning the dish three times. If bulges appear, gently press down with fingers protected by oven gloves. Brush all over with the egg yolk to seal holes. Cook, uncovered, on Full for a further 1 minute. Set aside.

To make the filling, put the pumpkin on a plate. Cook, uncovered, on Full for 15–18 minutes until the flesh is very soft. Spoon away from the skin and leave to cool to lukewarm. Blend until smooth with the remaining ingredients. Spoon into the pastry case still in its dish. Cook, uncovered, on Full for 20–30 minutes until the filling is set, turning the dish four times. Serve warm with whipped cream. If preferred, use 425 g/15 oz/ 2 cups canned pumpkin instead of fresh.

Oaten Syrup Tart

SERVES 6–8

An up-to-date version of treacle tart.

For the flan case (pie shell):
225 g/8 oz ready-prepared
  shortcrust pastry (basic pie
  crust)
1 egg yolk
For the filling:
125 g/4 oz/2 cups toasted muesli
  with fruit and nuts
75 ml/5 tbsp golden (light corn)
  syrup
15 ml/1 tbsp black treacle
  (molasses)
Whipped cream, to serve

To make the flan case, roll out the pastry thinly and use to line a lightly buttered 23 cm/9 in diameter fluted flan dish. Prick well all over with a fork, especially where the side joins the base. Cook, uncovered, on Full for 6 minutes, turning the dish three times. If bulges appear, gently press down with fingers protected by oven gloves. Brush all over with the egg yolk to seal holes. Cook, uncovered, on Full for a further 1 minute. Set aside.

To make the filling, mix together the muesli, syrup and treacle and spoon into the baked flan case. Cook, uncovered, on Full for 3 minutes. Allow to stand for 2 minutes. Cook, uncovered, on Full for a further 1 minute. Serve with cream.

Coconut Sponge Flan

SERVES 8–10

For the flan case (pie shell):
225 g/8 oz ready-prepared shortcrust pastry (basic pie crust)
1 egg yolk
For the filling:
175 g/6 oz/1½ cups self-raising (self-rising) flour
75 g/3 oz/⅓ cup butter or margarine
75 g/3 oz/⅓ cup caster (superfine) sugar
75 ml/5 tbsp desiccated (shredded) coconut
2 eggs
5 ml/1 tsp vanilla essence (extract)
60 ml/4 tbsp cold milk
30 ml/2 tbsp strawberry or blackcurrant jam (conserve)
For the icing (frosting):
225 g/8 oz/1⅓ cups icing (confectioners') sugar, sifted
Orange flower water

To make the flan case, roll out the pastry thinly and use to line a lightly buttered 23 cm/9 in diameter fluted flan dish. Prick well all over with a fork, especially where the side joins the base. Cook, uncovered, on Full for 6 minutes, turning the dish three times. If bulges appear, gently press down with fingers protected by oven gloves. Brush all over with the egg yolk to seal holes. Cook, uncovered, on Full for a further 1 minute. Set aside.

To make the coconut filling, sift the flour into a mixing bowl. Rub in the butter or margarine. Toss in the sugar and coconut, then mix to a soft batter with the eggs, vanilla and milk. Spread the jam over the pastry case still in its dish. Spread evenly with the coconut mixture. Cook, uncovered, on Full for 6 minutes, turning the dish four times. The flan is ready when the top looks dry and no sticky patches remain. Allow to cool completely.

To make the icing, mix the icing sugar with enough orange flower water to make thickish icing; a few teaspoonfuls should be ample. Spread over the top of the flan. Leave until set before cutting.

Easy Bakewell Tart

SERVES 8–10

Prepare as for Coconut Sponge Flan, but use raspberry jam (conserve) and substitute ground almonds for the coconut.

Crumbly Mincemeat Pie

SERVES 8–10

For the flan case (pie shell):
225 g/8 oz ready-prepared shortcrust pastry (basic pie crust)
1 egg yolk
For the filling:
350 g/12 oz/1 cup mincemeat
For the nut crumble:
50 g/2 oz/¼ cup butter
125 g/4 oz/1 cup self-raising (self-rising) flour, sifted
50 g/2 oz/¼ cup demerara sugar
5 ml/1 tsp ground cinnamon
60 ml/4 tbsp finely chopped walnuts
To serve:
Whipped cream, custard or ice cream

To make the flan case, roll out the pastry thinly and use to line a lightly buttered 23 cm/9 in diameter fluted flan dish. Prick well all over with a fork, especially where the side joins the base. Cook, uncovered, on Full for 6 minutes, turning the dish three times. If bulges appear, gently press down with fingers protected by oven gloves. Brush all over with the egg yolk to seal holes. Cook, uncovered, on Full for a further 1 minute. Set aside.

To make the filling, spoon the mincemeat evenly into the baked flan case.

To make the nut crumble, rub the butter into the flour, then stir in the sugar, cinnamon and walnuts. Press over the mincemeat in an even layer. Leave uncovered and cook on Full for 4 minutes, turning the pie twice. Leave to stand for 5 minutes. Cut into wedges and serve hot with whipped cream, custard or ice cream.

Bread and Butter Pudding

SERVES 4

Britain's favourite pudding.
4 large slices white bread
50 g/2 oz/¼ cup butter at kitchen temperature or soft butter spread
50 g/2 oz/⅓ cup currants
50 g/2 oz/¼ cup caster (superfine) sugar
600 ml/1 pt/2½ cups cold milk
3 eggs
30 ml/2 tbsp demerara sugar
Grated nutmeg

Leave the crusts on the bread. Spread each slice with the butter, then cut into four squares. Thoroughly butter a deep 1.75 litre/3 pt/7½ cup square or oval dish. Arrange half the bread squares over the base, buttered sides up. Sprinkle with the currants and caster sugar. Cover with the remaining bread, again buttered sides up. Pour the milk into a jug or bowl. Warm, uncovered, on Full for 3 minutes. Thoroughly beat in the eggs. Slowly and gently pour over the bread. Sprinkle with the demerara sugar and nutmeg. Allow to stand for 30 minutes, loosely covered with a piece of greaseproof (waxed) paper. Cook, uncovered, on Defrost for 30 minutes. Crisp the top under a hot grill (broiler) before serving.

Lemon Curd Bread and Butter Pudding

SERVES 4

Prepare as for Bread and Butter Pudding, but spread the bread with Lemon Curd (page 345) instead of butter.

Baked Egg Custard

SERVES 4

Superb eaten on its own, with any kind of fruit salad combination or Cocktail of Summer Fruits (page 289).

300 ml/½ pt/1¼ cups single (light) cream or full-cream milk
3 eggs
1 egg yolk
100 g/3½ oz/scant ½ cup caster (superfine) sugar
5 ml/1 tsp vanilla essence (extract)
2.5 ml/½ tsp grated nutmeg

Thoroughly butter a 1 litre/1¾ pt/ 4¼ cup dish. Pour the cream or milk into a jug. Heat, uncovered, on Full for 1½ minutes. Whisk in all the remaining ingredients except the nutmeg. Strain into a dish. Stand in a second 2 litre/ 3½ pt/8½ cup dish. Pour boiling water into the larger dish until it reaches the level of the custard in the smaller dish. Sprinkle the top of the custard with the nutmeg. Cook, uncovered, on Full for 6–8 minutes until the custard is only just set. Remove from the microwave and allow to stand for 7 minutes. Lift the dish of custard out of the larger dish and continue to stand until the centre firms up. Serve warm or cold.

Semolina Pudding

SERVES 4

Nursery food but still popular with everyone.

50 g/2 oz/⅓ cup semolina (cream of wheat)
50 g/2 oz/¼ cup caster (superfine) sugar
600 ml/1 pt/2½ cups milk
10 ml/2 tsp butter or margarine

Put the semolina in a mixing bowl. Blend in the sugar and milk. Cook, uncovered, on Full for 7–8 minutes, whisking thoroughly every minute, until boiling and thickened. Stir in the butter or margarine. Transfer to serving dishes to eat.

Ground Rice Pudding

SERVES 4

Prepare as for Semolina Pudding, but substitute ground rice for the semolina (cream of wheat).

Steamed Suet Treacle Pudding

SERVES 4

45 ml/3 tbsp golden (light corn) syrup
125 g/4 oz/1 cup self-raising (self-rising) flour
50 g/2 oz/½ cup shredded suet (vegetarian if preferred)
50 g/2 oz/¼ cup caster (superfine) sugar
1 egg
5 ml/1 tsp vanilla essence (extract)
90 ml/6 tbsp cold milk

Thoroughly grease a 1.25 litre/ 2¼ pt/5½ cup pudding basin. Pour in the syrup until it covers the base. Sift the flour into a bowl and toss in the suet and sugar. Thoroughly beat together the egg, vanilla essence and milk, then fork into the dry ingredients. Spoon into the basin. Cook, uncovered, on Full for 4–4½ minutes until the pudding has risen to reach the top of the basin. Allow to stand for 2 minutes. Turn out and spoon on to four plates. Serve with any sweet dessert sauce (pages 333–7).

Marmalade or Honey Pudding

SERVES 4

Prepare as for Steamed Suet Treacle Pudding, but substitute marmalade or honey for the syrup.

Ginger Pudding

SERVES 4

Prepare as for Steamed Suet Treacle Pudding, but sift 10 ml/2 tsp ground ginger in with the flour.

Jam Sponge Pudding

SERVES 4

45 ml/3 tbsp raspberry jam (conserve)
175 g/6 oz/1½ cups self-raising (self-rising) flour
75 g/3 oz/⅓ cup butter or margarine
75 g/3 oz/⅓ cup caster (superfine) sugar
2 eggs
45 ml/3 tbsp cold milk
5 ml/1 tsp vanilla essence (extract)
Whipped cream or custard, to serve

Spoon the jam into a thoroughly greased 1.5 litre/2½ pt/6 cup pudding basin. Sift the flour into a bowl. Rub in the butter or margarine finely, then toss in the sugar. Thoroughly beat together the eggs, milk and vanilla essence, then fork into the dry ingredients. Spoon into the basin. Cook on Full for 7–8 minutes until the pudding has risen to the top of the basin. Allow to stand for 3 minutes. Turn out and spoon portions on to four plates. Serve with cream or custard.

Lemon Sponge Pudding

SERVES 4

Prepare as for Jam Sponge Pudding, but substitute lemon curd for the jam (conserve) and add the finely grated peel of 1 small lemon to the dry ingredients.

Crêpes Suzette

SERVES 4

Back in fashion after a long spell in the shadows.

8 conventionally cooked pancakes, each about 20 cm/8 in diameter
45 ml/3 tbsp butter
30 ml/2 tbsp caster (superfine) sugar
5 ml/1 tsp grated orange peel
5 ml/1 tsp grated lemon peel
Juice of 2 large oranges
30 ml/2 tbsp Grand Marnier
30 ml/2 tbsp brandy

Fold each pancake in four so that it looks like an envelope. Leave aside. Put the butter in a shallow 25 cm/10 in diameter dish. Melt on Defrost for 1½–2 minutes. Add all the remaining ingredients except the brandy and stir well. Heat on Full for 2–2½ minutes. Stir round. Add the pancakes in a single layer and baste with the butter sauce. Cook, uncovered, on Full for 3–4 minutes. Remove from the microwave. Pour the brandy into a cup and heat on Full for 15–20 seconds until tepid. Tip into a ladle and ignite with a match. Pour over the crêpes and serve when the flames have died down.

Baked Apples

For **1 apple:** score a line round a large cooking (tart) apple with a sharp knife, about one-third down from the top. Remove the core with a potato peeler or apple corer, taking care not to cut through the base of the apple. Fill with sugar, dried fruit, jam (conserve) or lemon curd. Place in a dish and cook, uncovered, on Full for 3–4 minutes, turning the dish twice, until the apple has puffed up like a soufflé. Allow to stand for 2 minutes before eating.

For 2 apples: as for 1 apple, but arrange the apples side by side on the dish and cook on Full for 5 minutes.

For 3 apples: as for 1 apple, but arrange in a triangle in the dish and cook on Full for 7 minutes.

For 4 apples: as for 1 apple, but arrange in a square in the dish and cook on Full for 8–10 minutes.

Chocolate Fondue

SERVES 3–4

200 g/7 oz plain (semi-sweet) chocolate
150 ml/¼ pt/⅔ cup double (heavy) cream
15 ml/1 tbsp whisky, rum, brandy or orange-flavoured liqueur or 5 ml/1 tsp vanilla essence (extract)
Small biscuits, marshmallows and/or pieces of fresh fruit, to serve

Break up the chocolate and place in a basin. Melt, uncovered, on Defrost for 4–5 minutes until soft. Stir in the cream and heat, uncovered, on Defrost for about 1½ minutes. Stir in the alcohol or vanilla essence. Serve warm with biscuits, marshmallows and/or fresh fruit pieces for dipping.

Orange Chocolate Fondue

SERVES 3–4

Prepare as for Chocolate Fondue, but use only Grand Marnier, Mandarine Napolean liqueur or Cointreau. Flavour with 5 ml/1 tsp finely grated orange peel.

Mocha Fondue

SERVES 3–4

Prepare as for Chocolate Fondue, but add 15 ml/1 tbsp instant coffee powder with the cream and use only Tia Maria, Kahlua or coffee essence (extract) to flavour.

White Chocolate Fondue

SERVES 3–4

Prepare as for Chocolate Fondue, but substitute white chocolate for the plain (semi-sweet) and add 30 ml/2 tbsp of the measured cream to the chocolate before melting. Flavour with vanilla essence (extract) or an orange liqueur instead of the suggested spirits.

Toblerone Fondue

SERVES 3–4

Prepare as for Chocolate Fondue, but substitute white, milk or dark Toblerone chocolate for the plain (semi-sweet) chocolate.

Royal Chocolate Mousse

MAKES 10–12

15 ml/1 tbsp powdered gelatine
150 ml/¼ pt/⅔ cup cold water
500 g/1 lb 2 oz plain (semi-sweet)
  chocolate (70% cocoa)
30 ml/2 tbsp butter
75 ml/3 fl oz/5½ tbsp strong hot
  coffee
4 eggs, at kitchen temperature,
  separated
A pinch of salt
Coffee or cocoa (unsweetened
  chocolate) powder, to serve

Soak the gelatine in a glass jug in cold water 5 minutes. Melt, uncovered, on Full for 1½–2 minutes until the liquid looks clear. Stir round, then set aside. Break up the chocolate and place in a fairly large bowl with the butter and coffee. Melt, uncovered, on Defrost for 6–7 minutes. Stir in the egg yolks and melted gelatine. Chill until just beginning to thicken and set slightly round the edges. Whisk together the egg whites and salt until they form stiff peaks. Beat one-third into the chocolate mixture, then gently and smoothly fold in the remainder. Divide between 10–12 ramekin dishes (custard cups). Chill for several hours until firm. Dust with coffee or cocoa powder before serving.

Dutch-style Pears with Chocolate Advocaat Mousse

SERVES 6

10 ml/2 tsp powdered gelatine
30 ml/2 tbsp cold water
100 g/3½ oz plain (semi-sweet)
  chocolate
2 eggs, at kitchen temperature,
  separated
150 ml/¼ pt/⅔ cup advocaat (egg
  liqueur)
425 g/15 oz/1 large can pear
  halves in juice or syrup, drained
30 ml/2 tbsp chopped pistachio
  nuts

Soak the gelatine in a glass jug in cold water for 5 minutes. Melt, uncovered, on Full for 1–1½ minutes until the liquid looks clear. Stir round and set aside. Break up the chocolate and place in a separate bowl. Melt, uncovered, on Defrost for 3–3½ minutes. Stir well. Mix in the dissolved gelatine, egg yolks and advocaat. Beat until smooth and evenly combined. Cover and chill until just beginning to thicken and set. Beat the egg whites to stiff peaks. Whisk one-third into the chocolate mixture, then fold in the remainder with a metal spoon. Divide the pears between six sundae glasses and top evenly with the chocolate mixture. Chill until set. Sprinkle with the nuts before serving.

Traditional Chocolate Mousse
SERVES 4

100 g/3½ oz plain (semi-sweet) chocolate
15 ml/1 tbsp unsalted (sweet) butter
4 eggs at kitchen temperature, separated
A pinch of salt
Sponge finger biscuits (cookies), to serve

Break up chocolate, then put in a 1.25 litre/2¼ pt/5½ cup basin with the butter. Heat, uncovered, on Defrost for 3½–4 minutes, stirring once or twice, until both have melted. Mix in the egg yolks. In a separate bowl, beat the egg whites and salt to stiff peaks. Beat one-third into the chocolate mixture, then smoothly stir in the remainder with a large metal spoon. Spoon into four stemmed wine glasses. Cover with kitchen paper and chill thoroughly. Eat with sponge fingers.

Chocolate Orange Mousse
SERVES 4

Prepare as for Traditional Chocolate Mousse, but add 10 ml/2 tsp finely grated orange peel with the egg yolks.

Mocha Mousse
SERVES 4

Prepare as for Traditional Chocolate Mousse, but add 10 ml/2 tsp instant coffee granules with the egg yolks.

Chocolate Peppermint Cream Mousse
SERVES 4

Prepare as for Traditional Chocolate Mousse, but add a few drops of peppermint essence (extract) with the egg yolks. Just before serving, decorate the top of each with whipped cream.

Berlin Air
SERVES 6–8

Germany's answer to Italy's *zabaglione* and Britain's syllabub.

4 large eggs, separated
A pinch of salt
150 g/5 oz/⅔ cup caster (superfine) sugar
5 ml/1 tsp vanilla essence (extract)
10 ml/2 tsp cornflour (cornstarch)
150 ml/¼ pt/⅔ cup sweet white wine
150 ml/¼ pt/⅔ cup double (heavy) cream
30 ml/2 tbsp brandy
Wafer biscuits (cookies) and mixed berry fruits (optional), to serve

Whisk the egg whites with the salt until stiff. Whisk together the yolks, sugar and vanilla in a large bowl until the mixture is pale and thick. Gently whisk in the whites. Mix the cornflour smoothly with a little of the wine, then stir in the remainder. Fold into the egg mixture. Cook, uncovered, on Full for 3½ minutes, whisking every 30 seconds, until the mixture is foaming and resembles thickish custard. Cover and leave until completely cold. In large bowl, whisk the cream with the brandy until thick. Gradually whisk in the egg mixture. Spoon into six to eight individual ramekin dishes (custard cups) and chill thoroughly. Serve with crisp wafer biscuits and accompany, in season, with fresh berry fruits.

Crème Caramel

SERVES 4

Prepare one quantity of Baked Egg Custard (page 296). Pour bought caramel sauce into four buttered ramekin dishes (custard cups) and top with the egg custard. Cook, uncovered, on Defrost for 8–9 minutes until the custard is set. Allow to cool, then chill thoroughly. Turn out on to individual plates and serve with cream.

Spicy Peaches and Oranges in Red Wine

SERVES 6–8

8 large ripe peaches, blanched and skinned
Lemon juice
300 ml/½ pt/1¼ cups dry red wine
175 g/6 oz/¾ cup caster (superfine) sugar
5 cm/2 in piece cinnamon stick
4 whole cloves
2 cardamom pods
2 oranges, unpeeled and thinly sliced

Halve the peaches and twist to separate. Remove the stones (pits). Brush the flesh all over with lemon juice. Put the remaining ingredients except the oranges in a deep 20 cm/ 8 in diameter dish. Cover with an inverted plate and heat on Full for 4 minutes. Stir to mix. Add the peaches, cut sides down, and arrange the orange slices randomly between. Cover with clingfilm (plastic wrap) and slit it twice to allow steam to escape. Cook on Full for 10 minutes, turning the dish twice. Cool and chill before serving.

Spicy Pears and Oranges in Red Wine

SERVES 6–8

Prepare as for Spicy Peaches and Oranges in Red Wine, but substitute 8 small dessert pears, peeled, halved and cored, for the peaches.

Store-cupboard Raspberry Mousse

SERVES 6

15 ml/1 tbsp powdered gelatine
30 ml/2 tbsp cold water
425 g/15 oz/1 large can raspberries in syrup, drained and syrup reserved
3 eggs, separated
45 ml/3 tbsp caster (superfine) sugar
A pinch of salt
150 ml/¼ pt/⅔ cup whipping cream
15 ml/1 tbsp toasted and chopped hazelnuts (page 205), to decorate

Put the gelatine in a jug with the cold water. Stir round and leave for 5 minutes to soften. Melt, uncovered, on Full for 2 minutes until the liquid is clear. Add the raspberry syrup to the gelatine. Gently beat in the egg yolks and sugar. Cover and chill until just beginning to thicken and set. Beat the egg whites and salt until stiff. Whip the cream until thick. Beat one-third of the egg whites into the gelatine mixture, then mix in two-thirds of the raspberries and three-quarters of the cream. Fold in the remaining whites with a metal spoon. When smooth and well-combined, transfer to six dessert dishes. Cover and chill until set. Before serving, stir the remaining cream into the remaining raspberries and use to decorate the top of the mousses.

Egg Custard, Apricot and Sherry Trifle

••••••••••••••••••••••••••••••
SERVES 8

600 ml/1 pt/2½ cups full-cream milk or half single (light) cream and half milk
15 ml/1 tbsp cornflour (cornstarch)
15 ml/1 tbsp cold water
4 large eggs
75 ml/5 tbsp caster (superfine) sugar
5 ml/1 tsp vanilla essence (extract)
2 jam (conserve)-filled Swiss (jelly) rolls, thinly sliced
425 g/15 oz/1 large can apricot halves, drained
30 ml/2 tbsp sweet sherry
60 ml/4 tbsp apricot syrup
150 ml/¼ pt/⅔ cup double (heavy) cream
Hundreds and thousands, to decorate

Pour the milk into a jug. Warm, uncovered, on Full for 2 minutes. Put the cornflour and water in a 1.25 litre/2¼ pt/5½ cup bowl and stir until smooth. Beat in the eggs one at a time. Add 45 ml/3 tbsp of the caster sugar and mix in the warm milk. Cook, uncovered, on Full for 5–6 minutes, whisking every minute, until the custard is of a thin coating consistency (it thickens on cooling). Mix in the vanilla. Cover and set aside. Stand eight slices of Swiss roll against the side of a deep 20 cm/8 in diameter glass serving dish. Reserve 8 apricot halves for decoration and coarsely chop the remainder. Use to cover the base of the dish with the remaining Swiss roll. Moisten with the sherry and apricot syrup. Coat with half the warm custard and let it soak well in. Pour the remaining custard over the top. Cover and chill for 4–5 hours. Before serving, beat together the cream and remaining caster sugar until thick. Use to decorate the top of the trifle, then arrange the reserved apricot halves on top. Dust with hundreds and thousands.

Short-cut Sherry Trifle

••••••••••••••••••••••••••••••••••
SERVES 6–8

1 jam (conserve)-filled Swiss (jelly) roll, thinly sliced
45 ml/3 tbsp sweet sherry
425 g/15 oz/1 large can peach slices or fruit cocktail, drained and syrup reserved
45 ml/3 tbsp custard powder
30 ml/2 tbsp caster (superfine) sugar
600 ml/1 pt/2½ cups cold milk
150 ml/¼ pt/⅔ cup whipped cream
Hundreds and thousands and red glacé (candied) cherries, halved (optional)

Arrange the Swiss roll slices over the base and half-way up the side of a shallow glass bowl. Moisten with the sherry and few spoonfuls of the reserved syrup. Cover with the drained fruit. Put the custard powder and sugar in a fairly deep dish and mix smoothly with a little of the cold milk. Blend in the remainder. Cook, uncovered, on Full for 8 minutes, whisking briskly every minute to keep the custard smooth. Allow to cool slightly, then pour over the trifle. Cover when cold and chill thoroughly. Before serving, decorate with the whipped cream, hundreds and thousands and glacé cherries.

Note: use up any left-over syrup in fresh fruit salad.

Chocolate Cream Trifle

SERVES 8

Prepare as for Egg Custard, Apricot and Sherry Trifle, but use 2 cream-filled chocolate Swiss (jelly) rolls instead of jam-filled. Substitute coffee liqueur for the sherry and canned pear halves for the apricots. Sprinkle with grated chocolate or a crushed flake bar instead of the hundreds and thousands.

Trifle with Sponge Cakes

SERVES 6–8

Make any of the three trifles above, but substitute bought sponge cakes (8 in a packet) for the Swiss (jelly) roll. Split and fill with jam (conserve), curd or chocolate spread.

Fluffy Lemon Clouds

SERVES 4–5

300 ml/½ pt/1¼ cups cold milk
25 ml/1½ tbsp custard powder
15 ml/1 tbsp caster (superfine)
* sugar*
2 large eggs, separated
1 packet lemon jelly (jello)
A pinch of salt
Seasonal fruits, to decorate

Blend some of the cold milk smoothly with the custard powder in a large bowl. Mix in the remainder. Cook, uncovered, on Full for 3–3½ minutes, whisking every minute to prevent lumps forming, until the mixture comes to the boil and thickens. Beat in the sugar and egg yolks. Cover with a piece of clingfilm (plastic wrap), placing it directly on the surface of the custard to stop a skin forming. Allow to cool. Break up the jelly into cubes. Put in a measuring jug with 60 ml/ 4 tbsp water. Cover with a saucer and melt on Defrost for 2–2½ minutes, stirring twice. Make up to 300 ml/ ½ pt/1¼ cups with cold water. Lift the clingfilm off the custard and beat in the melted jelly. Cover and chill until the mixture is beginning to thicken and set. Whisk the egg whites and salt until stiff. Beat one-third into the jelly mixture, then smoothly fold in the remainder with a large metal spoon or balloon whisk. Transfer to four or five dessert glasses or dishes. Cover and chill until firm and set. Decorate with fresh seasonal fruits.

Fluffy Lime Clouds

SERVES 4–5

Prepare as for Fluffy Lemon Clouds, but substitute lime jelly (jello) for the lemon.

Apple Snow

SERVES 4

30 ml/2 tbsp vanilla-flavoured blancmange powder
450 ml/¾ pt/2 cups cold milk
45 ml/3 tbsp caster (superfine) sugar
125 g/4 oz/½ cup smooth apple purée (apple sauce)
2 large eggs, separated
A squeeze of lemon juice
Grated lemon peel

Tip the blancmange powder into a 1.75 litre/3 pt/7½ cup bowl. Mix smoothly with 60 ml/4 tbsp of the measured milk. Pour the remaining milk into a basin. Heat, uncovered, on Full for 4 minutes. Blend into the blancmange mixture. Add the sugar and stir thoroughly. Cook, uncovered, on Full for about 2½ minutes, beating every minute, until smooth and thickened. Whisk in the apple purée and egg yolks. Cover and allow to cool to lukewarm. Beat together the egg whites and lemon juice to stiff peaks. Whisk one-third into the blancmange mixture, then gently fold in the remainder with a large metal spoon. Spoon into four dishes or glasses. Cover and chill for several hours. Sprinkle each lightly with lemon peel before serving.

Apricot Snow

SERVES 4

Prepare as for Apple Snow, but substitute apricot purée (sauce) for the apple purée.

Lemon Meringue Spiced Pears

SERVES 6

Altogether a surprise package.

75 g/3 oz/⅓ cup light soft brown sugar
300 ml/½ pt/1¼ cups water
60 ml/4 tbsp dry white wine
5 cm/2 inch piece cinnamon stick
4 whole cloves
6 firm dessert pears
1 packet lemon meringue filling mix
150 ml/¼ pt/⅔ cup milk, at kitchen temperature
Finely grated peel of 1 small lemon
Basil leaves, to decorate

Put the sugar, water, wine, cinnamon stick and cloves in a 1.75 litre/3 pt/7½ cup dish. Heat, uncovered, on Full for 3 minutes. Set aside. Peel the pears, leaving the stalks in place. Arrange upright in the dish and baste with the spicy syrup mixture. Slide the dish into a roasting bag and tie up with string. Cook on Full for 7 minutes. Remove from the microwave and take the dish from the bag. Carefully strain the syrup into a measuring jug. Stir in the lemon filling mix. Cover with saucer and cook on Full for 2–3 minutes, whisking every 30 seconds, until the mixture comes to the boil. Allow to cool for 5 minutes. Whisk in the milk and lemon peel. Cover and chill both the pears and the lemon sauce for several hours. Before serving, coat the pears with about half the sauce and decorate with basil leaves. Pour the remainder into a jug and pass separately.

Finnish Cranberry Whip

SERVES 6

225 g/8 oz cranberries, thawed if frozen
150 ml/¼ pt/⅔ cup water
175 g/6 oz/¾ cup caster (superfine) sugar
5 ml/1 tsp finely grated lemon peel
150 ml/¼ pt/⅔ cup whipping cream
150 ml/¼ pt/⅔ cup double (heavy) cream
2 large egg whites

Put the cranberries, water, sugar and lemon peel in a 1.25 litre/2¼ pt/ 5½ cup dish. Cover with a plate and cook on Full for 8½ minutes, stirring twice and crushing the fruit against the side of the dish. Allow to cool completely. Whip the creams together until thick. Beat the egg whites to stiff peaks. Fold the cream and egg whites alternately into the cranberries. Transfer to six individual dishes. Chill lightly before serving.

Cranberry and Orange Whip

SERVES 6

Prepare as for Finnish Cranberry Whip, but add 10 ml/2 tsp grated orange peel with the lemon peel

Kissel

SERVES 4

Russia's answer to blancmange, made from fruits growing wild in the countryside around country *dachas* or wooden holiday homes.

450 g/1 lb mixed soft berry fruits
60 ml/4 tbsp red wine, apple juice or water
75 g/3 oz/⅓ cup caster (superfine) sugar
5 ml/1 tsp vanilla essence (extract)
Peel of 1 lemon, cut into strips
15 ml/1 tbsp cornflour (cornstarch) or potato flour
30 ml/2 tbsp cold water
Single (light) cream or Home-made Yoghurt (page 306), to serve

Purée the fruit in a blender or food processor. Sieve to remove the seeds. Pour the wine, juice or water into a mixing bowl. Add the sugar, vanilla and lemon strips. Cover with a plate and cook on Full for 3½ minutes, stirring twice to ensure the sugar has dissolved. Add the berry purée. Cover as before and cook on Full for 2 minutes. Strain into a clean bowl. Blend the cornflour or potato flour smoothly with the water. Add to the fruit mixture. Cook, uncovered, on Full for 2–3 minutes, stirring three times, until thickened. Allow to cool slightly. Transfer to four dessert dishes, then cover and chill for several hours. Float cream or yoghurt over the top of each before serving.

Home-made Yoghurt
•••••••••••••••••••••••••••••••••••
MAKES ABOUT 900 ML/1½ PT/3¾ CUPS

900 ml/1½ pts/3¾ cups full-cream milk
60 ml/4 tbsp skimmed milk powder (non-fat dry milk)
150 ml/¼ pt/⅔ cup plain yoghurt

Pour the milk into a bowl. Heat, uncovered, on Defrost for about 4–5 minutes until lukewarm but not hot. Whisk in the skimmed milk and yoghurt. Cover. Leave to stand in a warm place for 12 hours until set – a linen cupboard is ideal. Store in the refrigerator when cold.

Apricot Pots
•••••••••••••••••••••••••••••••••••••
SERVES 8

350 g/12 oz/2 cups dried apricot halves
600 ml/1 pt/2½ cups boiling water
30 ml/2 tbsp orange flower water
60 ml/4 tbsp icing (confectioners') sugar, sifted
225 g/8 oz/1 cup thick Greek-style plain yoghurt
Raspberry Coulis (page 334)

Thoroughly wash the apricots, then soak in boiling water, covered with a plate, for at least 6 hours. Drain and transfer to a bowl. Add the measured boiling water. Cover with clingfilm (plastic wrap) and slit it twice to allow steam to escape. Cook on Defrost for 25–30 minutes, turning the bowl three times. Remove from the microwave and allow to cool to lukewarm. Tip into a food processor with the orange flower water and sugar and run the machine until the mixture forms a fairly smooth purée. Combine with the yoghurt and spoon evenly into eight ramekin dishes (custard cups). Cover and chill. Before serving, cover each with the coulis.

Prune Pots
•••••••••••••••••••••••••••••••••••
SERVES 8

350 g/12 oz dried stoned (pitted) prunes
600 ml/1 pt/2½ cups boiling water
30 ml/2 tbsp orange flower water
60 ml/4 tbsp icing (confectioners') sugar, sifted
30–45 ml/2–3 tbsp Armagnac
225 g/8 oz/1 cup thick Greek-style plain yoghurt
Chopped pecan nuts and demerara sugar, to serve

Thoroughly wash the prunes, then soak in boiling water, covered with plate, for at least 6 hours. Drain and transfer to a bowl. Add the measured boiling water. Cover with clingfilm (plastic wrap) and slit it twice to allow steam to escape. Cook on Defrost for 25–30 minutes, turning the bowl three times. Remove from the microwave and allow to cool to lukewarm. Tip the drained prunes, orange flower water, sugar and Armagnac into a food processor and run the machine until the mixture forms a fairly smooth purée. Combine with the yoghurt and spoon evenly into eight ramekin dishes (custard cups). Cover and chill. Before serving, sprinkle each with pecan nuts and demerara sugar.

Cherries Jubilee

SERVES 6

One of North America's prize specimens and a show-off designed to impress.

*400 g/14 oz/1 large can black
    cherry fruit filling*
30 ml/2 tbsp cold water
30 ml/2 tbsp Kirsch or brandy
Vanilla ice cream

Put the fruit filling in a bowl and stir in the water. Heat, uncovered, on Defrost for 3 minutes. Stir round. Spread evenly into a shallow serving dish. In a separate dish, warm the spirit, uncovered, on Defrost for 45 seconds. Pour over the cherries and carefully ignite. Serve immediately over scoops of ice cream.

Fruits of the Forest Jubilee

SERVES 6

Prepare as for Cherries Jubilee, but substitute apple and blackberry fruit filling for black cherry and strawberry ice cream for vanilla.

Dutch Chocolate Sundaes

SERVES 4

90 ml/6 tbsp advocaat
75 ml/5 tbsp single (light) cream
2 small bananas, thinly sliced
Vanilla or chocolate ice cream
1 chocolate flake bar, crushed

Pour the advocaat into a dish and stir in the cream. Add the bananas. Heat, uncovered, on Defrost for 3 minutes. Mix gently. Spoon over scoops of ice cream in sundae dishes or dessert glasses and sprinkle with the chocolate flake. Eat straight away.

Cream Liqueur Sundaes

SERVES 4

Prepare as for Dutch Chocolate Sundaes, but substitute any cream liqueur, quantity to taste, for the advocaat.

Grape and Raspberry Jelly

SERVES 4

1 packet raspberry jelly (jello)
*225 g/8 oz mixed black and green
    seedless grapes, rinsed and
    drained*
Wafer biscuits (cookies), to serve

Snip the jelly into cubes with kitchen scissors and put in a measuring cup with 60 ml/4 tbsp cold water. Melt, uncovered, on Defrost for 2–2½ minutes. Make up to 450 ml/¾ pt/2 cups with cold water. Cover and chill until just beginning to thicken and set – it must not be at all runny. Fold the grapes into the thickened jelly with a spoon. Divide equally between four dessert dishes or stemmed glasses. Cover loosely with kitchen paper and chill until set. Serve with wafer biscuits.

Mandarin and Lemon Jelly

SERVES 4

Prepare as for Grape and Raspberry Jelly, but substitute lemon jelly (jello) for the raspberry and peeled fresh mandarin, clementine or satsuma segments, halved, for the grapes.

Black Cherry Rice Cream

SERVES 4

1 packet black cherry jelly (jello)
400 g/14 oz/1 large can rice
pudding
75 ml/5 tbsp single (light) cream
30 ml/2 tbsp black cherry jam
(conserve)

Snip the jelly into cubes with kitchen scissors and put in a measuring cup. Melt, uncovered, on Defrost for 2–2½ minutes. Fold in the rice pudding and cream, whisking gently without beating. Make up to 600 ml/1 pt/ 2½ cups with cold water. Cover lightly and chill until just beginning to thicken and set, stirring frequently. Divide equally between four sundae glasses and allow to set completely. Top each with 7.5 ml/1½ tsp jam before serving.

Banana Splits

SERVES 4

The return of something special after a long time away.

Peel 4 large bananas, then halve each lengthways. Arrange on four plates. Put 2 scoops of vanilla ice cream in between each to make a 'sandwich', then top with any of the hot chocolate sauce recipes (pages 334, 337). Pipe or spoon on softly whipped cream and serve straight away.

Spicy Prune Froth

SERVES 4

450 ml/¾ pt/2 cups prune juice
15 ml/1 tbsp powdered gelatine
8 cm/3 in piece cinnamon stick
2 star anise
30 ml/2 tbsp fine-shred orange
marmalade
2 large egg whites
A pinch of salt
30 ml/2 tbsp whipped cream
Ground cinnamon

Pour 45 ml/3 tbsp of the prune juice into a small bowl. Add the gelatine and stir round. Stand for 5 minutes to soften. Melt, uncovered, on Defrost for 2–2½ minutes. Set aside. Pour the remaining prune juice into a large jug and add the cinnamon stick, star anise and marmalade. Heat, uncovered, on Full for 6 minutes or until the liquid just begins to bubble. Gently beat in the dissolved gelatine. Strain into a clean bowl. Cover with a plate and allow to cool, then chill until just beginning to thicken and set. Whisk the egg whites and salt until stiff. Beat one-third into the part-set prune jelly, then fold in the remaining whites thoroughly with large metal spoon or spatula. Spoon into four glass dishes, cover loosely and allow to set for several hours in the refrigerator. Before serving, decorate each with cream and dust with cinnamon.

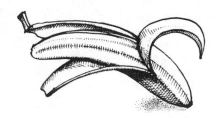

Chilled Oranges with Hot Chocolate Peppermint Sauce

SERVES 4

4 large oranges, peeled and very thinly sliced
Hot Chocolate Peppermint Sauce (page 334)
Mint sprigs

Peel and very thinly slice the oranges, ensuring any pips (pits) are removed. Arrange on four side plates, then cover and chill until almost icy. Immediately before serving, drizzle the sauce over each, then garnish with mint sprigs.

Summer Fruit Mould

SERVES 4

A sort of summer pudding in an instant. It is markedly sweet-sour and benefits from a drizzle of custard or sweetened cream.

500 g/1 lb 2 oz frozen mixed summer fruits
1 packet raspberry jelly (jello)

Tip the fruit into a bowl. Cover with a plate and thaw on Defrost for 7–8 minutes. Remove from the microwave. Snip the jelly into cubes and put in a bowl or jug. Melt, uncovered, on Defrost for 2½ minutes. Stir into the fruits. Chill until just beginning to thicken and set, stirring frequently so that the fruit stays suspended in the jelly. Transfer to a wetted mould or basin and cover. Chill until firm and completely set. Invert on to a plate and serve.

Watermelon and Apricot Chill with Frosted Grapes

SERVES 4

150 ml/¼ pt/⅔ cup sweet white wine
150 ml/¼ pt/⅔ cup white grape juice
Peel of 1 lime, cut into narrow strips
175 g/6 oz/1 cup dried apricots, well washed and cut into strips
5 ml/1 tsp vanilla essence (extract)
2.5 ml/½ tsp almond essence (extract)
1 large wedge red watermelon
4 clusters black seedless grapes
1 small egg white, lightly beaten
Caster (superfine) sugar

Pour the wine and grape juice into a 1.25 litre/2¼ pt/5½ cup bowl. Add half the lime peel. Heat, uncovered, on Full for 4 minutes. Add the apricot strips. Cook, uncovered, on Full for 2 minutes. Stir in the vanilla and almond essence (extract). Cover and allow to cool. Thoroughly chill when cold. Slice the watermelon flesh away from its skin and remove all the black seeds. Cut the flesh into small cubes. Set aside. Wash and dry the grapes but leave attached to their stalks. Dip them in egg white to cover, then coat thickly with caster sugar. Leave to dry and set for at least an hour. Add the melon to the apricot mixture and transfer to four glass dessert dishes. Top each with a bunch of frosted grapes and the remaining lime peel, cut into narrow strips.

Rhubarb and Mandarin Cups

••••••••••••••••••••••••••••••••

SERVES 6

450 g/1 lb rhubarb, trimmed and chopped
300 g/11 oz/1 large can mandarin oranges in syrup
60 ml/4 tbsp granulated sugar
5 ml/1 tsp finely grated orange peel
Raspberry or strawberry sorbet

Put the rhubarb in a 1.25 litre/ 2¼ pt/5½ cup dish with 30 ml/2 tbsp syrup from the mandarins and all the sugar. Cover with a plate and cook on Full for 7–9 minutes until the rhubarb is tender. Uncover and stir in the drained mandarins and orange peel. Cover and cool, then chill for several hours. Spoon into six glasses over scoops of sorbet and eat straight away

Rhubarb and Mandarin Cups with Ginger Cream

••••••••••••••••••••••••••••••••

SERVES 6

450 g/1 lb rhubarb, trimmed and chopped
300 g/11 oz/1 large can mandarin oranges in syrup
60 ml/4 tbsp granulated sugar
5 ml/1 tsp finely grated orange peel
5 ml/1 tsp ginger jam (conserve)
90 ml/6 tbsp double (heavy) cream, whipped
Vanilla ice cream

Put the rhubarb in a 1.25 litre/ 2¼ pt/5½ cup dish with 30 ml/2 tbsp syrup from the mandarins and all the sugar. Cover with a plate and cook on Full for 7–9 minutes until the rhubarb is tender. Uncover and stir in the drained mandarins and orange peel. Cover and cool, then chill for several hours. Mix the jam lightly into the cream. Spoon the rhubarb and mandarin mixture into six glasses over scoops of ice cream and top each with 25 ml/1½ tbsp of the ginger cream. Eat straight away.

Chocolate Strawberries on Pineapple Sorbet

••••••••••••••••••••••••••••••••

SERVES 4

175 g/6 oz plain (semi-sweet) chocolate
15 g/½ oz/1 tbsp unsalted (sweet) butter
16–20 large unhulled strawberries, washed and dried
Pineapple sorbet

Break up the chocolate and place in a dish with the butter. Melt, uncovered, on Defrost for about 3½ minutes. If the chocolate stays on the firm side, give it 10-second bursts on Defrost until just runny – do not overheat or the chocolate will become granular. Holding each strawberry by its green hull and stalk, swirl it round in the chocolate until three-quarters covered. Stand on a baking tray lined with greaseproof (waxed) paper and leave in the cool to set. To serve, put scoops of sorbet into four glass dessert dishes and top each with the strawberries.

Danish Apple 'Cake'
SERVES 4–6

An old friend from Denmark, and a distinguished and handsome-looking sundae – not remotely like a cake.

750 g/1½ lb cooking (tart) apples, peeled and sliced
45 ml/3 tbsp boiling water
90 ml/6 tbsp caster (superfine) sugar
125 g/4 oz/½ cup butter
100 g/3½ oz/1¾ cups fresh white breadcrumbs
30 ml/2 tbsp light soft brown sugar
150 ml/¼ pt/⅔ cup double (heavy) cream
15 ml/1 tbsp milk
20–60 ml/4–6 tsp red jam (conserve)

Put the apple slices in a 1.75 litre/3 pt/7½ cup dish with the boiling water. Cover with a plate and cook on Full for 7–8 minutes until very soft. Beat to a pulp, then stir in the caster sugar. Set aside. Melt the butter in a frying pan (skillet). Add the breadcrumbs and fry (sauté) conventionally until lightly browned. Stir in the brown sugar. Allow to cool. Fill four to six sundae or other tall glasses with alternate layers of apples and crumbs, ending with crumbs. Whip the cream and milk until softly stiff. Pile on top of each portion, then add 5 ml/1 tsp of jam to each.

Peasant Girl with Veil
SERVES 4–6

A variation on Danish Apple Cake, this is also Danish but uses 5 slices of crumbled rye bread instead of white breadcrumbs. Otherwise the ingredients and method are the same.

Imperial Rice
SERVES 6–8

An old French traditional recipe, simplified by the use of store cupboard ingredients.

400 g/14 oz/1 large can rice pudding
400–450 g/14–16 oz/1 large can custard
25 ml/1½ tbsp powdered gelatine
125 ml/4 fl oz/½ cup cold water
60 ml/4 tbsp smooth apricot jam (conserve)
5 ml/1 tsp vanilla essence (extract)
2.5 ml/½ tsp almond essence (extract)
30 ml/2 tbsp assorted coloured glacé (candied) cherries, coarsely chopped

Combine the rice pudding and custard in a 2 litre/3½ pt/8½ cup bowl. Put the gelatine into a small bowl and stir in half the water. Heat, uncovered, on Defrost for 1¾–2 minutes until melted and the liquid is clear. Add the remaining water. Stir gently into the rice and custard mixture. Spoon the jam into the emptied small bowl. Warm, uncovered, on Defrost for 1–1½ minutes. Stir into the rice mixture with the vanilla and almond essence (extract). Cover and chill until just on the point of setting. Stir in the cherries. Rinse a 1.5 litre/2½ pt/6 cup jelly (jello) mould with cold water, then fill with the rice mixture. Cover and chill until firm and set. Turn out and serve with any of the fruit sauces (pages 334–7).

Children's Fruity Mousse

••••••••••••••••••••••••••••••••
SERVES 4–6

An easy and economical sweet that reached its heyday in the fifties.

1 packet strawberry jelly (jello)
300 ml/½ pt/1¼ cups cold water
175 ml/6 fl oz/1 small can full-cream evaporated milk, chilled overnight in the refrigerator
30 ml/2 tbsp fresh or bottled lemon juice
Whipped cream and fruit, to decorate (optional)

Snip the jelly into cubes and put in a measuring jug. Cover with a plate and melt on Defrost for 2–2½ minutes. Gradually stir in the water. Keep covered and leave in the cool until just beginning to thicken. Beat the chilled evaporated milk until light and frothy. Add the lemon juice, a little at a time, and continue whisking until the milk thickens to the consistency of whipped cream. Whisk in the still liquid jelly lightly but smoothly. Transfer to four to six small dishes and chill until set. Decorate with cream and/or canned or fresh fruit, if liked.

Raspberry and Blackcurrant Mousse

••••••••••••••••••••••••••••••••••
SERVES 4

A more sophisticated version of Children's Fruity Mousse that can confidently be served to adults.

1 packet raspberry jelly (jello)
150 ml/¼ pt/⅔ cup cold water
150 ml/¼ pt/⅔ cup raspberry purée made from fresh or frozen raspberries
175 ml/6 fl oz/1 small can full-cream evaporated milk, chilled overnight in the refrigerator
30 ml/2 tbsp fresh or bottled lemon juice
Whipped cream and fresh blackcurrants, to decorate

Snip the jelly into cubes and put in a measuring jug. Cover with a plate and melt on Defrost for 2–2½ minutes. Gradually stir in the water and raspberry purée. Keep covered and leave in the cool until just beginning to thicken. Beat the chilled evaporated milk until light and frothy. Add the lemon juice, a little at a time, and continue whisking until the milk thickens to the consistency of whipped cream. Whisk in the still liquid jelly lightly but smoothly. Swirl into four wine glasses and chill until set. Decorate with cream and blackcurrants.

Breakfast Foods and Snacks

This chapter is all about food for breakfast, lunch, tea and supper – tasty morsels that cook in the microwave in next-to-no-time for fast meals when you're in a hurry and all you want is an easy snack. There are quick 'things on toast', tasty rarebits and a delicious and crackling DIY granola cereal, originally from North America, which makes a pleasing change from morning muesli. Instructions for cooking hassle-free porridge and a guide to preparing bacon can also be found.

Welsh Rarebit

SERVES 2

125 g/4 oz/1 cup Cheddar cheese, grated
5 ml/1 tsp mustard powder
5 ml/1 tsp cornflour (cornstarch)
1 egg yolk
10 ml/2 tsp milk
Salt and freshly ground black pepper
2 large slices freshly made toast
Paprika

Mix the cheese with the mustard, cornflour, egg yolk and milk. Season to taste. Spread over the toast. Transfer to individual plates. Cook one at a time, uncovered, on Full for 1 minute. Sprinkle lightly with paprika and eat straight away.

Mixed Cheese Rarebit

SERVES 2

Prepare as for Welsh Rarebit, but substitute 50 g/2 oz/½ cup crumbled Stilton cheese for half the Cheddar.

Buck Rarebit

SERVES 2

Prepare as for Welsh Rarebit, but top each slice with a fried (sautéed) egg, cooked either in the microwave (page 99) or conventionally.

Bacon Rarebit

SERVES 2

Put 4 streaky bacon rashers (slices) on a plate and cover with kitchen paper. Cook on Full for 2½ minutes. Prepare the Welsh Rarebit and top each slice with 2 bacon rashers.

Beer Rarebit

Slightly more ornate, this is a substantial snack for midday or the evening.

25 g/1 oz/2 tbsp butter or
margarine, at kitchen
temperature
5 ml/1 tsp mild made mustard
2.5 ml/½ tsp Worcestershire sauce
5 ml/1 tsp tomato ketchup
(catsup)
225 g/8 oz/2 cups Cheddar cheese,
grated
45 ml/3 tbsp dark ale
4 slices freshly made toast
1 large tomato, sliced
Chopped parsley
Bacon and fried (sautéed) or
poached eggs (page 99)
(optional), to serve

Combine the butter or margarine with the mustard, Worcestershire sauce, ketchup, cheese and ale. Spread equal amounts over the toast. Transfer to four individual plates. Cook, uncovered one at a time, on Full for 1 minute. Add the tomato slices and a sprinkling of parsley. If liked, top with bacon and/or eggs.

Open-topped Hungarian Salami Sandwiches

These are based on a recipe found in a leaflet at a Hungarian trade fair held in London. The subtle smokiness of the salami gives the sandwiches a continental flair.

4 spring onions (scallions), finely
chopped
75 g/3 oz Hungarian salami,
rinded and finely chopped
175 g/6 oz/1½ cups Emmental
cheese, finely grated
2 egg yolks
4 large slices freshly made toast
Pickled cucumber slices, to
garnish

Put the onions and salami in a bowl and combine with the cheese and egg yolks. Spread over the toast. Cook one at a time, uncovered, on Full for 1–1½ minutes until the cheese melts. Serve straight away.

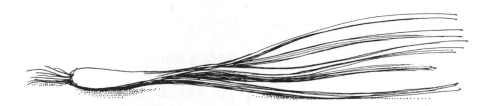

Granola

•••••••••••••••••••••••••••••••
MAKES ABOUT 750 G/1½ LB/6 CUPS

Like dry and sweet muesli with a distinctive crackle and a crunch, this is an import from North America where it is eaten as a breakfast cereal with milk or as a nibble instead of biscuits (cookies). Diet food it isn't, but it can be enjoyed as an occasional weekend treat.

125 g/4 oz/½ cup butter or margarine
90 ml/6 tbsp golden (light corn) syrup
250 g/9 oz/2¼ cups porridge oats
45 ml/3 tbsp coarse bran
100 g/3½ oz/scant ½ cup light soft brown sugar
75 g/3 oz/¾ cup chopped nuts
100 g/3½ oz/⅔ cup raisins

Put the butter or margarine in a 25 cm/10 in diameter casserole dish (Dutch oven). Add the syrup. Melt, uncovered, on Defrost for 4 minutes. Mix in all the remaining ingredients except the raisins. Cook, uncovered, on Full for 9½ minutes, stirring four or five times, until the granola is lightly browned. Add the raisins and mix in thoroughly. Allow to stand until cold and crisp, then break up with a fork until crumbly. Store in an airtight container.

Honey Granola

•••••••••••••••••••••••••••••••
MAKES ABOUT 750 G/1½ LB/6 CUPS

Prepare as for Granola, but substitute clear honey for the syrup.

Porridge

•••••••••••••••••••••••••••••••
For 1 portion: put 25 g/1 oz/¼ cup porridge oats in a cereal bowl. Add 150 ml/¼ pt/⅔ cup cold milk or water and a pinch of salt. Cook, uncovered, on Full for 1¾–2 minutes, stirring twice. Allow to stand for 1½ minutes before eating.
For 2 portions in 2 bowls: prepare as for 1 portion, but cook on Full for 3–3½ minutes.
For 3 portions in 3 bowls: prepare as for 1 portion, but cook on Full for 3½–4 minutes.

Bacon

•••••••••••••••••••••••••••••••
Bacon reacts well to microwave cooking and shrinks less than if grilled (broiled) or fried (sautéed) conventionally. Place the rasher or rashers (slices) in a single layer on a plate and cover lightly with kitchen paper to prevent spluttering and soiling the oven. The cooking time needed will vary according to the type and thickness of the bacon, but this is a general guide:

1 rasher: cook on Full for 45–60 seconds
2 rashers: cook on Full for 1½–1¾ minutes
3 rashers: cook on Full for 2–2¼ minutes
4 rashers: cook on Full for 2½–2¾ minutes
5 rashers: cook on Full for 3–3½ minutes
6 rashers: cook on Full for 4–4½ minutes

Drain the bacon on clean kitchen paper after cooking.

Sauces and Bastes

Even professional chefs grudgingly admit the microwave is a sauce-making marvel. It will produce smooth and creamy white sauces, mayonnaises, zippy salsas, and the essential cranberry, apple, gooseberry, mint and bread sauces. Gravies and bastes to add colour to roast poultry and meat are also here.

Basic White Sauce

SERVES 4

The multi-purpose and versatile coating sauce known and appreciated internationally for its smooth and velvety texture and glossy appearance.

300 ml/½ pt/1¼ cups milk
25 g/1 oz/2 tbsp butter or margarine
25 g/1 oz/¼ cup plain (all-purpose) flour
Salt and freshly ground black pepper or caster (superfine) sugar

Pour the milk into a jug and warm, uncovered, on Full for 2 minutes. Put the butter or margarine in a 900 ml/1½ pt/3¾ cup bowl. Melt, uncovered, on Defrost for 1 minute. Stir in the flour to form a roux. Heat, uncovered, on Full for 30 seconds. Remove from the microwave and gradually blend in the warm milk. Cook, uncovered, on Full for 3–4 minutes, beating every minute for maximum smoothness, until the sauce comes to the boil and thickens. Season to taste with salt and pepper for a savoury sauce and caster sugar for a sweet one.

Béchamel Sauce

SERVES 4

This the aristocratic version of Basic White Sauce, named after a steward of Louis XIV. It is important in the great kitchens of the western world and is deceptively easy to make. Use only for savoury dishes.

300 ml/½ pt/1¼ cups milk
1 bouquet garni sachet
1 bay leaf
1 small onion, peeled and quartered
2 large parsley sprigs
1.5 ml/¼ tsp grated nutmeg
25 g/1 oz/2 tbsp butter or margarine
25 g/1 oz/¼ cup plain (all-purpose) flour
Salt and freshly ground black pepper

Pour the milk into a 900 ml/1½ pt/ 3¾ cup jug. Add the bouquet garni, bay leaf, onion, parsley and nutmeg. Cover with a saucer and bring just up to the boil, allowing 5–6 minutes on Defrost. Remove from the microwave, keep covered, and allow to cool to lukewarm. Strain. Put the butter or margarine in a 900 ml/1½ pt/3¾ cup bowl. Melt, uncovered, on Defrost for 1 minute. Stir in the flour to form a roux. Heat, uncovered, on Full for 30 seconds. Remove from the microwave and gradually blend in the flavoured milk. Cook, uncovered, on Full for 3–4 minutes, beating every minute for maximum smoothness, until the sauce comes to the boil and thickens. Season to taste with salt and pepper.

Caper Sauce
SERVES 4

For skate, herring, mackerel and lamb.

Prepare as for Basic White Sauce, but add 20 ml/4 tsp drained and chopped capers half-way through the cooking time.

Cheese Sauce
SERVES 4

For bacon and gammon, fish, poultry and vegetables.

Prepare as for Basic White Sauce, but add 50–75 g/2–3 oz/½–¾ cup grated hard cheese and 5 ml/1 tsp made mustard half-way through the cooking time.

Mornay Sauce
SERVES 4

A close relation of Cheese Sauce, also for bacon and gammon, fish, poultry and vegetables.

Prepare as for Basic White Sauce, but use milk seasoned with salt and freshly ground black pepper and add 50–75 g/2–3 oz/½–¾ cup grated Gruyère (Swiss) cheese half-way through the cooking time.

Egg Sauce
SERVES 4

Also known as Dutch Egg Sauce or Mock Hollandaise. For fish and poultry.

Prepare as for Basic White Sauce, but add 2 chopped hard-boiled (hard-cooked) eggs (pages 98–9) with the seasoning.

Mushroom Sauce
SERVES 4

For fish and poultry and egg dishes such as omelettes.

Heat 50 g/2 oz/½ cup thinly sliced mushrooms with 10 ml/2 tsp butter on Full for 1½ minutes. Mix into the prepared Basic White Sauce half-way through the cooking time. Season to taste with ground nutmeg.

Mustard Sauce
SERVES 4

Serve with pork and gammon, offal and oily fish such as mackerel and herring.

Prepare as for Basic White Sauce, but add 10–15 ml/2–3 tsp English made mustard and 10 ml/2 tsp lemon juice with the seasoning.

Onion Sauce
SERVES 4

For grilled (broiled) and roast lamb.

Chop 1 onion and put into a small dish with 25 ml/1½ tbsp cold water and 1.5 ml/¼ tsp salt. Cover with cling-film (plastic wrap) and slit it twice to allow steam to escape. Cook on Full for 4–5 minutes until soft. Mix into the prepared Basic White Sauce.

Parsley Sauce

SERVES 4

For fish, vegetables, poultry and boiled bacon.

Prepare as for Basic White Sauce, but add 45–60 ml/3–4 tbsp chopped parsley with the seasoning.

Watercress Sauce

SERVES 4

For fish and poultry.

Prepare as for Basic White Sauce (page 316), but add 45–60 ml/3–4 tbsp chopped watercress with the seasoning.

Pouring Sauce

SERVES 4

Prepare as for Basic White Sauce (page 316), but reduce the flour to 15 g/½ oz/1 tbsp. Either season with salt and pepper and use as a white 'gravy', or sweeten with sugar and serve over steamed or baked pudding.

All-in-one Sauce

SERVES 4

A high-speed version of Basic White Sauce.

25 g/1 oz/¼ cup plain (all-purpose) flour
300 ml/½ pt/1¼ cups milk
25 g/1 oz/2 tbsp butter or margarine
Salt and freshly ground black pepper or caster (superfine) sugar

Whisk the flour into the milk in a bowl, then add the butter or margarine. Cook, uncovered, on Full for 6–6½ minutes, whisking four or five times, until thick and smooth. Flavour to taste.

Hollandaise Sauce

SERVES 6–8

One of the great sauces of our time, Hollandaise made conventionally needs skill and culinary artistry. In the microwave it behaves as though you were a chef of unquestionable brilliance. Use it with poached salmon and trout, broccoli and cauliflower, with artichokes and asparagus.

125 g/4 oz/½ cup slightly salted butter
15 ml/1 tbsp lemon juice, strained
2 egg yolks
Salt and freshly ground black pepper
A pinch of caster (superfine) sugar

Put the butter in a 900 ml/1½ pt/3¾ cup jug or dish. Melt, uncovered, on Full for 1½ minutes until hot and bubbling. Add the lemon juice and egg yolks and whisk thoroughly. Return to the microwave and cook on Full for 30 seconds. Stir briskly. The sauce is ready when it is as thick as cold custard and clings to the whisk; if not, cook for a further 15 seconds. Season to taste, then add the sugar to counteract the sharpness of the lemon juice. Serve warm. Watch the cooking time very carefully because Hollandaise that refuses to thicken and looks curdled has been overcooked. One remedy is to beat in 30–45 ml/2–3 tbsp very cold water; a second is to beat in 30 ml/2 tbsp double (heavy) cream; a third is to beat the curdled sauce into a fresh egg yolk and return to the microwave for a few seconds until thick and smooth.

Short-cut Béarnaise Sauce

SERVES 6–8

Recommended for steaks and rare roast beef.

Prepare as for Hollandaise Sauce, but substitute wine vinegar for the lemon juice and add 2.5 ml/½ tsp dried tarragon with the seasoning and sugar.

Maltese Sauce

SERVES 6–8

For freshwater fish and poultry.

Prepare as for Hollandaise Sauce, but stir in 5 ml/1 tsp very finely grated orange peel with the seasoning and sugar.

Mayonnaise Sauce

MAKES 600 ML/1 PT/2½ CUPS

Because of the current disquiet associated with eating raw egg yolk, the eggs in this mayonnaise are blended with very hot liquid, which is equivalent to being partially cooked and is therefore safer than standard homemade mayonnaise based on entirely raw yolks. The texture is thinner than traditional mayonnaise but, when cold, is thick enough to coat foods satisfactorily. It is also excellent as a mixer sauce with coleslaw and potato salad.

600 ml/1 pt/2½ cups sunflower or safflower oil
30 ml/2 tbsp lemon juice
15 ml/1 tbsp wine or cider vinegar
2.5 ml/½ tsp caster (superfine) sugar
15–20 ml/3–4 tsp salt
5 ml/1 tsp made mustard
2 large eggs

Spoon 75 ml/5 tbsp of the oil into a small bowl. Add the lemon juice, vinegar, sugar, salt and mustard. Heat, uncovered, on Defrost for 3–4 minutes until very hot. Break the eggs into a blender and add the hot oil mixture. Run the machine until smooth. With the machine still running but the lid removed, add the remaining oil in a thin steady stream. Transfer to a bowl. Cover and chill until cold and thick. Keep refrigerated in screw-topped jar and use as required.

Cocktail Sauce

MAKES 600 ML/1 PT/2½ CUPS

A classic for seafood.

Prepare as for Mayonnaise Sauce. After it has thickened, stir in 30 ml/2 tbsp tomato purée (paste), 10 ml/2 tsp horseradish, a dash of hot pepper sauce such as Tabasco and 5 ml/1 tsp Worcestershire sauce.

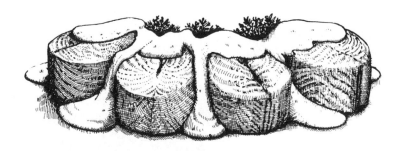

Louis Sauce

••••••••••••••••••••••••••••••••
MAKES 600 ML/1 PT/2½ CUPS

A sauce from San Francisco created in the early twentieth century by a chef called Louis Diat. It is specially for crab salad.

600 ml/1 pt/2½ cups sunflower or safflower oil
30 ml/2 tbsp lemon juice
15 ml/1 tbsp wine or cider vinegar
2.5 ml/½ tsp caster (superfine) sugar
15–20 ml/3–4 tsp salt
5 ml/1 tsp made mustard
2 large eggs
Chilli or hot pepper sauce
60 ml/4 tbsp whipping cream, softly whipped
¼ green (bell) pepper, seeded and finely chopped
15 ml/1 tbsp finely chopped spring onion (scallion)
Juice of ½ small lemon

Spoon 75 ml/5 tbsp of the oil into a small bowl. Add the lemon juice, vinegar, sugar, salt and mustard. Heat, uncovered, on Defrost for 3–4 minutes until very hot. Break the eggs into a blender and add the hot oil mixture. Run the machine until smooth. With the machine still running but the lid removed, add the remaining oil in a thin steady stream. Transfer to a bowl. Cover and chill until cold and thick. Stir in chilli or hot pepper sauce to make it gently hot, then add the cream, green pepper, spring onion and lemon juice. Keep refrigerated in a screw-topped jar and use as required.

Thousand Island Dressing

••••••••••••••••••••••••••••••••
MAKES 600 ML/1 PT/2½ CUPS

600 ml/1 pt/2½ cups sunflower or safflower oil
30 ml/2 tbsp lemon juice
15 ml/1 tbsp wine or cider vinegar
2.5 ml/½ tsp caster (superfine) sugar
15–20 ml/3–4 tsp salt
5 ml/1 tsp made mustard
2 large eggs
A dash of chilli or hot pepper sauce
1–2 hard-boiled (hard-cooked) eggs (pages 98–9), finely chopped
30–45 ml/2–3 tbsp tomato ketchup (catsup)
15 ml/1 tbsp finely chopped onion
15 ml/1 tbsp chopped parsley
30 ml/2 tbsp chopped stuffed olives (optional)
30 ml/2 tbsp whipped cream (optional)

Spoon 75 ml/5 tbsp of the oil into a small bowl. Add the lemon juice, vinegar, sugar, salt and mustard. Heat, uncovered, on Defrost for 3–4 minutes until very hot. Break the eggs into a blender and add the hot oil mixture. Run the machine until smooth. With the machine still running but the lid removed, add the remaining oil in a thin steady stream. Transfer to a bowl. Cover and chill until cold and thick. Stir in the chilli or hot pepper sauce, chopped eggs, tomato ketchup, onion, parsley and olives and cream, if using. Keep refrigerated in a screw-topped jar and use as required.

Green Sauce

●●●●●●●●●●●●●●●●●●●●●●●●●●●●●●●●●●●
MAKES 600 ML/1 PT/2½ CUPS

Designed for fish.

Prepare as for Mayonnaise Sauce (page 319). After it has thickened, stir in 15 ml/ 1 tbsp chopped parsley, 15 ml/1 tbsp snipped chives and 15 ml/ 1 tbsp watercress. A little chopped tarragon may also be added.

Rémoulade Sauce

●●●●●●●●●●●●●●●●●●●●●●●●●●●●●●●●●●●
MAKES 600 ML/1 PT/2½ CUPS

Superb with cold meats, beef in particular, and fish dishes.

Prepare as for Mayonnaise Sauce (page 319). After it has thickened, mix in 4 chopped anchovy fillets in oil, 5 ml/1 tsp French mustard, 5 ml/1 tsp chopped tarragon and 5 ml/1 tsp chopped parsley, 10 ml/2 tsp chopped gherkins (cornichons) and 10 ml/2 tsp chopped capers. A little chopped chervil may also be added.

Sauce Tartare

●●●●●●●●●●●●●●●●●●●●●●●●●●●●●●●●●●●
MAKES 600 ML/1 PT/2½ CUPS

For fish.

Prepare as for Mayonnaise Sauce (page 319). After it has thickened, stir in 45 ml/ 3 tbsp chopped gherkins (cornichons), 30 ml/2 tbsp chopped parsley and 15 ml/1 tbsp finely chopped capers.

No-egg Mayonnaise-style Dressing

●●●●●●●●●●●●●●●●●●●●●●●●●●●●●●●●●●●
SERVES 4

60 ml/4 tbsp cold water
90 ml/6 tbsp sunflower oil
1 oz/25 g/⅓ cup milk powder (non-fat dry milk)
2.5 ml/½ tsp salt
2.5 ml/½ tsp mustard powder
20 ml/4 tsp wine or cider vinegar
10 ml/2 tsp lemon juice
A pinch of sugar

Pour the water into a small bowl. Heat, uncovered, on Full for 1 minute until hot. Pour into blender or food processor and add all the remaining ingredients. Run the machine until smooth. Spoon into small bowl, cover and chill until cold. The dressing thickens up considerably if left overnight but can be thinned down to the desired consistency with warm water.

Mint Sauce

●●●●●●●●●●●●●●●●●●●●●●●●●●●●●●●●●●●
SERVES 4–5

A very British sauce for roast lamb.

60 ml/4 tbsp finely chopped fresh mint leaves
60 ml/4 tbsp water
15 ml/1 tbsp caster (superfine) sugar
75 ml/5 tbsp malt vinegar
Salt and freshly ground black pepper

Put all the ingredients into a measuring cup. Heat, uncovered, on Full for 3 minutes. Serve cold.

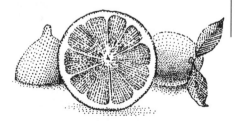

Orange Sauce

••••••••••••••••••••••••••••••
SERVES 6–8

For cold meats and barbecued foods.

225 g/8 oz/1 cup redcurrant jelly
(clear conserve)
Finely grated peel and juice of 1
orange
10 ml/2 tsp Grand Marnier

Put the redcurrant jelly with the orange peel and juice in a 1.25 litre/ 2¼ pt/5½ cup measuring jug. Heat, uncovered, on Defrost for 5–6 minutes, stirring three or four times, until the jelly melts. Allow the sauce to cool, then mix in the Grand Marnier. Serve cold.

Jellied Mixed Herb Sauce

••••••••••••••••••••••••••••••
SERVES 8–10

For lamb.

450 ml/¾ pt/2 cups white grape or
apple juice
15 ml/1 tbsp powdered gelatine
2.5 ml/½ tsp salt
30 ml/2 tbsp chopped mint
45 ml/3 tbsp snipped chives
40 ml/2½ tbsp chopped coriander
(cilantro) leaves

Pour 45 ml/3 tbsp of the fruit juice into a 1.25 litre/2¼ pt/5½ cup bowl. Stir in the gelatine. Allow to stand for 5 minutes to soften. Melt, uncovered, on Defrost for 2–2½ minutes. Stir in the remaining juice with the salt. Cover when cold and chill until just beginning to thicken and set round the edge. Mix in all the remaining ingredients. Transfer to a small serving dish and chill until set completely. Spoon out on to plates to serve.

Jellied Herb Sauce with Lemon

••••••••••••••••••••••••••••••
SERVES 8–10

For fish.

Prepare as for Jellied Mixed Herb Sauce, but substitute chopped parsley for the coriander (cilantro) and add 10 ml/2 tsp grated lemon rind with the other ingredients.

Salsa

••••••••••••••••••••••••••••••
SERVES 6

A simple version of the trendy Mexican sauce-cum-condiment which can be used as a dip or eaten with Mexican-style food. It also adds a bit of character to roasts and grilled (broiled) foods, bland cheeses like Mozzarella and omelettes. Some salsas are left uncooked, but heating this rather chunky version has a mellowing effect on the flavours.

3 large tomatoes, blanched,
skinned, seeded and chopped
1 sweet or Spanish onion, finely
grated
1–2 whole green chillies, seeded
and finely chopped
1–2 garlic cloves, crushed
30 ml/2 tbsp chopped coriander
(cilantro) leaves
5–10 ml/1–2 tsp salt

Place the tomatoes in a 1.25 litre/ 2¼ pt/5½ cup bowl with the onion, chilli and garlic. Cover with a plate and heat on Full for 3 minutes. Allow to cool completely. Stir in the coriander and salt before serving.

Smooth Salsa

SERVES 6

Prepare as for Salsa, but transfer the ingredients to a blender after cooking and work to a smooth purée before adding the coriander and salt.

Extra-hot Salsa

SERVES 6

Prepare as for Salsa, but double or even treble the quantity of green chillies. Take care when eating.

Coriander Salsa

SERVES 6

Prepare as for Salsa, but increase the quantity of coriander (cilantro) to 25 g/1 oz/¼ cup.

Apple Sauce

SERVES 4

Obligatory for roast pork, duck and goose.

450 g/1 lb cooking (tart) apples, peeled, quartered, cored and thinly sliced
45 ml/3 tbsp boiling water
10–15 ml/2–3 tsp granulated sugar
10 ml/2 tsp butter or margarine

Put the apples in a 1.25 litre/2¼ pt/ 5½ cup bowl with the water. Cover with a plate and cook on Full for 7–8 minutes until soft and pulpy, stirring twice. Beat until smooth. Mix in the sugar and butter or margarine. Serve warm or cold.

Mrs Beeton's Brown Apple Sauce

SERVES 4

Prepare as for Apple Sauce, but cook the apples with a thin gravy (page 327) instead of water.

Gooseberry Sauce

SERVES 4

An old English sauce, traditionally served with goose, duck and mackerel.

Prepare as for Apple Sauce, but substitute 225 g/8 oz/2 cups trimmed gooseberries for the apples and add 5 ml/1 tsp finely grated lemon peel with the other ingredients.

Salsa with Sweetcorn

SERVES 4

For barbecued foods.

10 ml/2 tsp corn oil
3 spring onions (scallions), finely chopped
30 ml/2 tbsp finely chopped coriander (cilantro) leaves
1 canned red pimiento, drained and chopped
2 large beef tomatoes, blanched, skinned, seeded and chopped
175 g/6 oz/1½ cups frozen sweetcorn (corn), thawed
10 ml/2 tsp jalapeno sauce
10 ml/2 tsp fresh lime juice
5 ml/1 tsp salt

Pour the oil into a 1.25 litre/2¼ pt/ 5½ cup bowl. Add the onions, coriander and pimiento. Cook, uncovered, on Full for 2½ minutes, stirring once. Mix in the tomatoes and sweetcorn. Cover with a plate and heat on Full for 2 minutes. Allow to cool completely. Stir in the remaining ingredients.

Austrian Apple and Horseradish Sauce

SERVES 6–8

An example of the unusual and the unexpected, a remarkable hot sauce for beef.

450 g/1 lb cooking (tart) apples, peeled, quartered, cored and thinly sliced
30 ml/2 tbsp boiling water
10 ml/2 tsp icing (confectioners') sugar, sifted
30 ml/2 tbsp blanched and finely chopped almonds
15–45 ml/1–3 tbsp finely grated fresh horseradish or 30–45 ml/ 2–3 tbsp creamed horseradish
2.5–5 ml/½–1 tsp salt
10 ml/2 tsp malt vinegar

Put the apples in a 1.25 litre/2¼ pt/ 5½ cup bowl with the water. Cover with a plate and cook on Full for 7–8 minutes until soft and pulpy, stirring twice. Stir in all the remaining ingredients. Cover as before and cook on Full for 1½ minutes. Serve hot.

Garlic Sauce

SERVES 4–6

An extremely garlicky sauce from Italy, designed for tossing into hot pasta dishes.

45 ml/3 tbsp olive oil
50 g/2 oz/¼ cup butter
6 garlic cloves, crushed
30 ml/2 tbsp finely chopped parsley
2.5 ml/½ tsp dried basil
2.5–5 ml/½–1 tsp salt
Freshly ground black pepper, to taste

Put all the ingredients in a 600 ml/ 1 pt/2½ cup bowl. Cover with a plate and warm on Defrost for 3–4 minutes, stirring once. Toss with piping hot spaghetti or other pasta and eat straight away.

Apple and Horseradish Sauce

SERVES 6–8

An apple sauce from Romania, to serve with chicken.

50 g/2 oz/¼ cup butter
2 large cooking (tart) apples, peeled and grated
50 g/2 oz/½ cup plain (all-purpose) flour
450 ml/¾ pt/2 cups hot chicken stock
5–10 ml/1–2 tsp grated horseradish or 10 ml/2 tsp horseradish sauce
Salt
150 ml/¼ pt/⅔ cup whipping cream, whipped until thick
Sifted icing (confectioners') sugar (optional)

Put the butter in a 1.5 litre/2½ pt/ 6 cup bowl and heat, uncovered, on Full for 1¼ minutes. Mix in the apples and cook, uncovered, on Full for 3 minutes, stirring once. Stir in the flour and cook on Full for 20 seconds. Gradually blend in the hot stock. Cook, uncovered, on Full for 4–5 minutes, whisking every minute, until smoothly thickened. Stir in the horseradish, season to taste with salt, then fold in the cream. If the sauce is too sour for personal taste, stir in a little icing sugar. Serve straight away.

Bread Sauce
SERVES 6–8

A vintage tradition with poultry.

300 ml/½ pt/1¼ cups milk
1 bouquet garni sachet
1 bay leaf
1 small onion, peeled and
quartered
2 large parsley sprigs
1.5 ml/¼ tsp grated nutmeg
65 g/2½ oz fresh white
breadcrumbs from crustless
bread
15–25 g/½–1 oz/1–2 tbsp butter or
margarine
Salt and freshly ground black
pepper

Pour the milk into a 900 ml/1½ pt/
3¾ cup jug. Add the bouquet garni,
bay leaf, onion, parsley and nutmeg.
Cover with a saucer and bring just to
the boil on Defrost, allowing about 5–6
minutes. Remove from the microwave,
keep covered and allow to cool to
lukewarm. Strain. Add the crumbs.
Cook, uncovered, on Defrost until
thickened, allowing about 4–6 minutes
and stirring every minute. Mix in the
butter or margarine and season to
taste. Reheat, uncovered, on Defrost
for 1 minute.

Brown Bread Sauce
SERVES 6–8

Prepare as for Bread Sauce, but substitute fresh breadcrumbs from
crustless brown bread in place of the
white.

Cranberry Sauce
SERVES 6–8

A sweet-sour, fruity winter sauce and a
sparkling and brilliant accompaniment
for poultry.

225 g/8 oz/2 cups cranberries,
thawed if frozen
150 ml/¼ pt/⅔ cup water
175 g/6 oz/¾ cup granulated sugar
5 ml/1 tsp finely grated lemon peel

Put all the ingredients in a 1.25 litre/
2¼ pt/5½ cup bowl. Cover with a
plate and cook on Full for 8–8½ minutes, stirring twice and crushing the
fruit against the side of the bowl, until
the fruit is soft. Remove from the
microwave, keep covered and serve
when cold. Keep any leftovers refrigerated in a covered container.

Cranberry Wine Sauce
SERVES 6–8

Prepare as for Cranberry Sauce, but
substitute red wine for the water.

Cranberry Orange Sauce
SERVES 6–8

Prepare as for Cranberry Sauce, but
substitute orange juice for the
water.

Cranberry and Apple Sauce
SERVES 6–8

Prepare as for Cranberry Sauce,
but substitute 1 sliced cooking
(tart) apple for half the cranberries.

Cumberland Sauce

SERVES 6

A full-bodied and typically English sauce for ham, pork and tongue.

5 ml/1 tsp mild made mustard
30 ml/2 tbsp light soft brown sugar
1.5 ml/¼ tsp ground ginger
A pinch of cayenne pepper
300 ml/½ pt/1¼ cups dry white wine or port
2 whole cloves
15 ml/1 tbsp cornflour (cornstarch)
30 ml/2 tbsp cold water
60 ml/4 tbsp redcurrant jelly (clear conserve)
5 ml/1 tsp grated orange peel
5 ml/1 tsp grated lemon peel
Juice of 1 small orange
Juice of 1 lemon

Put the mustard, sugar, ginger, cayenne, wine or port and cloves in a 1.25 litre/2¼ pt/5½ cup bowl and heat, uncovered, on Full for 6 minutes, stirring three times. Meanwhile, mix the cornflour smoothly with the cold water. Mix into the wine mixture with the remaining ingredients. Heat, uncovered, on Full for 4–6 minutes, stirring every minute, until the sauce is thickened and smooth and the jelly has melted. Serve hot.

Slovenian Wine Sauce

SERVES 4–6

A vegetable purée and wine sauce enriched with cream. It goes particularly well with venison and pigeon.

50 g/2 oz/¼ cup salted butter
2 carrots, finely grated
30 ml/2 tbsp plain (all-purpose) flour
300 ml/½ pt/1¼ cups dry white wine
100 g/3½ oz mushrooms, sliced
1 small bay leaf
Salt and freshly ground black pepper
150 ml/¼ pt/⅔ cup soured (dairy sour) cream

Put the butter in a 1.25 litre/2¼ pt/ 5½ cup bowl and heat, uncovered, on Full for 1¼ minutes. Add the carrots. Two-thirds cover with a plate and cook on Full for 4 minutes, stirring twice. Mix in the flour, wine, mushrooms and bay leaf. Cover with a plate and cook on Full for 6–7 minutes until the ingredients are tender. Remove the bay leaf and season to taste. Transfer to a blender or food processor and work to a smooth purée. Return to the dish and stir in the cream. Reheat on Full for 1–1½ minutes.

Thin Gravy for Poultry

SERVES 6

*15 ml/1 tbsp cornflour
(cornstarch)*
25 ml/1½ tbsp cold water
*1 chicken or vegetable stock cube
or 7.5 ml/1½ tsp brown gravy
powder*
*300 ml/½ pt/1¼ cups stock,
including pan juices from a
roast chicken or turkey*
*Salt and freshly ground black
pepper*

Blend the cornflour smoothly with the cold water in a 900 ml/1½ pt/ 3¾ cup bowl or jug. Crumble in the stock cube or mix in the gravy powder. Stir in the stock. Cook, uncovered, on Full for 4–6 minutes, stirring every minute, until the gravy has thickened slightly. Season to taste before serving.

Thick Gravy for Meat

SERVES 6

Prepare as for Thin Gravy for Poultry, but use 30 ml/2 tbsp cornflour (cornstarch) mixed with 40 ml/2½ tbsp cold water.

Short-cut Oriental Sauce

SERVES 6–8

A cross between an Indian and a Malaysian sauce, this is a marvellous vehicle for adding flavour to leftover cold meat and sausages.

*300 ml/10 fl oz/1 can condensed
cream of celery or mushroom
soup*
150 ml/¼ pt/⅔ cup boiling water
30 ml/2 tbsp tomato purée (paste)
*15 ml/1 tbsp mild or hot curry
paste*
1 garlic clove, crushed
5 ml/1 tsp turmeric
30 ml/2 tbsp fruit chutney
*15 ml/1 tbsp crunchy peanut
butter*
*20 ml/4 tsp desiccated (shredded)
coconut*

Pour the soup into a 1.25 litre/ 2¼ pt/5½ cup bowl with half the water. Add all the remaining ingredients except the coconut. Cover with a plate and heat on Full for 4 minutes, whisking every minute. Allow to stand for 2 minutes. Whisk in the remaining water and the coconut. Reheat, uncovered on Full for 1 minute.

Indonesian-style Peanut Sauce

SERVES 6–8

In the Far East this sauce is served over assorted cold cooked vegetables, rather like a salad dressing, but it can also be used as a punchy sauce for barbecued foods and meat on skewers.

15 ml/1 tbsp corn oil
2 onions, finely chopped
1 garlic clove, crushed
350 g/12 oz/1½ cups smooth
    peanut butter
10 ml/2 tsp light soft brown sugar
Juice of 1 small lemon
600 ml/1 pt/2½ cups boiling water
30 ml/2 tbsp brown table sauce
Salt and freshly ground black
    pepper

Pour the oil into a 1.25 litre/2¼ pt/ 5½ cup bowl. Heat on Full for 30 seconds. Stir in the onions and garlic. Cook, uncovered, on Full for 6 minutes, stirring three times. Mix in the peanut butter, sugar, lemon juice and half the water. Cook, uncovered, on Full for 2–3 minutes, stirring three times, until the sauce looks like porridge in texture. Remove from the microwave. Thin down the sauce by whisking in the remaining water, then season with the brown sauce and salt and pepper to taste.

Creole Sauce

SERVES 6–8

A jazzy sauce from the Mississippi, featuring sunset colours and an abundance of Mediterranean produce. It goes well with eggs, poultry, beef and even makes a vegetarian topping for fluffy mashed potatoes or rice.

20 ml/4 tsp corn oil
1 large onion, grated
1 garlic clove, crushed
30 ml/2 tbsp stoned (pitted) green
    olives, chopped
½ small green (bell) pepper, seeded
    and finely chopped
50 g/2 oz mushrooms, chopped
1 small bay leaf
400 g/14 oz/1 large can chopped
    tomatoes
15 ml/1 tbsp chopped basil leaves
15 ml/1 tbsp chopped parsley
10 ml/2 tsp dark soft brown sugar
5 ml/1 tsp salt
5 ml/1 tsp Tabasco or any other
    hot pepper sauce
5 cm/2 inch strip lemon peel

Put the oil, onion and garlic in a 2 litre/3½ pt/8½ cup bowl. Cook, uncovered, on Full for 6 minutes, stirring three times. Mix in the olives, green pepper and mushrooms. Cook, uncovered, on Full for 2 minutes. Stir in all the remaining ingredients. Cover with clingfilm (plastic wrap) and slit it twice to allow steam to escape. Cook on Full for 6–7 minutes, turning the bowl three times, until the sauce is hot. Allow to stand for 2 minutes before using.

Quick Creole Sauce

SERVES 4–6

*30 ml/2 tbsp dried (bell) pepper
    flakes*
*300 ml/10 fl oz/1 can condensed
    tomato soup*
75 ml/5 tbsp boiling water
2.5 ml/½ tsp dried oregano
5 ml/1 tsp light soft brown sugar
5 ml/1 tsp Worcestershire sauce

Cover the pepper flakes with boiling water and leave for 3 minutes. Drain thoroughly. Put the soup and measured boiling water in a 1.25 litre/ 2¼ pt/5½ cup dish and beat until smooth. Mix in the remaining ingredients. Heat, uncovered, on Full for 4–5 minutes, stirring three times, until very hot.

Newburg Sauce

SERVES 4

Associated primarily with lobster, this grandiose sauce goes equally well with many other shellfish, crab in particular.

25 g/1 oz/2 tbsp butter
1 small onion, grated
*30 ml/2 tbsp plain (all-purpose)
    flour*
*300 ml/½ pt/1¼ cups single (light)
    cream, heated to lukewarm*
3 egg yolks
*60 ml/4 tbsp dry sherry or white
    port*
*Salt and freshly ground black
    pepper*

Melt the butter, uncovered, on Full for 1 minute in a 900 ml/1½ pt/ 3¾ cup bowl. Add the onion and cook, uncovered, on Full for 1 minute, stirring once. Stir in the flour and cook, uncovered, on Full for 1 minute. Gradually blend in the cream. Cook, uncovered, on Full for 4–4½ minutes, whisking every minute, until thickened and smooth. Beat together the egg yolks and sherry or port. Add to the sauce and season to taste. Return to the microwave and cook, uncovered, on Defrost for 1–1½ minutes. Whisk and serve.

Piquant Brown Sauce

SERVES 4–6

Based on a classic French sauce, this is a cheat's version that turns up trumps for grilled (broiled) foods and roasts and old family friends like sausages, toad-in-the-hole and corned beef.

*300 ml/10 fl oz/1 can condensed
    oxtail soup*
75 ml/5 tbsp boiling water
*15 ml/1 tbsp chopped coriander
    (cilantro) leaves*
15 ml/1 tbsp chopped parsley
15 ml/1 tbsp chopped capers
*15 ml/1 tbsp chopped gherkins
    (cornichons)*
2.5 ml/½ tsp dried mixed herbs
15 ml/1 tbsp brown table sauce
15 ml/1 tbsp port
*Salt and freshly ground black
    pepper*

Put all the ingredients in a 1.25 litre/ 2¼ pt/5½ cup bowl and heat, uncovered, on Full for 5 minutes, whisking every minute, until hot and smooth.

Piquant Sauce with Pickled Walnuts

SERVES 4–6

Prepare as for Piquant Brown Sauce (page 329), but substitute 15 ml/ 1 tbsp chopped pickled walnuts for the capers.

Portuguese Sauce

SERVES 6

The lovely flavour of this fresh tomato sauce does wondrous things to salmon and also cheers up roasted chicken and turkey.

30 ml/2 tbsp olive oil
1 onion, finely grated
2 rashers (slices) streaky bacon,
  finely chopped
1–2 garlic cloves, crushed
1 small carrot, grated
30 ml/2 tbsp plain (all-purpose)
  flour
5 tomatoes, blanched, skinned and
  chopped
45 ml/3 tbsp tomato purée (paste)
150 ml/¼ pt/⅔ cup boiling meat or
  vegetable stock
10 ml/2 tsp pickling spice, tied in
  a piece of muslin
10 ml/2 tsp dark soft brown sugar
5 ml/1 tsp salt
5 cm/2 in strip lemon peel
10 ml/2 tsp fresh lemon juice
Freshly ground black pepper

Put the oil, onion, bacon, garlic and carrot in a 2 litre/3½ pt/8½ cup bowl. Cook, uncovered, on Full for 4 minutes, stirring twice. Mix in the flour and cook on Full for 1 minute. Stir in all the remaining ingredients, adding pepper to taste. Cover with clingfilm (plastic wrap) and slit it twice to allow steam to escape. Cook on full for 7 minutes, turning twice. Allow to stand

for 3 minutes. Strain into a clean dish. Cover with a plate and reheat on Full for 2–3 minutes before serving.

Rustic Tomato Sauce

SERVES 4–6

30 ml/2 tbsp olive oil
1 onion, very finely chopped
2 celery stalks, finely chopped
1 rasher (slice) streaky bacon,
  finely chopped
1 small carrot, grated
1 garlic clove, crushed
25 ml/1½ tbsp plain (all-purpose)
  flour
400 g/14 oz/1 large can plum
  tomatoes, mashed
30 ml/2 tbsp tomato purée (paste)
10 ml/2 tsp dark soft brown sugar
1.5 ml/¼ tsp grated nutmeg
2.5 ml/½ tsp salt
150 ml/¼ pt/⅔ cup boiling stock or
  water

Put the oil in a 2 litre/3½ pt/8½ cup bowl. Mix in the onion, celery, bacon, carrot and garlic. Cook, uncovered, on Full for 4½ minutes, stirring twice. Mix in the flour. Cook, uncovered, on Full for 30 seconds. Add all the remaining ingredients and stir thoroughly to mix. Part-cover with a plate and cook on Full for 7 minutes, stirring three times. Allow to stand for 2 minutes.

Curried Turkey Sauce for Jacket Potatoes

SERVES 6

15 ml/1 tbsp corn oil
2 onions, chopped
20 ml/4 tsp mild, medium or hot
  curry powder
350 g/12 oz/3 cups minced
  (ground) turkey
20 ml/4 tsp plain flour
150 ml/¼ pt/⅔ cup canned coconut
  milk
150 ml/¼ pt/⅔ cup water
30 ml/2 tbsp tomato purée (paste)
15 ml/1 tbsp fruit chutney
5 ml/1 tsp salt
Juice of 1 lime
30 ml/2 tbsp apple juice
150 ml/¼ pt/⅔ cup thick plain
  yoghurt

Pour the oil into a 1.25 litre/2¼ pt/ 5½ cup bowl. Heat on Full for 30 seconds. Mix in the onions and curry powder. Cook, uncovered, on Full for 5 minutes, stirring three times. Stir in the turkey. Cover with a plate and cook on Full for 6 minutes, stirring with a fork three or four times to keep the turkey crumbly. Mix in all the remaining ingredients except the yoghurt. Cover as before and cook on Full for 4 minutes, stirring twice. Allow to stand for 4 minutes. Spoon into split jacket potatoes (page 226) and top each with a dollop of thick yoghurt.

Tandoori Turkey Sauce for Jacket Potatoes

SERVES 6

Prepare as for Curried Turkey Sauce for Jacket Potatoes, but substitute tandoori powder for curry powder.

Hot Chilli Beef Sauce for Jacket Potatoes

SERVES 6

60 ml/4 tbsp corn or sunflower oil
2 onions, chopped
2 cloves garlic, crushed
350 g/12 oz/3 cups lean minced
  (ground) beef
30 ml/2 tbsp plain (all-purpose)
  flour
2.5–10 ml/½–2 tsp chilli powder
30 ml/2 tbsp tomato purée (paste)
300 ml/½ pt/1¼ cups hot water
5 ml/1 tsp salt
45 ml/3 tbsp dry cider

Pour the oil into a 1.25 litre/2¼ pt/ 5½ cup dish. Mix in the onions and garlic. Cook, uncovered, on Full for 5 minutes, stirring twice. Stir in the beef. Cover with a plate and cook on Full for 6 minutes, stirring with a fork three or four times to keep the meat crumbly. Stir in the remaining ingredients. Cover with clingfilm (plastic wrap) and slit it twice to allow steam to escape. Cook on Full for 6 minutes, turning the dish twice, until bubbling. Allow to stand for 5 minutes. Stir round, then spoon into split jacket potatoes (page 226).

Chop House Sauce

SERVES 4

An assertive sauce from Edwardian days for grilled chops, chicken and steaks. A little goes a long way, which is why the quantities are small.

15 ml/1 tbsp tomato ketchup (catsup)
5–10 ml/1–2 tsp anchovy essence (extract)
5 ml/1 tsp English made mustard
15 ml/1 tbsp wine vinegar
45 ml/3 tbsp double (heavy) cream
2.5 ml/½ tsp Worcestershire sauce
A dash of hot pepper sauce

Put all the ingredients in a 600 ml/ 1 pt/2½ cup measuring jug. Warm through, uncovered, on Full for 1¼–1½ minutes, stirring twice, until hot but not boiling. Use straight away.

Hot Cheese and Carrot Sauce for Jacket Potatoes

SERVES 4

A vegetarian sauce with a zippy temperament.

25 g/1 oz/2 tbsp butter or margarine
1 large carrot, grated
30 ml/2 tbsp plain (all-purpose) flour
300 ml/½ pt/1¼ cups warmed milk
5 ml/1 tsp mustard powder
1.5 ml/¼ tsp cayenne pepper
A pinch of ground nutmeg
2.5 ml/½ tsp salt
2.5 ml/½ tsp dried marjoram
50 g/2 oz/½ cup grated cheese

Put the butter or margarine in a 1.25 litre/2¼ pt/5½ cup dish. Melt, uncovered, on Defrost for 1 minute. Stir in the carrot. Cook, uncovered, on Full for 4 minutes, stirring twice. Mix in the flour. Cook, uncovered, on Full

for 30 seconds, then gradually blend in the warmed milk. Cook, uncovered, on Full for 4 minutes, stirring vigorously every minute. Stir in the remaining ingredients. Cook on Full for 30 seconds. Stir round and spoon into split jacket potatoes (page 226).

Basting Sauces

Brushed over meat joints, poultry and foods on the barbecue, bastes increase browning and make them look more appetising. They also add to the flavour and can be used as a basis for gravy and savoury sauces.

Butter Baste

MAKES ABOUT 60 ML/4 TBSP

25 g/1 oz/2 tbsp butter or margarine, at kitchen temperature
15 ml/1 tbsp tomato purée (paste)
5 ml/1 tsp paprika
5 ml/1 tsp Worcestershire sauce
5 ml/1 tsp light soft brown sugar

Melt the butter, uncovered, on Defrost for 1–1½ minutes. Stir in the remaining ingredients. Reheat on Defrost for 30 seconds and use as required.

Spicy Curry Baste

MAKES ABOUT 60 ML/4 TBSP

Prepare as for Butter Baste, but stir in 5 ml/1 tsp mild curry powder, 5 ml/1 tsp mustard powder, 2.5 ml/½ tsp garlic salt and a pinch of turmeric with the remaining ingredients.

Jalapeno Mexican Barbecue Baste

SERVES 6

You can't mistake the south-of-the-border kick from this one, which perks up barbecued pork and chicken like nothing else.

150 ml/¼ pt/⅔ cup French dressing
45 ml/3 tbsp tomato ketchup (catsup)
15 ml/1 tbsp soy sauce
15 ml/1 tbsp Worcestershire sauce
15 ml/1 tbsp jalapeno sauce
15 ml/1 tbsp fresh lime juice
2.5 ml/½ tsp dried mixed herbs

Put all the ingredients in a 600 ml/ 1 pt/2½ cup dish. Cover with a saucer and heat on Full for 2½ minutes. Stir round and use for basting.

Tomato Baste

MAKES ABOUT 60 ML/4 TBSP

A non-fat baste, ideal for slimmers and those on low-fat diets and also with rich meats such as pork, duck and goose.

15 ml/1 tbsp tomato purée (paste)
5 ml/1 tsp English made mustard
5 ml/1 tsp malt vinegar
5 ml/1 tsp Worcestershire sauce

Thoroughly mix together all the ingredients in a jug and heat, uncovered, on Full for 10 seconds.

Dessert Sauces

Dutch Butter Blender Cream

SERVES 4–6

Lush to eat and a cream that can be made when you run out of fresh or fancy something a bit different. It can be whipped to peaks like whipping cream and melts over hot food like ice cream.

150 ml/¼ pt/⅔ cup full-cream milk
150 g/5 oz/⅔ cup Dutch unsalted (sweet) butter

Pour the milk into a bowl. Cut in the pieces of butter. Heat, uncovered on Full for 2½ minutes. Transfer carefully to a blender and run the machine for 1 minute. Return to the washed and dried bowl, cover and chill for 2–3 hours. Spoon over puddings or whip softly, if preferred.

Dutch Butter Blender Cream with Vanilla

SERVES 4–6

Prepare as for Dutch Butter Blender Cream (page 333), but add 5 ml/1 tsp vanilla essence (extract) to the milk and butter in the blender.

Hot Chocolate Sauce

SERVES 6

An old classic for ice cream, ice cream sundaes and profiteroles.

25 g/1 oz/2 tbsp butter
30 ml/2 tbsp light soft brown sugar
30 ml/2 tbsp cocoa (unsweetened chocolate) powder
30 ml/2 tbsp golden (light corn) syrup
30 ml/2 tbsp single (light) cream
5 ml/1 tsp vanilla essence (extract)

Put the butter in a 600 ml/1 pt/2½ cup dish. Melt, uncovered, on Full for 1 minute. Thoroughly stir in all the remaining ingredients. Cook, uncovered, on Defrost for 5 minutes, stirring every minute, until the sauce is smooth and hot.

Mocha Sauce

SERVES 6

Prepare as for Hot Chocolate Sauce, but add 20 ml/4 tsp instant coffee powder or granules before heating.

Hot Chocolate and Orange Sauce

SERVES 6

Prepare as for Hot Chocolate Sauce, but stir in 10 ml/2 tsp finely grated orange peel after cooking.

Hot Chocolate Peppermint Sauce

SERVES 6

Prepare as for Hot Chocolate sauce, but add a few drops of peppermint essence (extract) after cooking.

Raspberry Coulis

SERVES 6–8

A clear – almost glassy – brilliant red sauce beloved by chefs for its stunning effect.

350 g/12 oz/3 cups fresh raspberries
45 ml/3 tbsp caster (superfine) sugar
15 ml/1 tbsp cornflour (cornstarch)
75 ml/5 tbsp cold water
5 ml/1 tsp vanilla essence (extract)
5 ml/1 tsp lemon juice

Carefully rinse the raspberries, then put in a food processor or blender and work to a purée. Strain through fine-mesh sieve (strainer) to remove the seeds. Transfer to a 900 ml/1½ pt/3¾ cup bowl with the sugar. Mix the cornflour smoothly with the water. Add to the purée in the bowl. Cook, uncovered, on Full for 2½–3½ minutes, whisking every 30 seconds, until the mixture has thickened and is clear and bubbling gently. Stir in the vanilla and lemon juice and use cold.

Summer Fruit Coulis

SERVES 6–8

Prepare as for Raspberry Coulis, but substitute a mixture of summer fruits for the raspberries.

Apricot Coulis

SERVES 6–8

450 g/1 lb stoned (pitted) apricots
200 ml/7 fl oz/scant 1 cup cold
water
60–75 ml/4–5 tbsp caster
(superfine) sugar
15 ml/1 tbsp cornflour
(cornstarch)
5 ml/1 tsp vanilla essence (extract)
5 ml/1 tsp lemon juice

Place the apricots in a dish with 60 ml/4 tbsp of the water. Cover with clingfilm (plastic wrap) and slit it twice to allow steam to escape. Cook on Full for 8–9 minutes until the fruit is tender. Transfer to a food processor or blender and work to a purée with another 60 ml/4 tbsp of the water. Transfer to a 900 ml/1½ pt/3¾ cup bowl with the sugar. Mix the cornflour smoothly with the remaining water. Add to the purée in the bowl. Cook, uncovered, on Full for 2½–3½ minutes, whisking every 30 seconds, until the mixture has thickened and is clear and bubbling gently. Stir in the vanilla and lemon juice and use cold.

Home-made Caramel Sauce

SERVES 4

50 g/2 oz/¼ cup dark soft brown
sugar
30 ml/2 tbsp cold water
15 ml/1 tbsp boiling water

Put the sugar and cold water into a measuring jug or bowl. Cook, uncovered, on Full for 2 minutes until boiling, watching carefully in case it starts to burn. Remove from the microwave and stir in the boiling water. Use hot as an ice cream topping or for Crème Caramel (page 301).

Egg Custard Sauce

SERVES 4–6

A golden, glowing sauce, bliss over sweets like Summer Fruit Mould (page 309), steamed puddings, stewed fruits, even trifle.

600 ml/1 pt/2½ cups full-cream
milk or half milk and half
single (light) cream
10 ml/2 tsp cornflour (cornstarch)
15 ml/1 tbsp cold water
4 large eggs
45 ml/3 tbsp caster (superfine)
sugar
5 ml/1 tsp vanilla essence (extract)

Pour the milk into a 1.25 litre/ 2¼ pt/5½ cup measuring jug and heat, uncovered, on Full for 2 minutes. Place the flour in a 1.25 litre/2¼ pt/ 5½ cup bowl and mix smoothly with the water. Break in the eggs, then add the sugar. Whisk until smooth, then gradually blend in the hot milk. Cook, uncovered, on Full for 5–5½ minutes, whisking every minute, until the sauce clings to the spatula or wooden spoon used for whisking. Mix in the vanilla essence.

Flavoured Egg Custard Sauce

SERVES 4–6

Prepare as for Egg Custard Sauce, but substitute rum, sherry, almond or rose essence (extract) for the vanilla essence.

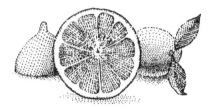

Lemon or Orange Custard

SERVES 4–6

Prepare as for Egg Custard Sauce (page 335), but substitute 10 ml/2 tsp finely grated orange or lemon peel for the vanilla essence.

Brandy Sauce

SERVES 4

Traditionally served on Christmas Pudding, also for mince pies.

25 g/1 oz/2 tbsp butter or margarine
30 ml/2 tbsp plain (all-purpose) flour
300 ml/½ pt/1¼ cups warmed milk
25–30 ml/1½–2 tbsp caster (superfine) sugar
25–30 ml/1½–2 tbsp brandy

Put the butter or margarine in a 900 ml/1½ pt/3¾ cup bowl. Melt, uncovered, on Defrost for 30–45 seconds. Stir in the flour. Cook on Full for 30 seconds. Gradually blend in the milk. Cook, uncovered, on Full for 4–5 minutes, beating every minute, until thickened and smooth. Mix in the sugar and cook, uncovered, on Full for 30 seconds. Stir in the brandy and serve.

Rum Sauce

SERVES 4

Prepare as for Brandy Sauce, but substitute rum for the brandy.

Orange Sauce

SERVES 4

An elusively scented sauce for any kind of light steamed pudding.

Prepare as for Brandy Sauce, but add 5 ml/1 tsp finely grated orange rind with the flour and substitute 15 ml/1 tbsp orange flower water for the brandy.

Sundae Sauces

Sticky Toffee Sauce

SERVES 4

Setting chewily on impact with ice cream, this is a heavenly sauce for any kind of sundae.

50 g/2 oz/¼ cup butter
40 g/1½ oz light soft brown sugar
50 g/2 oz marshmallows
15 ml/1 tbsp milk

Put all the ingredients in a 1.75 litre/3 pt/7½ cup bowl (the large size is necessary because the mixture rises as it cooks). Melt, uncovered, on Defrost for 2 minutes. Stir thoroughly. Heat on Full for a further 2½ minutes, stirring carefully three times. Use straight away as this sauce sets quickly.

Fresh Raspberry Sauce
SERVES 4

Fresh and fragrant, a superior summer sauce for sundaes based on nectarines or peaches and vanilla ice cream.

10 ml/2 tsp cornflour (cornstarch)
150 ml/¼ pt/⅔ cup single (light) cream
30 ml/2 tbsp caster (superfine) sugar
225 g/8 oz/2 cups fresh raspberries, carefully rinsed
15 ml/1 tbsp cherry brandy

Put the cornflour in a 1.5 litre/2½ pt/ 6 cup bowl and mix smoothly with some of the cream. Stir in the remaining cream with the sugar and half the raspberries. Cook, uncovered, on Full for 4 minutes, stirring every minute. Fold in the remaining raspberries with the cherry brandy. Serve warm.

Chocolate Honey Raisin Sauce
SERVES 6–8

Wonderful over coffee ice cream or orange sorbet.

50 g/2 oz/⅓ cup raisins
15 ml/1 tbsp boiling water
100 g/3½ oz plain (semi-sweet) chocolate
25 g/1 oz/2 tbsp butter
30 ml/2 tbsp single (light) cream
30 ml/2 tbsp thick honey
5 ml/1 tsp vanilla essence (extract)

Soak the raisins in the boiling water. Break up the chocolate and place in a small bowl with the butter. Melt, uncovered, on Defrost for about 3½ minutes. Stir in the cream, honey and vanilla. Heat, uncovered, on Full for 30–40 seconds. Drain the raisins and stir in.

Sweets and Candies

Microwave ovens have a magical touch where sweet-making is concerned and it is a constant source of pleasure and surprise to discover how quick and fuss-free it is to produce the kind of confectionery one can wrap up and give as gifts, offer round at home, or sell from stalls at garden fêtes, school open days and fund-raising charity events. The main advantages are that sweets can be prepared in dishes instead of pans so there is less messy washing up, the mixtures seldom boil over, the danger of burns is reduced, and the mixtures don't have to be watched and stirred continuously.

Walnut Chocolate Drops
MAKES 24

Wonderful Christmas gifts, these are also a superb after-dinner nibble to accompany coffee.

400 g/14 oz plain (semi-sweet) chocolate (70% cocoa)
175 g/6 oz/1½ cups coarsely chopped walnuts, lightly toasted (page 205)

Break up the chocolate and place in a mixing bowl. Melt, uncovered, on Defrost for about 5 minutes, allowing an extra 30 seconds if taken from the refrigerator. Stir twice, then mix in the nuts. Drop 24 heaped teaspoonfuls of the mixture on to baking trays lined with greaseproof (waxed) paper. Chill until hard. Carefully lift off the paper and store in an airtight tin in the refrigerator for up to three weeks.

Orange Nut Drops
MAKES 24

Prepare as for Walnut Chocolate Drops, but stir in 10 ml/2 tsp grated orange peel with the chocolate and nuts.

Mixed Nut Chocolate Drops
MAKES 24

Prepare as for Walnut Chocolate Drops, but substitute lightly toasted chopped mixed nuts for chopped walnuts on their own.

Nut Candy

MAKES 450 G/1 LB

350 g/12 oz/1½ cups light soft
brown sugar
150 ml/¼ pt/⅔ cup milk
50 g/2 oz/¼ cup golden (light
corn) syrup
30 ml/2 tbsp butter
5 ml/1 tsp vanilla
50 g/2 oz/½ cup walnuts, coarsely
chopped

Thoroughly butter a shallow round, square or oval 1 litre/1¾ pt/4½ cup dish. Place all the ingredients except the nuts in a 1.75 litre/3 pt/7½ cup dish. Cook, uncovered, on Full for 14 minutes, stirring with a wooden spoon four or five times. Remove from the microwave, then stand in the sink with enough cold water to come half-way up the outside of the dish. Leave for 8 minutes, then lift out and wipe the base and sides dry. Add the walnuts and beat the candy vigorously for several minutes until it starts to lighten in colour. (This is hard work!) Spread into the prepared dish and leave to set. Remove from the dish by lifting with a knife, then break the candy into pieces. Store in an airtight tin or jar.

Nut and Honey Candy

MAKES 450 G/1 LB

Prepare as for Nut Candy, but substitute clear honey for the syrup.

Almond and Honey Candy with Orange

MAKES 450 G/1 LB

Wash 50 g/2 oz/½ cup almonds in their brown skins. Toast as directed on page 205. Prepare the Nut Candy, but substitute honey for the syrup and add 5 ml/1 tsp finely grated orange peel with the other ingredients. Add the almonds before beating.

Choc-a-bloc Candy

MAKES 900 G/2 LB

A cross between fudge and crisp candy, this sets quite solidly yet cuts through easily enough with a sharp knife. Only for those with a sweet tooth!

450 g/1 lb plain (semi-sweet)
chocolate
50 g/2 oz/⅓ cup butter
45 ml/3 tbsp double (heavy) cream
5 ml/1 tsp vanilla essence (extract)
450 g/1 lb/2⅔ cups sifted icing
(confectioners') sugar

Break up the chocolate and place in a bowl with the butter. Melt, uncovered, on Defrost for 5½–7 minutes. Stir in the cream and vanilla essence. Gradually work in the icing sugar with a wooden spoon. (This takes time and effort.) When large crumbles form, press evenly with the fingers into a buttered 25 × 18 cm/ 10 × 7 in shallow rectangular dish. Smooth the top with a knife dipped in and out of hot water. Score deeply into about 70 pieces and leave to set firmly before cutting up. Store in a cool place.

Mocha Choc-a-bloc Candy

MAKES 900 G/2 LB

Prepare as for Choc-a-bloc Candy (page 339), but add 20 ml/4 tsp instant coffee powder or granules to the chocolate and butter before melting.

Decorated Choc-a-bloc Candy

MAKES 900 G/2 LB

Prepare as for Choc-a-bloc Candy (page 339), but score the fudge into pieces while still in its tin and press a toasted hazelnut (page 205) into each piece.

Marshmallow Ginger Fudge

MAKES 350 G/12 OZ

Fast and foolproof.

50 g/2 oz/¼ cup butter
50 g/2 oz/¼ cup light soft brown sugar
30 ml/2 tbsp milk
100 g/3½ oz marshmallows
100 g/3½ oz icing (confectioners') sugar, sifted
50 g/2 oz preserved ginger, chopped

Put the butter in a 1.75 litre/3 pt/7½ cup dish with the sugar and milk. Melt, uncovered, on Defrost for 4 minutes, stirring twice. Cook on Full for a further 4 minutes, stirring twice. Mix in the marshmallows and cook, uncovered, on Full for 30 seconds. Stir round and continue to cook for a further 30 seconds. Work in the icing sugar with a wooden spoon. Stir briskly, then add the ginger. Spread into a buttered 1 litre/1¾ pt/4¼ cup dish. When cold, cover and chill for 2–3 hours until set. Cut into pieces and store in an airtight container.

Marshmallow Raisin Fudge

MAKES 350 G/12 OZ

Prepare as for Marshmallow Ginger Fudge, but substitute 50 g/2 oz/⅓ cup raisins for the chopped ginger.

Marshmallow Nut Fudge

MAKES 350 G/12 OZ

Prepare as for Marshmallow Ginger Fudge, but add 50 g/2 oz/½ cup chopped nuts.

Chocolate Truffles

MAKES 15

100 g/3½ oz plain (semi-sweet) chocolate
50 g/2 oz/¼ cup butter
50 g/2 oz/⅓ cup icing (confectioners') sugar, sifted
30 ml/2 tbsp ground almonds
5 ml/1 tsp vanilla essence (extract)
Cocoa (unsweetened chocolate) powder

Break up the chocolate and put into a bowl with the butter. Melt, uncovered, on Defrost for 5–5½ minutes. Mix in the icing sugar with a wooden spoon, then stir in the almonds and vanilla. Transfer to a shallow dish, cover and chill until firm but not hard. Roll into 15 balls, toss in cocoa powder and drop into paper sweet cases (candy cups).

Coffee Truffles

MAKES 15

Prepare as for Chocolate Truffles, but add 15 ml/1 tbsp instant coffee powder or granules to the chocolate and butter before melting. Omit the vanilla essence (extract).

Sherry or Rum Truffles

MAKES 15

Prepare as for Chocolate Truffles, but substitute 5 ml/1 tsp sherry or rum for the vanilla essence (extract).

Orange Truffles

MAKES 15

Prepare as for Chocolate Truffles, but add 5 ml/1 tsp finely grated orange peel to the chocolate and butter before melting. Omit the vanilla essence (extract).

Petit Fours with Cherries

MAKES 12

100 g/3½ oz plain (semi-sweet) chocolate
50 g/2 oz/½ cup plain digestive biscuit (Graham cracker) crumbs
6 assorted colour glacé (candied) cherries, halved

Break the chocolate into a bowl. Melt, uncovered, on Defrost for 3–3½ minutes. Stir in the biscuit crumbs, then spoon equally into 12 paper sweet cases (candy cups). Top each with a cherry half and allow to set for at least an hour in the refrigerator.

Peppermint Fondants

MAKES 550 G/1¼ LB

50 g/2 oz/¼ cup unsalted (sweet) butter
30 ml/2 tbsp milk
5 ml/1 tsp peppermint essence (extract)
450 g/1 lb/2⅔ cups icing (confectioners') sugar, sifted, plus extra for dusting

Put the butter, milk and peppermint essence in a 1.75 litre/3 pt/7½ cup bowl. Heat, uncovered, on Defrost for 3 minutes. Work in the measured icing sugar. Knead until smooth, then turn out on to a surface dusted with icing sugar. Roll out fairly thinly. Cut into 30 rounds with a 2.5 cm/1 in cutter. Leave for 2–3 hours to dry out, then transfer to paper sweet cases (candy cups).

Chocolate Peppermint Fondants

MAKES 550 G/1¼ LB

Prepare as for Peppermint Fondants, but after the fondants have dried out, brush the tops with melted milk or plain (semi-sweet) chocolate and leave until set before putting into cases.

Coffee Fondants

MAKES 550 G/1¼ LB

Prepare as for Peppermint Fondants, but substitute 20 ml/4 tsp instant coffee powder or granules for the peppermint. Decorate each with a piece of walnut or pecan nut.

Rose Fondants

MAKES 550 G/1¼ LB

Prepare as for Peppermint Fondants, but substitute 5 ml/1 tsp rose essence (extract) for the peppermint essence. Decorate each with a crystallised (candied) rose petal.

Fruit Fondants

MAKES 550 G/1¼ LB

Prepare as for Peppermint Fondants, but substitute any other fruit essence (extract), such as lemon or orange, for the peppermint essence.

Preserves and Chutneys

Making preserves in the microwave is quick, safe and clean. There are no pans of hot jam (conserve) or marmalade to contend with, no boiling over and minimal mess. The technique is reliable, the bright colour is preserved and the taste is impeccable.

Tips

The same maxims apply to preserves made in the microwave as those cooked conventionally and are as follows:

- Choose sound fruit, firm and not over-ripe.
- Wash and dry before cooking.
- Remove stones (pits) before cooking where possible to prevent waste.
- To test for setting, use a sugar thermometer which should register 110°C/220°F. Alternatively, pour a little of the preserve on to a cold saucer and leave for 2 minutes. If a skin forms on top that wrinkles when touched, the preserve is ready: if not, cook a little longer, checking every minute.

- Skim, then spoon into clean and dry jars. Top with waxed discs. Cover and label when cold.
- To sterilise and warm empty glass or pottery jars, pour 45 ml/3 tbsp water into each. Heat one at a time on Full for 1½–2 minutes. Pour away the water. Turn the jars upside-down on a clean, folded tea towel (dish cloth) to drain. If any traces of water remain inside, wipe dry with kitchen paper.
- Store preserves in a cool, dark and dry area.

Making Jam

MAKES ABOUT 750 G/1½ LB/2 CUPS

To make successful jam and other preserves in the microwave, keep to small quantities of fruit, using no more than 450 g/1 lb. Put the prepared fruit in a 2.25 litre/4 pt/10 cup dish. Cook to a pulp with water *but no sugar*, following the directions given in the table on pages 51–3. After cooking, add the extra water and granulated or preserving sugar in the quantities given below. Stir well, return to the microwave and cook, uncovered, on Full for 5–7 minutes, stirring three times with a wooden spoon to ensure the sugar has dissolved completely. Continue to cook, uncovered, on Full for 20–40 minutes (the time needed will depend on the fruit), stirring frequently with a wooden spoon throughout cooking, until setting point is reached. Test for setting. Skim after cooking, transfer to pots, cover and label.

Apple and Blackberry

To 450 g/1 lb fruit, add 15 ml/1 tbsp water and 450 g/1 lb/2 cups sugar.

Apricot (Fresh)

To 450 g/1 lb fruit, add 15 ml/1 tbsp water, the juice of ½ lemon and 450 g/1 lb/2 cups sugar.

Blackberry

To 450 g/1 lb fruit, add 15 ml/1 tbsp lemon juice, no water and 450 g/1 lb/2 cups sugar.

Blackcurrant

To 450 g/1 lb fruit, add 300 ml/½ pt/1¼ cups water and 525 g/1 lb 3 oz/2⅓ cups sugar.

Damson

To 450 g/1 lb fruit, add 300 ml/½ pt/1¼ cups water and 525 g/1 lb 3 oz/2⅓ cups sugar. Skim off the stones (pits) as they rise to the surface. Bottle the jam when warm, not hot.

Gooseberry

To 450 g/1 lb fruit, add 135 ml/4½ fl oz water and 450 g/1 lb/2 cups sugar.

Greengage

To 450 g/1 lb fruit, add 15 ml/1 tbsp water and 450 g/1 lb/2 cups sugar. If possible, remove the stones (pits) before cooking the fruit.

Peach

To 450 g/1 lb stoned (pitted) peaches, add 45 ml/3 tbsp water, the juice of 1 small lemon and 390 g/13½ oz/ scant 1¾ cups sugar.

Plum

To 450 g/1 lb fruit, add 15 ml/1 tbsp water and 450 g/1 lb/2 cups sugar. If possible, remove the stones (pits) before cooking the fruit.

Raspberry

Cook 450 g/1 lb fruit with no water on Full for 4–6 minutes. Add 450 g/1 lb/2 cups sugar.

Strawberry

Cook 450 g/1 lb fruit with no water on Full for 4–6 minutes. Add 450 g/1 lb/2 cups sugar and the juice of ½ lemon.

Dried Apricot Jam

MAKES 900 G/2 LB/2⅔ CUP

A fine-flavoured, fragrant jam, much used in haute cuisine.

225 g/8 oz dried apricots, quartered
600 ml/1 pt/2½ cups cold water
900 g/2 lb/4 cups granulated or
**   preserving sugar**
Juice of 1 large lemon, strained

Soak the apricots in water overnight. Drain and place in a 2.5 litre/ 4½ pt/11 cup bowl with the measured water. Cook, uncovered, on Full for 15–20 minutes until the fruit is very tender. Add the sugar and lemon juice. Return to the microwave and cook uncovered, on Full for 5–6 minutes, stirring three times with a wooden spoon, until the sugar dissolves. Continue to cook, still uncovered, for 20–30 minutes until setting point is reached. Allow to cool to lukewarm, then transfer to pots, cover and label.

Apricot Jam with Almonds

MAKES 900 G/2 LB/2⅔ CUP

Prepare as for Dried Apricot Jam, but add 45–60 ml/3–4 tbsp halved blanched almonds with the lemon juice.

Apricot Jam with Orange

MAKES 900 G/2 LB/2⅔ CUP

Prepare as for Dried Apricot Jam, but add the finely grated peel of 1 small orange with the sugar.

Apricot Jam with Whisky

MAKES 900 G/2 LB/2⅔ CUP

Prepare as for Dried Apricot Jam, but stir in 15–30 ml/1–2 tbsp whisky to the cooked but still warm jam.

Multi-fruit Marmalade

MAKES 1.5 KG/3 LB/4 CUPS

A superior marmalade, which does the microwave much credit. It is essential to leave the marmalade until almost cool before potting to prevent the peel from rising in the jar.

1 grapefruit
1 orange
1 lemon
450 ml/¾ pt/2 cups boiling water
1 kg/2¼ lb/4½ cups granulated or
**   preserving sugar**

Peel the fruit thinly and cut the rind into thin, medium or thick shreds, as preferred. Halve each piece of fruit and squeeze out the juice, reserving any pips (pits) and the white pith. Pour the juice into a 2.5 litre/4½ pt/11 cup bowl. Put the pips and pith in a piece of cotton cloth, tie securely and add to the bowl of juice. Add 300 ml/½ pt/ 1¼ cups of the boiling water, cover and leave to stand for 1 hour. Pour in the remaining water, then cover the bowl with clingfilm (plastic wrap) and slit it twice to allow steam to escape. Cook on Full for 20–30 minutes (the time will depend on the thickness of the fruit peel). Uncover and stir in the sugar. Cook, uncovered, on Full for 8 minutes, stirring at least four times, until the sugar dissolves. Return to the microwave and continue to cook, uncovered, for a further 30–35 minutes, stirring with a wooden spoon every 7–10 minutes, until setting point is reached. Skim off the scum. Allow to cool to lukewarm, then discard the bag of pips and pith and transfer to warmed jars. Top each jar with a waxed disc. Cover and label when cold.

Marmalade with Whisky

MAKES 1.5 KG/3 LB/4 CUPS

Prepare as for Multi-fruit Marmalade, but stir in 30 ml/2 tbsp whisky as soon as the marmalade reaches setting point.

Mature Marmalade

MAKES 1.5 KG/3 LB/4 CUPS

Prepare as for Multi-fruit Marmalade, cutting the peel into thick shreds. Add 30 ml/2 tbsp black treacle (molasses) with the sugar.

Lemon Curd

MAKES 450 G/1 LB/1⅓ CUPS

A very fresh, very lemony and immensely buttery traditional preserve. It should be stored in the refrigerator as it is highly perishable.

125 g/4 oz/½ cup butter
3 eggs
1 egg yolk
225 g/8 oz/1 cup granulated sugar
Finely grated peel and juice of
*   3 lemons*

Put the butter in a 1.25 litre/2¼ pt/ 5½ cup bowl and heat, uncovered, on Defrost for 4 minutes. Beat together the remaining ingredients and add to the butter. Cook, uncovered, on Full for 5 minutes, beating with a wooden spoon every minute. If the curd seems a little thin, cook for an extra 30–60 seconds. Remove from the microwave when the curd is thick and coats the back of a spoon smoothly and in an even layer. Allow to stand for 2 minutes. Spoon into two small jars and cover as for jam (page 342).

Orange Curd

MAKES 450 G/1 LB/1⅓ CUPS

Prepare as for Lemon Curd, but substitute the finely grated peel and juice of 2 oranges for 2 of the lemons.

Lime Curd

MAKES 450 G/1 LB/1⅓ CUPS

Prepare as for Lemon Curd, but substitute the finely grated peel and juice of 2 limes for 1 of the lemons.

Mixed Onion Marmalade

SERVES 4–6

Using red onions and red wine darkens the marmalade and bypasses the need for slow cooking. Serve with firm fish, poultry and meat dishes.

45 ml/3 tbsp butter
2 red onions, very thinly sliced
4 shallots, peeled and chopped
1 white onion, very thinly sliced
1 leek, very finely sliced into rings
2 garlic cloves, crushed
6 spring onions (scallions), finely
*   chopped*
45 ml/3 tbsp dry red wine
2.5 ml/½ tsp malt vinegar
25 ml/1½ tbsp dark soft brown sugar
10 ml/2 tsp chopped marjoram
5 ml/1 tsp salt
Freshly ground black pepper

Put the butter in a large dish and melt on Defrost for about 1–1½ minutes. Mix in the red onions, shallots, white onion, leek, garlic and spring onions. Cover with a plate and cook on Full for 15–20 minutes, stirring three times, until the onions have softened. Mix in all the remaining ingredients. Cover as before and cook on Full for 3 minutes. Serve warm or cold.

Apple Chutney

MAKES 900 G/2 LB

450 g/1 lb/4 cups coarsely chopped cooking (tart) apples
1 large onion, grated
15 ml/1 tbsp salt
60 ml/4 tbsp water
15 ml/1 tbsp mixed pickling spice
1 bay leaf
350 ml/12 fl oz/scant 1½ cups malt or cider vinegar
225 g/8 oz/1 cup dark soft brown sugar
1–2 garlic cloves, crushed
125 g/4 oz/1 cup chopped dates
125 g/4 oz/⅔ cup whole raisins
15 ml/1 tbsp ground ginger or a walnut-sized piece of fresh ginger, peeled and finely chopped
5 ml/1 tsp ground cinnamon
5 ml/1 tsp mixed (apple-pie) spice
1.5–2.5 ml/¼–½ tsp cayenne pepper (optional)

Put the apples and onion in a 2.5 litre/4½ pt/11 cup bowl. Mix in the salt and water. Cover with a plate and cook on Full for 5 minutes. Tie the pickling spice and bay leaf in a piece of cloth and add to the apple mixture with all the remaining ingredients. Cook, uncovered, on Full for 30–40 minutes, stirring every 6–7 minutes, until the chutney thickens to the consistency of jam (conserve). (The chutney can be cooked for a further 5–10 minutes if necessary until the desired thickness is reached.) Remove and discard the bag of spices. Cover when cold and leave overnight in the cool for the flavours to mature. Transfer to pots and cover and label as for jam (page 342).

Apple and Pear Chutney

MAKES 900 G/2 LB

Prepare as for Apple Chutney, but substitute 225 g/8 oz/2 cups coarsely chopped pears for half the chopped apples.

Apple, Red Tomato and Apricot Chutney

MAKES 900 G/2 LB

Prepare as for Apple Chutney, but substitute 225 g/8 oz/2 cups coarsely chopped red tomatoes for half the chopped apples and coarsely chopped apricots for the raisins.

Green Tomato Chutney

MAKES 900 G/2 LB

Prepare as for Apple Chutney, but substitute coarsely chopped green tomatoes for the apples.

Banana and Green Pepper Chutney

MAKES 900 G/2 LB

Prepare as for Apple Chutney, but substitute bananas for the apples and add a finely chopped seeded green (bell) pepper with all the remaining ingredients.

Dark Plum Chutney

MAKES 900 G/2 LB

Prepare as for Apple Chutney, but substitute stoned (pitted) plums for the apples and add 1 star anise to the pickling spice for a slightly oriental flavour.

Bread and Butter Pickles

••••••••••••••••••••••••••••••••••••
MAKES 750 G/1½ LB

A North American clear relish, slightly on the sweet side, with a distinctive personality and a brilliant golden hue from the turmeric. It goes beautifully with cold meats and hamburgers, cheese, poultry and fried fish but does best in sandwiches.

1 large cucumber (about 450 g/
1 lb), unpeeled and cut into
paper-thin slices
2 large onions, peeled and cut into
paper-thin slices
175 ml/6 fl oz/¾ cup colourless
distilled malt vinegar
175 g/6 oz/¾ cup caster (superfine)
sugar
10 ml/2 tsp mixed pickling spice
10 ml/2 tsp salt
1.5 ml/¼ tsp mustard powder
1.5 ml/¼ tsp turmeric
4–5 sprays dill (dill weed)

Put the cucumber and onion slices in a colander (strainer) and leave to stand for 30 minutes to drain. Meanwhile, pour the vinegar into a 2 litre/3½ pt/8½ cup bowl. Stir in the sugar, pickling spice, salt, mustard and turmeric. Heat, uncovered, on Full for 5 minutes, stirring twice. Mix in the cucumber, onions and dill. Heat, uncovered, on Full for 3 minutes, stirring twice. Allow to cool to lukewarm, then transfer to one large or two medium jam (conserve) jars. Cover when cold and store in the refrigerator.

347

Recipes for One

The microwave is so perfect for small quantities that this is one of the biggest chapters in the book. Young, old, students and busy families all want to be catered for and if it can be done in conjunction with the microwave, so much the better because microwaves are easy to use, economical and work quickly and safely.

Filled Croissants

The next two pages contain some delicious ideas with croissants.

Cream Cheese and Pickle

1 croissant
30 ml/2 tbsp full-cream or low-fat
*   cream cheese*
15 ml/1 tbsp sweet pickle
1 small tomato, thinly sliced

Halve the croissant and spread the cut sides with cheese. Sandwich together with pickle and tomato. Put on a plate and heat, uncovered, on Defrost for 30–35 seconds until warm.

Ham Mayonnaise with Salad

1 croissant
15 ml/1 tbsp mild wholegrain
*   mustard*
2 thin slices ham
15 ml/1 tbsp mayonnaise
1 small sliced cooked beetroot
*   (red beet)*

Halve the croissant and spread the cut sides with mustard. Sandwich together with the remaining ingredients. Put on a plate and heat, uncovered, on Defrost for 30–35 seconds until warm.

Turkey and Coleslaw

1 croissant
Butter or margarine
2 slices cold turkey from a roast
*   bird or a packet*
30 ml/2 tbsp coleslaw

Halve the croissant and spread the cut sides with butter or margarine. Sandwich together with the remaining ingredients. Put on a plate and heat, uncovered, on Defrost for 35–40 seconds until warm.

Savoury Peanut Butter and Lettuce

1 croissant
Smooth peanut butter
Yeast extract
Soft lettuce leaves

Halve the croissant and spread the cut sides with peanut butter followed by yeast extract. Sandwich together with 2 or 3 lettuce leaves. Put on a plate and heat, uncovered, on Defrost for 20–25 seconds until warm.

Camembert and Redcurrant Jelly

1 croissant
Butter or margarine
3 slices camembert cheese, outer
  crust removed
10–15 ml/2–3 tsp redcurrant jelly
  (clear conserve)

Halve the croissant and spread the cut sides with butter or margarine. Sandwich together with the cheese and spoonfuls of the redcurrant jelly. Put on a plate and heat, uncovered, on Defrost for 30–35 seconds until warm.

Cheddar and Piccalilli

1 croissant
Butter or margarine
2–3 thin slices Cheddar cheese
15 ml/1 tbsp piccalilli

Halve the croissant and spread the cut sides with butter or margarine. Sandwich together with the cheese and piccalilli. Put on a plate and heat, uncovered, on Defrost for 30–35 seconds until warm.

Beef and Pickled Onion

1 croissant
Creamed horseradish
2–3 slices cold roast beef
1 brown pickled onion, thinly
  sliced

Halve the croissant and spread the cut sides with creamed horseradish. Sandwich together with the beef and onion slices. Put on a plate and heat, uncovered, on Defrost for 30–35 seconds until warm.

Pizza Croissant

1 croissant
15–20 ml/3–4 tsp pesto
3 thin slices Mozzarella cheese
1 small tomato, thinly sliced
2 stoned (pitted) black olives
  (optional)

Halve the croissant and spread the cut sides with pesto. Sandwich together with the remaining ingredients. Put on a plate and heat, uncovered, on Defrost for 40 seconds until warm.

Cottage Cheese and Lemon

1 croissant
Lemon Curd (page 345, or use
  bought)
30 ml/2 tbsp cottage cheese
1 small apple, grated

Halve the croissant and spread the cut sides with lemon curd. Sandwich together with the cottage cheese and apple. Put on a plate and heat, uncovered, on Defrost for 25–30 seconds until warm.

Spicy Jam and Banana

1 croissant
15 ml/1 tbsp red jam (conserve)
1 small banana, sliced
Ground cinnamon

Halve the croissant and spread the cut sides with jam. Sandwich together with the banana slices and sprinkle with cinnamon. Put on a plate and heat, uncovered, on Defrost for 25–30 seconds until warm.

Chocolate and Banana

Prepare as for Spicy Jam and Banana (page 349), but substitute chocolate spread for the jam (conserve).

Toasted Snacks

Baked Beans on Toast

A traditional favourite, microwaved on Defrost to prevent the beans bursting.

1 large slice toast
Butter or margarine (optional)
150 g/5 oz/⅔ cup baked beans in
*   tomato sauce*

Put the toast on a plate. Leave plain or spread with butter or margarine. Top with the beans. Heat, uncovered, on Defrost for 3½ minutes until warm.

Cheesy Beans on Toast

SERVES 1

Prepare as for Baked Beans on Toast, but sprinkle 45 ml/3 tbsp grated Cheddar cheese on top of the beans. Cook for an extra 15–20 seconds.

Spaghetti on Toast

SERVES 1

1 large slice toast
Butter or margarine (optional)
213 g/7½ oz/1 small can spaghetti
*   in tomato sauce*

Put the toast on a plate. Leave plain or spread with butter or margarine. Top with the spaghetti. Heat, uncovered, on Full for 2–2¼ minutes until warm.

Fish Dishes for One

Tipsy Trout

1 whole trout, cleaned and washed
15 ml/1 tbsp butter or margarine
Salt and freshly ground black
*   pepper*
Paprika
30 ml/2 tbsp sherry

Put the trout on a plate. Melt the butter or margarine, uncovered, on Full for 30 seconds. Stir in all the remaining ingredients and spoon over the fish. Cover with clingfilm (plastic wrap) and slit it twice to allow steam to escape. Cook on Defrost for 8 minutes. Allow to stand for 1 minute before eating.

Tuna Rarebit with Mayonnaise

1 large slice white or brown toast
30 ml/2 tbsp mayonnaise
100 g/3½ oz canned tuna in oil,
*   flaked*
30 ml/2 tbsp grated Cheddar
*   cheese*
Paprika

Put the toast on a plate and spread with the mayonnaise. Top evenly with the tuna. Sprinkle with the cheese and dust with paprika. Heat through, uncovered, on Full for 2 minutes.

Buttered Soft Herring Roes with Garlic

125 g/4 oz soft herring roes, washed and drained
15 ml/1 tbsp butter or margarine
1 garlic clove, peeled
Salt and freshly ground black pepper
1–2 spring onions (scallions), chopped
Toast, to serve

Put the roes in a small but deep dish. Dot with small pieces of the butter or margarine and crush the garlic over the top. Season to taste. Cover with clingfilm (plastic wrap) and slit it twice to allow steam to escape. Cook on Defrost for 5 minutes. Allow to stand for 1 minute. Uncover and sprinkle with the onions. Eat with toast.

Plaice in Cocktail Dressing

30 ml/2 tbsp tomato ketchup (catsup)
45 ml/3 tbsp thick mayonnaise
5 ml/1 tsp Worcestershire sauce
5 ml/1 tsp medium-dry sherry
1.5 ml/¼ tsp Tabasco sauce
1 small plaice, about 225 g/8 oz, cleaned and trimmed
1 spring onion (scallion), chopped

Mix together the tomato ketchup, mayonnaise, Worcestershire sauce, sherry and Tabasco. Put the fish on a plate. Coat with the sauce and sprinkle with the onion. Cover with clingfilm (plastic wrap) and slit it twice to allow steam to escape. Cook on Full for 3½–4 minutes until the skin just begins to break. Allow to stand for 1 minute before eating.

Chinese Plaice

A home-style dish that teams well with egg noodles

1 walnut-sized piece fresh ginger, peeled and chopped
1 garlic clove, crushed
15 ml/1 tbsp teriyaki sauce
2.5 ml/½ tsp Worcestershire sauce
10 ml/2 tsp chopped coriander leaves
1 small plaice, about 225 g/8 oz, cleaned and trimmed
1 spring onion (scallion), chopped

Mix together the ginger, garlic, teriyaki sauce, Worcestershire sauce and coriander. Put the fish on a plate. Coat with the herb and sauce mixture and sprinkle with the onion. Cover with clingfilm (plastic wrap) and slit it twice to allow steam to escape. Cook on Full for 3½–4 minutes until the skin just begins to break. Allow to stand for 1 minute before eating.

Sweet-sour Herb Herring

A hot version of soused herring.

1 fresh herring, cleaned, head removed, and washed
Salt and freshly ground black pepper
15 ml/1 tbsp cider vinegar
2.5 ml/½ tsp mixed dried herbs
2.5 ml/½ tsp soft brown sugar

Put the herring on a plate, flesh side up. Sprinkle with salt and pepper. Beat the vinegar with the herbs and sugar and spoon over the fish. Cover with clingfilm (plastic wrap) and slit it twice to allow steam to escape. Cook on Defrost for 3½–4 minutes until the flesh is flaking and soft. Allow to stand for 1 minute before eating.

351

'Poached' Salmon

1 salmon steak, about 200 g/7 oz,
    washed and dried
30 ml/2 tbsp lemon juice
30 ml/2 tbsp white wine or water
Salt and white pepper
Melted butter or mayonnaise, to
    serve

Put the salmon in a shallow round dish. Coat with the lemon juice and wine or water. Sprinkle with salt and pepper. Cover with clingfilm (plastic wrap) and slit it twice to allow steam to escape. Cook on Defrost for 6–7 minutes. Allow to stand for 1½ minutes. Eat hot with melted butter or cold with mayonnaise.

Citrus Skate with Coriander

1 piece fan-shaped skate wing,
    about 200 g/7 oz
15 ml/1 tbsp groundnut (peanut)
    or corn oil
45 ml/3 tbsp freshly squeezed
    orange juice
30 ml/2 tbsp coriander (cilantro)
    leaves, finely shredded
Chinese egg noodles, freshly boiled
10 ml/2 tsp sesame oil
Baby sweetcorn (corn), to serve
    (optional)

Put the fish on a large dinner plate. Combine the groundnut or corn oil and orange juice and heat, uncovered, on Defrost for 1 minute. Spoon over the skate. Sprinkle with the coriander. Cover with clingfilm (plastic wrap) and slit it twice to allow steam to escape. Cook on Full for 4 minutes. Allow to stand for 1 minute. Add the sesame oil to the noodles in the saucepan and toss thoroughly. Eat the skate with the noodles and baby sweetcorn, if liked.

Pesto-dressed Mackerel

1 mackerel, cleaned, head removed,
    and washed
15 ml/1 tbsp tomato juice
5 ml/1 tsp pesto
2.5 ml/½ tsp grated lemon peel
Salt and freshly ground black
    pepper
Ciabatta bread or macaroni, to
    serve

Put the fish on a plate, flesh side up. Beat the tomato juice with the pesto and lemon peel and spoon over the fish. Sprinkle with salt and pepper. Cover with clingfilm (plastic wrap) and slit it twice to allow steam to escape. Cook on Defrost for 3½–4 minutes until the flesh is flaking. Allow to stand for 1 minute before eating with warmed ciabatta or boiled macaroni.

Tandoori Mackerel

1 mackerel, cleaned, head
    removed, and washed
15 ml/1 tbsp lemon juice
Salt
5 ml/1 tsp tandoori spice
Mixed salad
1 naan bread

Put the fish on a plate, flesh side up. Sprinkle with the lemon juice, salt to taste and the spice mix. Cover with clingfilm (plastic wrap) and slit it twice to allow steam to escape. Cook on Defrost for 3½–4 minutes until the flesh is flaking and soft. Allow to stand for 1 minute before eating with salad and naan bread.

Thousand Petal Haddock with Crab

....

*1 haddock steak or a piece of
skinned fillet, about 200 g/7 oz,
washed and dried*
45 ml/3 tbsp dressed crab
*2.5 cm/1 in piece fresh root
ginger, chopped*
1 spring onion (scallion), chopped
1 garlic clove, crushed
25 ml/1½ tbsp thick mayonnaise
2.5 ml/½ tsp soy sauce
2.5 ml/½ tsp chilli sauce
5 ml/1 tsp malt vinegar

Put the fish on a dinner plate. Tip the crab into a small basin with the ginger, onion and garlic. Work in the remaining ingredients and mix thoroughly. Spread over the fish with a knife. Cover with clingfilm (plastic wrap) and slit it twice to allow steam to escape. Cook on Defrost for 8½ minutes. Allow to stand for 1½ minutes before eating.

Lemon and Thyme Cod

....

A mild herb dressing complements the fish brilliantly. Use hake or haddock if preferred.

*1 cod steak, about 200 g/7 oz,
washed and dried*
10 ml/2 tsp butter or margarine
30 ml/2 tbsp single (light) cream
*30 ml/2 tbsp dry lemon and thyme
stuffing mix*
Paprika
30 ml/2 tbsp chopped parsley

Put the fish into a shallow round dish. Melt the butter or margarine on Defrost for about 30 seconds. Mix in the cream and pour round the fish. Sprinkle the stuffing mix over the top and dust with paprika for extra colour. Cover with clingfilm (plastic wrap) and slit it twice to allow steam to escape.

Cook on Defrost for 6–7 minutes. Allow to stand for 1½ minutes. Scatter the parsley over the fish before eating.

The Good Wife's Cod

....

A classic, also known as *bonne femme*. In culinary terms this means anything cooked with onions, mushrooms and unsmoked bacon.

30 ml/2 tbsp butter or margarine
1 small onion, roughly chopped
*4 closed-cap mushrooms, trimmed
and sliced*
*2 rashers (slices) lean unsmoked
bacon, cut into strips*
*1 large cod steak, about 225 g/
8 oz*
Chopped parsley, to garnish

Put the butter or margarine in a 600 ml/1 pt/2½ cup round shallow dish. Melt, uncovered, on Defrost for 1½ minutes. Mix in the onion, mushrooms and bacon. Cover with clingfilm (plastic wrap) and slit it twice to allow steam to escape. Cook on Full for 2 minutes. Stir round, then place the fish on top. Cover as before and cook on Full for 4½–5 minutes. Allow to stand for 1 minute. Uncover and sprinkle with parsley. Eat straight away.

French-style Cod

225 g/8 oz cod fillet, cut from the thicker end
50 g/2 oz mushrooms, sliced
15 ml/1 tbsp butter or margarine
1 garlic clove, crushed
5 ml/1 tsp French mustard
15 ml/1 tbsp dry white wine or calvados
Salt

Put the cod on a plate and sprinkle with the mushrooms. Place the remaining ingredients in a small dish, adding salt to taste, and heat, uncovered, on Defrost for 1½ minutes. Spoon over the fish and mushrooms. Cover with clingfilm (plastic wrap) and slit it twice to allow steam to escape. Cook on Full for 4 minutes. Allow to stand for 1 minute before eating.

Manhattan Cod

1 large cod steak, about 225 g/8 oz
50 g/2 oz cream cheese with garlic and herbs
25 g/1 oz/¼ cup strong Cheddar cheese, grated
15 ml/1 tbsp tomato ketchup (catsup)
15 ml/1 tbsp crushed cornflakes or potato crisps (chips)

Put the fish in a shallow 600 ml/1 pt/2½ cup round dish. Spread with the cream cheese and sprinkle with the Cheddar cheese. Trickle the ketchup over the top. Cover with clingfilm (plastic wrap) and slit it twice to allow steam to escape. Cook on Full for 5 minutes. Allow to stand for 1 minute. Uncover and sprinkle with the cornflakes or crisps. Eat straight away.

Curried Cod with Coconut

225 g/8 oz skinned cod fillet, cut from the thicker end
15 ml/1 tbsp butter or margarine, at kitchen temperature
2.5 ml/½ tsp mild curry powder
15 ml/1 tbsp fine desiccated (shredded) coconut
15 ml/1 tbsp single (light) cream
Salt and freshly ground black pepper
Paprika
Chopped coriander (cilantro) leaves, to garnish

Put the cod on a plate and leave aside. Put the butter or margarine, curry powder, coconut and cream in a small bowl and beat well together. Heat, uncovered, on Defrost for 1 minute. Spoon over the cod and sprinkle over salt and pepper to taste. Dust with paprika. Cover with clingfilm (plastic wrap) and slit it twice to allow steam to escape. Cook on Full for 4 minutes. Allow to stand for 1 minute. Uncover and sprinkle with coriander. Eat straight away.

Fish Vinaigrette

225 g/8 oz skinned cod or haddock fillet, cut from the thicker end
30 ml/2 tbsp bought garlic and herb vinaigrette
6 fresh tarragon or basil leaves or watercress sprigs

Put the fish on a plate and coat with the vinaigrette. Top with the herb leaves or watercress sprigs. Cover with clingfilm (plastic wrap) and slit it twice to allow steam to escape. Cook on Full for 4 minutes. Allow to stand for 1 minute before eating.

Jugged Kipper

Imagine… A kipper with no lingering smell! Once upon a time kippers were cooked by being left in a jug of hot water but this microwave method also does an immaculate and similar job.

1 medium kipper fillet, thawed if frozen
Butter or margarine

Place the kipper in a shallow 20 cm/ 8 in square dish. Add just enough cold water to cover the fish. Cover with clingfilm (plastic wrap) and slit it twice to allow steam to escape. Cook on Full for 6 minutes. Allow to stand for 2 minutes. Uncover and drain. Serve topped with a knob of butter or margarine.

Finnan Haddock

125 g/4 oz piece of smoked haddock fillet, cut from the thicker end
300 ml/½ pt/1¼ cups cold water
Butter or margarine or 1 poached egg (page 99), to serve (optional)

Put the fish in a shallow 600 ml/ 1 pt/2½ cup round dish. Add half the water. Cover with clingfilm (plastic wrap) and slit it twice to allow steam to escape. Cook on Full for 3 minutes. Uncover and drain. Repeat, using the remaining water and covering as before. Uncover and drain again, then cook on full for a further 2 minutes. Uncover and drain. Transfer to a plate and top with a knob of butter or margarine or, as is traditional, a poached egg.

Fish Pie

175 g/6 oz floury potatoes, peeled and cubed
45 ml/3 tbsp cold water
Salt
5 ml/1 tsp butter or margarine
15 ml/1 tbsp milk
15 ml/1 tbsp chopped parsley
225 g/8 oz any skinned white fish or salmon fillet
30 ml/2 tbsp crushed potato crisps (chips) or cornflakes

Put the potatoes in a 600 ml/ 1 pt/2½ cup round dish. Add 30 ml/ 2 tbsp of the water and 2.5 ml/½ tsp salt. Cover with clingfilm (plastic wrap) and slit it twice to allow steam to escape. Cook on Full for 4 minutes. Allow to stand for 1 minute. Drain and mash finely with the butter or margarine and milk. Stir in the parsley with a fork. Put the fish in a small round dish and season with salt. Add the remaining cold water. Cover as before and cook on Full for 3 minutes. Drain and flake. Combine with the potato mixture. Spread into a clean buttered dish. Sprinkle with the crisps or cornflakes. Reheat, uncovered, on Full for 2 minutes.

Chicken Dishes for One

Hungarian Chicken

A grand treat, based on a Magyar classic.

1 boned chicken breast, about
150 g/5 oz, skinned
15 ml/1 tbsp dried mixed pepper
flakes
15 ml/1 tbsp dried sliced
mushrooms
15 ml/1 tbsp dried onions
45 ml/3 tbsp boiling water
60 ml/4 tbsp soured (dairy sour)
cream
15 ml/1 tbsp tomato purée (paste)
5 ml/1 tsp paprika
Salt and freshly ground black
pepper
Cooked pasta or new potatoes, to
serve

Wash the chicken and dry with kitchen paper. Cut into narrow strips, then set aside. Put all the dried vegetables in a 600 ml/1 pt/2½ cup round dish and mix in the water. Cover with clingfilm (plastic wrap) and slit it twice to allow steam to escape. Cook on Defrost for 5 minutes. Allow to stand for 4 minutes. Top with the chicken strips. Cover as before and cook on Full for 2 minutes. Whisk together the remaining ingredients, seasoning to taste. Stir into the chicken and vegetables. Cover as before and cook on Full for 3 minutes. Allow to stand for 2 minutes. Stir round before eating with freshly cooked pasta or new potatoes.

Fast Chicken à la King

From the sixties and seventies, when food from North America was beginning to catch on over here. Eat with a plain scone (biscuit) or a toasted muffin or crumpet.

1 part-boned chicken breast, about
200 g/7 oz, skinned
15 ml/1 tbsp dried mixed pepper
flakes
15 ml/1 tbsp dried sliced
mushrooms
7.5 ml/1½ tsp cornflour
(cornstarch)
30 ml/2 tbsp medium-dry sherry
75 ml/5 tbsp single (light) cream
or full-cream milk
Salt and freshly ground black
pepper

Put the chicken in a 600 ml/1 pt/ 2½ cup round dish. Sprinkle with the pepper flakes and mushrooms. Cover with clingfilm (plastic wrap) and slit it twice to allow steam to escape. Cook on Full for 4 minutes. Mix the cornflour smoothly with the sherry, then stir in the cream or milk. Season to taste. Uncover the chicken and coat with the cornflour mixture. Cover as before and cook on Full for 2½ minutes. Allow to stand for 2½ minutes before eating.

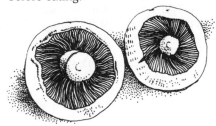

Hunter's Chicken

Originally Italian, this is a warm and characterful stew flavoured with black olives. Eat with rice, potato gnocchi or baby pasta.

1 part-boned chicken breast,
*   about 200 g/7 oz*
1 garlic clove, crushed
50 g/2 oz mushrooms, thinly
*   sliced*
8 black olives
2 tomatoes, blanched, skinned and
*   chopped*
10 ml/2 tsp chopped basil leaves
Salt

Wash the chicken and dry with kitchen paper. Place in a 600 ml/ 1 pt/2½ cup dish. Sprinkle with the garlic. Cover with clingfilm (plastic wrap) and slit it twice to allow steam to escape. Cook on Full for 4 minutes. Uncover. Top the chicken with all the remaining ingredients, adding salt to taste. Cover as before and cook on Full for 2 minutes. Allow to stand for 2 minutes before eating.

Chicken with Pumpkin

A Hallowe'en special.

1 boned chicken breast,
*   about 150 g/5 oz, skinned*
2 rashers (slices) streaky bacon,
*   chopped*
50 g/2 oz/¾ cup diced pumpkin
*   flesh*
50 g/2 oz mushrooms, sliced
5 ml/1 tsp cornflour (cornstarch)
5 ml/1 tsp stock powder or
*   10 ml/2 tsp gravy granules*
60 ml/4 tbsp apple juice or water
Salt and freshly ground black
*   pepper*

Wash the chicken and dry on kitchen paper. Cut into strips. Put in a 600 ml/1 pt/2½ cup round dish. Mix the bacon into the chicken with the remaining ingredients, seasoning to taste. Cover with clingfilm (plastic wrap) and slit it twice to allow steam to escape. Cook on Full for 6 minutes. Allow to stand for 1½ minutes, then stir round before eating.

Chicken in Kiev Sauce

An original adaptation of a super-market favourite.

1 part-boned chicken breast, about
*   200 g/7 oz, skinned*
Salt and freshly ground l ack
*   pepper*
15 ml/1 tbsp butter
30 ml/2 tbsp chopped parsley
1 garlic clove, crushed
10 ml/2 tsp lemon juice

Put the chicken in a 600 ml/1 pt/ 2½ cup round dish. Season to taste. Melt the butter or margarine on Defrost for about 1 minute. Mix in the remaining ingredients and spoon over the chicken. Cover with clingfilm (plastic wrap) and slit it twice to allow steam to escape. Cook on Full for 5 minutes. Allow to stand for 2 minutes before eating.

Penang Peanut Chicken

225 g/8 oz skinned chicken thighs
45 ml/3 tbsp smooth peanut butter
1.5 ml/¼ tsp paprika
1 garlic clove, crushed
15 ml/1 tbsp desiccated (shredded)
  coconut
75 ml/5 tbsp milk
15 ml/1 tbsp lime juice

Slash the flesh of each thigh in two places with sharp knife. Arrange in a 600 ml/1 pt/2½ cup round dish. Cover with clingfilm (plastic wrap) and slit it twice to allow steam to escape. Cook on Full for 4 minutes. Allow to stand for 2 minutes. Uncover. Mix together the remaining ingredients and spoon over the chicken. Cook, uncovered, on Defrost for 3½ minutes. Stir round. Cover as before and cook on Full for 2 minutes. Allow to stand for 3 minutes before eating.

Chicken Braise with Vegetables

15 ml/1 tbsp olive or corn oil
1 large carrot, grated
1 large onion, grated
2 celery stalks, thinly sliced
1 boned chicken breast, about
  150 g/5 oz, skinned
3 ripe tomatoes, blanched,
  skinned and chopped
45 ml/3 tbsp red or rosé wine
Salt and freshly ground black
  pepper
2.5 ml/½ tsp dried mixed herbs

Pour the oil into a 600 ml/1 pt/ 2½ cup round dish. Heat, uncovered, on Defrost for 1 minute. Mix in the vegetables. Cook, uncovered, on Full for 3 minutes. Slash the chicken flesh in two places with a sharp knife. Arrange on top of the vegetables. Coat with the tomatoes and wine. Season to taste and sprinkle the herbs on top. Cover with clingfilm (plastic wrap) and slit it twice to allow steam to escape. Cook on Full for 7½ minutes. Allow to stand for 4 minutes before eating.

Dieter's Pickled Onion Chicken

Trouble-free and very low fat.

225 g/8 oz skinned chicken thighs
1.5 ml/¼ tsp paprika
5 ml/1 tsp stock powder or
  10 ml/2 tsp gravy granules
10 ml/2 tsp hot water
2.5 ml/½ tsp Worcestershire sauce
2 brown pickled onions, thinly
  sliced

Place the chicken in a 600 ml/ 1 pt/2½ cup round dish. Dust with the paprika. Thoroughly combine the remaining ingredients except the onions. Pour round the chicken and top with the onion slices. Cover with clingfilm (plastic wrap) and slit it twice to allow steam to escape. Cook on Full for 5½ minutes. Allow to stand for 2 minutes before eating.

Spicy Chicken in Carrot Sauce
··

225 g/8 oz skinned chicken thighs
5 ml/1 tsp medium curry powder
200 g/7 oz/1 small can carrots,
  drained
2 pinches ground ginger
1.5 ml/¼ tsp garlic salt
2.5 ml/½ tsp cornflour
  (cornstarch)
15 ml/1 tbsp cold milk

Place the chicken in a 600 ml/
1 pt/2½ cup round dish and sprinkle
with the curry powder. Cover with
clingfilm (plastic wrap) and slit it twice
to allow steam to escape. Cook on Full
for 5 minutes. Meanwhile, mash the
carrots finely. Mix in the remaining
ingredients. Uncover the chicken and
coat with the carrot mixture. Cover as
before and cook on Full for 2½ minutes. Allow to stand for 3 minutes
before eating.

Bean Sprout Chicken
··

75 g/3 oz fresh bean sprouts,
  rinsed and drained
3 spring onions (scallions),
  chopped
225 g/8 oz skinned chicken thighs
7.5 ml/1½ tsp gravy granules or
  stock powder
30 ml/2 tbsp boiling water
10 ml/2 tsp medium-dry sherry
Salt and freshly ground black
  pepper
Cooked jasmine rice or Chinese
  noodles, to serve

Put the bean sprouts in a 600 ml/
1 pt/2½ cup round dish. Sprinkle
the spring onions over. Arrange the
chicken on top. Combine the gravy
granules or stock powder with the
water, then mix in the sherry. Season
to taste. Spoon over the chicken.
Cover with clingfilm (plastic wrap) and
slit it twice to allow steam to escape.
Cook on Full for 5½–6 minutes. Allow
to stand for 3 minutes before eating
with jasmine rice or noodles.

Chutney Chicken
··

225 g/8 oz chicken drumsticks,
  skinned
2 ripe peaches or nectarines,
  halved, stoned (pitted) and
  diced
Fresh lemon or lime juice
Paprika
Salt
45 ml/3 tbsp mango chutney
2 stoned dates

Slash the flesh of each drumstick in
three places with a sharp knife. Put
the diced fruit in the centre of a dinner
plate and sprinkle with the lemon or
lime juice. Arrange the drumsticks on
top, fleshy parts towards the edge of
the plate. Sprinkle with paprika and
salt and top with the chutney. Cover
with clingfilm (plastic wrap) and slit it
twice to allow steam to escape. Cook
on Full for 6 minutes. Allow to stand
for 4 minutes. Uncover and garnish
with the dates before eating.

Pineapple Chicken
··

For a taste of Hawaii, prepare as for
Chutney Chicken, but substitute 1
canned pineapple ring for the diced
peaches or nectarines. Sprinkle with
toasted coconut to garnish.

Tex-Mex and Avocado Chicken
....
225 g/8 oz chicken drumsticks, skinned
1 ripe small–medium avocado
5–10 ml/1–2 tsp chilli sauce
10 ml/2 tsp fresh lime juice
2 tomatoes, blanched, skinned and coarsely chopped
2.5 ml/½ tsp salt
Tortilla chips, to serve

Slash the flesh of each drumstick in three places with a sharp knife. Arrange in a 20 cm/7 inch diameter dish, fleshy parts towards the edge. Cover with clingfilm (plastic wrap) and slit it twice to allow steam to escape. Cook on Full for 4 minutes. Halve the avocado and scoop out the flesh. Mash finely with the chilli sauce and lime juice. Uncover the chicken and coat with the avocado mixture. Top with the tomatoes and sprinkle with the salt. Cover as before and cook on Full for 2½–3 minutes. Allow to stand for 3 minutes before eating with tortilla chips.

Sweet-sour Chicken with Chicory
....
225 g/8 oz chicken drumsticks, skinned
1 head chicory (Belgian endive), trimmed
1 celery stalk, thinly sliced
15 ml/1 tbsp soy sauce
15 ml/1 tbsp malt or rice vinegar
15 ml/1 tbsp clear honey

Slash the flesh of each drumstick in three places with a sharp knife. Arrange on a deep dinner plate, fleshy parts towards the edge. Remove a cone-shaped core from the base of the chicory to reduce bitterness. Halve the chicory lengthways and place, cut sides down, on each side of the chicken. Sprinkle the celery slices over the top. Beat together the remaining ingredients and pour over the chicken. Cover with clingfilm (plastic wrap) and slit it twice to allow steam to escape. Cook on Full for 6½–7 minutes. Allow to stand for 3 minutes before eating.

Fire Flung Chicken
....
225 g/8 oz chicken drumsticks, skinned
90 ml/6 tbsp thick creamy plain yoghurt
5 ml/1 tsp bottled creamed horseradish
5 ml/1 tsp continental mustard
2.5 ml/½ tsp paprika
2.5 ml/½ tsp onion or garlic salt
30 ml/2 tbsp salted peanuts, coarsely chopped
Boiled baby new potatoes and green salad, to serve

Slash the flesh of each drumstick in three places with a sharp knife. Arrange in a 600 ml/1 pt/2½ cup dish, fleshy parts towards the edge. Cover with clingfilm (plastic wrap) and slit it twice to allow steam to escape. Cook on Full for 5 minutes. Thoroughly mix together the yoghurt, horseradish, mustard, paprika and onion or garlic salt. Uncover the chicken and coat with the yoghurt mixture and the peanuts. Cover as before and cook on Full for 2 minutes. Allow to stand for 3 minutes before eating.

Portuguese Port Chicken

225 g/8 oz chicken drumsticks
1 garlic clove, crushed
1.5 ml/¼ tsp dried thyme
Salt and freshly ground black
* pepper*
Paprika
75 g/3 oz mushrooms, sliced
30 ml/2 tbsp port

Slash the flesh of each drumstick in three places with a sharp knife. Arrange in a 600 ml/1 pt/2½ cup dish, fleshy parts towards the edge. Sprinkle with the garlic and thyme and salt, pepper and paprika to taste. Cover with clingfilm (plastic wrap) and slit it twice to allow steam to escape. Cook on Full for 4 minutes. Uncover and surround with the mushrooms. Pour over the port. Cover as above and cook on Full for 3 minutes. Allow to stand for 3 minutes before eating.

Mock Chicken Stir-fry

1 courgette (zucchini), thinly
* sliced*
4 spring onions (scallions),
* chopped*
1 boneless chicken breast, about
* 150 g/5 oz, skinned*
15 ml/1 tbsp soy sauce

Arrange the courgette slices over the base of a 600 ml/1 pt/2½ cup dish and scatter the onions over. Slash the chicken flesh in two places with a sharp knife. Arrange on top of the vegetables and coat with the soy sauce. Cover with clingfilm (plastic wrap) and slit it twice to allow steam to escape. Cook on Full for 4–4½ minutes. Allow to stand for 3 minutes before eating.

Chicken and Rice Broth

200 g/7 oz chicken wings
15 ml/1 tbsp easy-cook long-grain
* rice*
15 ml/1 tbsp dried sliced onions
15 ml/1 tbsp chopped parsley or
* coriander (cilantro) leaves*
5 ml/1 tsp gravy granules or stock
* powder*
150 ml/¼ pt/⅔ cup hot water
Salt and freshly ground black
* pepper*

Put the chicken into a 600 ml/ 1 pt/2½ cup dish. Cover with cling-film (plastic wrap) and slit it twice to allow steam to escape. Cook on Full for 2½ minutes. Allow to stand for 2 minutes. Uncover and add the rice, onions, herbs and gravy granules or stock powder mixed with the water. Season to taste. Cover as before and cook on Defrost for 7 minutes. Allow to stand for 3 minutes before eating.

Chicken with Mushrooms

200 g/7 oz chicken breast meat,
* cubed*
150 ml/5 fl oz/½ can condensed
* cream of mushroom soup*
30 ml/2 tbsp toasted flaked
* (slivered) almonds (page 205)*

Arrange the chicken in a loose ring in a 600 ml/1 pt/2½ cup dish. Cover with clingfilm (plastic wrap) and slit it twice to allow steam to escape. Cook on Full for 2½ minutes. Uncover and thoroughly stir in the soup. Cover as before and cook on Defrost for 4 minutes. Allow to stand for 2 minutes. Uncover and sprinkle with the almonds. Eat straight away.

Rabbit Dishes for One

Mustard Rabbit
....

225 g/8 oz rabbit pieces
10 ml/2 tsp cornflour (cornstarch)
5 ml/1 tsp English mustard
 powder
Salt
25 ml/1½ tbsp tomato ketchup
 (catsup)
150 ml/¼ pt/⅔ cup full-cream milk

Arrange the rabbit in a 600 ml/ 1 pt/2½ cup dish. Cover with cling- film (plastic wrap) and slit it twice to allow steam to escape. Cook on Full for 3 minutes. Meanwhile, mix to- gether the cornflour (cornstarch), mustard and salt to taste. Gradually blend in the ketchup and milk and stir until smooth. Uncover the rabbit and coat with the mustard mixture. Cover as before and cook on Full for 3½ minutes. Allow to stand for 3 minutes before eating.

Bubbling Rabbit
....

225 g/8 oz rabbit pieces
1 small onion, very thinly sliced
 and separated into rings
25 ml/1½ tbsp cornflour
 (cornstarch)
½ can or small bottle sparkling
 mineral water flavoured with
 lime or lemon
5 ml/1 tsp gravy granules or stock
 powder
15 ml/1 tbsp hot water
Salt and freshly ground black
 pepper

Arrange the rabbit in a 600 ml/ 1 pt/2½ cup dish and place the onion rings on top. Cover with cling- film (plastic wrap) and slit it twice to allow steam to escape. Cook on Full for 3½ minutes. Whisk together the remaining ingredients until smooth. Uncover the rabbit and pour over the gravy mixture. Cover as before and cook on Full for 3½ minutes. Allow to stand for 3 minutes before eating.

Turkey Dishes for One

Turkey and Baby Peas
....

175 g/6 oz stir-fry turkey
15 ml/1 tbsp plain (all-purpose)
 flour
3 brown vinegar-pickled onions,
 thinly sliced
60 ml/4 tbsp petit pois, canned or
 frozen
30 ml/2 tbsp milk
Salt and freshly ground black
 pepper
30 ml/2 tbsp crushed potato crisps
 (chips)
1 Jacket Potato (page 226), to
 serve

Put the turkey in a 600 ml/1 pt/ 2½ cup dish. Cover with clingfilm (plastic wrap) and slit it twice to allow steam to escape. Cook on Full for 3 minutes. Uncover and stir round. Mix in all the remaining ingredients except the crisps. Cover as above and cook on Full for 2 minutes. Allow to stand for 2 minutes. Uncover, stir round and sprinkle with the crisps. Split the jacket potato and fill and partially coat with the turkey mixture.

Turkey with Prunes and Armagnac
....

12 stoned (pitted) prunes
45 ml/3 tbsp warm water
175 g/6 oz turkey breast fillet, cut
    into small cubes
1 leek, thinly sliced
15 ml/1 tbsp plain (all-purpose)
    flour
30 ml/2 tbsp Armagnac or other
    brandy
Salt and freshly ground black
    pepper

Soak the prunes in the warm water for 1 hour. Put the turkey and leek in a 600 ml/1 pt/2½ cup dish. Stir in the flour. Cover with clingfilm (plastic wrap) and slit it twice to allow steam to escape. Cook on Full for 4 minutes. Uncover and stir in the prunes, soaking water and all the remaining ingredients, seasoning to taste. Cover as before and cook on Full for 2 minutes. Allow to stand for 3 minutes before eating.

Turkey in Cider
....

10 ml/2 tsp butter or margarine
175 g/6 oz turkey breast fillet, cut
    into small cubes
1 garlic clove, crushed
15 ml/1 tbsp cornflour
    (cornstarch)
Salt to taste
5 ml/1 tsp gravy granules or stock
    powder
2.5–5 ml/½–1 tsp mustard powder
120 ml/4 fl oz/½ cup dry cider
Mashed potato and a green
    vegetable, to serve

Put butter or margarine in a 600 ml/ 1 pt/2½ cup dish. Melt, uncovered, on Defrost for 30–45 seconds. Mix in the turkey and garlic. Cover with clingfilm (plastic wrap) and slit it twice to allow steam to escape. Cook on Full for 3½ minutes. Combine the remaining dry ingredients smoothly with the cider. Uncover the turkey and stir in the cider mixture. Cover as before and cook on Full for 3 minutes. Allow to stand for 3 minutes before eating with mashed potato and a green vegetable.

Pink Turkey
....

10 ml/2 tsp butter or margarine
1 small onion, chopped
175 g/6 oz turkey breast fillet, cut
    into small cubes
15 ml/1 tbsp cornflour
    (cornstarch)
Salt and freshly ground black
    pepper
1.5 ml/¼ tsp paprika
120 ml/4 fl oz/½ cup rosé wine

Put the butter or margarine in a 600 ml/1 pt/2½ cup dish. Melt, uncovered, on Defrost for 30–45 seconds. Stir in the onion and turkey. Cover with clingfilm (plastic wrap) and slit it twice to allow steam to escape. Cook on Full for 3 minutes. Combine the remaining dry ingredients smoothly with the wine, seasoning to taste. Uncover the turkey and coat with the wine mixture. Stir thoroughly. Cover as before and cook on Full for 3½ minutes. Allow to stand for 3 minutes before eating.

Turkey Burger

*125 g/4 oz/1 cup minced (ground)
   turkey*
*15 ml/1 tbsp plain (all-purpose)
   flour*
1.5 ml/¼ tsp salt
15 ml/1 tbsp milk or stock
*1 hamburger bun, warmed, and
   pickles, to serve*

Thoroughly combine all the ingredients. Shape into a 9 cm/3½ in
round. Put on a plate. Cook, uncovered, on Full for 2½ minutes. Allow
to stand for 45 seconds. Split the
hamburger bun and place the burger
inside. Garnish with pickles of your
choice and eat.

Turkey Burger Variations

Curry: add 2.5 ml/½ tsp curry powder
to the turkey mixture before cooking.
Cajun: add 5 ml/1 tsp Worcestershire
sauce, 5 ml/1 tsp chilli sauce and 1
crushed garlic clove to the turkey
mixture before cooking.
Tomato: add 10 ml/2 tsp tomato
purée (paste) and a pinch of sugar to
the turkey mixture before cooking.
Italian: add 10 ml/2 tsp tomato purée
(paste) and 5 ml/1 tsp pesto to the
turkey mixture before cooking.
Oaten: substitute 30 ml/2 tbsp oats
for the flour. Increase the milk or stock
to 30 ml/2 tbsp.

Meat Dishes for One

It is important to remember that salt
toughens meat cooked in the
microwave. Therefore, where possible,
it is added either during or at the end
of the cooking cycle.

Fast Beef and Vegetable Stew

*125 g/4 oz/1 cup minced (ground)
   beef*
*75 g/3 oz/¾ cup packet coleslaw
   vegetable mix (with no dressing)*
*5 ml/1 tsp gravy granules or stock
   powder*
150 ml/¼ pt/⅔ cup hot water
Freshly ground black pepper

Put the beef in a 600 ml/1 pt/2½ cup
dish. Thoroughly mix in the
coleslaw. Cover with clingfilm (plastic
wrap) and slit it twice to allow steam
to escape. Cook on Full for 3 minutes.
Smoothly combine the remaining
ingredients. Uncover the meat and
vegetables and stir in the stock mixture. Cover as before and cook on Full
for 3 minutes. Allow to stand for 2
minutes before eating.

Beef Stew with Mixed Vegetables

Prepare as for Fast Beef and
Vegetable Stew, but substitute
15 ml/1 tbsp dried mushrooms and
15 ml/1 tbsp dried onions or mixed
(bell) peppers for the coleslaw.

Curried Beef Stew

Prepare as for Beef Stew with Mixed
Vegetables, but add 7.5–10 ml/
1½–2 tsp medium curry powder with
the dried vegetables.

Short-cut Bolognese Sauce

125 g/4 oz/1 cup minced (ground) beef
15 ml/1 tbsp dried onions
15 ml/1 tbsp dried mixed (bell) peppers
15 ml/1 tbsp dried sliced mushrooms
2.5 ml/½ tsp Italian seasoning or dried basil
15 ml/1 tbsp tomato purée (paste)
1.5 ml/¼ tsp sugar
10 ml/2 tsp plain (all-purpose) flour
5 ml/1 tsp gravy granules or stock powder
45 ml/3 tbsp hot water
3 tomatoes, blanched, skinned and chopped
Salt and freshly ground black pepper
Boiled pasta, to serve

Thoroughly mix together the beef, onions, peppers, mushrooms, Italian seasoning or basil, tomato purée, sugar and flour in a 600 ml/ 1 pt/2½ cup dish. Cook, uncovered, on Full for 2 minutes. Break up the meat with a fork. Mix the gravy granules or stock powder smoothly with the water and stir into the beef mixture. Mix in the tomatoes. Cover as before and cook on Full for 4½ minutes. Allow to stand for 2 minutes. Uncover and season to taste. Eat straight away with pasta.

Bolognese Sauce with Wine

Prepare as for Short-cut Bolognese Sauce, but substitute red wine for the water.

Stuffed Pepper

A speciality from Eastern Europe, the Balkans and Israel.

1 large red or green (bell) pepper
125 g/4 oz/1 cup minced (ground) beef, lamb or pork
15 ml/1 tbsp easy-cook long-grain rice
1 small onion, grated
5 ml/1 tsp gravy granules or stock powder
45 ml/3 tbsp hot water
1.5 ml/¼ tsp dried mixed herbs
45 ml/3 tbsp hot stock

Cut off the top of the pepper and reserve. Remove and discard the inside fibres and seeds. If necessary, cut a thin slice off the base so the pepper can stand upright. Combine the meat, rice, onion, gravy granules or stock powder, hot water and herbs. Pack into the pepper and top with the reserved 'lid'. Transfer to a 600 ml/ 1 pt/2½ cup pudding basin. Pour the stock around. Cover with clingfilm (plastic wrap) and slit it twice to allow steam to escape. Cook on Full for 7½ minutes. Allow to stand for 3 minutes before eating.

Gammon-stuffed Pepper

Prepare as for Stuffed Pepper, but substitute minced gammon for the beef, lamb or pork.

Minced Pork Goulash

175 g/6 oz/1½ cups minced
(ground) pork or beef
30 ml/2 tbsp dried onions
30 ml/2 tbsp mixed dried (bell)
peppers
10 ml/2 tsp plain (all-purpose)
flour
200 g/7 oz/1 small can chopped
tomatoes
2.5 ml/½ tsp paprika
Salt and freshly ground black
pepper

Put the meat in a 600 ml/1 pt/2½ cup dish. Work in the dried vegetables and flour. Cover with clingfilm (plastic wrap) and slit it twice to allow steam to escape. Cook on Full for 3 minutes. Uncover and mash down with a fork. Add the tomatoes and paprika and season to taste. Cover as before and cook on Full for 2½ minutes. Allow to stand for 2 minutes before eating.

Hungarian Meat Paprikas

Prepare as for Minced Pork Goulash, but stir in 30–45 ml/2–3 tbsp soured (dairy sour) cream or crème fraîche immediately before eating.

Beefburger

125 g/4 oz/1 cup lean minced
(ground) beef
15 ml/1 tbsp plain (all-purpose)
flour
Salt and freshly ground black
pepper
15 ml/1 tbsp milk or stock
1 hamburger bun or chips (fries)
and salad, to serve

Mix the beef thoroughly with the remaining ingredients. Shape into a 9 cm/3½ in round. Put on a plate. Cook, uncovered, on Full for 2 minutes. Allow to stand for 1 minute before eating in a split bun or with chips and salad.

Beefburger Variations

Tandoori: add 2.5 ml/½ tsp tandoori spice mix to the meat mixture.
Chinese: add 2.5 ml/½ tsp Chinese five spice powder to the meat mixture.
Mustard: add 4 ml/scant 1 tsp English made mustard to the meat mixture.
Cheese: after the burger has cooked and stood for 1 minute, top with a slice of processed cheese. Cook, uncovered, on Full for 30 seconds.

King Burger

For hefty appetites. Eat with lettuce and sliced tomatoes, a jacket potato (page 226) or chips (fries). The burger will make its own delicious gravy.

225 g/8 oz/2 cups coarsely minced
(ground) steak
Salt
30 ml/2 tbsp crusty white
breadcrumbs
15 ml/1 tbsp milk or stock
2.5 ml/½ tsp Bovril or other meat
extract

Thoroughly combine all the ingredients. Shape into a 12 cm/4½ in round. Transfer to a plate. Cook, uncovered, on Full for 4 minutes. Allow to stand for 1½ minutes before eating.

Giant Cheeseburger

Prepare as for King Burger, but when cooked top the burger with 1–2 slices processed cheese. Cook on Full for 45–60 seconds until melted.

Corned Beef Hash

225 g/8 oz potatoes, peeled and
  cubed
40 ml/2½ tbsp hot water
1.5 ml/¼ tsp salt
10 ml/2 tsp butter or margarine
125 g/4 oz corned beef, coarsely
  mashed
15 ml/1 tbsp milk or stock
2.5 ml/½ tsp English made
  mustard

Put the potatoes in a large serving dish with the water and salt. Cover with clingfilm (plastic wrap) and slit it twice to allow steam to escape. Cook on Full for 6–7 minutes until tender. Drain and mash. Beat in the butter or margarine. Mix in the remaining ingredients. Clean the edges of the dish with kitchen paper. Cover as before and cook on Full for 2 minutes. Allow to stand for 1 minute before eating directly from the dish.

Hash with Egg

Prepare as for Corned Beef Hash, but top with a fried (sautéed) or poached egg (page 99).

Fake Chinese Ribs

4 pork rib bones, about 225 g/8 oz
  in total
15 ml/1 tbsp orange or lemon
  marmalade
10 ml/2 tsp rice vinegar
10 ml/2 tsp soy sauce
Salt

Arrange the ribs on a large plate like the spokes of a wheel. Put the remaining ingredients in a small bowl. Warm on Defrost for 45–60 seconds. Spread smoothly over the ribs. Cover with clingfilm (plastic wrap) and slit it twice to allow steam to escape. Cook on Full for 4½ minutes. Allow to stand for 1½ minutes before eating.

Red Ribs

4 pork rib bones, about 225 g/8 oz
  in total
15 ml/1 tbsp tomato purée (paste)
1.5 ml/¼ tsp paprika
5 ml/1 tsp horseradish sauce
2.5 ml/½ tsp continental mustard

Arrange the ribs on a large plate like the spokes of a wheel. Mix together the remaining ingredients in small bowl, then spread over the ribs. Cover with clingfilm (plastic wrap) and slit it twice to allow steam to escape. Cook on Full for 4½ minutes. Allow to stand for 1½ minutes before eating.

Fruited Gammon

1 round gammon steak, about
  225 g/8 oz
75 ml/5 tbsp cold water
30 ml/2 tbsp lime cordial
1 dessert pear, peeled, halved and
  cored

Snip the gammon all the way round the edge at regular intervals to prevent it curling as it cooks. Put in a 600 ml/1 pt/2½ cup round dish and add the water. Cover with clingfilm (plastic wrap) and slit it twice to allow steam to escape. Cook on Full for 3½ minutes. Drain and transfer to a dinner plate. Coat with the cordial. Thinly slice the pear halves and arrange on top of the gammon. Cover as before and cook on Full for 1¼ minutes. Allow to stand for 1½ minutes before eating.

Devilled Pork

A peppy dish that goes admirably with sweetcorn and rice.

1 fleshy pork chop, about 200 g/7 oz
5 ml/1 tsp tomato ketchup
  (catsup)
5 ml/1 tsp brown table sauce
5 ml/1 tsp Worcestershire sauce
2.5 ml/½ tsp mild curry powder
1.5 ml/¼ tsp salt
1.5 ml/¼ tsp mustard powder
Cooked sweetcorn (corn) and
  boiled rice, to serve

Place the chop on a plate. Beat together the remaining ingredients and spread over the chop. Cover with clingfilm (plastic wrap) and slit it twice to allow steam to escape. Cook on Full for 4 minutes. Allow to stand for 1 minute before eating.

Pork in Spaghetti with Sauce

200 g/7 oz/1 small can spaghetti
  in tomato sauce
1 fleshy pork chop, about
  200 g/7 oz
1.5 ml/¼ tsp dried mixed herbs
1.5 ml/¼ tsp paprika
Salt and freshly ground black
  pepper

Spoon the spaghetti into a 600 ml/ 1 pt/2½ cup dish. Place the chop on top. Sprinkle with the herbs, paprika and pepper to taste. Cover with clingfilm (plastic wrap) and slit it twice to allow steam to escape. Cook on Full for 7 minutes. Allow to stand for 1½ minutes. Uncover and sprinkle with salt to taste before eating.

Lamb Kebab

175 g/6 oz lamb fillet, cubed
1 wooden skewer, soaked in water
  for about 1 hour
5 ml/1 tsp Worcestershire sauce
5 ml/1 tsp tomato ketchup
  (catsup)
1 garlic clove, crushed

Thread the lamb cubes on to the skewer. Put on a dinner plate. Combine the remaining ingredients and brush over the meat. Cover loosely with kitchen paper to prevent spluttering. Cook on Full for 3 minutes, turning the skewer over once. Allow to stand for 1 minute before eating.

Sausage Kebab

Prepare as for Lamb Kebab, but substitute beef or pork sausages for the lamb. Cut each sausage into five pieces.

Victorian Lamb Cutlets

*3 lamb best end neck cutlets,
about 200 g/7 oz in total*
15 ml/1 tbsp brown table sauce

Arrange the cutlets on a dinner plate like the spokes of a wheel, fleshy ends towards the edge. Spread with the sauce. Cover loosely with kitchen paper to prevent spluttering. Cook on Full for 3½ minutes. Allow to stand for 45 seconds before eating.

Short-cut Liver and Onions

45 ml/3 tbsp dried sliced onions
65 ml/2½ fl oz/4½ tbsp water
125 g/4 oz lambs' liver, cut into strips
10 ml/2 tsp gravy granules or stock powder
Salt and freshly ground black pepper

Put the onions in a 600 ml/1 pt/ 2½ cup dish with 60 ml/4 tbsp of the water. Cook, uncovered, on Full for 1¾ minutes. Stir in the liver, gravy granules or stock powder and the remaining water, adding pepper to taste. Cover with clingfilm (plastic wrap) and slit it twice to allow steam to escape. Cook on Full for 3 minutes. Allow to stand for 1 minute. Uncover and sprinkle with salt.

Braised Liver with Bacon and Peas

125 g/4 oz lambs' or pigs' liver, cut into strips
1 rasher (slice) streaky bacon, coarsely chopped
60 ml/4 tbsp canned garden peas
10 ml/2 tsp gravy granules or stock powder

Put the liver and bacon in a 600 ml/ 1 pt/2½ cup dish. Mix in the remaining ingredients. Cover with clingfilm (plastic wrap) and slit it twice to allow steam to escape. Cook on Full for 4 minutes. Allow to stand for 1½ minutes. Uncover and stir round. Eat straight away.

Peppered Kidneys

2 very fresh lambs' kidneys
Black peppercorns
15 ml/1 tsp cornflour (cornstarch)
5 ml/1 tsp Worcestershire sauce
60 ml/4 tbsp cold water
1.5 ml/¼ tsp salt
Toast, to serve

Wash and dry the kidneys and cut into small cubes. Transfer to a 600 ml/1 pt/2½ cup dish. Grind over a layer of black pepper. Mix in the remaining ingredients except the salt. Cover with clingfilm (plastic wrap) and slit it twice to allow steam to escape. Cook on Full for 3 minutes. Allow to stand for 1 minute. Uncover, stir round and sprinkle with the salt. Eat spooned on to toast.

Apple Tree Kidneys

2 very fresh lambs' kidneys
50 g/2 oz mushrooms, cut into
narrow strips
5 ml/1 tsp cornflour (cornstarch)
1.5 ml/¼ tsp dried mixed herbs
1.5 ml/¼ tsp paprika
75 ml/5 tbsp apple juice
Salt

Wash and dry the kidneys and cut into small cubes. Put in a 600 ml/ 1 pt/2½ cup dish with the mushrooms. Mix in the cornflour, herbs, paprika and apple juice. Cover with clingfilm (plastic wrap) and slit it twice to allow steam to escape. Cook on Full for 3½ minutes. Allow to stand for 1½ minutes. Uncover, stir round and sprinkle with salt to taste.

Eggs and Cheese Dishes for One

Universal Cheese Sauce

Beautifully creamy and smooth, all-purpose and rich-tasting. A sauce for vegetables, burgers, chicken, turkey, jacket potatoes and pizza.

75 g/3 oz processed cheese slices
60 ml/4 tbsp full-cream milk
1.5 ml/¼ tsp mustard powder
Freshly ground black pepper

Break the cheese slices into fairly large pieces. Transfer to a small bowl and add the milk, mustard and pepper to taste. Put a small wooden spoon in the bowl. Cook, uncovered, on Defrost for 4 minutes, stirring briskly every minute. Remove from the microwave, stir round and use as wished.

Pepper Cheese Sauce

Prepare as for Universal Cheese Sauce, seasoning after cooking with 5 ml/1 tsp canned or bottled Madagascan green peppercorns.

Chutney Cheese Sauce

Prepare as for Universal Cheese Sauce, seasoning after cooking with 10–15 ml/2–3 tsp chutney.

Chilli Cheese Sauce

Prepare as for Universal Cheese Sauce, seasoning after cooking with 5–10 ml/1–2 tsp chilli sauce.

Anchovy Cheese Sauce

Prepare as for Universal Cheese Sauce, seasoning after cooking with 5–10 ml/1–2 tsp anchovy essence (extract).

Cheese Rarebit

Prepare 1 quantity Universal Cheese Sauce, using only 30 ml/2 tbsp liquid, which can be milk, cream, beer or cider. Place a slice of toast on a plate and spoon the sauce over. Dust with paprika. Reheat on Defrost for 1½ minutes.

Imitation Fried Eggs

For 1 egg: break 1 large egg carefully into a buttered small shallow dish. Puncture the yolk gently in two places with the tip of a knife. Season to taste with salt and freshly ground black pepper. Cover with a plate, saucer or plastic lid. Cook on Full for 1 minute. Allow to stand for 1 minute. Cook on Full for a further 20–30 seconds until the white is set (allow an extra few seconds if necessary).

For 2 eggs: as for 1 egg, but cook on Full for 1¼ minutes and allow to stand for 1 minute. Cook for a further 35–50 seconds until the white is set (allow an extra few seconds if necessary).

Soft-boiled (Soft-cooked) Egg

Line a teacup closely with clingfilm (plastic wrap). Carefully break in 1 large egg. Puncture the yolk gently in two places with the tip of a knife. Cover with a saucer. Cook on Defrost for 1 minute. Twirl the egg round in the cup and cook on Defrost for a further 30–60 seconds until the white is lightly set (allow an extra few seconds if necessary). Allow to stand for 30 seconds, then eat from the cup.

Medium-boiled (Medium-cooked) Egg

Prepare as for Soft-boiled Egg, but cook on Defrost for 2 minutes. Allow to stand for 30 seconds.

Hard-boiled (Hard-cooked) Egg

Prepare as for Soft-boiled Egg, but cook on Defrost for 2½ minutes. Allow to stand for 45 seconds.

Egg with Mayonnaise

When hard-boiled (hard-cooked) eggs (page 98) are cold, turn out on to a plate lined with salad. Coat with mayonnaise and eat plain or garnished with capers, anchovies and a dusting of paprika or sprinkling of chopped parsley.

Thousand Island Egg

Prepare as for Egg Mayonnaise, but substitute Thousand Island dressing for the mayonnaise.

Poached Egg on a Crumpet with Cheese Sauce

1 Poached Egg (page 99)
1 toasted crumpet
Universal Cheese Sauce (page 370)
Paprika

Cook the Poached Egg as directed. Transfer to the crumpet and coat with the cheese sauce. Dust with paprika and eat straight away.

Plain Omelette

5 ml/1 tsp butter or margarine
2 large eggs
Salt and freshly ground black
*   pepper*
10 ml/2 tsp water

Melt the butter or margarine on Full for 30 seconds in a shallow 18 cm/7 cm diameter pottery dish. Beat together the remaining ingredients until light and fluffy. Pour into the dish. Cook, uncovered, on Full for 1½ minutes. Stir round with a fork. Cook on Full for a further 30–45 seconds until the omelette has risen to the top of the dish. Allow to stand for 30 seconds, then turn out and eat straight away.

Omelette Variations

Fresh Herb: beat 40 ml/2½ tbsp chopped parsley into the eggs and water. Cook for 45–60 seconds after stirring with a fork.
Mixed Herb: beat 40 ml/2½ tbsp chopped mixed fresh herbs into the eggs and water.
Cheese: cover half the cooked omelette with 30 ml/2 tbsp grated cheese, fold over and slide on to a plate.
Mushroom: cover half the cooked omelette with 45 ml/3 tbsp thinly sliced and cooked mushrooms.
American: prepare as for plain omelette, but substitute milk for the water.

Scrambled Eggs in a Glass

For 1 egg: beat 1 large egg thoroughly with 10 ml/2 tsp milk and salt and freshly ground black pepper to taste. Pour into a buttered teacup or small! bowl, preferably clear glass so you can watch the egg cooking. Cover with a saucer and cook on Full for 30 seconds. Stir round. Cover as before and cook on Full for a further 15–18 seconds until the egg is lightly set and filling the container. Stir again and eat straight away.
For 2 eggs: as for 1 egg, but cook for 40 seconds, stir round, then cook for a further 20–24 seconds or until the eggs are lightly set.

Vegetable Dishes for One

Creamed Potatoes

175 g/6 oz floury potatoes, peeled
*   and cut into small chunks*
30 ml/2 tbsp hot water
2.5 ml/½ tsp salt
5–10 ml/1–2 tsp butter or
*   margarine*
15 ml/1 tbsp milk or single (light)
*   cream*

Put the potatoes in a 600 ml/ 1 pt/2½ cup dish with the water and salt. Cover with clingfilm (plastic wrap) and slit it twice to allow steam to escape. Cook on Full for 4½ minutes until the potatoes are soft. Drain and mash thoroughly. Add the butter or margarine and milk or cream and beat thoroughly until smooth and creamy. Return to a clean dish. Reheat, uncovered, on Full for 15–20 seconds.

Cheese Potatoes

Prepare as for Creamed Potatoes, but beat in 30 ml/2 tbsp grated cheese with the butter or margarine and milk or cream. Reheat on Full for 15–20 seconds.

Jacket Potato

Wash and dry a potato and prick with a fork in six places to prevent the skin bursting. Stand on a plate or piece of kitchen paper and cover with more paper. Cook on Full for 7–8 minutes, depending on the size, until the potato is tender when pressed. Wrap in a clean tea towel (dish cloth) and allow to stand for 5 minutes. Slit open and fill with butter or margarine.

Jacket Potato Variations

Guacamole: split open the cooked potato and place on a plate. Fill with mashed avocado, 30–45 ml/2–3 tbsp soured (diary sour) cream, plenty of salt and freshly ground black pepper and a dusting of chilli powder.

Baked Beans: split open the cooked potato and place on a plate. Fill with 60 ml/4 tbsp baked beans in tomato sauce. Heat through, uncovered, on Full for 1½–2 minutes.

Canned Spaghetti: split open the cooked potato and place on a plate. Fill with 60 ml/4 tbsp canned spaghetti in tomato sauce. Heat through, uncovered, on Full for 1½–2 minutes.

Cream and 'Caviare': split open the cooked potato and place on a plate. Fill with 45 ml/3 tbsp crème fraîche and 10 ml/2 tsp orange or black Scandinavian lumpfish caviare.

Ploughman's: split open the cooked potato and place on a plate. Fill with 30 ml/2 tbsp brown pickle or chutney and 60 ml/4 tbsp grated orange-coloured Cheddar cheese. Cook, uncovered, on Full for 1–1½ minutes or until the cheese melts and bubbles.

Greek-style: split the cooked potato and open out on a plate. Fill one side with zatziki and the other with hummous.

Mexicana: split open the cooked potato and place on a plate. Fill with bought guacamole dip and 15 ml/ 1 tbsp canned red kidney beans. Reheat, uncovered, on Full for 30 seconds.

Potato 'Pizza'

A quickie pizza topping on a potato base, a change from bread.

250 g/9 oz potatoes, peeled and
*   cut into small chunks*
30 ml/2 tbsp water
2.5 ml/½ tsp salt
30 ml/2 tbsp milk
10 ml/2 tsp butter or margarine
75 ml/5 tbsp orange-coloured
*   Cheddar cheese*
5 ml/1 tsp pesto
15 ml/1 tbsp tomato ketchup
*   (catsup)*
6 black olives (optional)

Put the potatoes in a 600 ml/ 1 pt/2½ cup dish with the water and salt. Cover with clingfilm (plastic wrap) and slit it twice to allow steam to escape. Cook on Full for 6 minutes. Uncover and drain. Mash finely, then beat in the milk and butter or margarine. Smooth the top and clean the side of the dish with kitchen paper. Sprinkle thickly with the cheese. Mix together the pesto and ketchup and trickle over the cheese. Cook, uncovered, on Full for 1–1¼ minutes. Garnish with the olives, if using, and eat straight away.

Broccoli with Herbed Cheese Sauce

175 g/6 oz broccoli florets
45 ml/3 tbsp boiling water
Salt
50 g/2 oz cream cheese with garlic and herbs
10 ml/2 tsp cornflour (cornstarch)
110 ml/3¾ fl oz/scant ½ cup full-cream milk
1 slice freshly made toast
15 ml/1 tbsp toasted flaked (slivered) almonds (page 205)

Put the broccoli in a 600 ml/1 pt/2½ cup dish with the water. Sprinkle with salt. Cover with clingfilm (plastic wrap) and slit it twice to allow steam to escape. Cook on Full for 2½–3 minutes until the broccoli is tender but still has some bite. Put the cream cheese in a small basin. Blend the cornflour smoothly with the milk and gradually stir into the cheese. Uncover the broccoli and drain. Coat with the cheese mixture. Cover as before and cook on Full for 2 minutes. Spoon on to the toast and sprinkle with the nuts. Eat hot.

Nut-stuffed Pepper

1 large red or green (bell) pepper
15 ml/1 tbsp easy-cook long-grain rice
90 ml/6 tbsp orange-coloured Cheddar cheese, grated
45 ml/3 tbsp chopped walnuts or peanuts
2.5 ml/½ tsp made mustard
1.5 ml/¼ tsp paprika
45 ml/3 tbsp hot water
Salt and freshly ground black pepper
60 ml/4 tbsp tomato juice

Cut the top off the pepper and reserve. Discard the inside fibres and seeds. Stand the pepper upright in a small dish, cutting a thin slice off the base if necessary. Mix together the rice, cheese, nuts, mustard, paprika and hot water. Season to taste with salt and pepper. Pack into the pepper and replace the 'lid'. Pour the tomato juice round the pepper. Cover with clingfilm (plastic wrap) and slit it twice to allow steam to escape. Cook on Full for 6 minutes. Allow to stand for 3 minutes before eating.

Hot Avocado

1 large ripe avocado
5 ml/1 tsp Worcestershire sauce
75 ml/5 tbsp soured (dairy sour) cream
Salt and freshly ground black pepper
30 ml/2 tbsp garlic croûtons, broken up into small pieces

Peel the avocado as you would peel a pear, starting from the stem end. Halve and remove the stone (pit). Dice the flesh with a stainless steel knife. Transfer to a bowl and mix in the Worcestershire sauce and cream. Season to taste with salt and pepper. Spoon into a 600 ml/1 pt/2½ cup dish and sprinkle with the croûtons. Cook, uncovered, on Full for 2 minutes. Eat straight away.

Cauliflower in Marinade

A zippy side dish for meat, sausages and poultry.

175 g/6 oz cauliflower florets
Salt
30 ml/2 tbsp cold water
15 ml/1 tbsp olive or sunflower oil
10 ml/2 tsp raspberry vinegar
1.5 ml/¼ tsp bottled mint sauce
5 ml/1 tsp Worcestershire sauce
Salt and freshly ground black
  pepper

Break up the cauliflower, sprinkle with salt and add the water. Cover with clingfilm (plastic wrap) and slit it twice to allow steam to escape. Cook on Full for 3 minutes. Thoroughly beat together the remaining ingredients. Uncover the cauliflower and drain. Coat with the marinade and allow to cool. Cover and chill until really cold before eating.

Broccoli in Marinade

Prepare as for Cauliflower in Marinade, but substitute broccoli florets for the cauliflower.

Cauliflower Cheese with Parsley

200 g/7 oz cauliflower florets
Salt
45 ml/3 tbsp cold water
50 g/2 oz/¼ cup cream cheese
15 ml/1 tbsp milk
10 ml/2 tsp chopped parsley
2.5 ml/½ tsp made mustard
Paprika

Put the cauliflower in a serving dish. Sprinkle with salt and add the water. Cover with clingfilm (plastic wrap) and slit it twice to allow steam to escape. Cook on Full for 4 minutes. Put all the remaining ingredients except the paprika in a bowl. Heat, uncovered, on Defrost for 1 minute. Stir round. Drain the cauliflower and coat with the sauce. Reheat, uncovered, on Full for 1 minute. Sprinkle with paprika before eating.

Cauliflower and Stilton with Cranberry

Prepare as for Cauliflower Cheese with Parsley, but substitute crumbled Stilton cheese for the cream cheese and 5 ml/ 1 tsp cranberry sauce for the mustard. Omit the parsley and use fresh coriander (cilantro) instead.

Braised Celery with Bacon and Cheese

200 g/7 oz fresh celery, thinly sliced
Salt
45 ml/3 tbsp boiling water
50 g/2 oz/½ cup gammon, chopped
30 ml/2 tbsp grated Cheddar
  cheese
15 ml/1 tbsp any chopped salted
  nuts

Put the celery in a 600 ml/1 pt/ 2½ cup dish. Sprinkle with salt and add the water. Cover with clingfilm (plastic wrap) and slit it twice to allow steam to escape. Cook on Full for 7 minutes. Allow to stand for 1 minute. Drain. Stir in the gammon and cheese. Wipe the sides of the dish clean with kitchen paper. Sprinkle with the nuts. Cover as before and cook on Full for 1 minute. Allow to stand for 30 seconds before eating.

Braised Onions with Parma Ham and Parmesan Cheese

2 onions, sliced
Salt
45 ml/3 tbsp boiling water
50 g/2 oz/⅓ cup Parma ham,
  chopped
15 ml/1 tbsp grated Parmesan
  cheese
15 ml/1 tbsp any chopped salted
  nuts

Put the onions in a 600 ml/1 pt/
2½ cup dish. Sprinkle with salt and
add the water. Cover with clingfilm
(plastic wrap) and slit it twice to allow
steam to escape. Cook on Full for 7
minutes. Allow to stand for 1 minute.
Drain. Stir in the ham and cheese.
Wipe the sides of the dish clean with
kitchen paper. Sprinkle with the nuts.
Cover as before and cook on Full for 1
minute. Allow to stand for 30 seconds
before eating.

Egg-stuffed Aubergine with Pine Nuts

1 aubergine (eggplant), about
  250 g/9 oz
Salt
15 ml/1 tbsp lemon juice
10 ml/2 tsp olive oil
1 hard-boiled (hard-cooked) egg
  (page 98), shelled and chopped
30 ml/ 2 tbsp pine nuts
Chopped parsley, to garnish
Sesame seed bread, to serve

Prick the aubergine skin all over
with a fork. Wrap loosely in kitchen
paper and stand on a plate. Cook on
Full for 5 minutes. Allow to stand for 3
minutes. Transfer to a board. Cut off
and discard the green stalk at the top.
Halve the aubergine lengthways.
Scoop the flesh out on to the board,
retaining the shells, and chop coarsely.
Transfer to a bowl and season to taste
with salt. Mix in the lemon juice, oil,
egg and pine nuts and stir thoroughly.
Adjust the seasoning. Stand the
aubergine shells on plate and fill with
the egg mixture. Sprinkle thickly with
parsley and eat at room temperature
with sesame seed bread.

Piquant Bean Sprouts

An adventurous sidekick for fish and
poultry.

125 g/4 oz fresh bean sprouts
45 ml/3 tbsp tomato relish or
  brown pickle
2.5 ml/½ tsp Worcestershire sauce
2.5 ml/½ tsp salt

Mix together all the ingredients in a
600 ml/1 pt/2½ cup dish. Cover
with clingfilm (plastic wrap) and slit it
twice to allow steam to escape. Cook
on Full for 3 minutes. Allow to stand
for 1 minute, then stir round and eat.

Buttered Pumpkin

This microwaved pumpkin dish can be eaten as a sweet or savoury dish.

450 g/1 lb wedge of pumpkin in its skin
Butter or margarine
Demerara sugar or golden (light corn) syrup, or salt and freshly ground black pepper

Remove the strands and seeds from the pumpkin. Lay on its side on a plate. Cover with clingfilm (plastic wrap) and slit it twice to allow steam to escape. Cook on Full for 7 minutes. Allow to stand for 2 minutes. Put on a plate with the skin underneath and flesh facing up. Top with butter or margarine, then coat with sugar or syrup for sweet pumpkin or salt and pepper for savoury.

Warm Salad with Avocado

75 ml/5 tbsp ready-to-eat salad leaves
½ ripe avocado
8 tortilla chips, coarsely crushed
30 ml/2 tbsp any-flavour bought salad dressing

Arrange the salad leaves over the base of a plate. Scoop the avocado flesh on top. Sprinkle with the tortilla chips and coat with the dressing. Warm through, uncovered, on Defrost for 45 seconds. Eat warm.

Creamed Mushrooms with Roquefort and Garlic

125 g/4 oz button mushrooms
1 garlic clove, crushed
50 g/2 oz/½ cup Roquefort cheese, crumbled
45 ml/3 tbsp whipping cream
2.5 ml/½ tsp paprika
Boiled new potatoes or French bread, to serve

Wipe the mushrooms and put in a 600 ml/1 pt/2½ cup dish. Mix in the remaining ingredients. Cover with clingfilm (plastic wrap) and slit it twice to allow steam to escape. Cook on Full for 2½ minutes. Allow to stand for 30 seconds. Stir round and eat with hot new potatoes or pieces of crusty French bread.

Rice Dishes for One

Basic Rice

75 g/3 oz/scant ½ cup easy-cook long-grain rice
1.5 ml/¼ tsp salt
300 ml/½ pt/1¼ cups boiling water

Stir together all the ingredients in a 600 ml/1 pt/2½ cup dish. Cover with clingfilm (plastic wrap) and slit it twice to allow steam to escape. Stand the dish on a plate to catch any water that may boil over. Cook on Full for 10 minutes. Allow to stand for 3 minutes, then stir round before eating.

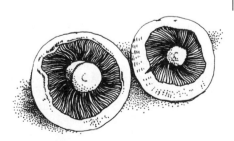

Yellow Rice

To eat with curries.

Prepare as for Basic Rice (page 377), but add 2.5 ml/½ tsp turmeric to the other ingredients.

Spiced Rice

To eat with Eastern food.

Prepare as for Basic Rice (page 377), but add 2 split cardamom pods, ½ small dried bay leaf and 1 cm/½ inch piece of cinnamon stick to the other ingredients.

Chinese Egg Rice

Prepare as for Basic Rice (page 377). After cooking, fork in 2–3 chopped spring onions (scallions), 30 ml/2 tbsp cooked and shelled prawns and 1 chopped hard-boiled (hard-cooked) egg (page 98). Cover as before and reheat on Full for 45–60 seconds.

Herb Rice

Prepare as for Basic Rice (page 377). After cooking, fork in 30 ml/2 tbsp finely chopped fresh herbs, using either one variety only or a combination of two or three. Cover as before and reheat on Full for 30 seconds.

Brown Butter Rice

Brown 15–30 ml/1–2 tbsp salted butter in a small frying pan (skillet). Prepare the Basic Rice (page 377) and stir in the butter after cooking.

Mock Mushroom Risotto

Fry (sauté) 6 sliced closed-cap mushrooms in a little butter. Prepare the Basic Rice (page 377). After cooking, stir in the mushrooms, 30 ml/2 tbsp Parmesan cheese and 10 ml/2 tsp butter. Cover as before and reheat on Full for 1½ minutes.

Winter Muesli Rice

Prepare as for Basic Rice (page 377), but add 30 ml/2 tbsp sweet fruit and nut muesli with the other ingredients. Cook on Full for 11 minutes. Stir round and eat with milk for breakfast. Chopped fresh or canned fruit and some honey or golden (light corn) syrup may also be added to the cooked rice.

Hot Rice Salad

75 g/3 oz/scant ½ cup easy-cook long-grain rice
Salt and freshly ground black pepper
300 ml/½ pt/1¼ cups boiling water
100 g/3½ oz/½ cup cottage cheese
30 ml/2 tbsp toasted sunflower seeds (page 206)
5 cm/2 in piece cucumber, peeled and chopped
1 tomato, chopped

Stir together the rice, 1.5 ml/¼ tsp salt and the boiling water in a 600 ml/1 pt/2½ cup dish. Cover with clingfilm (plastic wrap) and slit it twice to allow steam to escape. Stand the dish on a plate to catch any water that may boil over. Cook on Full for 10 minutes. Allow to stand for 3 minutes. Fork in the cheese, sunflower seeds, cucumber and tomato. Adjust the seasoning to taste. Cover as before and reheat on Full for about 2½ minutes.

Rice Cheese

A pre-World War Two favourite, made much more speedily here than it used to be.

75 g/3 oz/scant ½ cup easy-cook long-grain rice
1.5 ml/¼ tsp salt
300 ml/½ pt/1¼ cups boiling water
50 g/2 oz/½ cup Red Leicester cheese, grated
30 ml/2 tbsp milk or single (light) cream
2.5–5 ml/½–1 tsp mild made mustard
1–2 drops Tabasco or other hot pepper sauce
15 ml/1 tbsp toasted brown breadcrumbs
Paprika

Stir together the rice, salt and water in a 600 ml/1 pt/2½ cup dish. Cover with clingfilm (plastic wrap) and slit it twice to allow steam to escape. Stand the dish on a plate to catch any water that may boil over. Cook on Full for 10 minutes. Allow to stand for 3 minutes. Fork in the cheese, milk or cream, mustard and hot pepper sauce to taste. Sprinkle with the breadcrumbs, then dust with paprika. Reheat, uncovered, on Full for 1 minute. Allow to stand for 30 seconds before eating.

Pasta Dishes for One

Cooked in its own serving dish, microwaved pasta saves using and washing up a saucepan. Pasta holds it shape very well and stays perfectly *al dente*. Any of these pasta dishes may be cooked in boiling stock instead of water.

Plain Pasta

50 g/2 oz any pasta such as broken-up spaghetti, shells, bows, twists, macaroni
1.5–2.5 ml/¼–½ tsp salt
225 ml/8 fl oz/1 cup boiling water

Put the pasta in a large individual serving dish with the salt and water. Stand the dish on a plate in case the water boils over. Cook, uncovered, on Full for 7 minutes. Remove from the microwave, cover with a plate and allow to stand for 2 minutes. Drain, if necessary, before eating.

Pasta with Garlic

Prepare as for Plain Pasta. While standing, fry (sauté) 2–3 crushed garlic cloves in 15–30 ml/1–2 tbsp extra virgin olive oil until golden. Stir into the pasta.

Creamed Pasta with Ham

50 g/2 oz any pasta such as broken-up spaghetti, shells, bows, twists, macaroni
1.5–2.5 ml/¼–½ tsp salt
225 ml/8 fl oz/1 cup boiling water
60 ml/4 tbsp lean chopped ham
30 ml/2 tbsp chopped parsley
30 ml/2 tbsp double (heavy) cream
30 ml/2 tbsp tomato juice

Put the pasta in a large individual serving dish withthe salt and water. Stand the dish on a plate in case the water boils over. Cook, uncoverd, on Full for 6 minutes. Remove from the microwave, cover with a plate and allow to stand for 2 minutes. Drain. Stir in the remaining ingredients. Cover as before and reheat on Full for 1½ minutes.

Italian-style Tortellini Soup

12 fresh filled tortellini
300 ml/½ pt/1¼ cups boiling water
1 chicken, beef or vegetable stock
  cube
10 ml/2 tsp grated Parmesan
  cheese

Place the tortellini in a large soup bowl with the water. Crumble in the stock cube. Cook, uncovered, on Full for 4 minutes. Allow to stand for 1 minute. Sprinkle with the Parmesan before eating.

Desserts for One

Stewed Apples

2 medium or 1 large cooking (tart)
  apples, peeled, cored and sliced
40 ml/2½ tbsp granulated sugar
25 ml/1½ tbsp cold water
1 or 2 whole cloves
Cream or custard, to serve
  (optional)

Put the apple slices in a serving bowl with the sugar, water and cloves. Cover with clingfilm (plastic wrap) and slit it twice to allow steam to escape. Cook on Defrost for 4½–5 minutes until tender. Allow to stand for 1 minute. Eat hot, warm or cold, either plain or with cream or custard.

Stewed Apricots

6 fresh apricots, halved and stoned
  (pitted)
30 ml/2 tbsp granualted sugar
30 ml/2 tbsp cold water
Cream or custard, to serve
  (optional)

Put the apricot halves in a serving bowl with the sugar and water. Cover with clingfilm (plastic wrap) and slit it twice to allow steam to escape. Cook on Defrost for 4½–5 minutes until tender. Allow to stand for 1 minute. Eat hot, warm or cold, either plain or with cream or custard.

Warm Fruit Fluff

225 g/4 oz canned fruit purée
  (canned baby food is ideal)
1 large egg, separated
A pinch of salt
Crisp biscuits (cookies), to serve

Tip the pureé into a bowl. Gently beat in the egg yolk. Whisk the egg white with the salt to stiff peaks. Fold into the fruit mixture with a large metal spoon. Transfer to a lightly buttered 600 ml/1 pt/2½ cup basin. Cook, uncovered, on Full for 1½ minutes until the pudding is puffed up almost to the top of the basin. Eat straight away with biscuits.

Stewed Rhubarb

125 g/4 oz rhubarb, chopped
45 ml/3 tbsp granulated sugar
25 ml/1½ tbsp cold water
1.5 ml/¼ tsp ground ginger
Cream or custard, to serve
(optional)

Put the rhubarb in a serving bowl with the sugar, water and ginger. Cover with clingfilm (plastic wrap) and slit it twice to allow steam to escape. Cook on Defrost for 4½–5 minutes until tender. Allow to stand for 1 minute. Eat hot, warm or cold, either plain or with cream or custard.

Baked Apple Stuffed with Lemon Curd

1 large cooking (tart) apple
30 ml/2 tbsp Lemon Curd (page 345)
9 chocolate polka dots (chips)
45 ml/3 tbsp apple or grape juice

Score a line round the apple with a sharp knife, about one-third down from the top. Remove the core with a potato peeler or apple corer, taking care not to cut through the base of the apple. Pack with lemon curd and top with the chocolate polka dots. Transfer to a bowl large and deep enough to accommodate the apple comfortably. Pour the apple juice around. Cover with clingfilm (plastic wrap) and slit it twice to allow steam to escape. Cook on Defrost for 10 minutes, turning the dish twice, until the apple has puffed up like a soufflé. Allow to stand for 2 minutes before eating.

Date and Honey Apple

Prepare as for Baked Apple Stuffed with Lemon Curd, but instead of lemon curd, fill with 40 g/1½ oz/¼ cup chopped dates and 15 ml/1 tbsp demerara sugar. Put in a dish and coat with 30 ml/2 tbsp clear honey instead of pouring apple juice around.

Apricot Apple

Prepare as for Baked Apple Stuffed with Lemon Curd, but substitute 30 ml/2 tbsp chunky apricot jam (conserve) for the lemon curd. Sprinkle with 10 ml/2 tsp toasted flaked (slivered) almonds (page 205) and pour cider or wine into the dish instead of apple juice.

Peppercorn Strawberries

A startling combination, in keeping with modern food trends.

10 ml/2 tsp unsalted (sweet) butter
125 g/4 oz strawberries, halved lengthways
Black peppercorns
Vanilla ice cream

Put the butter in a serving dish. Melt, uncovered, on Defrost for 1 minute. Add the strawberries to the butter and grind a dusting of pepper over the top. Cover with a saucer or plate and cook on Defrost for 1 minute. Top with ice cream and eat straight away.

Ground Rice Milk Pudding

No sticky pan, no burning and no lumps!

15 ml/1 tbsp ground rice
10 ml/2 tsp caster (superfine)
  sugar
150 ml/¼ pt/⅔ cup milk
Ground cinnamon or mixed
  (apple-pie) spice

Put the ground rice and sugar in a 1.5 litre/2½ pt/6 cup basin (it will rise during cooking).Work in the milk smoothly with a plastic spoon or spatula. Cook, uncovered and with the spatula still in the basin, on Full for 1½ minutes, stirring three or four times. Allow to stand for 1 minute. Sprinkle with cinnamon or mixed spice before eating.

Semolina or Polenta Pudding

Prepare as for Ground Rice Milk Pudding, but substitute semolina (cream of wheat) or polenta for the ground rice.

Easy Custard

Prepare as for Ground Rice Milk Pudding, but substitute custard powder for the ground rice.

Tea Bun Pudding in Egg Custard

150 ml/¼ pt/⅔ cup milk
15 ml/1 tbsp butter or margarine
1 large egg, at kitchen
  temperature
2 fruited tea buns, halved
30 ml/2 tbsp demerara sugar

Pour the milk into a glass measuring cup or bowl. Add the butter or margarine. Heat together on Full for 1¼ minutes until the butter has melted and the milk is warm. Whisk in the egg. Place the buns in a shallow dish, cut sides up, in a single layer. Spoon over the milk mixture and sprinkle with the sugar. Cook, uncovered, on Full for 3½–4 minutes. Allow to stand for 2 minutes before eating.

Croissant Egg Custard Pudding

Prepare as for Tea Bun Pudding in Egg Custard, but substitute 2 large chocolate-filled or plain croissants for the buns. Add 10 ml/2 tsp caster (superfine) sugar instead of the demerara sugar.

Baked Egg Custard

1 large egg, at kitchen temperature
60 ml/4 tbsp milk
10 ml/2 tsp caster (superfine)
  sugar
2.5 ml/½ tsp vanilla essence
  (extract)
2.5 ml/½ tsp cornflour (cornstarch)
2.5 ml/½ tsp grated nutmeg

Thoroughly beat together all the ingredients except the nutmeg in a small basin. Pour into a pudding bowl and sprinkle with the nutmeg. Cook, uncovered, on Defrost for 4½ minutes. Eat warm or cold.

Perfumed Egg Custard

Prepare as for Baked Egg Custard, but substitute 5 ml/1 tsp orange flower water for the vanilla essence (extract) and nutmeg.

Jam Sponge Pudding

50 g/2 oz/½ cup self-raising (self-rising) flour
25 g/1 oz/2 tbsp caster (superfine) sugar
25 g/1 oz/2 tbsp butter or margarine
1 large egg, beaten
30 ml/2 tbsp cold milk
2.5 ml/½ tsp vanilla essence (extract)
30 ml/2 tbsp any red jam (conserve)
Ice cream, cream or custard, to serve

Thoroughly grease a 600 ml/1 pt/2½ cup pudding basin. Sift the flour into a bowl and toss in the sugar. Finely rub in the butter or margarine. Using a fork, mix to a soft consistency with the egg, milk and vanilla essence. Put the jam in the prepared basin. Heat, uncovered, on Full for 25 seconds. Spoon in the pudding mixture. Cook, uncovered, on Full for 1¼–1½ minutes until the pudding is well risen and spongy-looking. Allow to stand for 1 minute. Turn out on to a plate and eat with cream, ice cream or custard.

Marmalade Sponge Pudding

Prepare as for Jam Sponge Pudding, but substitute marmalade for the jam (conserve).

Syrup and Ginger Sponge Pudding

Prepare as for Jam Sponge Pudding, but sift in 5 ml/1 tsp ground ginger with the flour and substitute golden (light corn) syrup for the jam.

Mixed Fruit Sponge Pudding

Prepare as for Jam Sponge Pudding, but add 30 ml/2 tbsp mixed dried fruit (fruit cake mix) to the rubbed-in ingredients.

Castle Pudding

Prepare as for Jam Sponge Pudding, but add 5 ml/1 tsp grated lemon peel to the rubbed-in ingredients.

Fruit Bubbles

4 cubes (¼ packet) any flavour jelly (jello)
150 g/5 oz/⅔ cup any fruit purée
1 large egg, separated
A pinch of salt

Snip the jelly into four individual cubes with kitchen scissors dipped in and out of cold water. Put into a measuring jug and make up to 75 ml/5 tbsp with cold water. Heat, uncovered, on Defrost for about 2½–3 minutes until the jelly melts. Stir until clear. Gently whisk in the fruit purée and egg yolk. Chill until cold and just beginning to thicken and set round the edge. Whisk together the egg white and salt until stiff. Gently whisk in the jellied mixture. Spoon into a glass serving dish and chill for about 4 hours before eating.

Canadian Maple Pudding with Pecans

30 ml/2 tbsp maple syrup
50 g/2 oz/½ cup wholemeal self-raising (self-rising) flour
25 g/1 oz/2 tbsp light soft brown sugar
25 g/1 oz/2 tbsp butter or margarine
30 ml/2 tbsp coarsely chopped pecans
1 large egg, at kitchen temperature
30 ml/2 tbsp cold milk
Cream, to serve

Thoroughly grease a 600 ml/1 pt/ 2½ cup pudding basin. Pour in the syrup. Warm, uncovered, on Full for 30 seconds. Tip the flour into a bowl and toss in the sugar. Finely rub in the butter or margarine. Toss in the nuts. Beat together the egg and milk, then stir with a fork into the dry ingredients. Spoon into the basin over the syrup. Cook, uncovered, on Full for 2 minutes until the pudding is well risen and spongy-looking. Allow to stand for 1 minute. Turn out on to a plate and eat with cream.

Chocolate Sponge Pudding

40 g/1½ oz/½ cup self-raising (self-rising) flour
15 ml/1 tbsp cocoa (unsweetened chocolate) powder
25 g/1 oz/2 tbsp light soft brown sugar
25 g/1 oz/2 tbsp butter or margarine
1 large egg, at kitchen temperature
45 ml/3 tbsp cold milk
2.5 ml/½ tsp vanilla essence (extract)
Cream or ice cream, to serve

Thoroughly grease a 600 ml/1 pt/ 2½ cup pudding basin. Sift the flour and cocoa into a bowl and toss in the sugar. Finely rub in the butter or margarine. Beat together the egg, milk and vanilla essence, then stir with a fork into the flour mixture. Spoon into the prepared basin. Cook, uncovered, on Full for 1½ minutes. Allow to stand for 1 minute. Cook on Full for a further 30 seconds until the pudding is well risen and spongy-looking. Allow to stand for 30 seconds. Turn out on to a plate and eat with cream or ice cream.

Suet Pudding with Syrup

30 ml/2 tbsp golden (light corn) syrup
50 g/2 oz/½ cup self-raising (self-rising) flour
25 g/1 oz/¼ cup beef or vegetable suet
15 ml/1 tbsp caster (superfine) sugar
1 large egg, at kitchen temperature, beaten
30 ml/2 tbsp cold milk
Cream or custard, to serve

Thoroughly grease a 600 ml/1 pt/ 2½ cup pudding basin. Pour in the syrup. Heat, uncovered, on Full for 30 seconds. Sift the flour into a bowl and toss in the suet and sugar. Mix to a soft consistency with the egg and milk. Spoon into the basin. Cook, uncovered, on Full for 1½ minutes until the pudding is well risen and spongy-looking. Allow to stand for 1½ minutes. Turn out on to a plate and eat with cream or custard.

Suet Pudding with Marmalade

Prepare as for Suet Pudding with Syrup, but substitute coarse-cut marmalade for the syrup.

Suet Pudding with Lemon

Prepare as for Suet Pudding with Syrup, but substitute lemon curd for the syrup.

Suet Pudding with Fruit

Prepare as for Suet Pudding with Syrup, but add 30 ml/2 tbsp mixed dried fruit (fruit cake mix) to the mixture before the egg and milk. If liked, sift 2.5 ml/½ tsp ground mixed (apple-pie) spice in with the flour.

Individual Christmas Pudding

A perfect one-person pudding, rich without being cloying, and not too sweet.

15 g/½ oz/2 tbsp wholemeal flour
2.5 ml/½ tsp ground allspice
15 g/½ oz/¼ cup fresh brown breadcrumbs
15 g/½ oz/2 tbsp beef or vegetable suet
25 g/1 oz/2 tbsp dark soft brown sugar
125 g/4 oz/⅔ cup mixed dried fruit (fruit cake mix)
1 large egg, lightly beaten
15 ml/1 tbsp medium-sweet sherry or brandy
Rum or brandy butter, custard or cream, to serve

Thoroughly grease a 600 ml/1 pt/ 2½ cup pudding basin. Tip the flour, allspice, breadcrumbs, suet, sugar and fruit into a mixing bowl. Toss over and over with a spoon until thoroughly combined. Mix to a soft mixture with the egg and alcohol. Spoon into the prepared basin. Cook, uncovered, on Full for 1 minute. Allow to stand for 1 minute. Cook on Full for a further 40 seconds. Allow to stand for 1 minute. Turn out on to a plate. Eat with rum or brandy butter, custard or cream.

Tropical Sunshine

4 cubes (¼ packet) any flavour jelly (jello)
1 mango or papaya (pawpaw), peeled and flesh diced

Snip the jelly into four individual cubes with kitchen scissors dipped in and out of cold water. Put into a measuring jug and make up to 75 ml/ 5 tbsp with cold water. Heat, uncovered, on Defrost for about 2½–3 minutes until the jelly melts. Stir until clear. Chill until cold and just beginning to thicken and set round the edge. Transfer the diced fruit to a dessert dish and coat with the liquid jelly. Chill until set before eating.

Minted Chocolate Mousse

100 g/3½ oz chocolate peppermint creams, at kitchen temperature
1 large egg, at kitchen temperature, separated
A pinch of salt

Break up the chocolate and put in a basin. Melt, uncovered, on Defrost for 1½–2 minutes. Stir the egg yolk into the melted chocolate. Whip the egg white and salt until stiff. Fold into the chocolate mixture with a metal spoon. Transfer to a dessert dish Cover with saucer or plate and chill for about 4 hours before eating.

Chocolate Mousse with Coffee

Prepare as for Minted Chocolate Mousse, but substitute coffee chocolate creams for chocolate peppermint creams.

Honeypot Bananas with Rum and Coconut

1 ripe banana
15 ml/1 tbsp clear honey
10 ml/2 tsp rum
5 ml/1 tsp demerara sugar
5 ml/1 tsp toasted desiccated
    (shredded) coconut (page 205)

Slice the peeled banana into a dessert dish. Coat with the honey and rum and sprinkle with the sugar. Heat on Defrost for 1 minute. Sprinkle with the coconut before eating.

Orange with Sherry

1 large orange
30 ml/2 tbsp demerara sugar
45 ml/3 tbsp sweet sherry

Peel the orange, discarding all traces of white pith. Thinly slice. Transfer to a glass dessert dish. Put the sugar and sherry in a cup or small bowl. Heat, uncovered, on Defrost for 3 minutes. Stir briskly until the liquid is clear. Spoon over the orange. Cover with clingfilm (plastic wrap) and chill thoroughly before eating.

Figs Marinated in Lime Tea

An innovative sweet which can also double as a breakfast compôte.

1 tea bag
150 ml/¼ pt/⅔ cup cold water
10 ml/2 tsp caster (superfine)
    sugar
30 ml/2 tbsp lime cordial
6 dried figs, well washed

Put the tea bag into a cup with the water and sugar. Heat, uncovered, on Full for 1¾ minutes. Pour into a serving dish, discarding the tea bag. Stir in the cordial and add the fruit. Cover and leave to stand overnight in the refrigerator before eating.

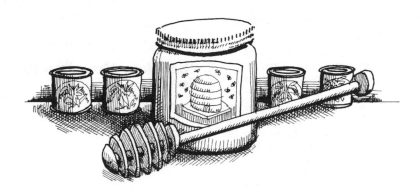

Drinks

Punches, nogs, a potent Scandinavian Christmas *glögg* and hot chocolate and cocoa are just some of the drinks perfectly made in the microwave. You'll also find instructions for heating milk, making safe drinks for drivers, a revival of egg nog with and without alcohol, and making your own gimmick-free Cappucino.

Grapefruit and Cider Punch

SERVES 8–12

4 large grapefruit
1.25 litres/2¼ pts/5½ cups sweet cider
60 ml/4 tbsp granulated sugar
2 cinnamon sticks
4 whole cloves
4 maraschino cherries
90 ml/6 tsp maraschino syrup

Halve 3 of the grapefruit and squeeze out the juice. Put the juice in a large bowl with all the remaining ingredients. Cover with a plate and heat on Full for about 20 minutes, stirring twice, until bubbling. Meanwhile, peel the remaining grapefruit and cut the flesh into segments between the membranes. Ladle the punch into handled cups or mugs and add grapefruit segments to each.

Grapefruit and Apple Juice Punch

SERVES 8–12

Prepare as for Grapefruit and Cider Punch, but substitute apple juice for the cider.

Grapefruit and Cranberry Punch

SERVES 8–12

Prepare as for Grapefruit and Cider Punch, but substitute cranberry juice for the cider.

Ale and Cider Punch

SERVES 8

A potent old English drink.

600 ml/1 pt/2½ cups pale ale
600 ml/1 pt/2½ cups cider
45 ml/3 tbsp black treacle (molasses)
5 ml/1 tsp ground ginger
2.5 ml/½ tsp grated nutmeg
1 wineglass whisky

Put all the ingredients except the whisky in a large bowl. Cover with a plate and heat on Full for 15 minutes until bubbling. Stir in the whisky and ladle into handled cups or mugs. Serve straight away.

Scandinavian Christmas Glögg

SERVES 4–5

Pronounced 'glerg', this is an indisputable *tour de force*, a punch like no other.

1 litre/1¾ pts/4¼ cups rosé or red wine
1 cinamon stick
5 whole cloves
Seeds from 5 cardamom pods
75 g/3 oz granulated sugar
Peel of ½ lemon, cut into strips
50 g/2 oz/½ cup blanched almonds, cut into strips
75 ml/5 tbsp raisins
1 liqueur glass brandy

Pour the wine into a large bowl. Add all the remaining ingredients except the brandy. Cover with a plate and heat through on Full for about 15–20 minutes, stirring four times, until hot and the sugar is dissolved. Add the brandy, ladle into handled cups or glasses and serve straight away.

Port Punch

SERVES 6

A civilised punch for winter festivities.

450 ml/¾ pt/2 cups apple juice
300 ml/½ pt/1¼ cups freshly squeezed orange juice
150 ml/¼ pt/⅔ cup ruby port
1 cinnamon stick

Put all the ingredients in a large bowl. Cover with a plate and heat on Full for 5–8 minutes until hot but not boiling. Allow to stand for 5 minutes. Stir round and ladle into handled glasses, cups or mugs. Serve hot.

Swedish Christmas Punch

SERVES 6–8

Beware! *Julglogg*, as it is known in its native country, is very strong.

1 bottle red wine
½ bottle vodka or Scandinavian or Dutch schnapps
6 whole cloves
1 cinnamon stick
Seeds from 3 cardamom pods
225 g/8 oz/1 cup granulated sugar
Peel of 1 large orange, cut into strips
Peel of 1 small lemon, cut into strips
60 ml/4 tbsp raisins

Pour the wine and vodka into a large bowl. Add all the remaining ingredients. Cover with a plate and heat through on Defrost for 25–30 minutes, stirring several times, until the sugar is dissolved. Ladle into handled cups or glasses and serve hot.

Heating Milk

Milk is easily heated in the microwave and runs less risk of boiling over than when warmed conventionally in a saucepan.

To warm: pour 300 ml/½ pt/1¼ cups cold milk into a glass or pottery jug. Heat, uncovered, on Full for 1½–2 minutes.

To bring just to the boil: pour 300 ml/½ pt/1¼ cups cold milk into a glass or pottery jug. Heat, uncovered, on Full for 2½–3 minutes.

Honey Milk

SERVES 2

450 ml/¾ pt/2 cups milk
30 ml/2 tbsp clear honey
30 ml/2 tbsp double (heavy) cream
Ground cinnamon

Pour the milk into a glass or pottery jug and add the honey. Heat, uncovered, on Full for 4½–5½ minutes until hot. Pour into two handled mugs. Float the cream on to each by carefully and slowly pouring it over the back of a teaspoon into the cups. Sprinkle with cinnamon.

Spicy Milk with Treacle

SERVES 3–4

900 ml/1½ pts/3¾ cups milk
15 ml/1 tbsp golden (light corn) syrup
15 ml/1 tbsp black treacle (molasses)
4 ml/¾ tsp mixed (apple-pie) spice

Pour the milk into a 1.25 litre/2¼ pt/5½ cup jug or deep bowl. Add the syrup and treacle. Heat, uncovered, on Full for 8–9 minutes until hot but not boiling. Pour into handled cups, mugs or glasses and sprinkle with the mixed spice.

Milky Marshmallow Melts

SERVES 3–4

A mocha milk drink that makes an acceptable parting shot for drivers at the end of an evening out.

900 ml/1½ pts/3¾ cup milk
30 ml/2 tbsp drinking chocolate
15 ml/1 tbsp instant coffee powder or granules
2.5 ml/½ tsp finely grated orange peel
6–8 marshmallows

Pour the milk into a 1.75 litre/3 pt/7½ cup deep bowl. Heat, uncovered, on Full for 8–9 minutes until hot but not boiling. Whisk in the drinking chocolate and coffee. Pour into handled cups, mugs or glasses and sprinkle with the orange peel. Float 2 marshmallows on top of each and drink as soon as they begin to melt.

Victorian Milk Punch

SERVES 8

A nineteenth century speciality for the new Millennium.

1.25 litre/2¼ pts/5½ cups milk
30 ml/2 tbsp ground almonds
125 g/4 oz/½ cup caster (superfine) sugar
5 ml/1 tsp finely grated orange peel
2 egg whites
75 ml/5 tbsp dark rum
75 ml/5 tbsp whisky

Pour the milk into a 2 litre/3½ pt/8½ cup bowl. Heat, uncovered, on Full for 10–11 minutes until hot. Stir in the almonds, sugar and orange peel. Reheat, uncovered, on Full for 1½ minutes. Beat the egg whites until stiff. Stir the rum and whisky into the hot sweetened milk, then gently whisk in the beaten egg whites. When the milk mixture is light and foamy, pour into handled cups and serve while still fairly hot.

Egg Nog

SERVES 1

1 egg, separated
15 ml/1 tbsp caster (superfine) sugar
300 ml/½ pt/1¼ cups milk

Beat the egg white until stiff. In a separate large bowl, beat together the egg yolk and sugar until thick and creamy. Pour the milk into a jug and heat, uncovered, on Full for 3–3½ minutes. Whisk gently into the beaten yolk and sugar, then fold in the egg white. Pour into a handled mug and drink while still foamy.

Brandy Nog

SERVES 1

Prepare as for Egg Nog, but add 15–30 ml/1–2 tbsp brandy to the mixture just before the egg white is folded in. (Whisky, rum or sherry may be substituted if preferred.)

Cocoa

SERVES 1

15–20 ml/3–4 tsp cocoa (unsweetened chocolate) powder or carob powder
200 ml/7 fl oz/scant 1 cup cold milk
Sugar

Put the cocoa or carob powder in a large cup or mug. Mix smoothly with 45 ml/3 tbsp of the milk. Whisk in the remaining milk. Heat, uncovered, for 1¾–2 minutes until hot or the cocoa just comes to the boil. Allow to stand for 45 seconds. Sweeten to taste.

Coffee with Milk
•••••••••••••••••••••••••••••••
SERVES 1

Prepare as for Cocoa, but substitute 5–10 ml/1–2 tsp instant coffee powder or granules for the cocoa (unsweetened chocolate) powder.

Hot Chocolate
•••••••••••••••••••••••••••••••
SERVES 1

Prepare as for Cocoa, but substitute drinking chocolate for the cocoa (unsweetened chocolate) powder.

Hot Chocolate Cream
•••••••••••••••••••••••••••••••
SERVES 1

Prepare as for Hot Chocolate. Top with 15–30 ml/1–2 tbsp softly whipped cream, then sprinkle with a crushed flake bar or grated chocolate.

Hot Liqueur Chocolate
•••••••••••••••••••••••••••••••
SERVES 1

Prepare as for Hot Chocolate, but mix in 15–30 ml/1–2 tbsp liqueur to taste. Leave plain or top with cream and chocolate.

Mock Cappucino
•••••••••••••••••••••••••••••••
SERVES 1

Fill a fairly large cup or mug with cold strong coffee. Add 15–20 ml/ 3–4 tsp milk powder (non-fat dry milk) mixed smoothly with 10 ml/2 tsp cold water. Heat, uncovered, on Full for 1½ minutes until hot and foamy. Allow to stand for 25 seconds. Sweeten if liked, then sprinkle with cocoa (unsweetened chocolate) powder or grated chocolate.

Reheating Leftover Coffee
•••••••••••••••••••••••••••••••
Because of the speed of the microwave, there is no stale flavour when cold coffee is reheated. Pour into cups and heat one at a time, uncovered, on Full for about 1 minute. Sweeten if liked and add milk or cream to taste.

Hints and Tips

Baby Food

To warm jars of baby food, remove the metal lids. Cover loosely with kitchen paper. Warm jars one at a time on Defrost, allowing about 1½ minutes. Test the warmth before using.

Cheese

To bring chilled cheeses to room temperature, warm on Defrost, allowing 15–30 seconds for every 100–175 g/3½ –6 oz. If the cheese still feels cold and too firm for personal taste, allow a few seconds more but watch carefully to ensure it does not start to melt.

Chicken and Turkey Livers

To prevent livers from popping during cooking, pierce each piece once or twice with the tip of a knife.

Citrus Fruits

To extract more juice from citrus fruits, warm each piece on Full for 10–30 seconds (the time needed will depend on the size of the fruit). Allow to stand for 5 minutes.

Cleaning

To clean the interior of a microwave easily, dampen a clean cloth and heat on Defrost for 30–45 seconds. Wipe over the interior of the microwave, then dry with a tea towel (dish cloth). Do this frequently to prevent food spills and splashes from sticking. As an alternative and also to freshen the microwave, wipe over with a specially formulated microwave cleaner. If you like the smell of citrus, put a few slices of fresh lemon or lime into a bowl with 300 ml/½ pt/1¼ cups cold water. Heat on Full for about 3–4 minutes until boiling rapidly. Wipe the interior with a cloth followed by a tea towel. Glass cleaner is ideal for the outside.

Containers

To check if a specific container is suitable for use in the microwave, test by placing a glass of water into it and transfer both together to the microwave. Heat on Full for 1 minute. If the container becomes hot in this time, it is absorbing too much heat and an alternative should be used. Important: sometimes dishes in the microwave become too hot to handle with bare hands and therefore oven gloves should always be worn.

Dinner Rolls

To refresh day-old rolls, place in a napkin-lined basket and warm through on Defrost for about 1–3 minutes, depending on the number and size of the rolls, until their surfaces feel slightly warm.

Dried Fruits

To rehydrate dried fruits such as apple rings, apricots and prunes without soaking overnight, put about 225 g/8 oz/1⅓ cups washed fruit into a glass bowl. Just cover with water and bring to the boil on Full for about 5½–8 minutes. Cover with a plate and leave to stand for 10 minutes. Drain before using. You can use the soaking water for sauces or for stewing fresh fruit. To plump up raisins, currants and sultanas (golden raisins), treat as for dried fruit, but reduce the cooking time to about 4–6 minutes on Full. Allow to stand for 5 minutes. Drain and thoroughly dry.

Ice Cream and Jellies

To soften ice cream and loosen jellies (not in metal tins or moulds), heat on Defrost for 45 seconds. Allow to stand for 2–3 minutes.

Lotions and Potions

To warm baby and beauty lotions, shampoos and hair conditioners before use, remove the caps and heat each container on Defrost for about 45–50 seconds.

Plate Meals

To have frozen plate meals ready in advance, arrange cooked foods – such as meat and two or three vegetables – on individual dinner plates. Place meat, fish and dense vegetables towards the outside of the dish without piling up, then arrange smaller vegetables, pasta or rice in the centre. Coat with gravy or sauce. Cover with clingfilm (plastic wrap) and slit it twice. When ready to serve, reheat each plate individually from frozen,

allowing 5–6 minutes on Full, depending on the dish. The food is ready when the base of the plate feels piping hot in the centre. Allow to stand for 3–5 minutes before serving.

Pomegranates

To soften and extract more juice, follow the directions for Citrus Fruits above.

Ring Mould

To improvise a ring mould, cover the outside of a narrow, straight-sided smooth tumbler closely with clingfilm (plastic wrap). Stand upright in the middle of any round dish.

Steam

To prevent the danger of steam rushing into your face, tilt any container away from you when uncovering.

Sugar

To soften lumpy or hard brown sugar, put 225 g/8 oz/1 cup in a dish with half a slice of very fresh bread or a wedge of fresh pear or apple. Cover with kitchen paper and warm on Defrost for 1½ minutes. Alternatively, cover the surface of the sugar with a piece of wet kitchen paper before heating.

Syrup

To melt syrups or honey that have become grainy and crystallised, remove the metal caps and warm the jars, individually, on Defrost for about 3 minutes, stirring once. Syrup in metal containers must be decanted into a microwaveable container before heating.

Index

Everyday Eating made more exciting

			QUANTITY	AMOUNT
Classic 1000 Recipes	0-572-01671-9	£5.99		
Classic 1000 Chinese	0-572-01783-9	£5.99		
Classic 1000 Indian	0-572-01863-0	£5.99		
Classic 1000 Italian	0-572-01940-8	£5.99		
Classic 1000 Pasta & Rice	0-572-02300-6	£4.99		
Classic 1000 Vegetarian	0-572-02375-8	£5.99		
Classic 1000 Quick and Easy	0-572-02330-8	£5.99		
Classic 1000 Cakes & Bakes	0-572-02387-1	£5.99		
Classic 1000 Calorie-counted Recipes	0-572-02405-3	£5.99		

*Please allow 75p per book for post & packing in UK
Overseas customers £1 per book.*

* POST & PACKING

TOTAL

Foulsham books are available from local bookshops. Should you have any difficulty obtaining supplies please send Cheque/Eurocheque/Postal Order (£ sterling only) made out to **BSBP** or debit my credit card:

☐ ACCESS ☐ VISA ☐ MASTER CARD

EXPIRY DATE   SIGNATURE

ALL ORDERS TO:
Foulsham Books, PO Box 29, Douglas, Isle of Man IM99 1BQ
Telephone 01624 675137, Fax 01624 670923, Internet http://www.bookpost.co.uk.

NAME

ADDRESS

Please allow 28 days for delivery.
Please tick box if you do not wish to receive any additional information ☐
Prices and availability subject to change without notice.